Essential French Grammar

Essential French Grammar is a student-friendly French grammar designed to give learners a firm foundation on which to build a real understanding of both spoken and written French. Clear explanations of grammar are supported by contemporary examples, lively cartoon drawings and a variety of exercises.

Key features of the second edition include:

+ each grammar point explained initially with reference to English

+ parallels between English and French provided where relevant

+ 'Key points' boxes and tables that summarize grammar concepts

+ real-life language examples in French, with English translations

+ a variety of exercises to reinforce learning

+ a contemporary primary source or literary extract to illustrate grammar in context

+ more detailed coverage of punctuation, accents, spelling and the specific sounds of French.

This second edition includes an introductory chapter that describes the lexical and grammatical differences between French and English. A glossary of grammatical terms in French and English, useful verb tables, and a key to the exercises are also provided, making this an ideal resource for both independent and class-based learners.

Essential French Grammar is an innovative reference grammar and workbook for intermediate and advanced undergraduate students of French. This text is ideal for students at CEFR levels B1 to C1, or Intermediate High to Advanced on the ACTFL scale.

Mike Thacker was Director of the Language Centre at the University of Surrey from 1991 to 2005 and has taught at all degree levels.

Casimir d'Angelo was Director of the Language Unit at the University of Cambridge from 1998 to 2014, and has taught at all degree levels. He is presently Director of the Global Training Centre at the China UK Development Centre.

Essential Language Grammars

A Spanish Learning Grammar, 3rd Edition
Pilar Muñoz and Mike Thacker

Essential German Grammar, 2nd Edition
Martin Durrell, Katrin Kohl, Claudia Kaiser and Gudrun Loftus

Essential French Grammar, 2nd Edition
Mike Thacker and Casimir d'Angelo

For more information about this series, please visit: www.routledge.com/Essential-Language-Grammars/book-series/ELG

ESSENTIAL
FRENCH GRAMMAR

Second edition

MIKE THACKER AND CASIMIR D'ANGELO

Routledge
Taylor & Francis Group

LONDON AND NEW YORK

Second edition published 2019
by Routledge
2 Park Square, Milton Park, Abingdon, Oxon, OX14 4RN

and by Routledge
52 Vanderbilt Avenue, New York, NY 10017

Routledge is an imprint of the Taylor & Francis Group, an informa business

© 2019 Mike Thacker and Casimir d'Angelo

First edition published by Routledge 2013

British Library Cataloguing in Publication Data
A catalogue record for this book is available from the British Library

Library of Congress Cataloging in Publication Data
Names: Thacker, Mike, author. | d'Angelo, Casimir, author.
Title: Essential French grammar / Mike Thacker and Casimir d'Angelo.
Description: Second edition. | Milton Park, Abingdon, Oxon ; New York, NY : Routledge, 2019. | Series: Essential Language Grammars | Includes index.
Identifiers: LCCN 2018031123 (print) | LCCN 2018040616 (ebook) | ISBN 9780429807398 (pdf) | ISBN 9780429807381 (ePub) | ISBN 9780429807374 (Kindle) | ISBN 9781138338166 (hardback : alk. paper) | ISBN 9781138338180 (pbk. : alk. paper) | ISBN 9780429441882 (ebook)
Subjects: LCSH: French language—Grammar. | French language—Textbooks for foreign speakers—English.
Classification: LCC PC2112 (ebook) | LCC PC2112 .T49 2019 (print) | DDC 445—dc23
LC record available at https://lccn.loc.gov/2018031123

ISBN: 978-1-138-33816-6 (hbk)
ISBN: 978-1-138-33818-0 (pbk)
ISBN: 978-0-429-44188-2 (ebk)

Typeset in Sabon
by Swales & Willis Ltd, Exeter, Devon, UK

Visit the companion website: www.routledge.com/cw/thacker

CONTENTS

ACKNOWLEDGEMENTS

We wish to express our gratitude to Camille Burns, Laura Sandford and Rosie McEwan of Routledge, for their encouragement and advice in preparing this second edition of *Essential French Grammar*. We would also like to thank reviewers for their invaluable feedback, which has given rise to important additions to the book.

The publishers would like to thank Éditions Gallimard and the Estate of Jacques Prévert for their permission to reproduce 'Inventaire' by Jacques Prévert. Please advise the publisher of any errors or omissions, and these will be corrected in subsequent editions.

INTRODUCTION

Essential French Grammar was written out of a conviction that grammar is the key to attaining a real understanding of both spoken and written French. While it is possible to communicate with native speakers at a basic phrase book level using a limited number of structures, knowledge of the grammar of the language is essential to hold a conversation of any complexity or to write a letter or an essay successfully. In our long experience of teaching and examining, grammar plays a fundamental part in the learning process of students who aspire to higher levels of competence.

Our aim in writing *Essential French Grammar* is to provide a clear description of French grammar, together with practice exercises, for English-speaking undergraduate students of French and for those who are studying French in preparation to go to university. University students of French will benefit from using this book, whether they are specialist linguists or non-specialists studying a module in French as part of another degree. In terms of the commonly accepted European system for assessing achievement in a language, the book corresponds approximately to levels B1 to C1 of the *Common European Framework Reference for Languages* (Independent User to Proficient User).

The new first chapter aims to give a brief account of the historical development of the French and English languages and then to compare major lexical and grammatical aspects in each language which show how they have diverged over time. In each of the chapters that cover a specific grammatical point (Chapters 2–16) we explain briefly how grammar works in English and then in French. This method enables students to grasp the fact that French has different ways of creating its grammatical rules, which derive from a distinctive cultural and linguistic tradition. Chapter 17 extends significantly the description in the first edition of punctuation, accents, spelling and specific sounds in French, giving a more detailed account of, for example, the rules of spelling and liaison, which are of great importance in the writing and speaking of French respectively.

The structure of each of Chapters 2–16 follows a sequence:

▶ each grammar point is explained initially with reference to English

▶ parallels between English and French are then pointed out in a contrastive way

▶ *Key points* relating the grammar in question are explained

▶ a description of how the grammar is formed, where appropriate, and its main uses are then explored, with translated *examples.*

In the final section of each chapter,

▶ the grammar point is exemplified in passages that show how it works *in context*

▶ a sequence of *exercises* gives ample practice for students to test themselves.

Occasional illustrations show grammar 'in action'.

The book also includes:

▶ a *Glossary*, provided at the beginning of the book, for those who are less familiar with grammar terms

▶ as an Appendix, a glossary of computing terminology

▶ *Answers* to the exercises

▶ an *Index.*

In general, we have followed the conventions for explaining French grammar found in English grammars of French, pointing out some conceptual differences where appropriate (e.g. in Chapter 9, Verbs 1).

In 1990, new rules for spelling were agreed by Francophone countries, which are set out in the *Rectifications de l'orthographe de 1990.* These rules, which we have summarized in Chapter 17, affect such aspects as the hyphenation of numbers, the use of the circumflex accent and compound words. Although this reform of spelling is not prescriptive, in recent years it has become more acceptable and so we have decided to adopt it in this new edition.

It is often the case that incorrect usage of a given structure in the spoken language has become so widespread it is generally accepted. In cases of this kind we have pointed out that the structure is confined to speech. Similarly, we have indicated language that is employed only in formal circumstances or used in a literary or legal register. Where we feel the need to point to language that is ungrammatical, an asterisk is placed before the example, e.g. **trois gens.*

Casimir d'Angelo
Mike Thacker
April 2018

GLOSSARY OF GRAMMATICAL TERMS

Active and passive voice

Sentences are either active or passive. In an active sentence, the subject carries out the action of the verb, e.g. *Un juge l'a mis en examen* (A judge investigated him). In the passive version of this example, what was the *object* of the active sentence, *l'* (him), becomes the *subject* of the passive verb, *il* (he), and the **agent**, *juge* (judge), appears after *par: Il a été mis en examen par un juge* (He was investigated by a judge). Verbs which take a direct object (transitive verbs) can be used in either an active or a passive way.

Adjective

Adjectives are words used to describe nouns. In French, adjectives agree with nouns in gender and number, e.g. *dix bouteilles vertes* (ten green bottles). *Vertes* is a feminine plural adjective. Adjectives can either be *attributive*, i.e., stand next to the noun as in *dix bouteilles vertes* or *predicative*, i.e., separated from the noun they describe, e.g. *Les bouteilles sont vertes* (The bottles are green).

Adverb

Adverbs give more information about a verb or another element in a sentence, such as an adjective or another adverb. Adverbs can tell you how, when, where and to what degree something happens or is, e.g. *Elle travaille bien / tard / là / trop* (She works well / late / there / too much); *Il est complètement fou* (He's quite mad).

Affirmative sentence

An affirmative sentence is one in which we assert a fact or state agreement to something, as opposed to a *negative* one in which we refuse, deny, or contradict something.

Agreement

Words change their form to 'be in agreement with' other words.

▶ **Verbs** change according to whether the person speaking is 'I', 'you', 's/he', etc.: *aller* (to go) becomes *je vais* (I go), *tu vas* (you go). *il / elle va* (he / she goes), etc.

▶ **Determiners** agree with nouns in gender and number: e.g. 'this' can be translated by three different forms according to the noun which follows: *ce garçon* (this boy), *cet homme* (this man), *cette femme* (this woman).

▶ **Adjectives** also agree with nouns in gender and number: e.g. the adjective *blanc* in its masculine singular form is *un vin blanc* (a white wine) and in its feminine plural form *des chemises blanches* (white shirts).

▶ A **past participle** in a compound verb agrees with a preceding direct object: *Ta grand-mère ? Je l'ai vue hier* (Your grandmother? I saw her yesterday).

Antecedent

In a relative clause the antecedent is the preceding element to which the relative pronoun or adjective refers. In *La fille que vous avez rencontrée hier est ma cousine* (The girl you met yesterday is my cousin), the noun *la fille* is the antecedent and *que* the relative pronoun.

Article

See Definite article, Indefinite article, Partitive article

Aspect

'Aspect' is a linguistic term which defines actions in relation to time, as perceived by the speaker. There is an opposition between those verb tenses that express actions in terms of the flow of time and those which are 'bounded' by time, i.e., do not have a sense of time passing. *Je travaillais* (I was working) describes the first type, *J'ai travaillé* (I worked) the second.

Auxiliary verb

An auxiliary verb is a verb which combines with a participle or an infinitive, e.g. to form a compound tense. The two auxiliary verbs used in French are *avoir*, which precedes the majority of verbs, and *être*, which is used with twenty or so intransitive verbs, pronominal verbs and to form the passive voice: *Elle a apporté les disques* (She has brought the disks); *Il est arrivé* (He has arrived).

Cardinal number

Cardinal numbers are those which refer to quantity, and are used for counting: *dix* (10), *vingt-trois* (23), *huit cent quatre-vingt-douze* (892), etc.

Clause

A clause is part of a sentence which contains its own verb, but which does not necessarily make complete sense. There are two types of clause, 'main' and 'subordinate'. A main clause has an independent meaning within the sentence; a subordinate clause cannot function independently without another clause. In **Ils sont revenus parce qu'ils avaient oublié les clés de la maison** (They came back because they had forgotten the house keys), the main clause *Ils sont revenus* can stand as the sentence on its own; the subordinate clause *parce qu'ils avaient oublié les clés de la maison* cannot stand independently.

Comparative

Comparatives are adjectives and adverbs which emphasize a particular quality by comparing the *degree* to which two nouns possess that quality: *La France est plus grande que la Belgique* (France is bigger than Belgium); *La plupart des fromages anglais sont moins forts que les français* (Most English cheeses are less strong than French ones).

Complement

A complement is a word or phrase that completes the meaning of a noun, verb, adjective or adverb.

▶ Verb: *Beaucoup de touristes visitent la cathédrale de Chartres* (Many tourists visit Chartres cathedral)

▶ Noun: *La voiture de mon père est en panne* (My father's car has broken down)

▶ Adjective: *Il est jaloux de son frère* (He's jealous of his brother)

▶ Adverb: *Il a bu trop de vin* (He's drunk too much wine)

Compound tense

See Tense

Conditional sentence

A conditional sentence is a sentence which usually consists of two clauses, a subordinate clause introduced by the conjunction *si* (if) and a main clause: *Si vous ne savez pas comment aller au centre sportif* [subordinate clause] *il faut demander à Charles* [main clause] (If you don't know how to get to the sports centre, you should ask Charles).

Conjugation	A conjugation is a group of verbs. There are three such groups of regular verbs in French, which are distinguished by their infinitive endings. These endings are: (1) *-er*, e.g. ***parler*** (to speak), (2) *-ir*, e.g. ***finir*** (to finish), and (3) *-re*, *-oir* and some verbs in *-ir*, e.g. ***vendre*** (to sell) / ***concevoir*** (to conceive) / ***venir*** (to come).
Conjunction	Conjunctions are words like *et*, *mais* and *parce que*, which link words, phrases or clauses, e.g. *Georges **et** Amélie sont venus **parce que** tu voulais parler avec eux des vacances* (Georges and Amélie have come because you wanted to talk to them about the holidays).
Copula	A copula is a link verb, such as *être* and *sembler*, which joins the subject of a sentence to the predicate: *Louis Pasteur était un fameux chimiste français* (Louis Pasteur was a famous French chemist); *Ça **semble** triste* (That seems sad).
Demonstrative	We use demonstrative determiners and pronouns when we wish to point to a particular person, thing, etc.: *ce*, *cet*, *cette*, etc. (this, that, etc.).
Demonstrative adjectives	See Determiners
Demonstrative pronouns	See Pronouns
Determiner	Determiners are words placed before a noun to give it a context. Indefinite article: *un / une / des* (a, an, some); definite article: *le / la / les* (the); demonstrative adjective: *ce / cet / cette / ces* (this, that, those); possessive adjective: *mon / ma / mes*, etc. (my, etc.)
Direct object	See Object
Exclamation	Exclamations are words or sentences which express emotions, such as surprise, wonder, urgency, horror. *J'en ai marre !* (I'm fed up!); *Allez !* (Come on!)
Gender	Words in French are either masculine or feminine in gender, e.g. *le tapis* (carpet), *la vache* (cow).

Gerund	The gerund in French has the same form as the present participle: *parlant*, *finissant*, *écrivant*. It is preceded by *en* and expresses an action which is simultaneous with that of the verb: *En réfléchissant il souriait* (While thinking he smiled).
Imperative	See Mood
Impersonal verb	Impersonal verbs are verbs whose subject has no particular identity, e.g. *Il neige* (It is snowing); *Il est difficile de savoir quoi faire* (It is difficult to know what to do).
Indefinite article	The indefinite article (English: a / an / some) is used to indicate a person, animal, thing or idea that has not been previously mentioned e.g. *un **ordinateur*** (a computer), *une **voiture*** (a car), *des **pommes de terre*** ([some] potatoes).
Indefinite pronoun	Indefinite pronouns are words that do not refer to a specific person or thing, like *quelqu'un* (someone), *personne* (nobody, anybody).
Indicative	See Mood
Indirect object	See Object
Infinitive	The infinitive is the form of the verb given in dictionaries and which is not inflected. In English the infinitive consists of the word 'to' plus the verb, e.g. 'to grow'. French infinitives end in either *-er*, *-ir*, *-re* or *-oir*, e.g. *regarder* (to look at), *choisir* (to choose), *écrire* (to write), *apercevoir* (to perceive, to notice).
Infix	An infix is an element inserted into a verb, e.g. *-iss-* inserted into ***finir*** (to finish), to make the present participle, ***finissant***.
Interrogative pronoun	Interrogative pronouns are words used to introduce questions, like *qui?* (who?), *combien?* (how much / many?) and *pourquoi?* (why?).
Intransitive verb	See Transitive and intransitive verbs
Inversion	Inversion takes place when the normal order of words is inverted, as in questions: *As-tu vu le film le plus récent de Klapisch ?* (Have you seen the latest film by Klapisch?)
Irregular verb	See Regular and irregular verb

Main clause	See Clause
Modal verb	Modal verbs are **semi-auxiliary** verbs, like *pouvoir* (can, to be able to) and *devoir* (must, to have to), which are followed by the infinitive. Modal verbs communicate a particular mood or intention to the verb which follows. *Je ne **peux** pas venir* (I can't come); *Je ne **dois** pas venir* (I mustn't come).
Mood	The following three moods of the verb are used to express differing ideas and emotions. These are:

▶ Indicative. This mood is used for statements of fact and certainty: *Il **boit** du café tous les matins* (He drinks coffee every morning).

▶ Imperative. This mood is used for commands. Commands are made in both the positive and the negative: *Regarde !* (Look!); *Ne regarde pas en bas !* (Don't look down!)

▶ Subjunctive. This mood is for uncertainty, unreality, necessity, wishes and hopes: *J'aimerais qu'ils viennent **nous voir demain*** (I would like them to come and see us tomorrow).

Negative sentence	A negative sentence is one in which we refuse, deny, contradict or say 'no', e.g. *Nous n'allons jamais au théâtre* (We never go to the theatre).
Noun	A noun is the name that we give to a person, animal, thing or idea. There are two types of noun: common, e.g. *passager* (passenger), *renard* (fox), *chambre* (room), *philosophie* (philosophy) and proper, which refer to particular persons, places, or objects, e.g. *Depardieu, les Alpes, Marseille, Crédit Agricole*.
Number	Number refers to words being singular or plural, e.g. *le chien* (dog), *les chiens* (dogs), *la rue* (street), *les rues* (streets).
Object	A direct object is a word which receives the action of the verb directly, e.g. *le repas* in **Elle a préparé** *le repas* (She prepared the meal). An indirect object is one which receives the action of the verb indirectly, e.g. *au policier* in **J'ai donné mon passeport** *au policier* (I gave my passport to the policeman).

Ordinal number	Ordinal numbers are used to arrange things in order: *premier* (first), *deuxième* (second), etc.
Participle	See Past participle, Present participle
Partitive article	The partitive article, *du*, *de l'*, *de la*, *des*, is a determiner expressing the idea of 'some' with mass nouns and abstract nouns: *du pain* ([some] bread), *de la beauté* ([some] beauty).
Passive voice	See Active and passive voice
Past participle	The past participle is the form of the verb ending, for regular verbs, in *-é* (*-er* verbs) *-i* (*-ir* verbs) or *-u* (*-re* verbs): *parler* (to speak) → *parlé* (spoken); *finir* (to finish) → *fini* (finished); *vendre* (to sell) → *vendu* (sold). It has two main functions: as an adjective, e.g. *la langue parlée* (the spoken language) and as part of a verb, as in the compound past tense, e.g. *J'ai vendu mon appartement* (I've sold my flat).
Person	Verb endings are always related to a subject, which can be in the first, second or third person, singular or plural:

▶ *je / j'* (I) first person singular

▶ *tu* (you) familiar second person singular

▶ *il*, *elle* (he, she, it) third person singular

▶ *nous* (we) first person plural

▶ *vous* (you) second person plural and polite second person singular

▶ *ils*, *elles* (they) third person plural.

Personal pronoun	See Pronoun
Possessive	Possessive determiners and pronouns tell us who is the possessor of something or show a relationship between different people, or people and things / ideas.
Possessive determiners	See Determiner
Possessive pronouns	See Pronoun
Preposition	A preposition links one part of a sentence (e.g. a noun) with the rest of the sentence, e.g. *près de* in *Le musée est près de la cathédrale* (The museum is near the cathedral). By changing the preposition we

change the meaning of the sentence, e.g. by replacing *près de* by *loin de* (far from), *dans* (in) or *en face de* (opposite) in the example.

Present participle

The present participle is the form of the verb ending in *-ant*: *regardant* (looking at), *disant* (saying), *écrivant* (writing).

Pronominal verb

These are verbs like *se laver*, that are accompanied by a reflexive pronoun like *me*, *te* and *se*, etc. See Pronoun. The verb is only reflexive if the subject is the same as the object, e.g. *Je me suis lavé très vite* (I washed [myself] / got washed quickly).

Pronoun

Pronouns stand in the place of nouns whenever it is unnecessary to refer to the noun. Personal pronouns appear in four main places in a sentence:

▶ as the subject, *je* (I)

▶ as the direct object, *me* (me)

▶ as the indirect object, *lui* (to him / her / it)

▶ after a preposition, **pour** *moi* (for me).

Other types of pronouns are:

▶ demonstrative: *celui*, *celle*, etc. (the one). See Demonstrative

▶ interrogative: *qui?* (who?), *quoi?* (what?), etc. See Interrogative pronoun

▶ possessive: *le mien* (mine), *le tien* (yours), etc. See Possessive

▶ reflexive: *me* (myself), *te* (yourself), *se* (himself, herself, itself, oneself, themselves), etc. See Pronominal verb

▶ relative: *qui* (who, which, that), *que* (who[m], which, that, what), *où* (where), etc. See Relative clause.

Quantifier

Quantifiers are determiners that are placed before a noun to indicate amount or quantity: *assez de* (enough), *beaucoup de* (much, many), *peu de* (few).

Question words	See Interrogative pronoun
Radical	The radical of a verb is the part of the verb that does not normally change; the variable part of the verb is the ending, which changes with person, tense and mood. In *parler* (to speak), *parl-* is the radical and *-er* the ending; in *choisir* (to choose), *chois-* is the radical and *-ir* the ending. The radical carries the meaning of the verb.
Reciprocal sentence	A reciprocal sentence is one in which the subjects of the verb are doing something to one another: *Ils se félicitent* (They congratulate each other).
Regular and irregular verb	Regular verbs, e.g. *parler* (to speak), *finir* (to finish), *vendre* (to sell), conform to predictable models in the formation of the different tenses. If you know that a verb is regular you can work out from the model the form that you need. Irregular verbs do not always conform to a predictable model for their formation and so it is important to learn their forms. Many common verbs, such as *aller* (to go), *venir* (to come), *savoir* (to know) are irregular. Tables of irregular verbs are on p. 422.
Relative clause	Relative clauses are subordinate clauses introduced by relative pronouns like *qui* (who, which, that). They refer back to a previous element in the sentence, called the **antecedent,** and they link two clauses together, e.g. *Le garçon qui m'a accompagné au match s'appelle Pierre* (The boy who / that went with me to the match is called Pierre). The antecedent is **Le garçon.**
Semi-auxiliary verb	Semi-auxiliary verbs such as *aller* (to go), *devoir* (to have to), *pouvoir* (to be able to), *venir* (to come) lose their full meaning when followed by another verb in the infinitive. They express nuances of tense and mood: *Le train va partir* (The train is about to depart); *Je ne peux pas chanter* (I can't sing).
Sentence	A sentence is a group of words arranged so as to make a comprehensible meaning. The order of words in a sentence varies from one language to another. Sentences can be: ▶ simple, i.e., consist of a single clause with a subject and a predicate, e.g. *Il a bu de l'eau* (He drank some water), which may be modified by additional

elements such as adverbs and prepositional phrases: *Après la course il a bu de l'eau à grands traits* (After the race he drank some water thirstily).

▶ compound, i.e., consist of two or more clauses: a *main* clause and one or more *subordinate* clauses. Typically, clauses are joined by conjunctions like *parce que: Il a bu de l'eau* [main clause], *parce qu'il avait soif* [subordinate clause] (He drank some water **because** he was thirsty). Relative pronouns are frequently used to join two clauses: *Les gens qui habitaient la vieille maison ne sortaient guère* (The people **who** lived in the old house scarcely went out).

The most important word in a sentence is normally the **verb**. Other components are **nouns, determiners, adjectives, adverbs, pronouns** and **prepositions**. Typical complements of the verb may be a **direct object**, an **indirect object** or a **prepositional phrase**.

Sentences may be affirmative or negative. They can take the form of questions and commands: *Qu'est-ce que tu fais là ? Sors !* (What are you doing here? Get out!)

Subject	The subject is the word or group of words which determines the verb ending, e.g. in *Les gosses jouaient dans la rue* (The kids were playing in the street), the subject *Les gosses* is plural so the verb is in the plural. In active sentences the subject usually carries out the action of the verb: *Gérard a construit le mur* (Gérard built the wall). In passive sentences the subject receives the action of the verb: *Le mur a été construit par Gérard* (The wall was built by Gérard).
Subjunctive mood	See Mood
Subordinate clause	See Clause
Superlative	The superlative is an adjective or adverb used when we are referring to a quality in its greatest possible degree, e.g. *la femme la plus âgée du monde* (the oldest woman in the world).
Tense	Tense refers to the time when an action took place, whether present, future or past. As in English, tenses

in French can be simple, i.e., consist of one word, e.g. *Je sais* (I know) or compound, i.e., consist of more than one word, e.g. *Je suis venu* (I have come).

▶ The simple tenses are: present, future, conditional, simple past and imperfect, e.g. the present: *Je sais* (I know); the imperfect: *Je savais* (I knew).

▶ Compound tenses consist of an **auxiliary verb**, either *avoir* or *être*, plus a **participle** e.g. the compound past: *Elle a commencé son travail* (She's started her job); the pluperfect: *Maurice était arrivé* (Maurice had arrived).

Transitive and intransitive verbs

A verb is called transitive when it has a direct object, as does the verb *voir* in *Tu vois cette peinture ?* (Do you see that painting?). An intransitive verb is one that does not have a direct object, as in *Il dort* (He's sleeping)

Verb

See Sentence

Voice

See Active and passive voice

THE FRENCH AND ENGLISH LANGUAGES COMPARED

1.1 French and English: a common origin

French and English belong to the Indo-European family of languages. According to recent research, about 8,000 years ago, people living in a region located somewhere between the east of Turkey and Azerbaijan spoke a language which can be reconstructed more or less entirely, and which today is known as 'Proto-Indo-European'. As a result of migration, this language spread over a territory stretching from India to the Atlantic.

Over millennia, Proto-Indo-European gave rise to more than a thousand languages, which are divided into groups, including, in Europe:

▶ the Germanic languages (German, Dutch, **English**, Swedish, Norwegian, Danish, Icelandic, etc.)

▶ the Italic languages (Latin, then the Romance languages such as Italian, **French**, Spanish, Portuguese, Romanian, etc.)

These languages contain a number of common features, the main ones being:

▶ **inflection**: words can undergo changes in their sound or appearance, even in their root, e.g. *sing, sings, sang, sung, song; firm, confirm, confirmed, confirming, confirmation, confirmations.* Each separate form carries a single meaning or contains a number of meanings: the word 'sings' tells you the category it belongs to (verb), its number (singular), its tense (present), its mood (indicative) and its aspect (non-continuous). Inflection is seen in:

  ▶ **declension**: between four and six cases, according to the language (German has four cases, Russian six). Today, in English as well as in French, there are only a few remnants of declension (e.g. in English, *I* versus *me*, *she* versus *her*; *who* versus *whose* versus *whom*; and in French, *je* versus *me* versus *moi*; *qui* versus *que* versus *quoi*).

  ▶ **conjugation**: the tenses, moods and persons of the verb, e.g. *être: je suis, nous étions, ils seront, que tu sois . . .*

  ▶ **gender**: masculine, feminine, neuter, e.g. *il* versus *elle*; *he* versus *she* versus *it*; *(la) main tendue* (f) (outstretched hand), *(le) muscle tendu* (m) (stretched muscle), *hand / foot* (n).

  ▶ **number**: singular and plural, e.g *un enfant / des enfants* (child / children)

▶ **articles,** definite, indefinite, partitive, e.g. *le vocabulaire, une grammaire, du lait.* In French, the article indicates the gender and number of a noun, e.g: *une page et un crayon.* In the plural, however, there is no distinction of the article between the two genders: *des pages et des crayons.*

From the fifteenth century onwards, as a result of the great discoveries of the Renaissance and colonization, half of the population of the world today speak an Indo-European language, and the Latin alphabet is used extensively outside the Indo-European family.

Today, the French and English languages are spoken on all five continents. French, with around 270 million speakers, is the fifth most-spoken language, the third language of business and the fourth of the internet.

French	English
Indo-European language family.	
Order of words in the sentence (subject–verb–object – SVO)	
6,000–7,000 years ago, the formation, from a common origin, of four language branches, two of which are Italo-Celtic and Germano-Balto-Slavic.	
The Italo-Celtic branch includes Latin, among others; French emerges from Latin after the sixth/seventh century.	The Germanic branch includes Anglo-Saxon among others, from which English emerges around the fifth/sixth century.
Until the Roman invasion (52 BCE), Gallic, a continental form of Celtic, which died out around the fifth century, was spoken in Gaul.	Until the Roman invasion (43 CE), insular Celtic languages, Gaelic, Welsh, Cornish, etc., were spoken in 'Britannia'. Some of these languages are still spoken in Scotland, Ireland, Wales and Brittany, in France.
52 BCE, the Roman invasion: Latin gradually replaced Celtic (the Gallo-Roman civilization).	43 CE: Celtic and Latin co-existed (Romano-British culture).
Up to this point, the two countries had a similar linguistic destiny.	
Fourth and fifth centuries: the invasion of Germanic tribes, the Franks, and in the 10th century, the Normans. The Franks, from whom the name 'France' is derived, spoke Latin but: (i) they influenced pronunciation and (ii) enriched the vocabulary (see below).	Fourth and fifth centuries: the invasion of Germanic tribes: Angles, Saxons, Frisians, Jutes. The Britons adopted their languages, from which English is derived. Later, colonization by the Vikings, some of whom invaded France.

French	English
The origins of French are in vulgar Latin spoken by Roman soldiers, traders and administrators.	The origins of English are in northern Germanic dialects.
842: the Oaths of Strasbourg is the first official document that testifies to a language, French, which is derived from Latin but is sufficiently independent from it. Latin continued to be used in written documents for several centuries.	731: Bede referred to the existence of five languages in Britain: English (of the Angles), Welsh (of the Britons), Gaelic (of the Scots), the language spoken by the Picts and Latin.

1.1.1 Comparison of French with English

1.1.2 French and English: reciprocal influences

Among the Germanic languages English has a special place. Over the centuries, its grammar was modified and its vocabulary enriched by Norman, then French and Latin. Most sources suggest that 50 to 70 per cent of English vocabulary is derived from these three languages.

For its part, French has incorporated around 1,200 English words.

The two languages, although they belong to different groups, have undergone reciprocal influences, one of which is Germanic, with the influence of Latin and French, the other Latin, with Germanic and English influence. The two languages have kept a large number of points in common in terms both of vocabulary and grammatical structure. However, both languages have developed along different pathways and it is useful to point out below some of the most notable differences.

1.2 Vocabulary

A very large number of words in the English language are derived from French; as a result, every learner of English acquires thousands of words of French origin.

1.2.1 Common vocabulary, French to English and vice versa (F = French; E = English)

▶ Sometimes exactly the same word but pronounced differently, e.g. *question, illusion, impression, social, distance, patience, bulldozer, pull-over, self-service, amateur*

▶ Sometimes the same word but retaining the original pronunciation:

▶ French: un *one-man show*, *le weekend*, *un boycott*, *le fair-play*, *une start-up*, *un T-shirt* . . .

▶ English: *cliché*, *au pair*, *amour-propre*, *avant-garde*, *art nouveau* . . .

▶ Sometimes with a slight change, e.g. ideal versus *idéal*; vocabulary versus *vocabulaire*; doctor versus *docteur*; biology versus *biologie*; *station-service*; apart versus *à part*

▶ Sometimes the word undergoes such a transformation that it is unrecognizable:

▶ e.g. from E to F packet boat → *paquebot*; bowling green → *boulingrin*

▶ e.g. from F to E *napperon* → an apron; F *caboche* (familiar for 'head') → E cabbage

▶ False Anglicisms, e.g. F *des baskets* / *des tennis* = E trainers / tennis shoes; F *recordman* = E record holder; F *planning* = E schedule; F *goal* = E goal-keeper; F *camping* = E camping-site.

▶ False Gallicisms, e.g. F *bon vivant* = E bon viveur; F *salle de bain attenante* = E en suite; F *jeune fille au pair* = E au pair; F *lieu* = E venue.

▶ Sometimes both words of Anglo-Saxon, Anglo-Norman, and even Latin, origin coexist:

▶ Doublets: Anglo-Saxon / Anglo-Norman e.g. ox / beef; sheep / mutton; withdraw / disengage; freedom / liberty; churchyard / cemetery;

▶ Triplets: Anglo-Saxon / Anglo-Norman / Latin e.g. begin / commence / initiate; end / finish / terminate; buy / purchase / acquire.

1.2.2 False friends

Hundreds of words are 'false friends', that is, they have a similar form to a word in one's native language but a different meaning.

French	English
location (renting)	location (i.e. place)
actuellement (now, at present)	actually (i.e. in fact)
comprehensif (understanding)	comprehensive (i.e. thorough)
éventuellement (possibly)	eventually (i.e. in the long run)
habit (clothes)	habit (i.e. custom)
passer un examen (to take an exam)	to pass an exam (i.e. be successful)
sensible (sensitive)	sensible (i.e. reasonable)
route (road)	route (i.e. itinerary)

1.3 Grammar

1.3.1 Time and tense (see also relevant sections in Chapter 10, Verbs 2)

While French and English tend to use the same tense to refer to periods of time, a number of differences exist between the two languages in the use of tenses.

The imperfect tense

The French imperfect tense does not have an exact equivalent in English and tends to be confused with the French compound past or simple past tenses. It refers to actions that were unfurling during a time period that has been completed, to habitual actions and to descriptions in the past. The closest equivalents in English are the notion of 'used to/ would (in the past)' and the past continuous (was + . . .ing).

*Avant on **avait** un téléphone fixe par famille.*	In the past we **had** (i.e. **used to have**) a fixed telephone line for every family.
*Tous les matins elle **lisait** le journal local.*	She **would read** the local newspaper every morning.
*Elle **dormait** dans le jardin quand le vent se leva et fit voler son chapeau.*	She **was sleeping** in the garden when the wind rose and blew her hat away.
*Son professeur lui a dit qu'elle **était** douée.*	Her teacher told her that she **was** gifted.

The compound past tense

The compound past expresses an action that has been completed in the past. Its nearest equivalent in English is the simple past. It may, however, also refer to events that continue into the present, which are expressed by the English compound past.

*Il a soudain **aperçu** le danger et **s'est écarté**.*	He suddenly **saw** the danger and **moved away**.
*J'**ai** toujours **su** que je ne suis pas fait pour ce genre de travail.*	I've always **known** that I'm not cut out for that sort of work.

The compound past differs from the imperfect in that the expression of the past moment is usually not precise : *Il a étudié le français* (He studied French). For the imperfect to be used, more information needs to be given: *Il étudiait le français à cette époque* (He studied (used to study) French at that time).

The simple past tense

This tense describes a single action in the past and corresponds to the simple past in English. It is hardly ever used in spoken French. Its use tends to be literary:

*Elle **prit** l'avion la première fois à 15 ans.*	She **flew** for the first time at the age of 15.

The simple past is often used to express a single action in contrast to a 'background' imperfect.

*Il contemplait le rivage quand soudain il **vit** un nageur en difficulté.*	He was looking at the coastline when suddenly he **saw** a swimmer in difficulty.

The future and conditional tenses

In most circumstances the future and conditional tenses in French perform as in English. One notable difference, however, is after conjunctions referring to time, such as *quand*, *dès que*, *aussitôt que*. In subordinate clauses introduced by these conjunctions, the tense is future if the main clause is in the future, and conditional if the main clause is in the conditional. In this type of sentence in English, the tense of the verb in the subordinate clause is present and past respectively.

*Je t'avertirai dès qu'on **aura** de ses nouvelles.*	I'll let you know as soon as we **have** news of him.
*Je lui ai dit qu'on en reparlerait quand son rapport **serait** sur ma table.*	I told her that we would speak about it again when her report **was** on my table.

Note

The English construction for making suggestions using 'shall' is translated using a present tense in French.

Est-ce que (tu veux que) j'apporte le vin ?	Shall I bring the wine?

Time expressions

Expressing time: *depuis*, *il y a*, *pendant* (for, since, ago)

To express the concept of time, the two languages do not always use the same tenses. This occurs especially when using the preposition *depuis,* which can mean either 'since' (referring back from now to the beginning of the action) or 'for' (referring to the time that has elapsed until the present moment).

In the case of actions that begin in the past and are still happening in the present or have consequences for the present moment:

▶ English views the action as **in the process of development,** from the past to the present, and so uses the **compound past tense.**

▶ French, on the other hand, only takes into account **the end of the process,** i.e. the present moment, and so it uses the **present tense.**

*Vous **taillez** ces arbres depuis ce matin.*	You've **been pruning** those trees since this morning.
*Vous **taillez** ces arbres depuis plusieurs heures !*	You've **been pruning** those trees for several hours!
*Je **connais** Sophie depuis des lustres.*	I've **known** Sophie for ages.
*Ils **marchent** depuis 2 heures.*	They've **been** walking **since** 2 o'clock/for 2 hours.

The starting-point can also be a place:

*Ma voiture **fait** ce drôle de bruit depuis Marseille.*	My car **has made** this funny noise since Marseilles.

If the action has no link with the present moment, i.e. is in past time, French uses a past tense, e.g. the imperfect, while English uses the pluperfect.

*Elle **était** en Espagne depuis le 30 juin.*	She **had been** in Spain since June 30th (but she isn't there any more).
*Je t'**attendais** depuis 20 minutes alors.*	I **had been waiting** for you for 20 minutes then.

Notes

▶ The time prepositions *pendant* and *durant* (during) use a past tense as in English:

▶ *On a parlé politique pendant une heure pendant/durant le repas.*	We talked politics for an hour during the meal.

▶ *il y a* + a period of time = 'ago':

▶ *Il est revenu il y a deux heures.*	He came back two hours ago.

The subjunctive

The subjunctive is a mood of the verb which expresses 'unreality': desires, wishes/will, doubt, fear, etc. It exists in four tenses: the present, the past, the imperfect, and the pluperfect. The present and past subjunctive are widely used; the imperfect and pluperfect are extremely formal and rarely used. There is no future subjunctive.

In English the subjunctive has practically disappeared. It exists in the odd construction, e.g. It is essential that they **be** aware of the new regulations; I insist that she **leave** immediately; If I **were** her father, I would speak to her; I wish I **were** you.

Apart from the occasional expression, such as *Vive la France !* (Long live France!) *Advienne que pourra* (Come what may), where the conjunction *que* is understood, the subjunctive is used with subordinate clauses introduced by *que*, *bien que*, *pour que*, *de peur que*, etc.):

*Faut-il que vous **fassiez** tous ces kilomètres ?*	Do you have to travel all those kilometres?
*Nettoyez bien avant qu'ils ne **viennent** !*	Clean up properly before they come!

Que may sometimes be replaced by the conjunction *de*, in which case the verb is in the infinitive:

*Il est important **que vous lisiez** toutes ces notes.* *Il est important **de lire** toutes ces notes.*	It is important that you read / for you to read all these notes.

If the subject of the main clause is the same as that of the subordinate clause the infinitive must be used and not the subjunctive:

Je voudrais partir plus tôt (and not **Je voudrais que je parte . . .*).	I'd like to leave earlier.

1.3.2 Agreement

Subject–verb agreement: collective nouns

A collective noun is a singular noun that designates a number of beings or things, e.g. a group, a crowd, the majority, a stack, a series, the police, the clergy, the family, the fleet. In French agreement with collective nouns is singular:

L'équipe a bien joué.	The team has played well.
La foule se disperse lentement.	The crowd disperses slowly.

In British English, agreement with a collective noun can be plural:

Le Paris Saint-Germain a bien joué.	Paris Saint-Germain **have** played well.

In American English, agreement tends to be singular:

Le New York Yankees a bien joué.	New York Yankees **has** played well.

Notes

▶ The word 'police' is always followed by the plural in English; the French equivalent is always followed by the singular.

▶ *La police **est** particulièrement occupée aujourd'hui.*	The police **are** particularly busy today.

▶ *la plupart* = most

    ▶ When used on its own, *la plupart* is followed by the plural.

    ▶ *La plupart étaient à l'heure.*   Most were on time.

    But agreement is singular, unlike in English, when it is used with a complement:

    ▶ *La plupart des trains* **était** *à l'heure.*   Most of the trains **were** on time.

Agreement of past participles

The essential difference between the past participle in French (e.g. *joué*, *appris*, *voulu*) and English (*played*, *learned*, *wanted*) is that the past participle in French adds an ending in certain circumstances, whereas the English past participle is invariable. For example: the past participle *né* adds 's' to make a plural in this sentence:

    Ils sont nés en l'an 2000.   They were born in the year 2000.

The past participle is made feminine plural to agree with a preceding direct object, as in the following phrase:

    les trois chansons qu'ils ont chantées   the three songs they sang

For a complete account of the agreement of past participles, see 11.6.4.

1.3.3 Word order

The sentence

SVO: The basic order of the components of a sentence in Indo-European languages is subject–verb–object.

Modifications of this pattern occur:

▶ for expressive reasons, as follows:

    a. use of introductory phrases such as *c'est . . . que*:

       C'est une ville que j'apprécie particulièrement.   It's a town that I particularly appreciate.

    b. apposition of personal pronouns:

       Lui, il gagne toujours, moi, je perds souvent.   He always wins and me, I often lose.

    c. placing of a complement before the verb for emphasis:

       L'avion, je déteste !   I really hate flying!

    d. inversion:

       Bien plus froide est la température quand il vente !   It gets a lot colder when it's windy!

▶ with direct and indirect object pronouns, which are placed before the verb in French:

*Je **les lui** ai offerts.*   I offered **them** to **him / her.**

▶ with prepositions, 'stranding', i.e. placing a preposition after the object it governs (usually at the end of a sentence), does not occur in French.

*Il n'a aucune idée **de** ce dont il parle.*   He has no idea what he is talking **about.**

*Je n'aime pas le garçon **près de** qui tu es assis.*   I don't like the boy (that) you are sitting **next to.**

▶ in interrogative and negative sentences:

  ▶ interrogative sentences

French	English
est-ce que ?	ASI: auxiliary + subject + infinitive
Est-ce que tu m'accompagnes ?	Will you come with me?
Est-ce que cela vous dérange ?	Do you mind?
Alternatively:	
Inversion of the subject: *M'accompagnes-tu ?*	
Rising intonation ↗: *Tu m'accompagnes ?*	

  ▶ negative sentences

French	English
Verb or auxiliary framed by a double negative word: *ne … pas, ne … rien,* etc.	SANI: subject + auxiliary + negation + infinitive
*Vous **ne** m'accompagnerez **pas**.*	You won't come with me.
*Elle **ne** m'a **pas** accompagné.*	She didn't go with me.

▶ 'back to front' constructions

In this type of construction, the direct object becomes the subject of the sentence in English and the subject becomes the object.

Il me manque.   I miss him.

Ça me plaît.   I like that.

Adjectives

Qualifying adjectives are usually placed after the noun, unlike in English:

la langue anglaise	the English language
une eau fraiche	fresh water

Note

In some English expressions the French order is followed: e.g. *court martial, notary public, secretary general.*

Adjectives, which are invariable in English, also vary in gender and number in French:

*un écolier **studieux***	a studious schoolboy
*une écolière **studieuse***	a studious schoolgirl
*des écolières **studieuses***	studious schoolgirls

Adverbs

If adverbs of frequency like *parfois, souvent, jamais* are not stressed, they are placed after the verb or the auxiliary in French. In English, they are placed between the subject and the verb or after the auxiliary:

*Je le voyais **souvent** mais je ne lui avais **jamais** parlé auparavant.*	I **often** saw him but I had **never** spoken to him before.

1.3.4 Nouns

Gender

All nouns in French, without exception, are either masculine or feminine. This affects articles, pronouns, adjectives and past participles that are connected to these nouns. Thus:

Le chocolat noir est meilleur, il est plus sain.	Dark chocolate is better; it's healthier.
La tasse était noire à l'intérieur, elle contenait probablement du café.	The cup was black inside; it probably contained coffee.

For masculine and feminine endings, see Chapter 2.

Number

Certain words are plural in English and singular in French and vice versa:

Plural in English	Singular in French	Plural in French	Singular in English
stairs	*un escalier* (or *les escaliers*)	*bagages*	baggage, luggage
physics, linguistics	*la physique, la linguistique*	*affaires*	business
scales	*la balance*	*cheveux*	hair
drums	*la batterie*	*prévisions*	forecast
to wash the dishes	*faire la vaisselle*	*pâtes*	pasta

Certain words have a different meaning in the plural:

Singular	Plural
l'économie = economics	*les économies* = savings
un échec = failure	*les échecs* = chess
le cuivre = copper	*les cuivres* = brass (musical instruments)
la lunette = telescope	*les lunettes* = glasses
une vacance = vacancy	*les vacances* = holiday(s)

1.3.5 Determiners

Nouns that have a general or abstract sense are normally preceded by an article in French, but not in English: *le courage* (courage), *la folie* (madness), *l'électronique* (electronics).

Possessive adjectives and pronouns agree in gender and number with the thing possessed in French, and not the possessor, as in English:

> *la tasse de Simon, sa tasse*   Simon's cup, his cup
>
> *le verre de Marie, son verre*   Mary's glass, her glass

Demonstratives

French adds the suffixes *-ci* and *-là* to nouns or pronouns, to indicate where objects are, nearer or further from the speaker:

> *ces gens-là*   those people (over there)
>
> *Je préfère celle-ci.*   I prefer this one (here).

1.3.6 Pronouns

There are no equivalents in English for the pronouns *en* and *y*, which are often not translated.

Il n'y en a pas.   There aren't any (i.e. of them).

J'y vais.   I'm going (i.e. there).

The distinction between the subject pronouns *tu* (singular, informal) and *vous* (plural or formal) is maintained in French. The equivalent in English of both pronouns is 'you'; the old informal pronoun 'thou' has all but disappeared.

1.3.7 Prepositions

The notion of 'belonging' in French is rendered by using the preposition *de*:

le pied de la table   the table leg

In English, this notion is rendered:

either by using the same structure as in French, with the preposition *of*: *le commencement de l'hiver* (the beginning of winter); *les mensonges des politiciens* (the lies of politicians);

or by using *'s* (singular) or *s'* (plural) after the thing 'possessed': *le livre de Marie* (Mary's book); *le journal d'hier* (yesterday's paper); *l'appartement de ses parents* (his parents' flat)

or by juxtaposing the thing possessed with the 'possessor': *une marche de deux jours* (a two-day walk).

In French, to avoid repetition, *celui de / celle de* + the possessor is used, where the equivalent in English is the possessor + *'s* or *s'*.

Ce n'est pas ton siège, c'est celui de Daniel.   This is not your seat, it's Daniel's.

The preposition *chez*, expressing the idea of 'at home' or 'at the shop' can also be translated using the above construction:

chez Lisa at Lisa's; *chez l'épicier* at the grocer's.

1.3.8 Relative pronouns

The conjunction *that* is often omitted in English, especially after verbs like *say*, *think*, *suggest*. In French, the equivalent *que* is never left out:

*J'ai pensé **que** vous seriez d'accord*   I thought (that) you would agree to
avec ma proposition.   my proposal.

1.3.9 Numbers

The Celtic, or possibly Norman, 'vigesimal' (or base 20) system is peculiar to numbers from 80 to 99 in French. Thus:

$80 = 4 \times 20$ *quatre-vingts*

$90 = 4 \times 20 + 10$ *quatre-vingt-dix*

$98 = 4 \times 20 + 18$ *quatre-vingt-dix-huit*

Numbers from 70 to 79 are a mix of the decimal and vigesimal systems: $60 + 10$.

$72 = 60 + 12$ *soixante-douze*

2 NOUNS

Nouns are words that we use to label living beings, things, feelings, ideas or actions:

Charles, enfant, chien, livre, poubelle, amour, économie, construction

KEY POINTS

✦ All nouns in French, without exception, are either masculine or feminine in gender:

lion (m), *lionne* (f), *bâtiment* (m), *maison* (f)

In some cases nouns may be of either gender:

un / une élève, un / une enfant, un / une artiste

✦ Nouns are either singular or plural; the plural is usually indicated by a change in the ending of the word:

lion (sing.) → *lions* (pl.)

lionne (sing.) → *lionnes* (pl.)

✦ Nouns decide the gender and number of any determiners that precede them, such as *mon, les, la*:

Mon frère aîné a peint les murs de la cuisine.	My older brother painted the kitchen walls.

✦ Nouns determine whether a following verb is singular or plural:

*Mon frère aîné **a peint** les murs de la cuisine; mes sœurs cadettes **ont peint** le plafond.*	My older brother painted the kitchen walls; my younger sisters painted the ceiling.

✦ When a noun is accompanied by determiners and adjectives a **noun phrase** is formed:

le petit cheval blanc	the little white horse

✦ All nouns are either **proper noun**s or **common nouns**

Nouns can be categorized in different types. These are:

1. Concrete and abstract nouns
2. 'Count' and 'mass' nouns
3. Collective nouns
4. Simple nouns and compound nouns

Proper nouns and common nouns

Proper nouns

Proper nouns designate things or beings that are unique, such as a specific person, country, town or place. They always begin with a capital letter, as in English: *Marie-France, Louis XIV, Marseille, l'Angleterre, Eurodisney.*

Some proper nouns are preceded by the definite article:

la Bretagne	Brittany
l'Amérique	America
le Mont-Blanc	Mont Blanc
la Nouvelle-Zélande	New Zealand
la Seine	the Seine
la Terre	the Earth

Common nouns

All other nouns are common nouns: they designate things or beings that are *not* unique. They are usually preceded by a determiner:

le lion; chaque lion; tous les lions; une élève; cette élève

Note

Some proper nouns can become common nouns, in which case they may be preceded by a determiner:

▶ *un bottin* is a telephone directory that derives from the name of its founder, Sébastien Bottin

▶ *un camembert* is a cheese that comes from the village of Camembert, in Normandy

▶ *un lycée* is named after the Lycée (Lyceum) in Ancient Greece, where Aristotle taught

and vice versa, some common nouns can become proper nouns:

▶ *le Débarquement*, from the word for 'disembarkation', refers to the Normandy landings in 1944

▶ *la Libération*, referring to the Liberation of Paris in 1944, derives from the common noun meaning 'freeing, release'

▶ *la Révolution française* is a particular revolution that began in 1789.

2.1 Types of nouns

While all nouns are either common or proper, various types of noun can be distinguished. The main ones are:

2.1.1 Concrete nouns and abstract nouns

Concrete nouns are nouns that have physical existence (i.e., you can see or touch them).

Abstract nouns are nouns that do not have a physical existence (i.e., you cannot see or touch them).

Concrete nouns		Abstract nouns	
livre	book	*bonheur*	happiness
maison	house	*connaissances*	knowledge
ordinateur	computer	*joie*	joy
vache	cow	*tristesse*	sadness

In general, all common nouns in French, including abstract nouns, are accompanied by the definite article.

*Tout le monde cherche **le** bonheur.*	Everyone looks for happiness.
*En vieillissant, **la** mémoire diminue.*	Memory deteriorates as we grow older.

But when the abstract noun has a complement, a definite article is also used in English:

Le *design des meubles suit les modes.*	**The** design of furniture follows fashion.

2.1.2 'Count' nouns and 'mass' nouns

In the following sentences:

Virginie avait plus de pommes que Jean-Charles.	Virginie had more apples than Jean-Charles.
Virginie avait plus de tact que Jean-Charles.	Virginie had more tact than Jean-Charles.

The noun *pommes* can be counted and is in the plural. This type of noun is called 'countable' or 'count' and can be used either in the singular or the plural.

The noun 'tact', on the other hand, designates an entity that cannot be counted (you cannot have *two 'tacts'), and is in the singular. This type of noun is called 'non-countable' or 'mass', and does not usually have a plural form.

Mass nouns frequently designate substances: *bois* (wood), *café* (coffee), *lait* (milk), *sel* (salt). These nouns may be used in the plural but in this case their meaning changes: *trois cafés* = three cups of coffee, or three different types of coffee.

Mass nouns cannot be preceded by the indefinite article or a number. They are preceded by other determiners such as the partitive article (see 3.5) *du / de la, des*, and expressions like *un peu de* and *plus / moins de*. You can say:

J'ai ajouté du sel / plus de sel / deux pincées de sel dans la soupe.	I've added some / more / two pinches of salt to the soup.

but NOT

*J'ai ajouté deux sels dans la soupe.	*I've added two salts to the soup.

2.1.3 Collective nouns

Collective nouns refer to groups of people, animals or things:

le bétail	cattle
l'équipe	team
le mobilier	furniture
la police	the police
une douzaine	a dozen
la majorité	the majority

These nouns are followed by a verb in the singular, unlike in English where they are often followed by the plural.

*La police **était** sur les lieux, **elle** a tout vu.*	The police **were** on the spot; **they** saw it all.
*Le bétail ne **transmet** la fièvre aphteuse que pendant une brève durée.*	Cattle only **transmit** foot-and-mouth disease for a short time.

Note

When a collective noun is followed by a complement in the plural it may be followed by the singular or the plural, depending on the focus of the speaker.

Un groupe de chômeurs plutôt réduit s'est présenté.	A rather small group of unemployed workers appeared.

Here the verb is in the singular. For the speaker, what matters is the idea of the group as a whole.

Un groupe de chômeurs bien indemnisés sont entrés dans la pièce.	A group of well-compensated unemployed workers entered the room.

Here the verb is in the plural. For the speaker it is the workers as individuals that matter and not the group.

The meaning or the intention of the speaker is therefore the prime factor in determining whether a singular or a plural verb is used. If the action is *collective*, a singular verb is used; if the speaker wants to focus on the action carried out by the *members* of the group, the plural is used.

2.1.4 Simple nouns and compound nouns

Nouns are either *simple* or *compound*:

▶ simple nouns consist of one word: *arbre* (tree), *agriculteur* (farmer), *engrais* (fertilizer)

▶ compound nouns may be written as:

  ▶ one word

gentilhomme (= gentil + homme) (archaic)	gentleman
passeport (= passe + port)	passport

  ▶ two words that are juxtaposed

État membre	Member state
cas limite	borderline case

  ▶ two words separated by a hyphen

sourd-muet	deaf-mute
après-midi	afternoon

  ▶ two words linked by a preposition, which may be hyphenated

pomme de terre	potato
brosse à dents	toothbrush
arc-en-ciel	rainbow
tête-à-tête	tête-à-tête

2.1.5 Gens

▶ The word *gens* is a mass noun which is found only in the plural form. You cannot say **trois gens* or **quelques gens*; in these cases *personnes* has to be used instead: *trois personnes, quelques personnes*.

▶ *Gens* has to be used when referring to people collectively:

| Aujourd'hui **les gens** ne croient plus à rien. | People don't believe in anything these days. |

▶ *Gens* may be preceded by *beaucoup / peu de, tous les . . ., tant de, la majorité des . . .* and *certaines . . .*

| Il y avait **tant de gens** qu'on ne pouvait pas respirer. | There were so many people that you couldn't breathe. |
| **Peu de gens** visitent le monument. | Few people visit the monument. |

2.1.6 Acronyms and abbreviations

Acronyms

There are two kinds of acronyms:

▶ words consisting of the first letter of each of several words. These acronyms (known as *acronymes* or *sigles* in French) are written in capital letters, each one nowadays rarely followed by a full stop. The letters are pronounced separately.

| HLM (habitation à loyer modéré) | (council housing estate) |
| SNCF (Société nationale des chemins de fer français) | (French railway company) |

▶ words that are pronounced like ordinary words. These acronyms do not have full stops.

OTAN or Otan (Organisation du traité de l'Atlantique Nord)	NATO
Ovni (objet volant non identifié)	UFO
Sida (syndrome d'immunodéficience acquise)	Aids (or AIDS)

Abbreviations

An abbreviation is the shortened part of a word: Mme = *Madame*.

The following rules apply:

▶ If the abbreviation does not include the final letter of the word, it finishes with a full stop:

Réf.= référence

M.= Monsieur

hab.= habitant

dép. = département

env. = environ

etc. = et cetera

adj. = adjectif

fém. = féminin

masc. = masculin

▶ If the abbreviation includes the last letter of the word, there is no full stop:

Dr = Docteur en médecine

bd = boulevard

ave = avenue

no = numéro

▶ If the abbreviations relate to measurements, they do not end in a full stop, even if they do not include the final letter:

min = minute(s)

V = volt(s)

kg = kilogramme(s)

km / h = kilomètre(s) par heure

A = ampère(s)

2.1.7 Shortened words

As in English, some long words are commonly used in a shortened form because of their frequency. There are two ways of shortening a word:

▶ the end of the word is cut off:

vélo (vélocipède)	bike
photo (photographie)	photo
métro (métropolitain)	metro, underground
auto (automobile)	car
ado (adolescent)	adolescent (informal)

▶ the beginning of the word is cut off:

car (autocar)	coach
bus (omnibus)	bus
chandail (this word has its origin in a special jumper worn by a marchand d'ail)	sweater

2.2 Gender

It is not always possible to predict the gender of a given noun and so students should get into the habit of learning the noun together with its article: for example, **un** *timbre* (a postage stamp) and **une** *forêt* (a forest), rather than *timbre* and *forêt*. Helpful guidelines exist for predicting the gender of groups of nouns, as explained in this section, but there are often exceptions to the rule.

Nouns may be classified in two broad groups: those referring to the gender of animate beings, and those referring to inanimate objects.

2.2.1 *Gender of animate beings*

▶ Generally nouns that refer to human beings are masculine or feminine according to their sex:

un homme	man
un fils	son
le père	father
une femme	woman
une fille	girl, daughter
la mère	mother

▶ Likewise the gender of some nouns that refer to animals is predictable:

un étalon	stallion
une jument	mare

    ▶ But most animals are either masculine or feminine without reference to their sex: for example, *une souris* (mouse) and *une baleine* (whale) have no separate masculine form; *un chimpanzé* (chimpanzee), *un crocodile* (crocodile) have no separate feminine form. If you want to refer to the other sex you have to say *une souris mâle, un chimpanzé femelle*.

▶ As a rule the names of species of animals are masculine:

un mammifère	mammal
un poisson	fish
un oiseau	bird
un dinosaur	dinosaur
un homme	man

▶ The young of animals are also usually masculine:

un chien	dog	une chienne	bitch	un chiot	puppy
un chat	cat	une chatte	female cat	un chaton	kitten
		une carpe	carp	un carpeau	young carp

But in some cases there are separate forms for masculine and feminine young:

un aigle	eagle	un aiglon	eaglet	une aiglonne	eaglet
un cheval	horse	un poulain	foal	une pouliche	filly
une vache	cow	un veau	calf	une génisse	heifer

▶ A few nouns are of either masculine or feminine gender only, but may refer to men or women:

une personne	person
un témoin	witness
une star	star (in the sense of a pop star)
une victime	victim

Paul était un témoin exceptionnel.	Paul was an exceptional witness.
Alain Souchon est une star encore appréciée en France aujourd'hui.	Alain Souchon is a star still liked in France today.

▶ Some nouns can be either masculine or feminine depending on whether they refer to the male or female sex:

un enfant, une enfant	child
un élève, une élève	pupil
un collègue, une collègue	colleague
un secrétaire, une secrétaire	secretary
un fonctionnaire, une fonctionnaire	civil servant
un journaliste, une journaliste	journalist

2.2.2 Gender of inanimate nouns

The gender of inanimate nouns is arbitrary:

un toit	roof	but	une toiture	roofing
le théâtre	theatre	but	la poésie	poetry
le cinéma	cinema	but	la littérature	literature
le pied	foot	but	la main	hand
le bras	arm	but	la jambe	leg
le genou	knee	but	la cheville	ankle

It is possible however to detect a certain logic in some cases: with objects that are related conceptually the bigger one is masculine, the smaller feminine.

un camion	lorry	une voiture	car
un bateau	boat, ship	une barque	small boat
un portail	gate	une porte	door

But

| un vélo | bike | une bicyclette | bicycle | une moto(cyclette) | motorbike |

2.2.3 Gender of products and means of transport

A useful way of remembering the gender of a product or a means of transport which derives from a noun is that it takes the gender of the 'group' noun it is identified with.

Product/means of transport		Origin	
Wines			
un bordeaux	un vin (wine)	Bordeaux	a city
un bourgogne	un vin	la Bourgogne	a region
un champagne	un vin	la Champagne	a region
Cheeses			
un camembert	un fromage (cheese)	Camembert	a village in Normandy
un brie	un fromage	la Brie	a region
un chèvre	un fromage	une chèvre	a she-goat
un hollande	un fromage	la Hollande	a country

Product/means of transport		Origin	
Means of transport			
une Renault	une voiture (car)	Renault	a car manufacturer
un Renault	un camion / un autobus (lorry / bus)	Renault	a car manufacturer
le Concorde	un avion (aeroplane)	la concorde	an abstract concept
le Titanic	un bateau (boat)	les Titans	Greek mythology
Other terms			
un canon	un appareil photos (camera)	Canon	a company
un MacIntosh	un ordinateur (computer)	une MacIntosh	a type of apple
une kanterbräu	une bière (beer)	Kanterbräu	a brasserie near Paris
un chine	un papier de luxe (paper)	la Chine	a country

2.2.4 Recognition of masculine gender by the endings of words

Nouns ending in the following letters are masculine:

Masculine endings		Main exceptions	
-ail, -eil, -ueil, -l, -al			
travail	work		
portail	gate		
soleil	sun		
réveil	wakening		
accueil	welcome		
cheval	horse		
journal	newspaper		
appel	call		
sol	ground		
-age		cage	cage
personnage	character	plage	beach
garage	garage	image	image
fromage	cheese	nage	swimming

(continued)

25

(continued)

Masculine endings		Main exceptions	
-c		*fac*	(short for '*faculté*') faculty (university)
trac	stage fright		
trafic	traffic		
parc	park		
sac	bag		
viaduc	viaduct		
-d, -ard			
canard	duck		
renard	fox		
retard	delay		
bord	edge		
-ège		*Norvège*	Norway
cortège	procession		
siège	seat, siege		
-er, -ier			
boucher	butcher		
danger	danger		
oranger	orange tree		
saladier	salad bowl		
couturier	couturier		
figuier	fig tree		
-eur			
voyageur	traveller		
serveur	waiter		
aviateur	aviator		
concepteur	designer		
-f		*nef*	nave
poncif	commonplace	*soif*	thirst

Masculine endings		Main exceptions	
-g			
blog	blog		
grog	toddy		
tag	tag		
-i		fourmi	ant
suivi	monitoring		
-isme			
fatalisme	fatalism		
sophisme	sophisme		
charisme	charisma		
-ment			
argument	argument		
développement	development		
ciment	cement		
-eau		eau	water
bureau	desk, office	peau	skin
château	castle		
-oi		foi	faith
émoi	commotion	loi	law
roiking		paroi	partition
emploi	job		
-oir			
comptoir	counter		
désespoir	despair		
miroir	mirror		
rasoir	razor		
soir	evening		
-on		leçon	lesson

(continued)

(continued)

Masculine endings		Main exceptions	
salon	sitting-room	façon	way
saucisson	sausage	prison	prison
cornichon	gherkin		
rayon	ray, shelf		
sermon	sermon		
soupçon	suspicion		
-t		forêt	forest
sabot	clog	nuit	night
habitat	habitat	dent	tooth
chocolat	chocolate	part	share
poulet	chicken	plupart	most

2.2.5 Masculine gender according to the meaning of the noun

▶ Days of the week, months and seasons

le lundi	Monday
le mardi	Tuesday
avril*	April
juillet*	July
le printemps	spring
un hiver	a / one winter

* Months are only used with the definite article when there is a complement.

Le janvier de l'année dernière était plus doux.	January last year was milder.

▶ Metals

le fer	iron
le plomb	lead
l'or	gold
le zinc	zinc

► Trees and shrubs

un pommier	apple tree
un oranger	orange tree
un olivier	olive tree
un citronnier	lemon tree
le chêne	chestnut tree
le hêtre	beech tree
le saule	willow tree

Exceptions

l'aubépine	hawthorn
la vigne	vine
la ronce	bramble

Note

Tree plantations are feminine:

une chênaie	oak grove
une oliveraie or *olivette*	olive grove
une orangeraie	orangery

► Numbers

un million	million
un milliard	billion
le un	number one
le sept	number seven
le mille	thousand

► Measurements

un centimètre	centimetre
un litre	litre
un hectare	hectare
un ampère	ampere
un volt	volt

(continued)

(continued)

un ohm	ohm
un joule	joule
un micron	micron
un nanomètre	nanometre

But

une année-lumière	light year

Note

Imperial weights and measures can be of either gender:

une once	ounce
un pied	foot
une livre	pound
un pouce	inch
une lieue	league
un mile	mile

▶ Languages

le japonais	Japanese
le turc	Turkish
le russe	Russian
le grec	Greek

▶ Paintings

un Rembrandt	a Rembrandt
un Picasso	a Picasso

▶ Cheeses (see also 2.2.3)

Cheeses are masculine but when referring to the shape of a cheese or to cooking, feminine words can be found:

une fourme	a blue-veined French cheese, cylinder-shaped
une brique	a brick-shaped cheese
une tomme	shaped like a thick disk: *la tomme de Savoie*
une rigotte	a small flat cylinder-shaped cheese

▶ Colours

Le Rouge et le noir	The Red and the Black (title of a novel by Stendhal)
le jaune	yellow

▶ Points of the compass

le nord	north
le sud	south
l'est	east
l'ouest	west

▶ Letters of the alphabet

un a	an 'a'
Afrique ne prend qu'un seul f	Africa has only one 'f'
l'alpha et l'oméga	alpha and omega

▶ Nouns designating an activity which is derived from an infinitive

le boire et le manger	eating and drinking
le déjeuner	lunch
le pouvoir	power
le devoir	homework
le savoir	learning, knowledge
un être	being
un avoir	asset
les dires	statements

2.2.6 Recognition of feminine gender by the endings of words

Nouns ending in the following letters are feminine:

Feminine endings		Exceptions	
-ade		jade	jade
limonade	lemonade	grade	rank
salade	salad	stade	stadium

(continued)

(continued)

Feminine endings		Exceptions	
une camarade female friend		*un camarade* male friend	
-aille, -eille, -ueille, -ouille		*Braille*	Braille
médaille	medal		
abeille	bee		
bouteille	bottle		
grenouille	frog		
-ison		*poison*	poison
saison	season	*vison*	mink
maison	house	*tison*	brand
raison	reason	*oison*	gosling
trahison	betrayal		
-ance, -anse, -ense			
circonstance	circumstance		
concordance	agreement		
défense	defence		
danse	dance		
-ce		*espace*	space
espace	space (printing)	*palace*	palace
hélice	propeller	*exercice*	exercise
audace	daring	*bénéfice*	profit, benefit
		service	service
		commerce	commerce
		office	duty, office
		dentifrice	toothpaste
-ence		*silence*	silence
patience	patience		
absence	absence		
présence	presence		

Feminine endings		Exceptions	
-ette		squelette	skeleton
pipette	pipette		
tablette	bar		
burette	burette		
-eur (abstract nouns)		bonheur	happiness
douceur	sweetness	malheur	misfortune
rancœur	resentment	honneur	honour
pâleur	pallor		
odeur	smell		
-ie		incendie	fire
penderie	wardrobe	génie	genius
anomalie	anomaly	foie	liver
allergie	allergy	parapluie	umbrella
-ière		arrière	rear
salière	salt cellar	derrière	bottom
chaumière	thatched cottage	cimetière	cemetery
fermière	woman farmer		
épicière	woman grocer		
-ine		domaine	estate
chaîne	chain	capitaine	captain
aubaine	windfall	ciné	cinema
popeline	poplin	pipeline	pipeline
marine	navy	patrimoine	patrimony
		magazine	magazine
-ion		ion	ion
religion	religion	million	million
passion	passion	billion	billion
fission	fission	camion	lorry

(continued)

(continued)

Feminine endings		Exceptions	
fusion	fusion	*scorpion*	scorpion
		espion	spy
		avion	aeroplane
-ite		*gîte*	self-catering home
(names of inflammatory illnesses)		*graphite*	graphite
otite	otitis	*satellite*	satellite
péritonite	peritonitis	*granite*	granite
méningite	meningitis	*rite*	rite
marmite	saucepan	*mérite*	merit
		site	site
-oire		*territoire*	territory
passoire	sieve	*laboratoire*	laboratory
armoire	cupboard, wardrobe	*conservatoire*	conservatory
		interrogatoire	cross-examination
		pourboire	tip
		accessoire	accessory
		observatoire	observatory
-ose, -oise, -ouse, -use, -euse, -ise			
osmose	osmosis		
blouse	overall		
excuse	excuse		
ardoise	slate		
franchise	frankness, franchise		
entreprise	company		
perceuse	drill		
marchandise	merchandise		
expertise	expertise		
-té		*été*	summer

Feminine endings		Exceptions	
société	society, business	*comité*	committee
identité	identity	*comté*	county
communauté	community	*député*	MP
absurdité	absurdity	*côté*	side
charité	charity	*traité*	treaty
acidité	acidity	*pâté*	pâté
-tion		*bastion*	bastion
nation	nation		
option	option		
question	question		
-ure		*mercure*	mercury
usure	usury	*sulfure*	sulphur
lasure	stain	*murmure*	murmur
texture	texture	*parjure*	betrayal
		augure	omen

2.2.7 Feminine gender according to the meaning of the noun (see also 2.2.3)

▶ Sciences, school and university subjects, arts, areas of knowledge

la géographie	geography
la chimie	chemistry
la physique	physics
la psychologie	psychology
l'informatique	computer science
la peinture	painting
l'architecture	architecture

2.2.8 Feminine nouns which are derived from masculine ones

▶ The usual way of forming feminine nouns is by adding *-e* to the masculine:

un Anglais	Englishman	une Anglaise	Englishwoman
un savant	wise man	une savante	wise woman
un étudiant	male student	une étudiante	female student
un voisin	male neighbour	une voisine	female neighbour

▶ Masculine nouns that end in *-e* have the same form in the feminine:

un camarade	(male) friend	une camarade	(female) friend
un élève	(male) pupil	une élève	(female) pupil
un secrétaire	(male) secretary	une secrétaire	(female) secretary

Exceptions

A number of masculine nouns ending in *-e* have their feminine in *-esse*:

un maître	master	une maîtresse	mistress
un tigre	tiger	une tigresse	tigress
un prince	prince	une princesse	princess
un comte	count	une comtesse	countess
un âne	ass	une ânesse	she-ass

▶ Masculine nouns ending in *-er* and *-ier* have their feminine in *-ère* and *-ière*:

le boulanger	(male) baker	la boulangère	(female) baker
le boutiquier	(male) shopkeeper	la boutiquière	(female) shopkeeper

▶ Masculine nouns ending in *-eur* have their feminine in *-euse*:

un vendeur – une vendeuse	salesman / -woman
un tricheur – une tricheuse	cheat

▶ Masculine nouns ending in *-teur* have their feminine in *-trice* or *-teuse*:

un spectateur – une spectatrice	spectator
un rédacteur – une rédactrice	editor
un directeur – une directrice	director
un admirateur – une admiratrice	admirer
un collaborateur – une collaboratrice	collaborator

un aviateur – une aviatrice	aviator
un tuteur – une tutrice	tutor
un chanteur – une chanteuse	singer
un acheteur – une acheteuse	buyer
un conteur – une conteuse	storyteller

Exception

un docteur – une doctoresse (or une femme médecin)	doctor

▶ Masculine nouns which double the final consonant to make the feminine:

un Colombien – une Colombienne	Colombian
un Bourguignon – une Bourguignonne	Burgundian
un Européen – une Européenne	European
un criminel – une criminelle	criminal
un cadet – une cadette	younger / youngest child

But nouns ending in **-an** and **-in** do not double the final consonant:

un faisan – une faisane	pheasant
un orphelin – une orpheline	orphan

Exception

un paysan – une paysanne	peasant

▶ Masculine nouns ending in **-at** and **-ot** do not double the *t*:

un candidat – une candidate	candidate
un scélérat – une scélérate	villain
un Hottentot – une Hottentote	Hottentot
un huguenot – une huguenote	Huguenot

Exceptions

un chat – une chatte	cat
un sot – une sotte	fool

▶ Masculine nouns ending in *-if* have their feminine *-ive*:

un sportif – une sportive	sportsman / -woman
un natif – une native	native

▶ Masculine nouns ending in *-eux* or *-oux* have their feminine in *-euse* or *-ouse*:

un chanceux – une chanceuse	a lucky person
un époux – une épouse	husband – wife

2.2.9 Irregular feminine nouns

un loup – une louve	wolf
un agneau – une agnelle	lamb
un héros – une héroïne	hero / heroine

2.2.10 Animate nouns which have separate forms for the male and the female

le père – la mère	father – mother
le fils – la fille	son – daughter
le parrain – la marraine	godfather – godmother
le mari – la femme	husband – wife
l'homme – la femme	man – woman
l'étalon – la jument	stallion – mare
le taureau – la vache	bull – cow
le frère – la sœur	brother – sister
l'oncle – la tante	uncle – aunt
un monsieur – une dame	gentleman – lady
un coq – une poule	cock – hen
un bélier – une brebis	ram – ewe
un neveu – une nièce	nephew – niece
un copain – une copine	(boy)friend – (girl)friend
un duc – une duchesse	duke – duchess
un roi – une reine	king – queen

2.2.11 The names of professions

Traditionally, most professions in France have not had feminine forms but recent changes in social attitudes have led to new feminine forms being created. These forms are gradually becoming accepted, despite some disagreement among linguists.

Notes

> *la ministre* (minister), as an alternative to *Madame le Ministre*
>
> *la juge* (judge), as an alternative to *Madame le Juge*
>
> *un médecin* (doctor). For a woman doctor, *une femme médecin* or *un médecin* is used (*médecine* refers to the science of medicine)
>
> *un écrivain* (writer); *une écrivaine* is in common use
>
> *un auteur* (author); *une auteure* is used in Quebec only

In Quebec, by contrast with France, the use of feminine titles is very widespread, accepted and often compulsory. There are uses that appear only rarely in France, such as *la docteure* (woman doctor), even though the feminine of *docteur*, *doctoresse*, already exists, *la médecin*, *la gouverneure* (woman governor), *la ministre* (female minister), *la première ministre* (woman prime minister), *la mairesse* (or *la maire*) (mayoress), etc.

2.2.12 Nouns which change their meaning according to their gender

Masculine		Feminine	
un aigle	eagle	*une aigle*	eagle (military insignia, e.g. *les aigles romaines* Roman eagles)
un crêpe	crepe	*une crêpe*	pancake
un geste	gesture	*la geste*	gest(e) (epic exploits, as in *chanson de geste*)
un critique	critic	*une critique*	criticism
un gîte	shelter, self-catering cottage	*la gîte*	bed (nautical term)
un greffe	office of Clerk of Court	*une greffe*	graft, transplant
un livre	book	*une livre*	pound in money and weight (approx. ½ kilo)
un manche	handle	*une manche*	sleeve; *La Manche* English Channel
un manœuvre	unskilled worker	*une manœuvre*	manœuvre

(continued)

(continued)

Masculine		Feminine	
un mémoire	dissertation, memo	*la mémoire*	memory
un mode	mode	*une mode*	fashion
un moule	mould	*une moule*	mussel
un mousse	ship's apprentice	*une mousse*	moss, foam
un page	page boy	*une page*	page (of book)
un parallèle	parallel (geog., e.g. of latitude)	*une parallèle*	a parallel line
un pendule	pendulum	*une pendule*	clock
le physique	physical appearance	*la physique*	physics
un poste	position	*la poste*	post office
un solde	credit /debit balance	*une solde*	pay
le pourpre	crimson	*la pourpre*	purple
un tour	turn, round, revolution (*le Tour de France* – annual cycle race)	*une tour*	tower e.g. *la Tour Eiffel*
un vase	vase	*la vase*	sludge
un voile	veil	*une voile*	sail

Notes

▶ *un hymne* (hymn) is masculine when it designates a song glorifying a hero or a people, and either masculine or feminine when it designates a religious chant / song.

▶ *Pâque* (Passover) without -*s*, designating the Jewish festival, is feminine: *la Pâque juive.*

▶ *Pâques* (Easter) with -*s*, designating the Christian festival, is masculine singular but it is always feminine when plural.

Quand Pâques sera venu ...	When Easter comes ...
Joyeuses Pâques !	Happy Easter!

▶ *personne* (person) is feminine when it designates an individual: *C'est une personne intelligente.* (S/he's an intelligent person), and masculine when it is an indefinite pronoun meaning 'no one':

Personne n'est venu.	No one has come.

2.2.13 Nouns of variable gender: amour, délice and orgue

These words are masculine in the singular and feminine in the plural:

le parfait amour	perfect love	les premières amours	first love
un vrai délice	a real delight	les vraies délices	(literary) true delight(s)
un petit orgue	a small organ	les grandes orgues	the great organ

2.2.14 Plural of gens

Adjectives following the noun *gens* (people) are masculine plural:

| des gens intelligents | intelligent people |

Adjectives preceding the noun are feminine plural:

| toutes ces vieilles gens | all these old people |

Note

When the adjective has the same form in the masculine and the feminine (e.g. *brave*), the adjective is in the masculine:

| tous ces braves gens | all these good people |

2.2.15 Countries, regions, towns

▶ Countries and regions

The names of countries and provinces which do not end in *-ie* or *-e* are masculine:

l'Iran, le Vietnam, le Japon, le Sri Lanka, le Sénégal, le Congo, le Vénézuéla, le Canada, le Québec

The names of countries and provinces which end in *-ie* or *-e* are feminine. They are the majority:

l'Allemagne, la Suisse, la Turquie, la Colombie, la Chine

Exceptions

le Cambodge, le Mexique, le Zaïre, le Maine, le Mozambique

▶ Towns

The proper names of towns are in principle masculine, but this is far from being a general rule. Sometimes the same town even has two genders.

Marseille est beau.	Marseilles is beautiful.
la Rome antique	Ancient Rome
le Rome des années 70	Rome of the 70s

The last syllable of the name can sometimes help to identify gender. If the last vowel of the word is silent [ə], as in the English word 'college', the town will usually be feminine.

la Florence des Médicis	the Florence of the Medicis
Bruxelles, ma belle	my beautiful Brussels (song)
Salamanque, si vieille et si belle.	Salamanca is an old Spanish town.

Exception

| le vieux Londres | old London |

If the last syllable of the name is 'sounded', the town is usually masculine.

| Alger est parfumé le soir et Paris est mystérieux la nuit. | Algiers is scented in the evening and Paris is mysterious by night. |

Towns which already have an article as part of their name keep the gender of the article:

Roche-la-Molière, La Ciotat, Le Caire, Le Puy-en-Velay, La Haye, La Rochelle, Le Mans

The gender of towns with adjectives or common nouns as part of their name is more easily identifiable:

Louvain-la-Neuve, Vieux-Condé, La Grande Motte, Port-Leucate, Port Bou, La Nouvelle-Orléans

Towns which are, or include, the names of saints have the gender of the saint in question:

Saint Etienne, Saintes-Maries-de-la-Mer, Sainte Ségolène, Saint Joseph

However, in literary language, you often find that names of towns are feminine. *Le Bon usage* (Grévisse, Duculot, Paris 1980) gives numerous examples (p. 267): *Strasbourg blessée* (wounded Strasbourg) (Fr. Ambrière, *Les Grandes vacances*, p. 376), whether they end with a silent or a voiced syllable.

There is a good deal of uncertainty in this area. The best way to get round the difficulty of gender is to say *la ville de Madrid, la ville de Marseille* (the town of . . .), etc.

2.2.16 Compound nouns

In general, compound nouns are masculine.

There are rules which help to identify the gender of a compound noun.

▶ If the compound noun is composed of two nouns it takes the gender of the first noun:

un chou-fleur	cauliflower
une station-service	petrol station
un timbre-poste	postage stamp
une pause-café	coffee break
un appui-tête	head-rest
un soutien-gorge	bra
un portrait-robot	identikit picture
un drap-housse	fitted sheet

▶ If the compound noun is composed of two feminine nouns it is usually feminine:

| une porte-fenêtre | French window |
| une moissonneuse-batteuse | combine harvester |

▶ If the first component is a verb the noun is usually masculine:

un chasse-neige	snowplough
un brise-glace	icebreaker
un allume-cigare	cigar lighter

(continued)

(continued)

un coupe-vent	windbreak
un essuie-tout	paper towel
un garde-boue	mudguard
un croque-madame	ham and cheese sandwich with a fried egg
un tire-bouchon	corkscrew
un coupe-faim	appetite suppressant
un rendez-vous	appointment, date

But

une garde-robe	wardrobe (masculine in Canadian French)

▶ If the first component is an adverb, an adjective or a preposition, the compound noun usually takes the gender of the second component:

un avant-bras	forearm
une arrière-garde	rearguard
un sous-sol	basement
une sous-tasse	saucer
un haut-parleur	loudspeaker
un beau-père	father-in-law
une grand-tante	great-aunt
une plate-bande	flower bed
un avant-poste	outpost
une demi-finale	semi-final
un demi-dieu	demigod

But

un (four) micro-onde	microwave (oven)
un en-tête	heading
un après-guerre	post-war years
un rouge-gorge	robin
un or une après-midi (masculine or feminine)	an afternoon

▶ If the first component is **mi-**, the noun is usually feminine:

la mi-décembre	mid-December
une mi-temps	half-time (sport)

But

| un mi-temps | part-time (at work) |

▶ If the compound noun is composed of loanwords (English, German, etc.), the word is usually masculine:

le hand-ball (or le handball)	handball
un attaché-case	attaché case
un week-end	weekend

But in the case of a man or a woman, the gender of his / her sex prevails:

une cover-girl; *une pin-up*; *un cow-boy*; *un businessman*

▶ If the compound noun is composed of two verbs or a phrase, its gender is masculine:

un va-et-vient	two-way switch; comings and goings
un laissez-passer	pass
un sot-l'y-laisse	oyster (poultry)

2.3 Number

▶ The plural of most nouns is formed as in English, by adding -s to the singular:

| un jour – des jours | day(s) |
| une semaine – des semaines | week(s) |

Note

French differs from English in that the final -*s* is not pronounced; singular and plural sound the same.

▶ The plural applies when the noun denotes two or more things:

| deux mètres | two metres |

But

| 1,9 mètre | 1.9 metres |

2.3.1 Nouns ending in -s, -z and -x

These nouns are the same in the singular and the plural:

un bus	des bus	bus(es)
une noix	des noix	nut(s)
un nez	des nez	nose(s)

2.3.2 Nouns ending in -au, -eau, -eu, -œu

These nouns add *-x* to form their plural:

un anneau	*des anneaux*	ring(s)
un jeu	*des jeux*	game(s)
un tuyau	*des tuyaux*	pipe(s)
un vœu	*des vœux*	vow(s)

Exceptions

un bleu	*des bleus*	blue colour(s); bruise(s)
un émeu	*des émeus*	emu(s)
un landau	*des landaus*	pram(s)
un pneu	*des pneus*	tyre(s)

Note

Les Bleus also is the popular name given to French national teams in a number of sports, especially football and rugby.

2.3.3 Nouns ending in -ou

In general these nouns form their plural with *-s*:

un clou	*des clous*	nail(s)
un coucou	*des coucous*	cuckoo(s)

Exceptions

The following seven nouns form their plural in *-oux*:

un bijou	*des bijoux*	jewel(s)
un caillou	*des cailloux*	stone(s)
un chou	*des choux*	cabbage(s)
un genou	*des genoux*	knee(s)
un hibou	*des hiboux*	owl(s)
un joujou	*des joujoux*	toy(s)
un pou	*des poux*	louse / lice

2.3.4 Nouns ending in -al

These nouns form their plural *-aux*:

un journal	des journaux	newspaper(s)
un cheval	des chevaux	horse(s)
un terminal d'ordinateur	des terminaux d'ordinateur	computer terminal(s)

Exceptions

The following nouns ending in *-al* form their plural in *-s*:

un bal	des bals	dance(s), ball(s)
un cal	des cals	callus(es)
un carnaval	des carnavals	carnival(s)
un cérémonial	des cérémonials	ceremonial(s)
un chacal	des chacals	jackal(s)
un étal	des étals	(market) stall(s)
un festival	des festivals	festival(s)
un récital	des récitals	recital(s)
un régal	des régals	delight(s)

Note

| un idéal | des idéaux or des idéals | ideal(s) |

2.3.5 Nouns ending -ail

Most of these nouns form their plural in *-ails*:

un chandail	des chandails	sweater(s)
un détail	des détails	detail(s)
un épouvantail	des épouvantails	scarecrow(s)

Exceptions

A number of nouns ending in *-ail* form their plural in *-aux*. The seven most common of these nouns are:

un bail	des baux	lease(s)
un corail	des coraux	coral(s)
un émail	des émaux	enamel(s)

(continued)

(continued)

un soupirail	des soupiraux	(cellar) window(s)
un travail	des travaux	work(s)
un vantail	des vantaux	(cupboard) door(s)
un vitrail	des vitraux	stained-glass window(s)

Notes

Le bétail (livestock) is a mass noun and so has no plural form.

L'ail (garlic) has two plural forms: *aulx* and *ails* (when referring to the botanic family)

2.3.6 Nouns with two plural forms: ciel, aïeul, œil

▶ *ciel*

un ciel	des ciels / des cieux	sky(ies), heaven(s)

Des ciels is the 'true' plural form. It is used especially for pictorial representation of the sky or for climate:

Les ciels de Van Gogh ont des couleurs plus vives que ceux de Monet.	Van Gogh's skies have brighter colours than Monet's.
Des ciels chargés de nuages menaçants.	Skies full of threatening clouds.

Des cieux is literary or religious. Its meaning is synonymous with the singular form.

Laissez venir à moi les petits enfants car le Royaume des cieux est à ceux qui leur ressemblent.	Let the little children come to me because the kingdom of heaven belongs to such as these.

▶ *aïeul*

un aïeul	des aïeuls	grandfather / grandparents

Notes

Bisaïeul/e (great-grandfather / -mother) and *trisaïeul/e* (great-great-grandfather / -mother) form their plural by adding *-s*: *bisaïeuls*, *trisaïeuls*.

Aïeux means 'ancestors' and has no singular form in this meaning.

Un de ses aïeux était viking.	One of her ancestors was a Viking.

▶ *oeil*

The plural of *un œil* (eye) is *des yeux*.

Il a les yeux bleus.	He has blue eyes.

The plural *des œils* exists but only in compound nouns: *des œils-de-bœuf* (bull's eyes).

2.3.7 Abbreviations, acronyms and symbols

▶ Abbreviations do not take -s in the plural except in a few cases:

un village de 1000 hab. (habitants)	a village of 1000 inhabitants
un livre de 250 p. (250 pages)	a book of 250 pages

Exceptions

Mmes (mesdames)	plural of 'madam', 'Mrs'
nos (numéros)	plural of 'number'
Drs (docteurs)	doctors
éts (établissements)	establishments

▶ If the abbreviation consists only of the first letter, that letter can be doubled to form the plural:

MM. (messieurs)	plural of 'monsieur', 'Mr'
pp. (pages)	plural of 'pages'

▶ Plurals of ordinal numbers:

1ers = premiers	first
2es = deuxièmes, second(e)s	second
3es = troisièmes	third

▶ Abbreviations of symbols do not have a plural form:

des km	plural of 'kilometre'
un immeuble de 30m	a 30-metre high building

▶ Acronyms in capital letters do not have a plural form, but if they are written like a normal noun they do form a plural:

Les ANPE ont été remplacées par les agences Pôle emploi.　The ANPE have been replaced by the Pôle emploi agencies (job centres).

Il y a des lasers de différentes couleurs.　There are lasers of different colours.

▶ Nouns which are shortened words form a plural:

des kilos de riz (kilogrammes)	kilos of rice
des dactylos (dactylographes)	typists
des autos (automobiles)	cars

2.3.8 Nouns not normally used in the plural

▶ Names of disciplines and branches of knowledge in science or the arts:

la politique	politics
l'économie	economics
l'informatique	information science
la physique	physics
la littérature	literature
la sculpture	sculpture

Note

These nouns may be used in the plural when qualified in some way:

les littératures africaines	African literatures
les sculptures de Rodin	Rodin's sculptures

Exceptions

les mathématiques	mathematics
les sciences humaines	human sciences
les sciences naturelles	natural sciences
les beaux-arts	fine arts

▶ Names of sports

le basket	basketball
le foot	football
le volley	volleyball

2.3.9 Nouns and expressions which have no singular form

▶ Common nouns:

des arrhes (f)	deposit
des chips (m)	crisps
des environs (m)	surroundings
des fiançailles (f)	engagement

des funérailles (f)	funeral
des gens (m or f)	people
des gravats (m)	rubble
des honoraires (m)	fees
des mœurs (f)	customs
des préparatifs (m)	preparations
des ténèbres (f)	darkness

▶ Expressions:

les pertes et profits	profit and loss
les dommages et intérêts	damages (law)
les Jeux olympiques	the Olympics

2.3.10 Nouns which have a singular form but are used more often in the plural

les applaudissements (m)	applause
les félicitations (f)	congratulations
les pourparlers (m)	negotiations
les représailles (f)	reprisals
les déchets (m)	refuse
les déboires (m)	problems
les broussailles (f)	brush

▶ The names of classifications of plants and animals:

les liliacées (f)	liliaceous plants
les mammifères (m)	mammals
les équidés (m)	the horse family

▶ A number of geographical names:

les Antilles	the West Indies
les Alpes	the Alps

2.3.11 Nouns which can have a different meaning in the plural

un ciseau	chisel	des ciseaux	scissors
une lettre	letter	les lettres	humanities, letters
une lunette	toilet seat	des lunettes	glasses
une vacance	vacancy	des vacances	holidays

2.3.12 Words used in both the singular and the plural

▶ Nouns like *jumelles* (f) (binoculars), *guillemets* (m) (inverted commas) indicating things composed of two similar parts, are generally used in the plural, but can be singular when the two parts are considered as a whole.

▶ Nouns related to clothing which covers the legs are singular but are often used in their plural form in the spoken language: *des shorts* (m), *des jeans* (m).

▶ Nouns designating objects consisting of a number of components are often in the plural, e.g. *escaliers* (m) (staircase).

▶ Nouns relating to toilets are generally in the plural (but in the singular in Belgium): (*les*) W-C (m), *toilettes* (f) (toilets).

2.3.13 The plural of compound nouns

In compound nouns only the noun and adjective components have a plural form; verbs, adverbs and prepositions which form part of compound nouns are invariable (see new spelling rules, 17.4).

2.3.14 Noun + noun or adjective + noun

In these two combinations it is usual for both components to become plural:

un bloc-moteur	des blocs-moteurs	engine block(s)
un chou-fleur	des choux-fleurs	cauliflower(s)
un grand-parent	des grands-parents	grandparent(s)
un rond-point	des ronds-points	roundabout(s)
un tiroir-caisse	des tiroirs-caisses	cash drawer(s)

But

un pur-sang	des purs-sangs or des pur-sang	thoroughbred(s)

Sometimes the components vary, according to the meaning:

▶ If the two components create a noun which has a different identity both components become plural:

une porte-fenêtre, des portes-fenêtres   French window(s) (doors which are at the same time windows)

▶ If the second component modifies the meaning of the first one, only the first noun becomes plural:

une année-lumière, des années-lumière   light year(s) (the distance travelled by light in a year)

un timbre-poste, des timbres-poste   postage stamp(s) (stamps used by the postal service)

Note

The adjectives *grand* and *franc* are invariable in the feminine singular: *un grand-père* (grandfather), *une grand-mère* (grandmother), *des grands-pères* (grandfathers); *des grands-mères* (grandmothers).

2.3.15 Noun + adjective, adjective + adjective

In general, both elements become plural:

un coffre-fort	*des coffres-forts*	safe(s)
un sourd-muet	*des sourds-muets*	deaf-mute(s)

Exception

un terre-plein	*des terre-pleins*	terreplein(s), platform(s)

2.3.16 Noun + preposition + noun

▶ When the second noun modifies the first one, only the first noun becomes plural:

un arc-en-ciel	*des arcs-en-ciel*	rainbow(s)
un chef-d'œuvre	*des chefs-d'œuvre*	masterpiece(s)

▶ When the second noun does not modify the first one, the two nouns are invariable:

un tête-à-tête	*des tête-à-tête*	tête-à-tête(s)

▶ Where the compound noun is not connected by a hyphen or hyphens, in general only the first noun becomes plural:

| un chemin de fer | des chemins de fer | railway(s) |
| une pomme de terre | des pommes de terre | potato(es) |

but the second noun is sometimes found in the plural:

| un jaune d'œuf | des jaunes d'œufs | egg yolk(s) |

2.3.17 Compound nouns with the adjectives or adverbs demi and nu

When placed before a noun or adjective, *demi* and *nu* are connected by a hyphen and are invariable:

une demi-finale	des demi-finales	semi-final(s)
une demi-heure	des demi-heures	half hour(s)
un nu-pieds	des nu-pieds	flip-flop(s)

2.3.18 Verb + noun

The verb is invariable but the noun adds -*s* in the plural:

un couvre-lit	des couvre-lits	bedspread(s)
un essuie-glace	des essuie-glaces	windscreen-wiper(s)
un tire-bouchon	des tire-bouchons	corkscrew(s)

Note

If the noun is preceded by an article or begins with a capital letter it does not add -*s* in the plural:

| un prie-Dieu | des prie-Dieu | prie-dieu(s) |
| un trompe-l'œil | des trompe-l'œil | trompe-l'œil(s) |

2.3.19 Verb + verb

The two components are invariable:

un laissez-passer	des laissez-passer	pass(es)
un savoir-faire	des savoir-faire	know-how(s)
un va-et-vient	des va-et-vient	two-way switch(es)

2.3.20 Invariable word + noun

Only the noun becomes plural:

une arrière-boutique	des arrière-boutiques	back-shop(s)
une avant-garde	des avant-gardes	vanguard(s)
un en-tête	des en-têtes	letter-head(s) (on notepaper)
un non-lieu	des non-lieux	dismissal(s)

2.3.21 Various

▶ Loanwords normally follow the rules for French words. These rules have not been fully assimilated and so there is some variation (see 17.4).

un post-scriptum	des post-scriptum	post-script(s)
un orang-outang	des orangs-outangs	orang-utang(s)
un minimum	des minimums or -a	minimum(a)
un sandwich	des sandwichs or -es	sandwich(es)

▶ The truncated first component of a compound word does not become plural:

un Anglo-saxon	des Anglo-saxons	Anglo-Saxon(s)
un Gallo-romain	des Gallo-romains	Gallo-Roman(s)
une tragi-comédie	des tragi-comédies	tragicomedy(ies)

NOUNS IN CONTEXT

Inventaire

Une pierre
deux maisons
trois ruines
quatre fossoyeurs
un jardin
des fleurs

un raton laveur

une douzaine d'huîtres un citron un pain
un rayon de soleil
une lame de fond
six musiciens
une porte avec son paillasson
un monsieur décoré de la légion
d'honneur

un autre raton laveur

un sculpteur qui sculpte des Napoléon
la fleur qu'on appelle souci
deux amoureux sur un grand lit
un receveur des contributions une chaise
trois dindons
un ecclésiastique un furoncle
une guêpe
un rein flottant
une écurie de courses
un fils indigne deux frères dominicains
trois sauterelles un strapontin
deux filles de joie un oncle Cyprien
une Mater dolorosa trois papas gâteau
deux chèvres de Monsieur Seguin
un talon Louis XV
un fauteuil Louis XVI
un buffet Henri II deux buffets Henri III
trois buffets Henri IV
un tiroir dépareillé

un veau marengo
un soleil d'Austerlitz
un siphon d'eau de Seltz
un vin blanc citron
un Petit Poucet un grand pardon un
calvaire de pierre une échelle de corde
deux sœurs latines trois dimensions
douze apôtres mille et une nuits
trente-deux positions six parties du
monde cinq points cardinaux
dix ans de bons et loyaux services sept
péchés capitaux deux doigts

une pelote de ficelle deux épingles de
sûreté un monsieur âgé
une Victoire de Samothrace un
comptable deux aides-comptables
un homme du monde deux chirurgiens
trois végétariens
un cannibale
une expédition coloniale un cheval entier
une demi-pinte de bon
sang une mouche tsé-tsé
un homard à l'américaine un jardin à la
française
deux pommes à l'anglaise
un face-à-main un valet de pied un
orphelin un poumon d'acier
un jour de gloire
une semaine de bonté
un mois de Marie
une année terrible
une minute de silence
une seconde d'inattention
et ...

cinq ou six ratons laveurs

un petit garçon qui entre à l'école en
pleurant
un petit garçon qui sort de l'école en
riant
une fourmi
deux pierres à briquet
dix-sept éléphants un juge d'instruction
en vacances assis sur un pliant
un paysage avec beaucoup d'herbe verte
dedans
une vache
un taureau
deux belles amours trois grandes orgues
de la main dix gouttes avant chaque
repas trente jours de prison
dont quinze de cellule cinq minutes
d'entr'acte

et ...

plusieurs ratons laveurs

Jacques Prévert
© Éditions Gallimard

Gender

Masculine	Feminine
un raton	une maison
un rayon	une douzaine
un monsieur	une légion
un sculpteur	une contribution
un lit	une chaise
un fils	une écurie
un frère	une fille
un gâteau	une sûreté
un fauteuil	une expédition
un buffet	une semaine
un tiroir	une bonté
un homme	des amours
un valet	une sœur
un orphelin	une dimension
un garçon	une position
un soleil	une partie
un paysage	
un taureau	
un veau	

I. Masculine nouns

Human beings are masculine or feminine according to their sex [2.2.1]: *un monsieur, un fils, un frère, un garçon, un homme, un valet, un orphelin*

The young of animals are usually masculine [2.2.1]: *un raton, un veau*

The gender of some animals is predictable [2.2.1]: *un taureau*

nouns ending in **-on** are masculine [2.2.4]: *un rayon*

nouns ending in **-eur** are masculine [2.2.4]: *un sculpteur*

nouns ending in **-euil** and **-eil** are masculine 1.2.4]: *un fauteuil, un soleil* nouns ending in **-oir** are masculine [2.2.4]: *un tiroir*

nouns ending in **-age** are masculine [2.2.4]: *un paysage*

2. Feminine nouns

Human beings are masculine or feminine according to their sex [2.2.1]: *une fille, une sœur*

nouns ending in **-ison** are feminine [2.2.6]: *une maison*

nouns ending in **-ine** are feminine [2.2.6]: *une dizaine, une semaine*

nouns ending in **-(t)ion** are feminine [2.2.6]: *une légion, une dimension, une contribution, une expédition, une position*

nouns ending in **-ie** are feminine [2.2.6]: *une écurie, une partie*

nouns ending in **-é** are feminine [2.2.6]: *une sûreté, une bonté*

nouns ending in **-ise** are feminine [2.2.6]: *une chaise*

amour is feminine in the plural: *deux belles amours*, but **masculine** in the singular [2.2.13].

3. Plurals of nouns

The plural of most nouns is formed by adding *-s* to the singular [2.3].	*une maison → des maisons* *une ruine → des ruines*
Nouns ending in **-s, -z** and **-x** are the same in the singular and the plural [2.3.1].	*un amoureux → des amoureux* *un fils → des fils* *un mois → des mois*
Nouns ending in **-au, -eau, -eu, -œu** add **-x** to form their plural [2.3.2].	*un gâteau → des gâteaux* *un taureau → des taureaux*
Nouns ending in **-al** form their plural **-aux** [2.3.4].	*un cheval → des chevaux*
In compound nouns which combine noun + noun it is usual for both components to become plural [2.3.14].	*un(e) aide-comptable → des aides-comptables*
In the combination noun + preposition + noun, when the second noun modifies the first one, only the first noun becomes plural [2.3.16].	*un face-à-main → des faces-à-main*

EXERCISES

1. Give the masculine or the feminine of the following words, as appropriate:

1 *un agneau*	→	_____
2 *une amie*	→	_____
3 *un conseiller*	→	_____
4 *un coq*	→	_____
5 *la directrice*	→	_____
6 *un élève*	→	_____
7 *un épicier*	→	_____
8 *la fermière*	→	_____
9 *mon grand-père*	→	_____
10 *cette jument*	→	_____
11 *une marchande*	→	_____
12 *ma mère*	→	_____
13 *son oncle*	→	_____
14 *un paysan*	→	_____

2. Read carefully the following list of nouns. Classify them in five categories corresponding to the columns below, placing them in the appropriate boxes. Bear in mind the definitions given (a, b, c, d, e) at the head of each table.

sentinelle, camarade, danseur, poste, grand-père, Anglais, pianiste, araignée, acrobate, oncle, infirmière, enfant, altesse, perroquet, concierge, stagiaire, jument, vache, chèvre, nièce, Russe, recrue, crocodile, critique, Espagnole, chat, brebis, mannequin, moule, Indienne, parallèle, artiste, pendule, secrétaire, victime, élève, architecte, livre, tigre, roi, mémoire, ami, coq, voile, boulanger, somme

a) Animate nouns which do not differentiate between male and female (e.g. *souris*)	b) Nouns which have only one form for masculine and feminine (e.g. *un* or *une artiste*)	c) Animate nouns having different words for male and female (e.g. *coq* and *poule*)	d) Nouns whose feminine form is a modification of the masculine form (e.g. *Écossais – Écossaise*)	e) Homonyms whose meaning varies according to the gender (e.g. *le mode*)

3. **Write the correct plural form of the words in brackets.**

Il y a eu trois incidents en deux _____ (après-midi) dans trois _____ (ville) des _____ (environ). J'ai pu lire tous les _____ (détail) dans les _____ (journal) locaux ce matin. Comme c'était l'époque des _____ (festival), de nombreux _____ (bus) transportaient les _____ (festivalier) à travers la ville. De jeunes _____ (cycliste) _____ (nu-tête), sur des _____ (vélo) aux _____ (pneu) usés, jouaient à des _____ (jeu) imprudents, comme par exemple faire des _____ (demi-tour) brusques sur la chaussée. Soudain, à 50 _____ (m) d'ici un bus fit irruption, et en moins de 2 _____ (sec.) il alla heurter légèrement l'un des _____ (jeune) avec son rétroviseur, au niveau des _____ (œil) et le fit tomber sur les _____ (genou). _____ Heureusement le jeune en fut quitte pour _____ (quelque) _____ (éraflure) et _____ (quelque) _____ (bleu). Il y eut plus de peur que de mal.

DETERMINERS

A **determiner** is a useful term to cover all those words which give a *context* to a noun. In English, these are words like *the*, *a*, *this*, *my*, *some*. Determiners are placed before the noun.

▶ The word 'the' in '**The** ring has been stolen', refers to a specific ring that is known to you.

▶ The word 'a' in 'I'm going to buy you **a** ring', refers to a ring which is unspecific, not 'known' to you.

▶ The words 'this' and 'that' in 'I want **this** ring, not **that** one', refer to objects that you are pointing to.

▶ The word 'his' in '**His** ring was expensive', tells you who possesses the ring.

▶ In this chapter the determiners covered are:

    ▶ the definite articles: *le, la, l', les*

    ▶ the indefinite articles: *un, une, des*

    ▶ the partitive articles: *du, de l', de la, des*

    ▶ the demonstrative adjectives: *ce, cet, cette, ces*

    ▶ the possessive adjectives: *mon, ma, mes*; *ton, ta, tes*, etc.

3.1 The three types of article

There are three types of determiner called 'article': definite, indefinite and partitive, as in the following table:

Definite article	Indefinite article	Partitive article
The noun referred to is known to the speaker.	The noun referred to exists but has not been specified.	The noun referred to is abstract (e.g. *l'amour* [love], *la peur* [fear]) or concrete (e.g. *eau* [water] and *pain* [bread]). The latter type of noun is referred to as a 'non-countable' or 'mass' noun.* This type is hardly ever used in the plural.

The noun referred to exists but has not been specified. |
| *Range le verre dans le buffet, s'il te plaît !*

Put **the** glass in the sideboard, please! | *Vous avez une belle robe aujourd'hui.*

You have **a** beautiful dress on today. | *Rajoute de la crème et du poivre dans ta sauce !*

Add **some** cream and (**some**) pepper to your sauce! |

* For an explanation of count and mass nouns, see 2.1.2.

Note

In French the same word is often used for the count noun referring to an animal as for the mass noun for the meat derived from it, whereas English employs a different word to express the mass noun:

le veau	the calf	*un veau*	a calf	*du veau*	veal
le bœuf	the bullock	*un bœuf*	a bullock	*du bœuf*	beef

3.2 Forms of the articles

The articles in French change their form according to the noun that follows. They take either the singular or plural form, and the masculine or feminine form.

The different forms of the article are:

		Singular		Plural
		Masculine	Feminine	Masculine and feminine forms
Definite article		*le* (*l'* before a vowel or silent *h*)	*la* (*l'* before a vowel or silent *h*)	*les*
Contracted forms of the definite article	With *à*	*au*		*aux*
	With *de*	*du*		*des*

		Singular		Plural
		Masculine	Feminine	Masculine and feminine forms
Indefinite article		*un*	*une*	*des*
Partitive article		*du* (*de l'* before a vowel or silent *h*)	*de la* (*de l'* before a vowel or silent *h*)	*des*

3.3 The definite article

The definite article is used with a noun that has been *specified*, i.e., has been mentioned before, or is evident from the context.

KEY POINTS

✦ The masculine singular article *le* contracts to:

  ○ *au* when preceded by the preposition *à* [*à* + *le* = *au*]

  ○ *du* when preceded by the preposition *de* [*de* + *le* = *du*]

✦ The masculine plural article *les* contracts to:

  ○ *aux* when preceded by *à* [*à* + *les* = *aux*]

  ○ *des* when preceded by *de* [*de* + *les* = *des*]

Aux premières heures du matin le bus des migrants sortit du bateau.	In the early hours of the morning the migrants' bus emerged from the boat.
Nous voyageons aux Antilles.	We are travelling to the West Indies.
Nous revenons du Puy.	We are returning from le Puy.

✦ Although the definite article is, for the most part, used in a similar way in French as in English, there are instances where French uses it and English does not. The most important of these uses is with nouns considered in **a general sense**, to refer to **a class** of things, or an **abstract idea or a unique concept**.

En France les ingénieurs sont mieux appreciés qu'en Angleterre.	In France engineers are better valued than in England.

(continued)

(continued)

*Moi je préfère **le** café **au** thé.*	I prefer coffee to tea.
***L'**homme est le plus évolué des mammifères.*	Man is the most evolved of the mammals.
*C'est de **la** folie !*	It's madness!

3.3.1 Elision of le and la

▶ *le* and *la* are shortened to *l'* before a word beginning with a vowel or silent *h*

Singular	Plural	
l'avion (m)	*les avions*	the aeroplane(s)
l'attitude (f)	*les attitudes*	(the) attitude(s)
l'hiver (m)	*les hivers*	the winter(s)
l'honneur (m)	*les honneurs*	honour(s)

▶ A number of words begin with aspirate *h*, for which *le* or *la* has to be used in the singular, and not *l'*.

le hibou	the owl
la haie	the hedge
la haine	hate
***L'**homme* [silent *h*] *en question avait **l'**habitude* [silent *h*] *de tailler **la** haie* [aspirate *h*] *de son jardin vers le début de **l'**été.*	The man in question was in the habit of cutting his garden hedge when summer was about to begin.

3.3.2 Uses of the definite article

▶ In most statements where the noun referred to is known to the speaker the definite article is used in a similar way to English.

*Avez-vous ouvert **la** porte?*	Have you opened the door?
***Le** train de 21.30 va arriver dans 10 minutes.*	The 21.30 train will arrive in 10 minutes.
***La** Révolution française*	The French Revolution

As well as with nouns considered in **a general sense** and with **abstract ideas**, French uses the definite article where English normally does not:

▶ with the names of countries, most large islands and geographical features:

La France, est-elle aussi grande que la Turquie ?	Is France as big as Turkey?
La Corse est située à 170 km au sud de la côte française.	Corsica is situated 170 km to the south of the coast of France.

Exception

Malte	Malta

▶ with the names of languages:

On dit que le chinois est plus difficile que le japonais.	They say that Chinese is more difficult than Japanese.

▶ with the seasons:

L'hiver sera plus froid que l'année dernière.	Winter will be colder than last year.

But when l'hiver, l'automne and l'été are preceded by en the article is omitted:

En éte, nous allons toujours en Catalogne.	We always go to Catalonia in summer.

▶ with titles:

Monsieur le Président	Mr Chairman
Madame le (or la) Maire	Madam Mayor
Monsieur le Ministre	Minister

▶ in superlatives, where the adjective comes after the noun, the article is repeated:

l'enfant le plus doué de la classe	the brightest child in the class

▶ with parts of the body and clothing, where English uses the possessive adjective:

Il se promène les mains dans les poches et la chemise ouverte.	He's walking with his hands in his pockets and his shirt open.

▶ with quantities, French uses the definite article, English the indefinite article.

> *Les abricots sont à 4 euros le kilo.* Apricots are 4 euros a kilo.

▶ with days of the week, when used habitually (English uses 'on' plus the day in the plural):

> *Nous jouons au tenis le samedi.* We play tennis on Saturdays.

▶ The definite article is repeated when in lists:

> *Elle a mis le livre, les billets et les passeports dans sa valise.* She put the book, tickets and passports in her suitcase.

3.4 The indefinite article

The indefinite article **un** (masculine), **une** (feminine) and **des** (plural) is used for a noun that has not been specified, or not individualized enough to warrant the definite article.

KEY POINTS

✦ The use of the indefinite article **un(e)** is similar to English in the singular but the plural **des** (some) is used where English commonly omits it. The sentence 'He's looking at samples' in French must contain the indefinite article: « *Il regarde **des** échantillons* ».

*Il a posé **des** questions pertinentes.*	He asked relevant questions.
*Je lui ai donné **des** chocolats.*	I gave her chocolates.
*Il est revenu avec **des** amis de son frère.*	He came back with (some) friends of his brother.

3.4.1 Uses of the indefinite article

▶ The indefinite article is used for things that are unspecified, in a similar way to English.

*Elle aimerait bien acheter **une** voiture plus puissante.*	She would like to buy a more powerful car.
*Il a vu **un** livre intéressant qu'il aimerait bien lui offrir.*	He saw an interesting book that he would like to give her.

Note

It is important not to confuse **un** and **une**, the indefinite article (*a, an* in English), with **un** and **une** meaning the number *one* in English.

▶ When coming after a negative, **un**, **une** and **des** become **de** (or **d'** before a vowel or silent h), except after the verb **être**.

Il y avait une tasse sur la table hier. Aujourd'hui il n'y a plus de tasse.	There was a cup on the table yesterday. Today there is no longer a cup (there).

But

*Ce ne **sont pas des** fraises que tu as vues mais **des** framboises.*	Those aren't strawberries that you saw but raspberries.

▶ The indefinite article is used with abstract nouns when accompanied by an adjective;

Cette actrice est d'une grande beauté. She's an actress/actor of rare beauty.

▶ The plural indefinite article *des* becomes *de* (or *d'* before a vowel or silent *h*) before a plural noun **preceded** by an adjective. Compare:

*Il a **des** affiches énormes sur son mur.* *Il a **d'**énormes affiches sur son mur.*	He has enormous posters on his wall.

▶ *Des* is omitted when preceded by *de / d'*:

Avec l'aide d'outils sophistiqués, le chirurgien a pu réussir son opération.	With the aid of sophisticated instruments, the surgeon was able to carry out his operation successfully.

▶ *Des* is omitted after most quantifiers:

Je voudrais un kilo de tomates.	I'd like a kilo of tomatoes.

▶ *Des* becomes *d'* before *autres:*

*Elle a bien **d'**autres chats à fouetter.*	She has other fish to fry. [lit. 'cats to whip']

▶ Be careful not to confuse:

*Il n'y a pas **de** chaises dans ce salon.*	There are no chairs in this sitting-room.

with

*Il n'y a pas **une** chaise dans son salon.*	There isn't a chair in his sitting room.

▶ Be careful not to confuse *des*, the indefinite article, with *des*, the contracted definite article [*de* + *les*].

The two uses can easily be distinguished, by replacing *des* by *un(e)*. If it is possible to make this replacement *des* will be the indefinite article; if not, it will be the contracted definite article.

*Il a ajouté **des** olives dans la sauce.* (*Il a ajouté **une** olive.*)	He has added (some) olives to the sauce. (He has added **one** olive.)

Therefore *des* = the indefinite article.

La cueillette des olives a lieu en automne.	Olive-picking takes place in the autumn.

*La cueillette une olive is not possible; this is the preposition *de* + the definite article *les* (*de* + *les* = *des*, the contracted definite article).

3.5 The partitive article

KEY POINTS

✦ The partitive article expresses the idea of 'some' in English with mass nouns such as *sucre* (sugar), *pain* (bread) or abstract nouns, such as *tristesse* (sadness), *colère* (anger), *peur* (fear), *joie* (joy). English often does not have a determiner with these nouns.

Donne-moi **du** lait !	Give me (some) milk!
On peut lire **de la** tristesse sur son visage.	You can see sadness in his face.

✦ As in the case of the indefinite article, *de / d'* is used without a following article, whether singular or plural, after a negative form such as *ne ... pas, ne ... plus, ne ... jamais*. In English this idea is expressed by '(not) ... any', 'no' or '(not) ... a':

Il n'a pas bu d'alcool.	He's had [lit. 'drunk'] no alcohol.
Je n'ai plus de papier.	I haven't got any more paper.
Il n'a jamais d'idées.	He never has any ideas.

But

after *être* this rule does not apply:

Ce n'est pas de la viande.	It's not meat.

3.5.1 Uses of the partitive article

The partitive article is used before:

▶ a mass noun:

Elle boit **du** champagne.	She's drinking (some) champagne.
Après trois jours, il ne leur restait que **du** pain et **de** l'eau.	After three days they had only bread and water left.

▶ an abstract noun:

Ils ont **de la** chance de s'en sortir à si bon compte.	They are lucky [lit. 'have some luck'] to get off so lightly.

▶ materials:

Pour faire **du** feu, il faut **du** bois et **du** papier.	To make fire, you need wood and paper.

Notes

▶ Since the partitive article is used with mass nouns, it is scarcely ever used in the plural. However, certain words such as *cendres* (ash), *ténèbres* (darkness), *vivres* (food) and *rillettes* (potted meat) are always used in the plural, and so the plural partitive article is used with them: ***des vivres***, ***des rillettes***, etc.

| Ils ont pris du bois et des vivres avec eux. | They took some wood and food with them. |

▶ Be careful not to confuse:

    ▶ the partitive article, *de*, with the preposition *de* before the singular definite article:

| Elle a bu **de** l'eau. | She drank some water. (**de l'** = partitive article) |
| Elle vient de sortir **de** l'eau. | She's just come out of the water. (preposition **de** + the definite article **l'**) |

    ▶ the partitive article, *du*, with the contracted form *du* (*de* + *le*) of the masculine definite article:

| Nous buvons **du** lait. | We are drinking (some) milk. (partitive article) |
| Il nous a parlé **du** Brésil. | He spoke about Brazil. (preposition **de** + **le**) |

3.6 Omission of the article

The article is normally omitted:

▶ before the names of people and towns, unless they are qualified:

| De Gaulle est enterré à Colombey. | De Gaulle is buried at Colombey. |
| À Lyon il a visité le Parc de la Tête d'Or et **le** vieux Lyon. | In Lyons he visited the Parc de la Tête d'Or and old Lyons. |

But

some proper nouns are preceded by the article: *Le Puy*, *Le Havre*, *La Haye* (the Hague).

Note that before masculine towns the definite article contracts:

*Demain nous allons **au** Havre en voiture.* We're going to Le Havre by car tomorrow.

▶ after the prepositions *en* or *de* with feminine continents, countries or regions:

en Asie	in Asia
en Bourgogne	in Burgundy
Il est passé **de** France **en** Espagne par le cirque de Gavarnie.	He went from France to Spain via the Cirque de Gavarnie.

But

with masculine nouns the article is kept:

les vins **du** Roussillon	wines from the Roussillon region

▶ before a noun in apposition:

Sa mère, artiste de talent, voyage beaucoup.	His mother, a talented artist, travels a lot.

▶ before nouns used in a rhetorical address:

Françaises, Français, il est temps de voter pour le bon parti !	Men and women of France, it is time to vote for the right party!

▶ before nouns following *être* unless the noun is modified by an adjective or a phrase:

Sa mère est avocate et son père ingénieur.	His mother is a lawyer and his father an engineer.

But

Sa mère est une avocate brillante.	His mother is a brilliant lawyer.

▶ before days of the week and months:

Rendez-vous mardi à midi.	Let's meet (on) Tuesday at midday.

But

when modified by a date, adjective or phrase it may be preceded by an article:

le samedi 20 novembre	on Saturday 20 November
Il est venu le juillet où il a fait si chaud !	He came that very hot July!

▶ with the names of kings, queens and popes:

François Ier (premier)	Francis the First
Elizabeth II (deux)	Elizabeth the Second
Louis XIV (quatorze)	Louis the Fourteenth
Pie XII (douze)	Pius the Twelfth

▶ in certain noun constructions, when the second noun functions as an adjective:

un château de cartes	a house of cards
un esprit de synthèse	a spirit of synthesis
un billet de théâtre	a theatre ticket
une station de ski	a ski resort

But

when the phrase is qualified, the definite article is used:

un billet du cinéma l'Eden	a ticket for the Eden cinema

▶ in certain verb constructions, phrases, set expressions and proverbs:

avoir faim	to be hungry
faire faillite	to go bankrupt
tirer satisfaction	to draw satisfaction
perdre patience	to lose patience
Chat échaudé craint l'eau froide.	Once bitten, twice shy.

3.7 Demonstrative determiners

We use demonstrative determiners, 'this, these' and 'that, those' when we wish to *point to* a particular thing, person or concept:

This shoe fits me better than **that** one.

Unlike in English, the simple form of the demonstrative in French makes no distinction between objects that are near us ('this') and objects that are further away ('that'). Demonstrative determiners agree with the noun in number and gender.

3.7.1 Forms

	Masculine	Feminine
Singular	ce	cette
Plural	ces	

KEY POINTS

✦ In the masculine singular **ce** is used before a word beginning with a consonant or aspirate **h**:

ce désavantage	this / that disadvantage
ce handicap	this / that handicap

(continued)

(continued)

✦ The form **cet** is used before a word beginning with a vowel or silent **h**:

*J'ai vu **cet** homme sortir de **cet** hôtel.*	I saw that man come out of this / that hotel.

✦ In the feminine singular there is one form, **cette**.

*Tiens ! Écoute **cette** chanson !*	Hey! Listen to this / that song!

✦ In the plural there is one form for the masculine and feminine.

*Range **ces** verres et **ces** tasses dans cette armoire.*	Put these / those glasses and cups away in that cupboard.

3.7.2 Emphatic forms

▶ To distinguish between objects that are near to the speaker and objects that are further away, the suffixes *-ci* or *-là* may be added to the noun:

***Ces temps-ci**, il me semble qu'il fait plus chaud.*	These days it seems to me to be hotter.
*En **ce temps-là**, nous n'avions pas de téléphones portables.*	In those days we didn't have mobile phones.

▶ When used in the same sentence, however, these emphatic forms don't really indicate proximity to, or distance from, the speaker, but are a means of contrasting two objects:

*Je mets **cette** cravate-**ci** ou **cette** cravate-**là** ce soir ?*	Should I wear this tie or that one tonight?

▶ In contemporary spoken language, the particle *-là* is used more and more often, and frequently replaces *-ci*, which is considered to be rather more formal:

*Je crois que je préfère **cette** version-**là**; l'autre est trop rapide.*	I think I prefer this version; the other one is too fast.

3.8 Possessive determiners

Possessive determiners indicate possession or show a relationship between the speaker and a thing, person or idea. In English, the possessive determiner agrees with the **possessor**: It's **our** house. She's **my** favourite singer. It's **their** idea.

3.8.1 Forms

		Masculine singular	Feminine singular	Plural
One 'possessor'	1st pers. sing.	*mon*	*ma* (*mon* before a vowel or silent *h*)	*mes*
	2nd pers. sing.	*ton*	*ta* (*ton* before a vowel or silent *h*)	*tes*
	3rd pers. sing.	*son*	*sa* (*son* before a vowel or silent *h*)	*ses*
Several 'possessors'	1st pers. plur.	*notre*		*nos*
	2nd pers. plur.	*votre*		*vos*
	3rd pers. plur.	*leur*		*leurs*

KEY POINTS

✦ Unlike in English, possessive determiners in French agree with the thing which is possessed. The possessive determiner chosen depends on whether the thing possessed is masculine or feminine, singular or plural.

Il aime **ses** *élèves.* [possessor 3rd person singular; thing possessed plural]	He loves his pupils.
Ils aiment **leur** *professeur.* [possessor 3rd person plural; thing possessed singular]	They love their teacher.
J'ai trouvé **son** *article et* **sa** *photo sur internet.*	I found his article and his photo on the internet.
Ma *trousse de maquillage;* **notre** *trousse de secours.*	My make-up kit; our first-aid kit.

✦ The possessive determiners *ma, ta, sa* are replaced by *mon, ton, son* immediately before a feminine noun beginning with a vowel or silent **h**.

Ton *idée est bonne –* **ta** *première idée était meilleure.*	Your idea is a good one; your first idea was better.
Le sport contribue à **mon** *hygiène mentale.*	Sport contributes to my mental health.
Son *hélice a trois pales –* **sa** *seconde hélice est tombée en panne.*	His propeller has three blades; his second propeller has broken.

Notes

▶ Take care not to confuse the possessive determiners *leur* and *leurs* with the invariable personal pronoun *leur* (the plural of *lui*). To distinguish between them, you can replace the possessive determiner *leur* by another possessive, such as *ses*, and the personal pronoun *leur* by another personal pronoun, such as *lui* (see 4.2).

*Ne **leur** (lui) dites pas où sont **leurs** (ses) bonbons.*	Don't tell them (him / her) where their (his / her) sweets are.

▶ The possessive determiner is replaced by the definite article with parts of the body and clothing, provided there is no ambiguity (see 3.3.2).

*Il se promène toujours un couteau à **la** ceinture, **les** mains dans **les** poches et **la** tête haute.*	He always walks with a knife in his belt, his hands in his pockets and his head held high.

▶ To emphasize possession the adjective *propre* may be added, in the same way as 'own' in English.

*Il a été trahi par son **propre** fils.*	He was betrayed by his own son.

DETERMINERS IN CONTEXT

I *The articles*

Une découverte insolite: les marchés de Lyon

À Lyon, les lieux de promenade sont variés. Que diriez-vous d'une escapade gastronomique en bateau sur la Saône ? Une marche sur plusieurs kilomètres de sentiers le long du Rhône ? Passer d'une rue à l'autre en s'engouffrant dans une mystérieuse « traboule » ? Flâner un après-midi entier dans le grand parc de la Tête d'Or ? Descendre un musée gallo-romain en colimaçon pour en sortir au cœur d'un théâtre romain ? Arpenter les ruelles du Vieux-Lyon, autour d'une cathédrale gothique ?

Mais la surprise vient des marchés qu'on n'a pas l'habitude de classer parmi les lieux de détente.

La ville offre de nombreux marchés biologiques, des marchés d'art et de loisirs et même des marchés du soir. Dans le 8e arrondissement, il y a même un « Marché biologique du soir » tous les mercredis de 15h à 20h. On y vend des fruits, des légumes, de la viande, du poisson, des fromages, du pain et du vin de la région dont les fameux Beaujolais et Côtes du Rhône.

Au « Marché des producteurs de pays », il faut être producteur et de la région proche pour avoir l'autorisation de vendre. On y trouve de la charcuterie, de la viande, des fruits et légumes, des produits laitiers, des œufs, du miel, du pain, du vin, des fleurs et des plantes.

On trouve des marchés d'articles manufacturés tels que chaussures, vêtements, sacs.

Dans le 4e arrondissement, les peintres lyonnais exposent leurs peintures sur toile, bois, métal, porcelaine ou soie.

Au marché des vieux papiers, on vend de vieux livres, des cartes postales et des revues.

Enfin, près de la gare de Perrache, on trouvera le « Marché aux chiens et aux chats ».

The definite, indefinite and partitive articles [3.1–3.6]

Determiner	Masculine singular	Feminine singular	Plural
Definite article	du Rhône	la Saône	les ruelles
	le parc	l'autre	les marchés
	au cœur	la Tête	les lieux
	du Vieux-Lyon	l'habitude	les mercredis
	le plus	la ville	les Beaujolais
	du soir	la région	des producteurs
	le 8e arrondissement	l'autorisation	les peintres
	au Marché	la gare	des vieux papiers
	le Marché		aux chiens
			aux chats
Indefinite article	un après-midi	une découverte	des lieux
	un musée	une escapade	des voies
	un théâtre	une marche	de nombreux marchés
	un Marché	une rue	des marchés
		une cathédrale	des fruits
		une traboule	des légumes
			des fromages
			des produits
			des œufs
			des fleurs
			des plantes
			de vieux livres
			des cartes postales des revues

(continued)

(continued)

Determiner	Masculine singular	Feminine singular	Plural
Partitive article	*du poisson* *du pain* *du vin* *du miel*	*de la viande* *de la charcuterie*	

2 Other determiners

Ces nouvelles technologies qui passionnent notre jeunesse !

Avec leurs laboratoires ultra modernes et leur savoir-faire commun, les sociétés « Disque Optique » et « Digi-Disc » ont battu tous leurs rivaux dans ce domaine si convoité du disque optique numérique.

Grâce à sa gamme de supports variée, « Disque Optique » est devenue numéro un mondial du DV PAL et ses 25 images par seconde et du DVD de studio professionnel. Quant à « Digi-Disc » et ses logiciels de création de DVD Blu-ray 3D, elle vient de réussir un beau coup marketing. En effet, cet après-midi, cette très jeune société annonçait une véritable révolution dans la technologie du disque optique et ce soir, le cours de son action grimpait en flèche.

Pourtant, ce logiciel n'est pas parfait. On lui reproche notamment son grand nombre d'automatismes. Dans son discours face aux médias, le PDG justifiait ainsi son produit: « Notre logiciel est adapté à vos attentes et celles de tous nos clients en général. Il est à la fois très performant et très facile d'utilisation. »

« Nous ne critiquons pas ses performances, répliquaient les journalistes, mais plutôt cette frustration de liberté imposée par ces trop nombreux automatismes. »

Les deux sociétés ont finalement promis de transmettre ces critiques à leur bureau de recherche et développement.

Demonstrative and possessive determiners

Demonstrative determiners [3.7]

masculine singular	**ce** *domaine;* **ce** *soir;* **ce** *logiciel*
masculine singular before a vowel or silent *h*	**cet** *après-midi*
feminine singular	**cette** *très jeune société;* **cette** *frustration*
plural	**Ces** *nouvelles technologies;* **ces** *trop nombreux automatismes;* **ces** *critiques*

Possessive determiners [3.8]

	Masc. sing	Fem. sing	Before a vowel	Plural
1st person singular				
2nd person singular				
3rd person singular	**son** grand nombre; **son** discours; **son** produit	**sa** gamme	**son** action (f)	**ses** 25 images; **ses** logiciels; **ses** performances
1st person plural	**notre** jeunesse; **notre** logiciel			**nos** clients
2nd person plural				**vos** attentes
3rd person plural	**leur** savoir-faire; **leur** bureau			**leurs** laboratoires; **leurs** rivaux

EXERCISES

1. Fill the gaps with an appropriate demonstrative determiner:

1. J'aime _____ série télévisée allemande.
2. J'aime _____ langage simple et _____ façon naturelle d'exprimer les émotions les plus intenses.
3. J'aime aussi _____ tons de pastel, et _____ campagne sereine.
4. J'aime _____ habits archaïques qui lui donnent _____ côté désuet.
5. Et puis _____ acteurs si talentueux, _____ actrices si subtiles.
6. Je verrais très bien _____ forme d'art entrer dans les programmes scolaires.
7. _____ genre est relativement nouveau, mais il a acquis une certaine maturité.
8. C'est _____ maturité qui m'étonne le plus.
9. Je regarderai l'épisode de _____ soir quoi qu'il arrive.
10. _____ fois, je ne me laisserai pas distraire par mes amis.

2. Fill the gaps with an appropriate possessive determiner:

1. _____ famille est assez grande.
2. _____ deux sœurs sont plus âgées que moi.
3. _____ distraction préférée c'est de me taquiner.
4. Et je passe _____ temps à me défendre.
5. _____ mère me protégeait quand j'étais plus jeune.
6. Mais maintenant elle a trop à faire avec _____ grand-mèreet _____ arrière grand-mère donc.
7. _____ frère est plus jeune que moi.
8. _____ journées à nous sont aussi mouvementées.

9. _____ sport favori, à _____ frère et à moi, c'est le frisbee.

10. Et _____ sport favori à vous, quel est-il ?

3. **Fill the gaps with a suitable determiner:**

Un malheur ne vient jamais seul !

1. Mais _____ journée ne fut qu'_____ suite de mésaventures.

2. _____ matin _____ voiture n'a pas voulu démarrer, j'ai dû prendre bus.

3. Mais j'avais oublié de prendre _____ argent.

4. J'avais bien _____ carte de crédit, mais pouvais-je payer _____ bus avec _____ carte bancaire?

5. Heureusement il me restait _____ monnaie. Juste ce qu'il fallait.

6. En traversant _____ avenue, _____ moto a failli me renverser. Elle m'a juste effleuré _____ bras.

7. _____ fois _____ restaurant, on m'a donné_____ place _____ plus incommode, près _____ cuisines.

8. J'ai commandé _____ agneau et _____ purée, mais il ne restait que _____ poulet et _____ haricots.

9. _____ viande et _____ légumes baignaient dans _____ huile.

10. Et j'ai dû rajouter _____ sel et _____ poivre; _____ goût pour _____ épices est prononcé.

11. _____ soir j'irai _____ cinéma plutôt, ils passent _____ film de Truffaut, _____ metteur en scène préféré.

4   PRONOUNS

Pronouns stand in the place of nouns. For example, in a conversation, you might give a friend's name first in order to identify him, and then use pronouns to replace nouns subsequently:

Matt flew to France yesterday. *He* went with Jim; *they* took two suitcases with *them*.

We all use pronouns as a kind of shorthand to avoid clumsy or needless repetition. A pronoun does not tell you anything more about the noun it is replacing; it simply acts as a neat and shorter substitute.

Pronouns may appear in four main places in a sentence:

▶ as the **subject** (English 'I', 'he')

▶ as the **direct object** (English 'me', 'them')

▶ as the **indirect object** (English 'you', 'us', preceded by a preposition like 'to')

▶ after a **preposition** (English 'after you', 'above it').

The following types of pronoun are covered in this chapter:

▶ **personal pronouns**, the equivalent of 'I', 'you', 'to him', etc. They can be subject, direct object, indirect object, or appear after prepositions.

▶ **demonstrative pronouns**, the equivalent of 'this one, 'that one', 'these ones, 'those ones'.

▶ **possessive pronouns**, the equivalent of 'mine', 'yours', etc.

▶ **indefinite pronouns**, the equivalent of 'someone', 'whoever', 'several', etc.

The following pronouns are covered elsewhere: **negative** (Chapter 8), **relative** (Chapter 15) and **interrogative** (Chapter 16).

Subject, direct object and indirect object pronouns

In French the personal pronouns refer to both people and things. The pronouns *y* and *en*, which have no exact equivalent in English, are widely used.

▶ *y* and *en*

▶ the pronoun *y* is the rough equivalent of 'there' and stands for phrases of location, beginning with *à, en, dans, sur,* etc.

*Il est à la piscine. Il **y** va toutes les deux semaines.*	He's at the pool. He goes there every fortnight.

▶ the pronoun *en* stands for phrases beginning with *de.*

*J'**en** reviens à l'instant.*	I've just come from there.

Note

The subject pronoun *je*, and the object pronouns *me, te, le / la* elide to *j', m', t'* and *l'* when a vowel follows:

*Il **m'**a demandé de venir mais **j'**ai dit non.*	He asked me to come but I refused.
*Je **l'** ai vu dans la rue.*	I saw him / her in the street.
*Tu **t'** en vas?*	Are you going?

Subject, direct object and indirect object pronouns

	Subject	Direct object	Indirect object
First person singular	*je / j'* I	*me / m'* me	*me / m'* to me
Second person singular	*tu* you	*te / t'* you	*te / t'* to you
Third person singular	*il* he, it	*le / l'* him, it	*lui* to him, to her, to it
	elle she, it	*la / l'* her, it	

	Subject	Direct object	Indirect object
First person plural	**nous** we	**nous** us	**nous** to us
Second person plural	**vous** you	**vous** you	**vous** to you
Third person plural	**ils** they	**les** them	**leur** to them
	elles they		

4.1 Subject pronouns

KEY POINTS

✦ A subject pronoun stands for the person, thing or idea which is the subject of the sentence:

J'arrive.	I'm coming.
Ils font du bruit.	They are making a noise.
Nous sommes fatigués.	We're tired.

✦ Subject pronouns agree in number and gender with the person(s) they stand for:

Michel est honnête. **Il** ne ment jamais.	Michel is honest. He never lies.
Rose est une bonne actrice dans ce film, et en plus **elle** est belle.	Rose is a good actor in that film; furthermore, she is beautiful.

✦ They are placed before the verb **except** where there is inversion, as when asking questions:

Pourquoi riez-**vous**?	Why are you laughing?
Ont- **elles** payé leur loyer?	Have they paid their rent?

✦ **il / elle / ils / elles** refer to persons, animals and things:

Le chien a l'air d'être malade. **Il** manque d'énergie.	The dog seems ill. He has no energy.
La ville est trop bruyante; **elle** est sale aussi.	The town is too noisy; it's dirty too.
Ce sont des vélos volés; **ils** ont été récupérés par la police.	They are stolen bikes; they've been recovered by the police.

✦ **on** refers to 'someone', 'people', 'they', 'you' 'we', 'one' depending on the context:

On ne sait jamais.	One never knows / You never know.
On habite à deux pas de l'arrêt de bus.	We live a few steps away from the bus stop.

4.1.1 tu *and* vous

▶ *tu* and *vous* are both used to address a person as 'you'. In order to choose the correct one to use in a given situation some understanding of French social relationships is necessary.

▶ *tu* is used when the relationship between you and the person addressed is a close one. It is mostly used for friends and family, but not exclusively: young people tend to address each other as *tu* (*tutoyer*), whether they are close friends or not; adults use *tu* to address young children.

▶ *vous* is used to address (a) a single person formally, e.g. a stranger, a work colleague (*vouvoyer*), and (b) more than one person, regardless of whether they are close to you or not.

Patrick, tu exagères! Tu as vu? Tu as une demi-heure de retard!	Patrick, this is too much! Can't you see that you're half an hour late?
Monsieur le député, irez-vous à Paris en taxi?	[addressing an MP] Are you going to Paris by taxi, sir?

4.1.2 ils *and* elles

Ils refers to either masculine plural nouns or mixed masculine and feminine nouns; *elles* refers to feminine plural nouns only.

Je n'aime pas les araignées; **elles** me font peur !	I don't like spiders; they frighten me!
La bière et le vin ? **Ils** ne sont pas produits dans les mêmes régions.	Beer and wine? They are not produced in the same regions.

4.1.3 on

The use of *on* is much more widespread than 'one' in English.

On is used:

▶ as the equivalent of 'people', 'someone', 'they', 'you', 'one':

On dit que les Français conduisent vite.	They say the French drive fast.
On m'a dit qu'en Angleterre on buvait du bon thé.	Someone told me that in England people drank good tea.

▶ as a replacement for *nous* in speech. In this case a qualifying adjective is in the plural:

On vient de faire 80 km à vélo, **on** est vannés.	We've just cycled 80 kilometres and we're knackered.
On a finalement décidé de prendre le train.	We finally decided to take the train.

▶ to express a passive idea:

| **On** a refait le pont entièrement l'année dernière. | The bridge was entirely rebuilt last year. |
| Je suis perdu ! **On** a changé le nom des rues dans ce quartier. | I'm lost! All the street names in this area have been changed. |

Note

In written French, *on* is sometimes replaced by *l'on*, especially after *et, ou, où, pourquoi, qui, quoi, si*:

| En Écosse, où que **l'on** aille le paysage est splendide. | Wherever you go in Scotland the landscape is magnificent. |
| Si l'on comprend bien, . . . | If one understands it correctly, . . . |

4.1.4 Subject–verb inversion

In French, the normal order of words is subject (noun or pronoun) + verb:

| Elles voyagent. | They're travelling. |

In certain circumstances, however, **inversion** of the **subject pronoun** and the verb is made. Inversion can be optional.

When inversion takes place, the pronoun is attached to the verb by a hyphen. If the verb ends in a vowel *-t-* is inserted between the verb and the pronoun:

| **A-t-elle** bien mesuré les conséquences? | Has she considered the consequences properly? |

Note

Liaison between the inverted pronoun and the verb is compulsory if the verb ends in a consonant. For example, in: *Elle a, dit-elle, bien mesuré les conséquences.* (She has considered the consequences properly, she says), the - *t* in *dit* is sounded.

Types of inversion

▶ In questions (see 16.1.1)

Avez-vous assez d'argent?	Have you got enough money?
Vos parents **ont-ils** de l'argent?	Have your parents any money?
Pourquoi **faut-il** autant d'argent?	Why do we need so much money?

▶ In short interpolated phrases after:

  ▶ *dire* (to say), *demander* (to ask), *penser* (to think)

  ▶ *sembler* (to seem), *paraître* (to appear), etc., when used impersonally

*Mes amis, **dit-elle**, je vous présente votre nouveau directeur.*	My friends, said she, I would like to introduce you to your new director.
*On a, **paraît-il**, restauré le Pont du Gard.*	We have, it seems, restored the Pont du Gard.
*« Avez-vous un stylo ? », **a-t-elle** demandé.*	'Have you got a pen?' she asked.

▶ In sentences beginning with certain adverbs or adverbial phrases, inversion can be mandatory or not, according to which adverb is used.

  ▶ Compulsory inversion

    After *à peine* (scarcely), *du moins* (at least), *encore* (still), *rarement* (rarely), *en vain* (in vain)

*À peine **était-il** arrivé qu'il partit aussitôt.*	Scarcely had he arrived than he left.
*Encore **faut-il** lui faire confiance.*	It's still necessary to have confidence in him.

It is important to note that if the subject is **not a personal pronoun** or *ce* or *on*, it is placed **before** the verb and duplicated after the verb by a personal pronoun attached to the verb by a hyphen.

*À peine **Camilla** était-elle arrivée qu'elle partit aussitôt.*	Scarcely had Camilla arrived than she left.

Note

Inversion in the expression *toujours est-il que*:

***Toujours est-il qu'**on ne l'a jamais retrouvé.*	The fact remains that we have never found it.

  ▶ Inversion or *que*

    After *peut-être* (perhaps) and *sans doute* (doubtless) it is necessary either to invert or use *que* without inversion:

***Peut-être connaissait-il** la solution / **Peut-être qu'il** connaissait la solution.*	Perhaps he knew the answer.

  ▶ Optional inversion

    After *ainsi* (so), *aussi* (also), *encore* (still), *en vain* (in vain) inversion is optional.

*Ainsi **fut-il** décidé qu'on se réunirait le lendemain. / Ainsi il fut décidé qu'on se réunirait le lendemain.*	So it was decided that we should meet the next day.

▶ An exclamation or a subjunctive, expressing a strong desire, can be replaced by an inversion.

| **Suis-je** stupide ! J'ai mal lu la notice. | How foolish I am! I misread the notice. (for *Que je suis stupide !*) |
| **Puissiez-vous** un jour enfin comprendre ! | It would be good if one day you could finally understand! (for *Si vous pouviez enfin comprendre !*) |

4.1.5 Impersonal il

Il ('it') is frequently used impersonally:

▶ in weather expressions:

Il pleut.	It's raining.
Il fait nuit.	It's night(-time).
Il fait du vent.	It's windy.
Il tonne.	It's thundering.

▶ for saying the time:

| Quelle heure est-**il?** | What time is it? |
| **Il** est trois heures. | It's 3 o'clock. |

▶ as the subject of an impersonal expression (see 9.5):

| **Il** est difficile de savoir ce qu'il pense. | It's difficult to know what he thinks. |

Note

Il est and *c'est*, when used as impersonal subjects, have the same meaning. *Il est* is more formal and common in written French whereas *c'est* is more common in everyday French. They have the same structure:

either

Il est / C'est + adjective + *que*

or

Il est / C'est + adjective + preposition + infinitive

| Il est clair qu'il s'est trompé. | It's clear that he's made a mistake. |
| C'est clair qu'il s'est trompé. | |

(continued)

(continued)

Il est facile de se tromper.	It's easy to make a mistake.
C'est facile de se tromper.	

▶ with certain very common phrases: *il y a* (there is / are), *il s'agit de* (it's a question of), *il faut* (it is necessary), *il vaut mieux* (it's better), *il se peut* (maybe)

Il semble qu'il y ait un problème de carburateur.	It seems that there's a problem with the carburettor.
Il s'agit de ne pas se tromper.	It's a question of not making a mistake.

Note
In spoken French *ça* is sometimes used instead of *il*:

Ça pleut.	It's raining.
Ça se peut qu'il vienne.	He may come.
Ça risque de barder!	Sparks may fly!

4.2 Direct and indirect object pronouns

KEY POINTS

✦ Object pronouns stand for the person, thing or idea which is the object of the sentence:

Apportez ces livres. Je vais **les** lire en vacances.	Bring those books. I'm going to read them on holiday.

✦ Object pronouns agree in number and gender with the person(s) they stand for:

Marianne va venir. Tu **la** connais ?	Marianne is coming. Do you know her?

✦ Object pronouns, unlike in English, are usually placed before the verb:

Il me l' a envoyé la semaine dernière.	He sent me it last week.

4.2.1 Direct object in English = indirect object in French

▶ It is important to recognize those French verbs which are followed by an indirect object where English requires a direct object, e.g. *apprendre à*, *téléphoner à*, *conseiller à*:

| Je **lui** ai téléphoné trois fois. | I've phoned her / him three times. |
| Il **lui** a appris à souder de petits objets. | He taught her / him how to weld small objects. |

▶ A number of verbs in English, like 'to give', 'to send', 'to tell', 'to offer', 'to teach' take two direct objects, where the French equivalent is a direct object plus an indirect object. The English construction can usually also be written as direct object + indirect object by placing 'to' before the relevant pronoun.

Elle le lui a donné hier.	She gave him it yesterday. [OR She gave it to him yesterday.]
Mon copain le leur a envoyé.	My friend sent them it. [OR My friend sent it to them.]
Il me l'a dit.	He told me [it]. [lit. *'He told it to me'.]

4.2.2 le *as a neutral pronoun*

Le functions both as a masculine pronoun and as a neutral one, referring usually to previously stated phrases or whole sentences, especially with *savoir* and *pouvoir*. There is sometimes no equivalent in English for *le* used in this way.

| On ne peut pas changer sa personnalité, je **le** sais. | You can't change your personality, I know. (**le** here refers to all of the previous statement, i.e., the fact of not being able to change one's personality) |
| Tu m'en demandes trop, je ne pourrai pas **le** faire. | You are asking too much of me; I will not be able to do it. (**le** refers to the thing that is being asked) |

4.2.3 lui *and* leur

Lui and *leur* refer to either masculine or feminine nouns:

| Je **lui** ai donné la clé de la voiture. | I've given him / her the car key. |
| Demandez- **leur** s'ils vont au marché. | Ask them if they are going to the market. (**leur** could refer to the masculine, feminine or a mixture of the two) |

4.2.4 *Position of object pronouns*

▶ Object pronouns are normally placed immediately before the verb:

| Je **leur** ai répété 100 fois ! | I've told them 100 times! |

Note

In negative sentences *ne* is placed before the object pronoun:

| Je ne l'ai pas vu(e). | I didn't see him / her. |

In compound tenses, object pronouns are placed immediately before the auxiliary verb *avoir*:

| Je **les** ai vus il y a cinq minutes à peine. | I saw them scarcely five minutes ago. |

(See also 11.6.4.)

▶ Where the verb that relates to the pronoun is an infinitive, the object is normally placed before the infinitive:

| Je voudrais **vous** inviter à diner chez moi ce soir. | I'd like to invite you to dine at my place this evening. |
| Arrêtez de m'ennuyer avec vos histoires ! | Stop annoying me with your nonsense! |

Note

When an infinitive is dependent on a verb such as *écouter*, *entendre*, *faire*, *laisser*, *regarder*, *sentir*, *voir*, the object of the infinitive is placed before the main verb:

| Je **les** vois faire tous les jours. | I see them do it every day. |
| Mes parents **m'**ont laissé partir seul. | My parents let me go away by myself. |

▶ With affirmative imperatives (see 11.1.1):

 ▶ object pronouns are placed immediately after the verb, and joined to the verb by a hyphen:

| Regardez-les ! | Look at them! |
| Taisez-vous ! | Be quiet! |

 ▶ the forms *me* and *te* are replaced by *moi* and *toi* respectively:

| Regardez-moi ! | Look at me! (**not** *Regardez-me !*) |

▶ After negative imperatives, the pronoun is placed before the verb:

| Ne le bois pas. | Don't drink it! |
| Ne lui donnez pas les billets. | Don't give him / her the tickets. |

4.2.5 Agreement of the direct object with the past participle in compound tenses

In compound tenses when using the auxiliary *avoir*, or with pronominal verbs in certain circumstances, the past participle agrees in number and gender with a preceding direct object (see 11.6.4).

| *Tu as vu mes **lunettes** de soleil ?* | Have you seen my sunglasses? No, I haven't |
| *Non, je ne les ai pas **vues**.* | seen them. (***vues*** agrees in gender and number with the feminine plural direct object *les* [= lunettes]) |

Elle s'est lavée.	She washed / has washed (i.e. herself).
Elle s'est lavé les mains.	She washed her hands.
Elle se **les** est **lavées**.	She washed them.
– Ont-ils bien sauvegardé les documents ? – Oui, pas de problème, ils **les** ont bien sauvegard**és**.	'Have they saved the documents properly?' 'Yes, don't worry. They've saved them properly.'

4.3 y

KEY POINTS

✦ **y**, meaning 'there' 'in it' 'to it', indicates location, and normally refers to things and not people:

– Vous êtes déjà revenus de France ? – Non, en fait c'est la semaine prochaine que nous **y** allons.	'You're already back from France?' 'No, in fact, we're going there next week.'

✦ **y** follows the same rules for position in relation to the verb as other object pronouns:

J'**y** vais.	I'm going (there).

4.3.1 y indicating location

y stands for phrases indicating location which are introduced by prepositions such as *à*, *dans*, *sur* and *devant*.

Nous allons **au musée** cet après-midi. Nous **y** allons cet après-midi.	We're going to the museum this afternoon. We're going there this afternoon.
Je dois vite aller **au** centre sportif, mes amis m'**y** attendent déjà !	I must go to the sports centre quickly; my friends are waiting for me there already.
– Envoie-moi un texto quand tu seras dans le train ! – Mais j'**y** suis déjà !	'Send me a text when you are on the train.' 'But I'm already on it!'
– Au tennis, est-ce que tu joues **sur** terre battue ? – Non, j'**y** joue jamais, je préfère le gazon.	'Do you play tennis on clay courts?' 'No, I never play on them; I prefer grass courts.'

4.3.2 y following certain verbs

With certain verbs, e.g. *penser à, songer à, tenir à, arriver à*, *y* replaces *à* plus a following infinitive.

– As-tu pensé à changer les draps ?	'Have you thought about changing the sheets?'
– J'**y** ai pensé.	'I have.'
– Est-ce que tu tiens vraiment à faire ce long voyage ?	'Are you really set on making that long journey?'
– J'**y** tiens.	'I am.'
– As-tu songé à fermer la porte à clé ?	'Have you considered locking the door?'
– Oui, j'**y** ai songé.	'Yes, I have.'
Il n'est pas arrivé à apprendre à conduire.	He hasn't managed to learn to drive.
Il n'**y** est pas arrivé.	He hasn't managed it.

4.3.3 Useful phrases with y

y is found in a number of useful phrases:

Allons-y.	Let's go.
Ça y est.	That's it (then).
Il n'y a pas de quoi.	Not at all / Don't mention it.
il y a longtemps	a long time ago
y compris	including
Vas-y ! Allez-y !	Go on!

4.4 en

KEY POINTS

✦ en, meaning 'of / about it', 'of / about them', stands for phrases introduced by *de*:

Nous avons parlé **de son projet**.	We spoke about his project.
Nous **en** avons parlé.	We spoke about it.

– *Combien de **kilos d'abricots** désirez-vous ?*	How many kilos of apricots do you want?
– *J'**en** veux trois.*	I want three.

✦ **en** follows the same rules for position in relation to the verb as other object pronouns.

✦ **en** may be used to refer to things and, in the spoken language, to people:

– *Est-ce que tu le connais ?*	'Do you know him?'
– *Non, j'**en** ai entendu parler simplement.* (entendre parler **de** quelqu'un)	'No, I've just heard about him.'
*On n'a recruté qu'une infirmière sur deux, pourtant on **en** a vraiment besoin.*	We've only recruited one out of two nurses, yet we really need them
De *la viande ? J'**en** mange parfois, pas souvent.*	Meat? I eat it sometimes, not often.

4.4.1 en *with numbers and quantifiers*

en is used with numbers and quantifiers. In most cases there is no pronoun equivalent in English.

*Voulez-vous un billet pour l'exposition ? J'**en** ai acheté deux.*	Do you want a ticket for the exhibition? I've bought two (of them).
*J'**en** ai trop.*	I've got too many.
*Il m'**en** restait sept hier, il ne m'**en** reste plus.*	I had seven over yesterday; I haven't got any left.

4.4.2 *Verbs and expressions with* en

Certain verbs and expressions are followed by *en*, whose equivalent is a direct object in English.

▶ *avoir besoin de:*

*Il nous a proposé un emprunt, mais nous n'**en** avons pas besoin.*	He offered us a loan but we don't need one.

▶ *se servir de:*

*On m'a prêté ces outils, mais je ne sais pas m'**en** servir.*	He's lent me these tools, but I don't know how to use them.

4.5 Reflexive pronouns

Reflexive pronouns are object pronouns which refer back to the subject of the sentence. In English, the reflexive pronouns are 'myself', 'yourself', etc. In 'She cut herself' the reflexive pronoun 'herself' refers back to the subject 'She' (see 9.4).

The reflexive pronouns are the same as direct object pronouns except in the third person.

First person singular	**me** (to) myself
Second person singular	**te** (to) yourself
Third person singular	**se** (to) himself, herself, itself, oneself
First person plural	**nous** (to) ourselves
Second person plural	**vous** (to) yourselves
Third person plural	**se** (to) themselves

KEY POINTS

Reflexive pronouns in French have four main uses:

✦ with pronominal verbs

Je **me** lève à six heures.	I get up at six o'clock.

✦ in a reciprocal meaning

Ils **se** sont félicités.	They congratulated each other.

✦ in constructions which in English would be in the passive

Les fraises **se** mangent avec de la crème.	Strawberries are eaten with cream.

✦ with parts of the body, where English would use a possessive adjective

Je **me** suis lavé les cheveux.	I washed my hair.

4.5.1 Pronominal verbs

Note that in pronominal verbs the reflexive pronoun does not usually have an equivalent in English (using 'myself', etc.), e.g. *s'asseoir* (to sit [down]), *se laver* (to wash), *se lever* (to get up), *se raser* (to shave) (see 9.4.1).

*Ils **s'**assoient sur l'herbe.*	They sit [lit. sit themselves] down on the grass.
*En rentrant du travail, je **me** change et je **me** mets un instant devant la télévision.*	When I come back from work, I get changed and I sit [lit. put myself] in front of the television for a while.

4.5.2 Reciprocal use

Note that in reciprocal sentences (see 9.4.1) the reflexive pronoun is often understood in English, and does not always have an equivalent, e.g. *se rencontrer* (to meet), *se dire au revoir* (to say goodbye), *se serrer la main* (to shake hands), *s'embrasser* (to hug), *se disputer* (to argue).

Nous nous sommes rencontrés tôt ce matin, nous nous sommes salués, puis nous nous sommes séparés très vite.	We met (each other) early this morning, we greeted each other, then we separated (from each other) very quickly.
Je crois bien qu'ils se sont disputés hier.	I think they had an argument yesterday.

4.5.3 Passive meaning

Note that the passive voice is used much less frequently in French than in English.

*Ce vin **se** boit avec du poisson.*	This wine is drunk with fish.
*De tels actes violents **se** voient rarement dans nos contrées.*	Such violent acts are rarely seen in our lands.
*Cette école **s'**appelle Lycée Victor Hugo.*	This school is called the Lycée Victor Hugo. (See 9.2.3.)

4.5.4 Use with parts of the body

When referring to parts of the body and clothing, the reflexive pronoun is used rather than the possessive determiner (see 3.8.1).

*Elle va **se** faire couper les cheveux.*	She's going to have **her** hair cut.
*Il **s'**est cassé la clavicule en tombant.*	He broke **his** collarbone when he fell.
*Elle **s'**est désinfecté le genou avec de l'alcool.*	She disinfected **her** knee with alcohol.

4.5.5 Reflexive pronouns which have no equivalent in English

Many pronominal verbs have no reflexive idea in the English equivalent: *se douter de* (to suspect), *s'écrier* (to shout), *s'évanouir* (to faint), *se fier à* (to trust), *s'occuper de* (to look after), *se réveiller* (to wake up), *se souvenir de* (to remember), *se taire* (to keep quiet), *se tromper* (to make a mistake).

Il s'est trompé d'heure et n'a pu s'occuper des enfants.	He forgot the time and wasn't able to look after the children.
À quelle heure se réveillent-ils d'habitude ?	At what time do they usually wake up?
Veuillez vous taire, s'il vous plaît ?	Will you keep quiet, please?

4.5.6 Addition of moi-même, etc.

The following pronouns are often added to a sentence containing a reflexive verb, for emphasis: *moi-même* (myself), *toi-même* (yourself), *lui-même* (himself), *elle-même* (herself), *soi-même* (oneself), *nous-mêmes* (ourselves), *vous-mêmes* (yourselves), *eux-mêmes* (themselves), *elles-mêmes* (themselves).

| Il s'est rendu compte lui-même du mensonge. | He himself realized it was a lie. |
| Je ne m'en souviens pas moi-même. | I don't remember it myself. |

4.6 Order of object pronouns

4.6.1 Object pronouns before the verb

▶ When two object pronouns, including *y* and *en*, come before the verb they follow the order in the table below:

Order of object pronouns

me	le	lui	y	en
te	la	leur		
se	les			
nous				
vous				

Il nous l'a montré avant.	He showed us it beforehand.
Elle s'en est acheté plusieurs.	She bought herself several of them.
Qui s'y frotte s'y pique !	If you go looking for trouble, you'll find it.

▶ When a direct and an indirect object come together before the verb:

  ▶ if both objects are in the third person, the direct object comes first:

Je le lui ai donné.	I gave him it.

  ▶ if only one of the objects is in the third person the direct object comes second:

Il me l'a donné.	He gave me it.
Ils me les ont prêtés et je les leur ai rendus immédiatement.	They lent me them and I gave them back straight away.

4.6.2 Object pronouns after the affirmative imperative

▶ When two object pronouns follow the affirmative imperative, the order they follow differs from that of the table in section 4.6.1 in one respect: third person pronouns **precede** first and second person pronouns. The pronouns are linked by hyphens:

Donne-les-moi.	Give me them.
Dites-le-nous.	Tell us (it).
Allez-vous-en.	Go away!
Donnez-le-leur.	Give it to them.

Note

The forms *me* and *te* are replaced by *moi* and *toi* respectively, except before *y* and *en*:

Va-t'en.	Go away!
Commence à t'y diriger pendant que j'attends.	Start going there while I wait.

Negative imperatives follow the order in the table in section 4.6.1:

Ne le leur donnez pas.	Don't give it to them.
Ne m'en parle plus jamais !	Don't ever speak to me about it!

4.6.3 Two object pronouns after certain verbs

When a number of verbs, including *faire*, *laisser* and *entendre*, are followed by the infinitive, two object pronouns normally come before the verb and not the infinitive:

Il me l'a fait boire.	He made me drink it.
Elle le lui a laissé croire.	She let him believe it.

4.6.4 Object pronouns after devoir and pouvoir

When *devoir* and *pouvoir* are followed by the infinitive, object pronouns normally precede the infinitive:

Vous pouvez me le donner quand nous serons chez nous.	You can give me it when we get home.
Vous devrez me l'avoir remboursé sous huitaine.	You will have to pay (it) me back within a week.

4.7 Stressed pronouns

Stressed (or 'disjunctive') pronouns are those used after prepositions, as in 'We went in after *them*' or for the purposes of emphasis, as in 'I haven't a clue, *me*'.

KEY POINTS

✦ Typically, these pronouns in French follow prepositions:

*Elle était debout devant **lui**.*	She was standing in front of him.
*Ils ont couru après **elle** sans succès.*	They ran after her in vain.

✦ They are used for emphasis:

***Lui**, il n'a aucune idée de quoi faire.*	He's no idea what to do.

✦ They are frequently used after **c'est**, often with a sense of possession:

*C'est à **vous**, cette voiture?*	Is that car yours?
*C'est **lui** le coupable.*	He's the culprit.
*Quand tu t'en iras, c'est **moi qui** organiserai la collecte.*	When you go it'll be me who'll organize the collection.

✦ They can stand alone:

*Qui est-ce qui a gagné? **Lui**.*	Who's won? Him. / He has.

Stressed pronouns

First person singular	***moi*** me
Second person singular	***toi*** you

Third person singular	*lui* him
	elle her
	soi oneself
First person plural	**nous** us
Second person plural	**vous** you
Third person plural	*eux* them
	elles them

Notes

Stressed pronouns are used:

▶ in comparisons:

| *Il est plus doué que* **moi**. | He's cleverer than I [am]. |

▶ for contrast:

| **Toi**, *tu prépares le repas et* **moi** *je fais la vaisselle*. | You get the meal and I'll wash up. |

▶ after positive imperatives:

| *Donnez-le-***moi**. | Give it to me. (See 11.1.1.) |

▶ with *même*, *seul*, *pas*, *non plus* and *aussi*:

Lui seul connaît la solution.	He alone knows the solution.
Êtes-vous déjà allés au Kenya ? Pas moi !	Have you already been to Kenya? Neither have I!
Moi aussi je veux y aller.	I'd like to go there too.
– *Je n'aime pas la nouvelle Renault.*	'I don't like the new Renault.'
– *Moi non plus.*	'Neither do I.'

4.7.1 soi

Soi is the stressed pronoun equivalent of *on*, referring to 'people', 'oneself':

Il est si bon comédien que dans ses films on rit et on pleure malgré **soi**.	He's such a good actor that in his films one laughs and cries despite oneself.
On *n'est jamais si bien servi que par* **soi-même**.	If you want something done, you'd better do it yourself.
On garde cela pour **soi-même**.	One keeps that to oneself.
À minuit, chacun rentra chez **soi**.	At midnight, everyone went home.

4.8 Coordination of personal pronouns

▶ Subject pronouns

  ▶ When linked by the coordinating conjunctions *et, ou* and *ni* the second pronoun may be omitted:

Je sors de la maison et (je) prends le bus à 8 heures du matin.	I leave the house and catch the bus at 8 am.

  ▶ In compound tenses the auxiliary verb is omitted:

Ils ont bu et chanté pour son anniversaire.	They drank and sang for his birthday.

▶ Object pronouns

  ▶ When linked by the coordinating conjunctions *et, ou* and *ni* the second pronoun is normally repeated:

*Georges **m'**a appelé ce matin et **m'**a dit qu'il ne viendrait pas.*	Georges called me this morning and told me that he wouldn't come.

▶ Stressed pronouns

  ▶ When two or more pronouns linked by *et* or *ou* are the subject of the verb, stressed pronouns are used. Note that in this case *subject* pronouns are used in English:

***Toi** et **moi** allons voyager ensemble demain.*	You and I are going to travel together tomorrow.
***Lui** et **moi** assisterons à la réunion de famille.*	He and I will go to the family reunion.

4.9 Demonstrative pronouns

We use demonstrative pronouns 'this one, these ones' and 'that one, those ones' when we wish to point to a particular thing, person or concept: 'That idea is better than this one', 'These shoes are trendier than those (ones).'

KEY POINTS

  ✦ The demonstrative pronouns *celui, celle, ceux* and *celles* are the equivalent of 'the one(s)'.

  ✦ Demonstrative pronouns agree in gender and number with the noun they stand for.

  ✦ The distinction in English between 'this one' and 'that one' is made by adding *-ci* or *-là* respectively to the pronoun: *celui-ci, celle-là*, etc.

Demonstrative pronouns

Masculine singular	*celui* the one	*celui-ci* this one	*celui-là* that one
Feminine singular	*celle* the one	*celle-ci* this one	*celle-là* that one
Masculine plural	*ceux* the ones	*ceux-ci* these ones	*ceux-là* those ones
Feminine plural	*celles* the ones	*celles-ci* these ones	*celles-là* those ones

Note

ce / c', *cela*, *ceci* and *ça* are demonstrative pronouns which do not stand for specific nouns. They refer to either general states of affairs or actions, or are simply impersonal.

– *Tu voudrais aller au cinema ?*	'Would you like to go to the cinema?'
– *Ce serait avec plaisir.*	'That would be a pleasure.' (The fact of going to the cinema would be a pleasure.)
C' est dommage.	It's a pity. (Here *c'* is impersonal; like 'it' in English, *c'* refers to no specific noun or idea.)
Ça va ?	All right / OK?

4.9.1 Use of demonstrative pronouns in relative clauses

The simple demonstrative pronoun cannot stand on its own. Typically, it is used to introduce relative clauses, *celui qui / celle que* etc. (see 15.4).

*Levez la main **ceux qui** savent qui a gagné la bataille d'Azincourt.*	Raise your hands those who know who won the battle of Agincourt.

4.9.2 Use of ce, cela, ceci, ça

The pronouns *ce*, *cela*, *ceci* and *ça* are neutral. *Ça* is more colloquial.

*Il ment, **cela** se lit sur son visage !*	He's lying; you can see that on his face.
Ceci n'est pas pour lui déplaire !	This suits him well.
*Pour **ce** faire, il faudrait parler chinois couramment.*	To do that you should be be fluent in Chinese.
Ça va faire trois ans qu'il n'est pas retourné dans son pays.	He hasn't been back to his country for three years.

Note

Ça is frequently used instead of *il* colloquially (see 4.1.5).

4.10 Possessive pronouns

Possessive pronouns indicate possession or show a relationship between the speaker and a thing, a person or an idea: 'Is that drink *mine* or *yours*?' 'The idea was *hers*.'

KEY POINTS

Possessive pronouns agree in number and gender with the thing possessed:

*Mon père habite Rouen. Où habite **le vôtre** ?*	My father lives in Rouen. Where does yours live?
– Où sont mes lunettes de soleil ? *– **Les tiennes** sont dans la voiture, avec **les miennes***	'Where are my sunglasses?' 'Yours are in the car with mine.'
*Ma femme et **la tienne** se connaissent depuis longtemps.*	My wife and yours have known each other for a long time.
*Une maison comme **la leur**, cela doit coûter cher, non ?*	A house like theirs must cost a lot, mustn't it?

Possessive pronouns

	Masc. singular	Fem. singular	Masc. plural	Fem. plural	
First person singular	*le mien*	*la mienne*	*les miens*	*les miennes*	mine
Second person singular	*le tien*	*la tienne*	*les tiens*	*les tiennes*	yours
Third person singular	*le sien*	*la sienne*	*les siens*	*les siennes*	his, hers
First person plural	*le nôtre*	*la nôtre*	*les nôtres*	*les nôtres*	ours
Second person plural	*le vôtre*	*la vôtre*	*les vôtres*	*les vôtres*	yours
Third person plural	*le leur*	*la leur*	*les leurs*	*les leurs*	theirs

Note

The possessive pronouns *le / la nôtre* and *le / la vôtre* are distinguished from the possessive adjectives *notre* and *votre* by the definite article and a circumflex accent on the letter *o*.

4.10.1 *à* plus a stressed pronoun indicating possession

The idea of possession may also be expressed by adding *à* plus a stressed pronoun to the thing possessed.

C'est **à lui**.	It's his.
Ces pommes ne sont pas **à vous**, cher voisin! Elles dépassent la clôture, elles sont légalement **à nous**.	Those apples are not yours, dear neighbour! They are on the other side of the hedge and so they are legally ours.

4.11 Indefinite pronouns

Indefinite pronouns are words that do not refer to a specific person or thing. In 'You can ask anyone you like; they are all helpful here', 'anyone' and 'all' are indefinite pronouns.

KEY POINTS

✦ As in English, indefinite pronouns refer to non-specific persons or things.

✦ Indefinites may be positive, e.g. *quelqu'un, tous, plusieurs*, or negative, e.g. *nul, personne, aucun, rien* (see Chapter 8).

The principal indefinite pronouns in French are:

aucun	any, none
l'(les) autre(s)	the other one(s)
le (la) (les) même(s)	the same
n'importe qui	no matter who
n'importe quoi	anything
nul	nobody
personne	nobody
plusieurs	several
quelque chose	something
quelqu'un	someone
qui que ce soit	whoever
quiconque	anyone
quoi que ce soit	anything
rien	nothing
tel(le)(s)	some

(continued)

(continued)

tous	all
tout le monde	everyone
tout	everything
un	one

Tu as vu les joueurs ! **Plusieurs** *ont été blessés pendant le match.*	Did you see the players! Several were injured during the match.
Tout *est bien qui finit bien.*	All's well that ends well.
J'ai perdu mon parapluie. Est-ce que **quelqu'un** *peut m'en prêter* **un** *?*	I've lost my umbrella. Can someone lend me one?

PRONOUNS IN CONTEXT

Nos enfants, l'électronique et l'informatique

Aujourd'hui, les jeunes baignent dans l'informatique. Dès la prime enfance on **leur** offre un ordinateur portable, puis **il leur** faut un téléphone portable et très vite **ils** ne jurent que par **lui**. Les textos, **ils les** composent 10 fois plus vite que **vous**. Le tout dernier modèle, **ils en** rêvent, et quand **ils l'ont**, **ils** ne manquent pas une occasion pour **le** comparer avec **celui** du copain. Même chose avec les ordinateurs portables:

– **Le mien** a un disque dur d'un téraoctet.

– Oui mais **le tien** n'a pas de carte graphique HD.

– Pour **moi ce** n'est pas **ça** qui compte. Mon ordi, je **le** veux rapide, mince, léger et avec beaucoup de mémoire. Je télécharge des films et je **les** regarde dans le train, le bus, partout. **Ça me** divertit. Si **tu** veux, viens chez **moi**, je **te** montrerai.

– **Toi, ce** qui **te** plaît **c'**est le cinéma, **moi, ce** sont les jeux. J'**en** ai des dizaines. J'**y** passe des heures entières. Si tu veux tu peux jouer avec **moi** !

Les jeunes deviennent inaccessibles. **Certains** passent des journées sur la toile. Que font-ils ? Qui est derrière l'écran ? **On** voudrait **les** mettre en garde, mais **ils se** rient de **nous**. Ajoutez à **cela** qu'**ils** passent les weekends et les vacances entre copains. Et de peur que vous ne **les** contrôliez, **ils** ne **vous** acceptent même pas comme amis sur Facebook.

On a vraiment l'impression qu'ils cherchent à **se** réfugier dans un monde virtuel. Pourtant, la toile est loin d'être un havre de paix. La violence de certains messages échangés est bien réelle et **celui** ou **celle** qui **la** subit vit un enfer.

Subject	**on** leur offre un ordinateur portable; Si **tu** veux **tu** peux [4.1]
Direct object	quand ils **l'** ont; ils ne **vous** acceptent; Mon ordi, je **le** veux rapide, mince, léger; celui ou celle qui **la** subit [4.2]
Indirect object	on **leur** offre un ordinateur portable; je **te** montrerai; ce qui **te** plaît [4.2]
y	J'**y** passe des heures entières [4.3]
en	ils **en** rêvent; J'**en** ai des dizaines [4.4]
Reflexive	**se** réfugier dans un monde virtuel [4.5]
Stressed	ils ne jurent que par **lui**; viens chez **moi**; **Toi**, ce qui te plait, c'est le cinéma [4.7]
Impersonal	**il** leur faut un téléphone portable [4.1.5]
Neutral	**Ça** me divertit; Ajoutez à **cela** [4.9.2]
Demonstrative	**celui** du copain; **celui** ou **celle** qui la subit [4.9]
Possessive	**Le mien** a un disque dur; mais **le tien** n'a pas de carte graphique HD [4.10]
Indefinite	**Certains** passent des journées sur la toile [4.11]

EXERCISES

1. **Replace the words underlined with personal pronouns:**

   1. _Une enfant_ joue sur la plage.
   2. Ses parents surveillent _l'enfant_.
   3. De temps en temps les parents jouent avec _l'enfant_.
   4. La famille passe l'été _sur cette plage_. _La famille_ part _de la plage_ à l'automne.
   5. Les parents ont offert _à l'enfant_ un petit bateau gonflable.
   6. _Les parents_ montrent _à l'enfant_ le bateau.
   7. _Le père_ fait monter l'enfant _sur le bateau_.
   8. _L'enfant_ ne veut pas garder _ses sandales_.
   9. « Donne _tes sandales_ _à ta sœur_ », disent _les parents_.
   10. _L'enfant_ ôte _ses sandales_. Puis _l'enfant_ tend _ses sandales_ _à ses parents_.

2. **Fill the blanks with pronouns that correspond to the nouns in square brackets:**

   1. [À William et Isabelle] elle _____ a offert un beau livre.
   2. Dans les poches, [à Paul] il ne _____ restait que 3 euros.
   3. [À ses amies] il _____ a réservé une surprise.
   4. [De France] il _____ a rapporté d'excellents souvenirs.
   5. [Des encouragements] il _____ a vraiment besoin.
   6. [À Londres] il _____ va tous les jours.
   7. [Ses enfants] on _____ aide habituellement.

8. [À ses enfants] on ne _____ ment pas en principe.

9. [Les faits], on _____ connaît.

10. [Eux-mêmes], ils _____ servent de cet outil sophistiqué.

3. **Fill the blanks with a suitable stressed pronoun:**

1. Et _____, comment allez-vous?

2. _____, je vais bien, je pars pour l'Afrique.

3. Ma cousine, _____, n'est jamais allée en Afrique.

4. Mon cousin, _____, ira au printemps prochain.

5. _____, nous y sommes allés trois fois.

6. _____, ils vont partir pour l'Irlande demain.

7. _____, elles y sont déjà allées.

8. Et _____, tu restes là ?

9. Oh, _____, je ne sais pas !

10. Allez, je t'emmène, accompagne-_____ !

4. **Fill the blanks with a suitable possessive pronoun:**

1. J'ai perdu mon parapluie, peux-tu me prêter _____?

2. Il ne connaît pas ma famille, je ne connais pas _____

3. La famille Martin et moi partageons le même parking. Ma voiture est à côté de _____

4. Nous avons nos problèmes, ils ont _____

5. Toi tu t'occupes de tes devoirs et lui s'occupe _____

6. Vous ne savez rien de mes études, et je ne sais rien _____

7. Je vais chercher mes affaires et il va chercher _____

8. Il a payé sa part, nous devons aussi payer _____

9. Hier tu as célébré ton anniversaire, aujourd'hui je célèbre _____

10. Je lui ai fait visiter mon appartement, elle m'a fait visiter _____

5 ADJECTIVES

An adjective is a word that gives more information about a noun or a pronoun.

When we say 'John has a computer', we communicate no information about the computer except that John possesses it. When we place an adjective before 'computer', e.g. 'John has a new computer', or after it, e.g. 'John's computer is new', we describe the computer further.

In English, adjectives are usually placed either before the noun or separate from it, as the complement of the verb. The English term for the former type of adjective is 'attributive' and the latter 'predicative'.

KEY POINTS

In French, adjectives are generally used in the same way as in English. They are *either*:

✦ **attributive** (*épithète* in French), i.e., next to the noun they describe:

une usine désaffectée	a disused factory
une Rolls-Royce blanche	a white Rolls-Royce

or:

(continued)

(continued)

✦ **predicative** (*attribut* in French), i.e., separated from the noun by a verb of 'state', like *être* or *sembler*:

L'usine semble désaffectée.	The factory appears disused.
La Rolls-Royce est blanche.	The Rolls-Royce is white.

There are three major differences between adjectives in French and English:

✦ Adjectives agree with the noun or pronoun in *gender*:

*un bulletin **blanc***	a blank vote [masculine singular]
*une maison **blanche***	a white house [feminine singular]
*une machine **volante***	a flying machine [feminine singular]
*Les musées sont **ouverts** le dimanche.*	The museums are open on Sundays. [masculine plural]
*Les écoles sont **fermées** le samedi.*	Schools are closed on Saturdays. [feminine plural]

✦ Adjectives agree with the noun or pronoun in *number*:

*une copie **blanche***	a blank script [feminine singular]
*des cahiers de textes **quadrillés***	exercise books with squared paper [masculine plural]
*Ils ont laissé toutes les fenêtres **ouvertes**.*	They left all the windows open. [feminine plural]

✦ Adjectives are normally placed *after* the noun, with the exception of a number of common adjectives which precede it:

un disque dur	a hard disk

But

un gros ordinateur	a large computer

5.1 The position of adjectives

5.1.1 *Position after the noun*

The following adjectives are normally placed after the noun:

▶ long adjectives (of more than three syllables) qualifying a short noun:

une vue bucolique	a bucolic view
un site enchanteur	an enchanting site

▶ adjectives followed by a complement or modified by a long adverb (more than one syllable):

un bateau vieux de 30 ans	a thirty-year-old boat
une fille vraiment jolie	a really pretty girl

▶ adjectives of colour or geometrical form:

une cour carrée	a square courtyard
des murs blancs	white walls
une route sinueuse	a winding route

Note

In figurative use, or in poetry, colour adjectives can be placed before the noun:

de noirs desseins	dark designs
les vertes collines du Maine	the green hills of Maine

▶ adjectives with an idea of time:

les générations futures	future generations
les pages suivantes	the following pages

▶ adjectives which are descriptive, or which classify:

▶ expressing a physical quality:

un sentier sablonneux	a sandy path
un divan confortable	a comfortable divan

▶ adjectives denoting nationality or regional identity:

la cuisine française	French cuisine
une crème anglaise	thin custard
un danseur espagnol	a Spanish dancer
un écrivain breton	a writer from Brittany

▶ adjectives relating to social, religious, historical, geographical, administrative and technical matters:

un syndicat réformateur	a reforming trade union
l'Église catholique	the Catholic Church
un décret royal	a royal decree
le plissement alpin	the Alpine fold mountains
un formulaire administratif	an administrative form
le droit romain	Roman law
un moteur électrique	an electric motor

▶ adjectives which describe a style, a look, a taste:

une église gothique	a Gothic church
un immeuble moderne	a modern building
un café amer	a bitter coffee
un air triste	a sad appearance

▶ adjectives derived from proper nouns or indicating an affiliation:

une tragédie shakespearienne	a Shakespearian tragedy
un parti gaulliste	a Gaullist party

▶ adjectives derived from past participles or forms of the verb ending in -*ant*:

un pré fleuri	a meadow full of flowers
un jeu amusant	an amusing game
un ordinateur performant	a high-performance computer
un livre apprécié	a much-loved book

5.1.2 Position before the noun

A few short and common adjectives are generally placed before the noun:

autre	another	haut	high
beau	beautiful	joli	pretty
bon	good	long	long
bref	brief	mauvais	bad, evil

double	double	*nouveau*	new
faux	false	*petit*	small
grand	large	*vaste*	vast
gros	fat	*vieux*	old

un beau visage	a beautiful face
une jolie maison	a pretty house
une longue route	a long journey
un gros orage	a big storm

▶ adjectives expressing a moral quality:

C'est une gentille fille.	She's a nice girl.
un vilain garçon	a naughty boy

▶ adjectives which qualify a proper noun:

le légendaire Docteur Mabuse	the legendary Doctor Mabuse
le célèbre professeur Tournesol	the famous Professor Calculus (in *Tintin*)

▶ cardinal and ordinal numbers:

les sept jours de la semaine	the seven days of the week
cent mille euros	a hundred thousand euros
le vingtième siècle	the twentieth century
le troisième jour	the third day

5.1.3 Adjectives which have a different meaning according to whether they are before or after the noun

The following adjectives change their meaning according to their position. Where the adjective precedes the noun its meaning is often figurative, and has moral rather than descriptive connotations.

ancien (old / former)	
un athlète ancien	an old athlete
un ancien athlète	a former athlete
brave (nice / courageous)	

(continued)

(continued)

un soldat brave	a courageous soldier
un brave homme	a nice man
certain (sure / certain)	
une influence certaine	a real influence
une certaine influence	a certain influence
cher (expensive / dear)	
une voiture chère	an expensive car
mon cher ami	my dear friend
curieux (inquisitive / strange)	
un enfant curieux	an inquisitive child
de curieuses façons	strange ways
dur (hard / difficult, strenuous)	
un disque dur	a hard disk
un dur labeur	a strenuous job
grand (big / great)	
un homme grand	a tall/big man
un grand homme	a great man (i.e., famous)
gris (grey, dull / unhappy)	
la matière grise	grey matter
faire grise mine	to look none too pleased
honnête (honest [doesn't cheat] / respectable, decent)	
un commerçant honnête	an honest shopkeeper
une honnête proposition	a decent proposal
juste (correct, not wrong / legitimate, righteous)	
une réponse juste	a correct answer
une juste colère	a legitimate anger
méchant (wicked / terrific)	
un chien méchant	a vicious dog
une méchante pluie	heavy rain
même (same / very)	
la même chose	the same thing

le jour même	the very day
nul (worthless / none)	
un devoir nul	a worthless piece of homework
nul doute	(although *aucun doute* is more common) no doubt
pâle (pale / insignificant)	
un teint pâle	a pale complexion
une pâle imitation	a pale imitation
parfait (perfect / total, complete)	
un travail parfait	a perfect job
un parfait gentleman	a complete gentleman
pauvre (poor)	
un homme pauvre	a poor man (without money)
un pauvre homme	a poor man (causing pity but can be rich)
propre (clean / own)	
une chambre propre	a clean room
ma propre chambre	my own room
pur (pure / total, sheer)	
de l'alcool pur	pure alcohol
de la pure méchanceté	sheer wickedness
riche (wealthy / excellent)	
un pays riche	a rich country
une riche idée	an excellent idea
sacré (holy / a hell of a . . .)	
un lieu sacré	a holy place
un sacré courage !	a hell of a brave act
sale (dirty / nasty)	
un endroit sale	a dirty place
un sale caractère	a nasty character
seul (lonely / only)	
une femme seule	a lonely woman

(continued)

(continued)

un seul homme	one man (only)
sévère (strict, rigorous / serious)	
un professeur sévère	a strict teacher
une sévère défaite	a heavy defeat
simple (simple, easy / mere, ordinary)	
une question simple	an easy (straightforward) question
une simple question	a mere question
sombre (dark / gloomy)	
un couloir sombre	a dark corridor
un sombre avenir	a gloomy future
triste (sad / sorry, dreadful)	
un enfant triste	a sad child
un triste état	a dreadful state
vrai (true / real, genuine)	
une histoire vraie	a true story
de vrais diamonts	genuine diamonds

5.1.4 Adjectives which accompany numbers

Several adjectives which accompany a number are placed after that number, unlike in English. These are: *premier* (first), *dernier* (last), *autre* (another), *prochains* (next) and *mêmes* (same).

les trois derniers jours	the last three days
les cinq dernières minutes	the last five minutes
les quatre prochains jours	the next four days
les deux autres dimanches	the other two Sundays

5.2 The feminine of adjectives

5.2.1 Adjectives which add -e to form the feminine

▶ As with nouns, the feminine of adjectives is usually formed by adding *-e* to the masculine:

Masculine	Feminine	
cru	crue	raw
joli	jolie	pretty
national	nationale	national
poli	polie	polite
régional	régionale	regional
vrai	vraie	true

▶ In most cases, the addition of the -e causes the final consonant (that appears in the written form of the word) to be pronounced:

étonnant	étonnante	surprising
fort	forte	strong
grand	grande	big
gris	grise	grey
inclus	incluse	inclusive
petit	petite	little
persan	persane	Persian

Note

The adjectives *grand* and *franc*, when used in compound nouns *in certain set expressions*, are invariable in the feminine singular: *une grand-mère* but *des grands-mères* (grandmother[s]). In these expressions:

▶ *grand* does not mean 'big' or 'tall' in physical stature (a grandmother is not necessarily 'big').

▶ *grand* is linked to a word by a hyphen to create a compound word. The most frequent of these words are:

grand-maman	(grandma)
grand-mère	(grandmother)
grand-route / grand-rue	(main / high street)
grand-tante	(great-aunt)
grand-vergue	(main yard)
grand-voile	(mainsail)
(ne) pas grand-chose	(not much, not a lot)
à grand-peine	(with great difficulty)
avoir grand-peur	(to be fear-stricken)

Otherwise, *grand* is not followed by a hyphen and agrees with its noun: *grande banlieue* (outer suburbs); *grandes vacances* (summer [i.e. long] holidays); *Grande Bretagne* (big compared with *Bretagne* [Brittany]); *Grande Ourse* (Great Bear); *grande surface* (hypermarket; large surface).

5.2.2 Adjectives which are invariable in the masculine and feminine

Adjectives which end in *-e* are the same in the masculine and feminine:

habile	*habile*	clever
riche	*riche*	rich
sale	*sale*	dirty
sincère	*sincère*	sincere
utile	*utile*	useful

Exceptions

maître	*maîtresse*	master, main
traître	*traîtresse*	treacherous

une poutre maîtresse	a main beam
une accalmie traîtresse	a deceptive lull

Note

drôle (funny), *ivrogne* (drunk), *pauvre* (poor), *suisse* (Swiss) are the same in the feminine: *une histoire drôle* (a funny story), *une montre suisse* (a Swiss watch), but nouns formed from them have a feminine form: *une drôlesse* (hussy), *une Suissesse* (Swiss woman).

5.2.3 Adjectives ending in -er

Adjectives ending in *-er* form the feminine in *-ère*:

Masculine	Feminine	
cher	*chère*	dear
entier	*entière*	whole
fier	*fière*	proud
léger	*légère*	light
printanier	*printanière*	spring(like)

Note

The masculine forms of *amer* (bitter) and *fier* are pronounced the same as the feminine *amère* [amɛʁ] and *fière* [fjɛʁ].

5.2.4 Adjectives ending in -el, -eil, gentil *and* nul

Adjectives ending in *-el*, *-eil*, *gentil* and **nul** double the final *l* in the feminine:

habituel	habituelle	habitual
nul	nulle	no, useless
pareil	pareille	same

5.2.5 Adjectives ending in -et

Adjectives ending in *-et* double the *t* before the final *-e* of the feminine:

muet	muette	dumb
net	nette	clear, net
fluet	fluette	slight, frail
violet	violette	violet, purple
propret	proprette	neat and tidy

Exceptions

▶ The following adjectives form the feminine in *-ète*:

complet	complète	complete
concret	concrète	concrete
discret	discrète	discreet
inquiet	inquiète	worried
secret	secrète	secret

▶ Adjectives ending in *-at* and *-ot* do not double the final *t*:

délicat	délicate	delicate
idiot	idiote	idiotic
bigot	bigote	bigoted

Exceptions

boulot	boulotte	tubby
pâlot	pâlotte	rather pale
sot	sotte	foolish
vieillot	vieillotte	quaint

5.2.6 Adjectives ending in -f

Adjectives ending in *-f* form the feminine in *-ve*:

vif	vive	bright, keen
collectif	collective	collective

Note

bref (brief) adds a grave accent in the feminine: *brève*.

5.2.7 Adjectives ending in -en and -on

Adjectives ending in *-en* and *-on* double the final *n*:

ancien	ancienne	old
bon	bonne	good
européen	européenne	European
mignon	mignonne	pretty

Exception

mormon	mormone	Mormon

Note

lapon (Lapp), *letton* (Latvian), *nippon* (Japanese) have two feminine forms: *lapone / laponne*; *lettone / lettonne*; *nippone / nipponne*.

5.2.8 Adjectives ending in -an, -in, -ain, -ein, -un

Adjectives ending in *-an, -in, -ain, -ein, -un* add *-e*:

voisin	voisine	neighbouring
plein	pleine	full
anglican	anglicane	Anglican
commun	commune	common

Exceptions

▶ *paysan* (peasant) doubles the final *n*: *paysanne*.

▶ *bénin* (benign, minor) and *malin* (malignant, clever) form the feminine in -*gne*: *bénigne, maligne*.

5.2.9 Adjectives ending in -c

Adjectives ending in -*c* form the feminine in -*que*:

Masculine	Feminine	
caduc	caduque	obsolete
public	publique	public
turc	turque	Turkish

Exceptions

blanc	blanche	white
franc	franche	frank, honest
sec	sèche	dry

Notes

▶ *grec* (Greek) becomes *grecque* in the feminine.

▶ *laïque* (lay / secular) is both masculine and feminine.

5.2.10 Adjectives ending in -g

Adjectives ending in -*g* form the feminine in -*gue*:

long	longue	long
oblong	oblongue	oblong

5.2.11 Adjectives ending in -gu

Adjectives ending in -*gu* form the feminine in -*guë* or, since 1990, -*güe* (see 17.4):

aigu	aigüe / aiguë	high-pitched
ambigu	ambigüe / ambiguë	ambiguous
exigu	exigüe / exiguë	cramped, confined

5.2.12 Adjectives ending in -x and -s

Adjectives ending in -x and -s form the feminine in -se (pronounced [z]):

clos	close	(en)closed
danois	danoise	Danish
français	française	French
gris	grise	grey
jaloux	jalouse	jealous
mauvais	mauvaise	bad
pluvieux	pluvieuse	rainy
ras	rase	short

Exceptions

▶ *doux* and *frais*

doux	douce	sweet
frais	fraîche	fresh

▶ the following adjectives ending in -s double the final letter:

bas	basse	low
gras	grasse	fat, greasy
gros	grosse	big, fat
épais	épaisse	thick
métis	métisse	mixed-race
las	lasse	weary
exprès	expresse	express

▶ the following adjectives ending in -x (*faus* and *rous* in Old French) form the feminine in -sse:

faux	fausse	false
roux	rousse	red, ginger

▶ *vieux* (see 5.3).

5.2.13 Adjectives ending in -eur

Adjectives ending in *-eur* (derived from verbs) form the feminine in *-euse*:

joueur	joueuse	playful
rieur	rieuse	cheerful, laughing

Exceptions

▶ *pécheur* and *vengeur*

pécheur	pécheresse	sinful
vengeur	vengeresse	vengeful

▶ Comparative adjectives ending in *-eur* form the feminine by adding *-e*:

meilleur	meilleure	better
supérieur	supérieure	upper, superior
majeur	majeure	main, major
mineur	mineure	minor
antérieur	antérieure	previous
inférieur	inférieure	lower, inferior
ultérieur	ultérieure	subsequent, ulterior
postérieur	postérieure	later, posterior
extérieur	extérieure	outer

▶ *vainqueur* has no feminine form; for the feminine, *victorieuse* (masculine *victorieux*) is used.

5.2.14 Adjectives ending in -teur

Adjectives ending in *-teur* (derived from verbs) form the feminine in *-teuse* or *-trice*:

▶ If you can make a present participle by changing *-teur* to *-tant*, the feminine ends in *-teuse*.

Verb	Present participle	Adjective	
flatter	flattant	flatteur → flatteuse	flattering
sauter	sautant	sauteur → sauteuse	jumping

(continued)

(continued)

une proposition flatteuse	a flattering proposal
une scie sauteuse	a jigsaw puzzle

▶ If you cannot make a present participle by changing *-teur* to *-tant*, the feminine ends in *-trice*:

Verb	Present participle	Adjective	
protéger	protégeant	protecteur → protectrice	protective
corrompre	corrompant	corrupteur → corruptrice	corrupting
perturber	perturbant	perturbateur → perturbatrice	disruptive
sauver	sauvant	salvateur → salvatrice	saving

une paroi protectrice	a protective wall
une intention corruptrice	an intention to corrupt
une action perturbatrice	a disruptive action

5.2.15 Special cases

coi	coite	speechless
favori	favorite	favourite
	mes lectures favorites	my favourite reading
rigolo	rigolote	funny
	une histoire rigolote	a funny story
tiers	tierce	third
	une tierce personne	a third party
andalou	andalouse	Andalusian
	la ville andalouse de Séville	the Andalusian town of Seville
esquimau	esquimaude	Eskimo
	une famille esquimaude	an Eskimo family

▶ the past participles *dissous* (dissolved) and *absous* (absolved), when used as adjectives, become *dissoute*, *absoute* respectively in the feminine.

▶ *pauvre* (poor) and *nègre* (black) do not have a separate feminine form as adjectives, but the feminine nouns derived from them have a separate form: *pauvresse* (pauper), *négresse* (negress).

▶ *hébreux* (Hebrew) becomes *hébraïque* in the feminine when describing things: *l'histoire hébraïque* (Hebrew history). When referring to people, *israélite* or *juif / juive* is used.

5.2.16 Adjectives that are invariable in the feminine

A few adjectives such as *chic* (smart, chic), *bougon* (grumpy), *fat* (conceited), *grognon* (bad-tempered), *kaki* (khaki), *snob* (snobbish) are invariable in the feminine.

une personne chic	a smart person
une voisine grognon	a bad-tempered neighbour

5.2.17 Adjectives without a feminine form

A few adjectives, such as *aquilin* (aquiline), *benêt* (simple-minded), *hongre* (gelded), *pers* (blue-green) have no feminine form and can only qualify masculine nouns.

un nez aquilin	an aquiline nose
des yeux pers	blue-green eyes
un cheval hongre	a gelded horse

5.2.18 An adjective without a masculine form

Bée (gaping) has no masculine form:

être bouche bée de surprise   to be open-mouthed with surprise

5.3 Adjectives with a second masculine form

A number of adjectives have a **second** masculine form, which is used before a noun beginning with a vowel or a silent *h*. The feminine derives from the old masculine form.

Masculine singular before a consonant	Masculine singular before a vowel or silent *h*	Masculine plural	Feminine singular	Feminine plural
beau (beautiful)	*bel*	*beaux*	*belle*	*belles*
fou (mad)	*fol*	*fous*	*folle*	*folles*
mou (soft)	*mol*	*mous*	*molle*	*molles*
nouveau (new)	*nouvel*	*nouveaux*	*nouvelle*	*nouvelles*
vieux (old)	*vieil*	*vieux*	*vieille*	*vieilles*

(continued)

(continued)

un vieil édifice	an old building
un édifice vieux	an old building (i.e. decrepit)
de vieux édifices	old buildings
un homme nouveau	a new man (changed character)
un nouvel homme	a new man (another man)
de nouveaux hommes	new men
un fol amour (or un amour fou)	crazy love

5.4 The plural of adjectives

5.4.1 Agreement

▶ An adjective takes the masculine plural form when:

  ▶ all the nouns it qualifies are masculine

  ▶ at least one of the nouns it qualifies is masculine

*La porte, la fenêtre et le portail sont **ouverts**.*	The door, the window and the gate are open.

Note

When this happens, it is preferable to place the masculine noun nearest to the adjective:

une viande et des légumes bien cuits (lit. a well-cooked piece of meat and well-cooked vegetables) rather than *des légumes et une viande bien cuits*.

▶ An adjective takes the feminine pural if all the nouns it qualifies are feminine:

La fenêtre et la porte sont ouvertes.	The window and the door are open.
Ma mère et ma sœur sont petites.	My mother and sister are small.

5.4.2 Formation of the plural

▶ In general adjectives, like nouns, form the plural by adding *-s* to the singular. This is the case with *all* feminine adjectives.

Singular	Plural	
un talon haut	*des talons hauts*	high heel(s)
une portière bleue	*des portières bleues*	blue door(s)

Note

The final *-s* is not pronounced, except where there is liaison [z]:

des murs jaunes [z] *et des rideaux bleus*	yellow walls and blue curtains

▶ Masculine adjectives ending in *-s* or *-x*.

   ▶ These adjectives are invariable in the plural:

un enfant heureux	*des enfants heureux*	a happy child / happy children
un enfant reclus	*des enfants reclus*	a reclusive child / reclusive children
un papier gris	*des papiers gris*	a grey piece of paper / grey pieces of paper

▶ Masculine adjectives ending in *-eau*.

   ▶ These adjectives add *-x* in the plural:

beau	*beaux*	beautiful
jumeau	*jumeaux*	twin
nouveau	*nouveaux*	new
Tourangeau	*Tourangeaux*	inhabitant of Tours

des frères jumeaux	identical twin brothers
de nouveaux textes de loi	new bills

Notes

▶ *esquimau* (Eskimo) and *hébreu* (Hebrew) also add *-x* in the plural:

des livres hébreux	Hebrew books
des chiens esquimaux	huskies

▶ *bleu* and *feu* add *-s* in the plural:

mes feus grands-parents	my late grandparents
des yeux bleus	blue eyes

But

When *feu* is placed **before** a determiner it is invariable:

feu mes oncles	my late uncles

▶ Masculine singular adjectives ending in *-al* become *-aux* in the plural:

un discours inaugural	an inaugural speech
des discours inauguraux	inaugural speeches
un palais royal	a royal palace
des palais royaux	royal palaces

Exceptions

▶ The masculine plural of *bancal* (rickety), *fatal* (fatal), *natal* (native), *naval* (naval) and *fractal* (fractal) add *-s* in the plural:

des chantiers navals	naval dockyards
des tabourets bancals	rickety stools

▶ The masculine plural of a number of adjectives, such as *final* (final), *glacial* (glacial), *idéal* (ideal), *pascal* (Easter), *tribal* (tribal), *jovial* (jolly) and *tonal* (tonal), ends either in *-als* or *-aux*:

des coups de vent glacials or glaciaux	glacial gales
des points finals or finaux	full stops

▶ The masculine plural of *banal* is *banals* in the modern meaning of 'commonplace', but *banaux* in the old meaning of 'communal', in a feudal society.

des textes banals	commonplace texts
les moulins banaux	communal mills

5.5 Compound adjectives

▶ Adjectives, like nouns, can have compound forms:

sourd-muet	deaf and dumb
aigre-doux	bitter-sweet

(See also 2.2.16.)

▶ If the compound adjective includes two adjectives, they both agree in gender and number:

des prunes aigres-douces	bitter-sweet plums
Hier, j'ai vu des étudiants ivres-morts.	I saw some students who were dead-drunk yesterday.
C'est une école pour filles sourdes-muettes.	It's a school for deaf and dumb girls.

▶ If the compound adjective includes an adjective and an invariable element, only the adjective agrees:

des théories anglo-saxonnes	Anglo-Saxon theories
Les relations franco-américaines s'améliorent.	Franco-American relations are improving.
Molière a écrit des pièces tragi-comiques.	Molière wrote tragicomedies.

5.6 Agreement of adjectives with *on*

Adjectives related to *on* are usually masculine singular. However, increasingly *on*:

▶ replaces *nous* in both colloquial French and standard French

▶ represents a woman or several people.

In these two cases, the adjective agrees with the person it represents. It can therefore be in the masculine or feminine or the singular or plural according to the gender and number of the person(s).

On est toutes arrivées en même temps.	We all arrived at the same time.
Alors, ma chère, on est pressée?	Well now, dear, are you in a hurry?
On était serrés comme des sardines.	We were packed tight like sardines.

5.7 Agreement of adjectives according to meaning

5.7.1 *Two nouns linked by* et *or* ou

▶ If the adjective qualifies two or more nouns it is plural:

une télévision et un ordinateur neufs	a new television and computer
une chemise ou un pull vieux	an old shirt or (an old) sweater

If the adjective qualifies one of the nouns it agrees with the noun that is nearest:

| Un ordinateur ou une télévision neuve | a computer or a new television (only the televison is new) |

▶ At times agreement is obvious:

| le père et la fille cadette | the father and the youngest daughter |
| Au petit déjeuner il prend des céréales ou un œuf brouillé. | He has cereal or scrambled egg for breakfast. |

Note

If the two nouns are synonymous or juxtaposed, the adjective is in the singular:

| un courage, une bravoure exemplaire | an exemplary courage, bravery |

5.7.2 Two nouns linked by de

The adjective agrees with the noun it qualifies:

| Ces cables de TGV sont torsadés. | Those TGV cables are twisted. |
| ces lignes de TGV bleu | those lines for the blue TGV |

5.8 Adjectives of colour

In general, straightforward adjectives of colour agree with the noun in gender and number:

| une cravate grise | a grey tie |
| des yeux verts | green eyes |

5.8.1 Adjectives of colour which derive from nouns

These are usually invariable (the word *couleur* is understood):

des portes marron (des portes de la couleur du marron)	brown doors
des couvertures orange	orange blankets
des chemises crème	a cream shirt
des taches olive et citron	olive and lemon stains
des yeux noisette	light-brown eyes

Exceptions

rose (pink), *mauve* (mauve), *pourpre* (purple), *écarlate* (scarlet) act like normal adjectives:

des rubans roses et des rideaux mauves	pink ribbons and mauve curtains

5.8.2 châtain

châtain often adds *-s* in the masculine plural:

des cheveux châtains	nut-brown hair

In the feminine it is sometimes variable:

des moustaches châtaines or *des moustaches châtain*	brown whiskers

5.8.3 Compound adjectives of colour

Compound adjectives of colour are invariable if they consist of two different adjectives or a colour adjective followed by a complement:

des yeux vert clair	light green eyes
des vestes bleu marine	navy blue jackets
des chemises jaune citron	lemon yellow shirts
des statues vert de gris	verdigris statues

Where two or more adjectives of different colours are used, they are linked by a conjunction or juxtaposed and are usually invariable:

des papillons rouge et blanc	red and white butterflies
des drapeaux bleu, blanc, rouge	blue, white, red flags

5.9 Foreign borrowings

5.9.1 'Compound' adjectives containing prefixes

In 'compound' adjectives which combine a prefix and an adjective, such as *hémi-*, *semi-*, *tragi-*, *pseudo-*, *franco-*, *anglo-*, *néo-*, the prefix is invariable.

des origines anglo-saxonnes	Anglo-Saxon origins
les plages néo-calédoniennes	New Caledonian beaches

(continued)

(continued)

des pièces tragi-comiques	tragicomic plays
les relations franco-allemandes	Franco-German relations

5.9.2 Other borrowings

Borrowings that have not been gallicized are usually invariable:

des cheveux auburn	auburn hair
des allures sexy	sexy looks
des livres sterling	pounds sterling
des gens cool	cool people

5.9.3 Minimum, maximum *and* optimum

Le Bon usage (M. Grevisse and A. Goosse, 14th edition, 2010 [p. 708]) advises that these words may vary in number, by adding *-s* for the plural, but not in gender: *des prix minimums* (minimum prices) but *une température maximum* (a maximum temperature).

5.10 Special cases

5.10.1 Invariable words used as adjectives

When words that are not adjectives, such as *Empire*, *bien* and *famille*, have an adjectival function, they are invariable.

des bureaux Empire	Empire-style [Napoleon III] desks
des gens bien	good people
des jeunes pas trop famille	young people who don't believe in family values

5.10.2 Adjectives employed as nouns

Adjectives are commonly used as nouns by placing an article in front of them:

les riches et les pauvres	the rich and the poor
des clairs-obscurs	chiaroscuros

5.10.3 Adjectives employed as adverbs

When adjectives are used as adverbs they do not agree with a noun:

Ils parlent fort.	They are speaking loudly.
Elle sent bon.	She smells good
Vous voyez clair.	You see clearly.

(See Chapter 7.)

5.10.4 Shortened adjectives

Shortened adjectives and abbreviations used adjectivally are invariable:

des gens sympa	friendly / nice people
des gens BCBG (bon chic, bon genre)	(ironic) respectable, upper middle-class people
des gens parano	paranoid people

5.11 Adjectival expressions

▶ The expression *seul à seul* has been invariable in the past:

| Je me suis retrouvé seul à seul avec Brigitte. | I found myself alone with Brigitte. |

but nowadays grammars tend to make this expression agree:

Je me suis retrouvé seul à seule avec Brigitte.

Je me suis retrouvée seule à seul avec Pierre.

Avoir l'air + adjective

Avoir l'air, a verb expressing a state, like *paraître*, is followed by an adjective which agrees with the subject:

| Ils ont l'air méchants. | They look nasty. |
| Elle a l'air intelligente. | She seems intelligent. |

▶ When, however, *avoir l'air* has its full sense of 'appearance', i.e., *avoir une physionomie*, the adjective agrees with *air*:

| Ils ont l'air méchant. | They have a nasty appearance. |
| Elle a l'air intelligent. | She has an intelligent look. |

▶ *Demi, semi, mi, nu*

   ▶ *Demi* (half), *semi* (half), *mi* (mid) and *nu* (naked) are invariable when they precede the noun, and they are linked to it by a hyphen (see 2.3.17):

des semi-remorques	articulated lorries
une demi-heure	a half-hour
la mi-saison	mid-season
nu-tête	bare-headed
nu-pieds	barefoot

▶ *Nu* agrees in gender and number when it is placed after the noun:

la tête nue	bare head
les pieds nus	bare feet

▶ *Demi* can be placed after the noun. It is then linked by *et* and agrees only in gender.

une heure et demie	an hour and a half
deux doses et demie	two and a half doses

▶ **Bon marché** and **meilleur marché**

  ▶ *Bon marché* (cheap) and *meilleur marché* (cheaper) are invariable:

Les maisons sont bon / meilleur marché en Belgique.	Houses are cheap / cheaper in Belgium.

▶ *Possible*

  ▶ *Possible* is invariable after a superlative:

Il souhaite travailler le plus d'heures possible.	He hopes to work for the most possible hours.
le moins d'erreurs possible	the least possible mistakes

5.12 Comparison of adjectives (see also 7.4)

When making comparisons using adjectives, various adverbs are used to indicate different degrees of intensity:

aussi . . . que	as . . . as
plus . . . que	more . . . than
le plus . . .	the most . . .
moins . . . que	less . . . than
le moins . . .	the least

▶ The comparative

Comparisons establish a connection between two elements in three different ways:

▶ comparison of equality

When the two elements are of equal value, *aussi . . . que* (as . . . as) is used:

| Le loup est **aussi** menacé **que** le rhinocéros. | The wolf is as endangered as the rhinoceros. |

▶ comparison of superiority

When one component is greater than the other, *plus . . . que* (more . . . than) is used. (For this type of comparison in English either *-er* is added to the adjective or 'more' precedes it.)

| Les pays d'Afrique sont **plus** chauds **que** ceux d'Europe. | African countries are hotter than European ones. |
| Le loup est **plus** menacé **que** l'éléphant. | The wolf is more endangered than the elephant. |

▶ comparison of inferiority

When one element is less than another *moins . . . que* (less . . . than) is used.

| L'éléphant est moins menacé que le loup. | The elephant is less endangered than the wolf. |

▶ The superlative

The superlative expresses a quality in its greatest possible degree. The superlative can be:

▶ absolute superlative

The equality is of the highest degree, without comparison. The adverbs used are *très* (very), *extrêmement* (extremely):

| Cet ordinateur est très performant. | This computer is very high performance. |

The absolute superlative can also be formed by adding the suffix *-issime* to the adjective: *rarissime* (extremely rare), *grandissime* (tremendous), *richissime* (fabulously rich).

▶ relative superlative

The quality of the adjective is of a very high degree or a very low degree when compared with all others. The adverbs used are *le plus . . .* (either adjective + -est or 'the most' + adjective in English) and *le moins . . .* (the least).

| Elle est la plus douée de sa promotion. | She is the most talented person in her year-group. |

Notes

▶ Adjectives like *meilleur* and *pire* are already comparatives and cannot therefore be preceded by *plus* or *moins* (*plus meilleur and *plus pire are not possible).

▶ Certain adjectives, such as *préféré* (favourite), *total* (total) and *entier* (whole), cannot be superlatives because the idea of highest quality is already present in them.

▶ Adjectives like *double, triple, parallèle* and *rectangulaire*, as well as *aîné* (older/-est), *cadet* (younger/-est), *principal* (principal) and *unique* (unique) are incompatible with the idea of degree. *Plus cadet, *plus principal* and *plus double* are therefore impossible.

▶ **Specific cases**

The adjectives *bon, mauvais* and *petit* have the irregular comparative forms *meilleur, pire* and *moindre* respectively. Note however that the alternatives *plus mauvais / le plus mauvais* and *plus petit / le plus petit* exist for *pire* and *moindre*.

Comparative	*bon*	*meilleur, -e, -s, -es . . .* (que)	*Cette fois les résultats étaient meilleurs.* This time the results were better.
	mauvais	*pire, -s / plus mauvais, -e, -es . . . (que)*	*Il a fait pire que la dernière fois.* He did worse than the last time.
	petit	*plus petit, -e, -s, -es / moindre, -s . . . (que)*	*dans une moindre mesure* to a lesser extent
Superlative	*bon*	*le meilleur, la meilleure, les meilleur(e)s*	*C'est à Lyon qu'on trouve les meilleurs restaurants.* It's in Lyons that you find the best restaurants.
	mauvais	*le, la, les pire(s) / le, la, les plus mauvais(e)s*	*Ce voyage fut la pire / la plus mauvaise chose qui me soit arrivée.* That journey was the worst thing to happen to me.
	petit	*le, la, les moindre(s) / le, la, les plus petit(e)s*	*C'est la moindre des choses.* It's the least we can say. *Michel est le plus petit des trois.* Michel is the smallest of the three.

5.13 Verbal adjectives

Verbal adjectives are derived from the present participle of verbs. The present participle is formed by adding *-ant* to the stem of the first person plural of the present indicative. The verbal adjective and the present participle are similar, but there is often a difference of spelling between them. A useful way of distinguishing the verbal adjective is by replacing it with an adjective (see 11.4.3).

Formation

Verb	1st person plural	Present participle	Verbal adjective
finir	*nous finiss-ons*	*finiss-ant*	*finiss-ant(e)s*
exceller	*nous excell-ons*	*excell-ant*	*excell-ent(e)s*
fatiguer	*nous fatigu-ons*	*fatigu-ant*	*fatig-ant(e)s*
convaincre	*nous convainqu-ons*	*convainqu-ant*	*convainc-ant(e)s*
briller	*nous brill-ons*	*brill-ant*	*brill-ant(e)s*

À Polytechnique on trouve des étudiants excellant en mathématiques.	At Polytechnique you find students excelling in mathematics.
À Polytechnique on trouve d'excellents étudiants.	At Polytechnique you find excellent students.

▶ Verbal adjectives ending in *-ent*

A number of verbal adjectives end in **-ent** instead of **-ant**: *excellent* (excellent), *différent* (different), *négligent* (negligent), *influent* (influential), *équivalent* (equivalent):

des idées convergentes	convergent ideas
des parents négligents	careless parents

▶ Verbal adjectives of verbs ending in *-guer*

The verbal adjective ends in **-gant**, whereas the present participle ends in **-guant**, e.g. *intriguer*:

un personnage intrigant	a scheming character

▶ Verbal adjectives of verbs ending in *-quer*

Some verbal adjectives end in **-cant**, others end in **-quant**, like the present participle: *paniquer*, *paniquant(e)(s)* (to panic / panicking), *communiquer*, *communicant(e)(s)* (to communicate / communicating):

une scène paniquante	a scary scene
Son attitude est provocante.	His attitude is provocative.

Notes

▶ The verbal adjective agrees with the noun in gender and number:

une cuisine excellente	an excellent cuisine
des femmes exigeantes	demanding women

▶ It can be modified by an adverb of degree:

| *Ce travail est plus fatigant que l'autre.* | This job is more tiring than the other one. |

▶ The verbal adjective can always be replaced by another adjective, unlike the present participle. In *L'année **suivante**, ils iront en Afrique* (The following year they will go to Africa), *suivante* can be replaced by *prochaine*: *L'année **prochaine**, ils iront en Afrique.*

But

In *Ils vécurent à Paris les trois années **suivant** leur mariage* (They lived in Paris for the three years following their marriage), *suivant* is a present participle; **les trois années prochaines leur mariage* is not possible.

ADJECTIVES IN CONTEXT

La Rempailleuse

On prit pour arbitre le docteur, **vieux** médecin **parisien** retiré aux champs, et on le pria de donner son avis.

Justement, il n'en avait pas: [. . .]

« C'est une affaire de tempérament; quant à moi, j'ai eu connaissance d'une passion qui dura cinquante-cinq ans sans un jour de répit, et qui ne se termina que par la mort. »

La marquise battit des mains.

« Est-ce **beau** cela ! Et quel rêve d'être aimé ainsi ! Quel bonheur de vivre cinquante-cinq ans tout enveloppé de cette affection **acharnée** et **pénétrante** ! Comme il a dû être **heureux** et bénir la vie celui qu'on adora de la sorte ! »

Le médecin sourit:

« En effet, madame, vous ne vous trompez pas sur ce point, que l'être aimé fut un homme. Vous le connaissez, c'est M. Chouquet, le pharmacien du bourg. Quant à elle, la femme, vous l'avez connue aussi, c'est la **vieille** rempailleuse de chaises qui venait tous les ans au château. Mais je vais me faire mieux comprendre. »

L'enthousiasme des femmes était tombé; et leur visage dégoûté disait: « Pouah ! » comme si l'amour n'eût dû frapper que les êtres **fins et distingués**, seuls **dignes** de l'intérêt des gens comme il faut.

Guy de Maupassant, *La Rempailleuse*, short story, extract

Adjective	
vieux	short adjective in the masculine singular placed before the noun [5.3]
parisien	adjective in the masculine singular denoting regional origin, placed after the noun [5.1.1]
beau	predicative adjective in the masculine singular qualifying *cela* [Key points and 5.3]
acharnée	adjective in the feminine singular: past participle of the verb *acharner* [5.2.1]
pénétrante	verbal adjective in the feminine singular derived from the verb *pénétrer* [5.13]
heureux	predicative adjective in the masculine singular after the verb *être* [Key points]
vieille	short adjective in the feminine singular placed before the noun; the feminine form of *vieux* [5.3]
fins et distingués	two masculine plural nouns linked by the conjunction *et*, agreeing with the noun *êtres* [5.4.1]
dignes	masculine plural noun placed after the noun [5.1]

EXERCISES

1. **Write the correct form of the adjectives in brackets using the following endings: -te, -que, -lle, -eure, -se, -ille, -s, -e, -ues, -rice, -ve, (-), -ne:**

   1. *Ma voisine est (turc) _____ ou (iranien) _____, je ne suis pas sûr.*
   2. *C'est ma voisine (favori) _____. La (meilleur) _____ des voisines.*
   3. *Elle a une (beau) _____ maison, avec des fleurs (multicolore) _____.*
   4. *Elle-même a toujours une mine (radieux) _____.*
   5. *Elle est directrice d'école, c'est dire si elle est (patient) _____ avec les (petit) _____ enfants.*
   6. *Elle est (jeune) _____ et pourtant elle n'a pas eu toujours de la chance dans sa (court)_____ vie.*
   7. *Elle a perdu sa (vieux) _____ grand-mère récemment.*
   8. *Et cela fait cinq (long) _____ années qu'elle est veuve et qu'elle vit (seul) _____.*
   9. *Pendant une (bref) _____ période, elle a connu quelqu'un, mais cela n'a pas duré.*
   10. *Avec ses yeux (vert clair) _____ ses joues (rose) _____ et son (épais) _____ chevelure (auburn) _____, elle ne restera pas seule longtemps.*

2. Translate the following phrases into French:

Example: *grand / homme*

A great man	*un grand homme*
A tall man	*un homme grand*

1. *seule / femme*

   (only) one woman

   a lonely woman

2. *jeunes / mariés*

   a newly married (couple)

   a young married people

3. *belle / famille*

   a beautiful family

   in-laws

4. *sale / tête*

   a nasty face

   a dirty face

5. *propre / voiture*

   his / her clean car

   his / her own car

6. *cher / bijou*

   my beloved jewel

   my expensive jewel

7. *ancienne / usine*

   a former factory

   an old (in age) factory

8. *sacré / endroit*

   a (hell of a) place

   a holy place

9. *curieux / enfant*

   a nosy / inquisitive child

   a strange child

10. *pauvre / homme*

the poor man!

a poor (not wealthy) man

3. **Using the vocabulary in the boxes, paint a physical and moral portrait of a female friend of yours. The adjectives used should all be either feminine singular or plural, or masculine plural.**

Example

1. *Ma meilleure amie est jolie mais un peu égoïste.*

2. *Elle a souvent une attitude agressive, mais elle est franche ...*

Apparence		vieux, jeune, joli, beau, athlétique, mince (thin, slim), maigre (skinny), gros (fat), grand (tall), petit
La face (le visage) / la figure / la tête:		rond, carré, long, allongé, poupin / potelé (chubby), joufflu (chubby-cheeked)
Les yeux	Couleur	marron, vert, gris, noir, bleu, bleu clair
	Forme	rond, en amande (almond-shaped), écarquillé (wide-eyed)
Les cheveux	Couleur	brun, blond, châtain / clair / foncé, roux, auburn
	Forme	court, long, frisé, bouclé, raide
Les bras		musclé, tatoué, mince
Description morale		calme, agressif, insolent, arrogant, posé, gentil combatif, gagneur, perdant, loser, débrouillard (resourceful) curieux, passif, actif amusant, drôle, ennuyeux franc, menteur, honnête egoïste, généreux, indifférent naïf, intelligent sportif

6 NUMBERS

There are three types of numbers:

▶ those we use for counting (7, 25, 302, 1000, etc.), called **cardinal** numbers

▶ those we use for placing things in order (1st, 6th, 21st, etc.), called **ordinal** numbers

▶ those we use for stating approximate quantities ('a dozen or so', 'a couple', etc.).

There are many differences between French and English in the way that numbers are formed and used.

But

l'an **2000**	the year 2000
Henri IV (**quatre**)	Henry the Fourth

✦ Numbers do not agree in gender with the exception of:

    ○ the cardinal number *un*(e) either standing alone or forming part of another number.

Parmi *les concurrents il n'y avait qu'***une** *fille.*	Among the contestants there was only one girl.
*J'ai cent-**un** amis sur Facebook.*	I've a hundred and one Facebook friends.
*Vingt-et-**une** bouteilles*	twenty-one bottles

✦ the ordinal numbers, *premier(s)* / *première(s)* and *second(e)(s)*

les **premières** *fleurs du printemps*	the first blossom of spring
voyager en **seconde** *classe*	to travel second class

6.1 Cardinal numbers

0	*zéro*
1	*un*
2	*deux*
3	*trois*
4	*quatre*
5	*cinq*
6	*six*
7	*sept*
8	*huit*
9	*neuf*
10	*dix*
11	*onze*
12	*douze*
13	*treize*
14	*quatorze*
15	*quinze*

(continued)

(continued)

16	seize
17	dix-sept
18	dix-huit
19	dix-neuf
20	vingt
21	vingt-et-un
22	vingt-deux
23	vingt-trois
24	vingt-quatre
25	vingt-cinq
26	vingt-six
27	vingt-sept
28	vingt-huit
29	vingt-neuf
30	trente
31	trente-et-un
40	quarante
41	quarante-et-un
50	cinquante
51	cinquante-et-un
60	soixante
61	soixante-et-un
70	soixante-dix
71	soixante-et-onze
72	soixante-douze
73	soixante-treize
80	quatre-vingts
81	quatre-vingt-un
82	quatre-vingt-deux
83	quatre-vingt-trois
90	quatre-vingt-dix

91	quatre-vingt-onze
92	quatre-vingt-douze
93	quatre-vingt-treize
100	cent
101	cent-un
102	cent-deux
103	cent-trois
200	deux-cents
201	deux-cent-un
300	trois-cents
1 000	mille
1 001	mille-un
1 100	mille-cent*
1 101	mille-cent-un
1 200	mille-deux-cents*
2 000	deux-mille
1 000 000	un million
1 200 000	un million-deux-cent-mille
1 000 000 000	un milliard
1 000 000 000 000	un billion

*onze-cents (1 100), douze-cents (1 200) etc. are alternatives.

Note

The forms *septante* (70) and *nonante* (90) are used in Belgium, Switzerland, Luxembourg, Val d'Aoste, and in the extreme south of Nova Scotia, in Canada. Otherwise the cardinal numbers are identical.

septante-et-un = 71, etc.; *nonante-et-un* = 91, etc.

Est-ce le tram nonante-quatre ou septante-quatre qui passe par l'avenue Louise ?	Is it the ninety-four or the seventy-four tram that goes along Louise Avenue?

These forms also survive in the former Belgian colonies of the Democratic Republic of Congo, Rwanda and Burundi.

They still co-exist in France among old people in Lorraine, Franche-Comté and the whole of the south of France, but they are disappearing.

Huitante (80) is used in the Vaud canton in Switzerland. *Octante* (80) is used by old people in Lorraine.

6.1.1 Linkage of numbers

▶ Use of *et*

   ▶ *et* is inserted where one is added to tens: *vingt-et-un*, *trente-et-un*, except *quatre-vingt-un* and *quatre-vingt-onze*

   ▶ *et* is not inserted after hundreds or thousands, where 'and' would be in English:

cent-dix	a hundred and ten
mille-soixante-deux	a thousand and sixty-two

▶ Use of hyphens

Hyphens link all compound numbers:

17	*dix-sept*
45	*quarante-cinq*
98	*quatre-vingt-dix-huit*
21	*vingt-et-un*
31	*trente-et-un*
71	*soixante-et-onze*
101	*cent-un*
1 001	*mille-un*

Note

Under the new rules for spelling (1990) it is proposed that hyphens be inserted for all compound numbers. For example: 1 328 = *mille-trois-cent-vingt-huit* (see 17.4).

6.1.2 Plurals

▶ *quatre-vingts* loses the final *-s* when another number is added:

88	*quatre-vingt-huit*

   ▶ but not when another noun follows:

quatre-vingts kilos	eighty kilos

▶ *cent* adds an *-s* when it is multiplied and not followed by another number.

Hundreds from *deux-cents* to *neuf-cents* lose the final *-s* when another number is added:

200	*deux-cents*
1 800	*mille-huit-cents*
777	*sept-cent-soixante-dix-sept*

but not when a noun follows:

quatre-cents habitants	four hundred inhabitants

▶ *un million, un milliard, un billion* are nouns and must be made plural when necessary:

trois-millions	three million
deux-millions-trois-cent-mille-cinq	two million three hundred thousand and five

but they must be followed by *de / d'* when they precede words other than numbers:

un million d'habitants	a million inhabitants
un milliard de livres	a billion pounds

6.1.3 huit, onze

When *le* precedes *huit* or *onze*, it is not elided to *l'*:

le onze mars	the 11th of March
*le numéro de mon billet est **le** huit.*	The number of my ticket is eight.

6.1.4 Pronunciation

▶ *six, dix* /sis/, /dis/

    ▶ the final letter is pronounced [s] when the number stands alone or at the end of a sentence:

Il en veut six. /sis/	He wants six.
Il y en avait dix. /dis/	There were ten of them.

    ▶ the final letter is pronounced [z] when the number precedes a word beginning with a vowel or silent *h*:

dix euros /diz/	ten euros
à six heures /siz/	at six o'clock

▶ the final letter is not pronounced before a word beginning with a consonant:

six jours /si/	six days
dix roubles /di/	ten roubles

▶ *huit* /ɥit/

   ▶ The final -*t* is pronounced when *huit* stands alone or precedes a word beginning with a vowel or silent *h*:

huit hommes /ɥit/	eight men
J'en veux huit. /ɥit/	I want eight.

   ▶ But it is not pronounced before a noun beginning with a consonant:

huit dollars /ɥi/	eight dollars

▶ *vingt* /vɛ̃/

The final -*t* is pronounced only in the numbers 21–29 and when *vingt* precedes a word beginning with a vowel or silent h:

vingt enfants /vɛ̃t/	twenty children

▶ *cent* /sɑ̃/

The final -*t* is not pronounced when another number follows, e.g. 101 *cent-un*, 108 *cent-huit*, but it is pronounced when *cent* precedes a word beginning with a vowel or silent h:

cent arbres /sɑ̃t/	a hundred trees

6.1.5 Placing of cardinal numbers after the noun

Cardinal numbers follow the noun when referring to a page, a line of text / a poem, a bus, a terminal, and a year. A definite article precedes the noun in these cases (see also 6.2.4).

Commence à la page 244.	Start on page 244.
Lis la ligne 3.	Read line 3.
Prends le 5.	Catch the number 5.
le Terminal 3	Terminal 3
le quai 6	Platform 6
l'an 2014	(the year) 2014

6.2 Ordinal numbers

1st	premier, première
2nd	deuxième, second(e)
3rd	troisième
4th	quatrième
5th	cinquième
6th	sixième
7th	septième
8th	huitième
9th	neuvième
10th	dixième
11th	onzième
12th	douzième
13th	treizième
14th	quatorzième
15th	quinzième
16th	seizième
17th	dix-septième
18th	dix-huitième
19th	dix-neuvième
20th	vingtième
21st	vingt-et-unième
22nd	vingt-deuxième
30th	trentième
40th	quarantième
50th	cinquantième
60th	soixantième
70th	soixante-dixième
71st	soixante-et-onzième
80th	quatre-vingtième

(continued)

(continued)

90th	quatre-vingt-dixième
91st	quatre-vingt-onzième
100th	centième
1000th	millième

Note

dernier, -ière(s) = last

| le **dernier** jour des vacances | the last day of the holidays |

6.2.1 Formation

Ordinal numbers are formed by adding *-ième* to the cardinal number. Note that:

▶ cardinal numbers, e.g. *quatre*, drop the final ending *-e*:

| la quatrième année de ses études | the fourth year of his studies |

▶ *cinq, vingt-cinq*, etc. insert *u* before *-ième*:

| le cinquième anniversaire | the fifth anniversary |

▶ The final *-f* of *neuf, dix-neuf*, etc. becomes *v*:

| au neuvième étage | on the ninth floor |

▶ The shortened forms of the ordinal numbers are as follows:

$1^{er/re}$, 2e, 3e, etc.

6.2.2 premier

▶ In dates *premier* is the only ordinal number used for the first day of the month:

| le premier juillet | the first of July |

　▶ Otherwise, unlike in English, cardinal numbers are used:

| le vingt-deux juillet | the twenty-second of July |

▶ *premier* is also used for the first of monarchs and popes of the same name:

| François premier (normally written François Ier) | Francis the First |
| Elizabeth première (Elizabeth Ire) | Elizabeth the First |

Otherwise, unlike in English, cardinal numbers are used:

| Louis seize (XVI) | Louis the Sixteenth |
| Jean-Paul deux (II) | John-Paul the Second |

6.2.3 second(e) *and* deuxième

These two words have the same meaning but *deuxième* is used more frequently. *Second* is for a maximum of two; *deuxième* is used for more than two.

| la Seconde Guerre mondiale | the Second World War |
| C'est la deuxième des quatre maisons à gauche. | It's the second of the four houses on the left. |

6.2.4 *Use of cardinal numbers to replace ordinals*

When cardinal numbers replace ordinals, e.g. *la page 8*, numbers which end in -*s* in the plural lose the -*s*. These numbers are *quatre-vingts* and multiples of *cent* (*deux-cents*, *trois-cents*):

| page trois-cents, ligne quatre-vingt | page three hundred, line eighty |
| l'année mille-neuf-cent | nineteen hundred |

6.3 Word order when a cardinal and ordinal number are together

Unlike in English, when a cardinal and an ordinal number, or *dernier / premier*, come together, the cardinal number always comes first:

| les trois premiers jours d'avril | the first three days of April |
| Les deux derniers coureurs étaient italiens. | The last two runners were Italian. |

6.4 Approximate numbers

Approximate numbers are formed, in general, by adding the suffix -*aine* to the cardinal number, dropping the final -*e*, where relevant.

une huitaine	about eight
une dizaine	about ten (note the -*x* of *dix* becomes -**z**)
une douzaine	about a dozen (but see note below)

(continued)

(continued)

une quinzaine	about fifteen
une vingtaine	about twenty
une trentaine	about thirty
une quarantaine	about forty
une cinquantaine	about fifty
une soixantaine	about sixty
une centaine	about a hundred
un millier	about a thousand

Note

The following numbers usually denote a specific quantity or time period:

une douzaine	(exactly) a dozen
une huitaine	a week
une quinzaine	a fortnight

As nouns, these numbers are followed by *de* when expressing an approximate quantity of something:

une douzaine d'œufs	a dozen eggs
Elle aura lu une trentaine de livres.	She'll have read about 30 books.
des centaines de personnes	hundreds of people

6.5 Time

▶ The full answer to the question *Quelle heure est-il ?* (What time is it?) begins *Il est . . .*

| Il est une heure. | It's one o'clock. |
| Il est trois heures vingt-cinq. | It's twenty-five past three. |

▶ For 'half past' the hour *et demi(e)* is added:

| Il est six heures et demie. | It's half past six. |
| Il est midi et demi. | It's half past twelve/midday. |

▶ For 'quarter past' and 'quarter to' the hour *et quart* and *moins le quart* are added; for times in between: for 'past' just add the number; for 'to' *moins* plus the figure is used:

Il est huit heures et quart.	It's a quarter past eight.
Il est huit heures dix.	It's ten past eight.
Il est neuf heures moins le quart.	It's a quarter to nine.
Il est neuf heures moins vingt-cinq.	It's twenty-five to nine.

▶ Figures may be used as an alternative to the above:

8.15	huit heures quinze
8.20	huit heures vingt
8.30	huit heures trente
8.45	huit heures quarante-cinq
8.55	huit heures cinquante-cinq

▶ The twenty-four-hour clock is used for timetables, opening hours, etc.

| Le magasin est ouvert de 14h00 à 17h30. | The shop is open from 14:00 to 17:30. |
| Le train part à 23h22. | The train departs at 23:22. |

▶ 'a.m.' and 'p.m.' are expressed in French by *du matin*, *de l'après-midi* and *du soir*:

| Je suis parti à 11 heures du matin. | I left at 11 a.m. |
| Viens à 7 heures et demie du soir. | Come at 7.30 p.m. |

▶ When stating distance in terms of time, the word *minute(s)* is often omitted:

| Le château est à 1 heure 35 de marche. | The castle is 1 hour 35 minutes' walk. |

6.6 Dates

▶ Cardinal numbers are used for days of the month, with the exception of *premier* (the first):

le 1er [premier] août	(on) 1st [the first of] August
le 15 [quinze] septembre	(on) 15th [the fifteenth of] September
le 31 [trente-et-un] octobre	(on) 31st [the thirty-first of] October

▶ There are two ways of expressing the year:

| 1998 | **mille neuf** cent quatre-vingt-dix-huit | [lit. one thousand nine hundred ninety-eight] |
| or | **dix-neuf** cent quatre-vingt-dix-huit | nineteen hundred ninety eight |

▶ **but** only the first way is used from 2000 onwards.

| 2013 | *deux mille treize* | (two thousand thirteen) |

▶ Decades are expressed by *les années* plus the number:

| *j'ai beaucoup voyagé dans les anneés soixante-dix.* | I travelled a lot in the seventies. |

6.7 Measurements

The adjectives *épais* (thick), *haut* (high), *large* (wide), *long* (long), and *profond* (deep) are used for measurements. Two structures may be used to express measurement:

▶ *être* + (adjective) + *de* + length, etc.

| *Cette piste est longue de 400 mètres.* | That track is 400 metres long. |
| *Le bâtiment est haut de 20 mètres.* | The building is 20 metres high. |

or

▶ *avoir* + length etc. + *de* + (adjective)

| *La table a 90 cm de large.* | The table is 90 centimetres wide. |

   ▶ In colloquial French *faire* + length etc. + *de* + (adjective) is commonplace:

| *Cette route fait 10 km (de long).* | This road is 10 kilometres (long). |

6.8 Fractions and calculations

▶ Fractions and decimals

   ▶ la moitié

La moitié is the equivalent of 'half' as a noun:

| *j'ai passé la moitié de ma vie en Afrique.* | I've spent half my life in Africa. |

   ▶ *demi* is the equivalent of 'half' when linked to another noun by a hyphen. It is invariable (see 5.11).

un demi-verre de vin blanc	half a glass of white wine
une demi-douzaine	half a dozen
une demi-heure	half an hour

When, however, it follows the noun and is linked by *et*, it agrees in gender with the noun:

| une heure et demie | an hour and a half |
| trois kilos et demi | three and a half kilos |

▶ *un quart* (a quarter), *trois quarts* (three quarters)

| Un quart des habitants n'ont pas voté. | A quarter of the inhabitants did not vote. (Note the plural agreement with 'habitants' here) |
| Les trois quarts des bouteilles étaient vides. | Three-quarters of the bottles were empty. |

▶ *un tiers* (a third), *les deux tiers* (two-thirds)

| Un tiers de la population est mal nourri. | A third of the population is malnourished. |
| Les deux tiers des grévistes sont retournés à la maison. | Two-thirds of the strikers have gone home. |

▶ Ordinal numbers are used for the remaining fractions: *un sixième* (a sixth), *un huitième* (an eighth), *un dixième* (a tenth), etc.

▶ When a number is followed by a decimal, a comma is used to separate them (unlike in English, which uses a full stop):

| 65,5% | 65.5% |
| 21,35 € | €21.35 |

▶ *sur* with numbers

sur is the equivalent of 'out of' in such phrases as *deux sur trois* (two out of three) and *dix sur vingt* (ten out of twenty).

▶ Calculations

2 + 2 = 4	deux et / plus deux font / égalent quatre	two and two make / are four
4 − 2 = 2	quatre moins deux égalent deux	four minus two makes two
3 × 3 = 9	trois fois trois font / égalent neuf	three times three makes nine
30 ÷ 6 = 5	trente divisé par six égalent cinq	thirty divided by six equals five

6.9 Quantifiers

Quantifiers are words or phrases used before a noun to indicate the amount or quantity. In English 'many', 'enough', 'all' are quantifiers. Like numbers, they are determiners.

▶ Quantifiers are words and phrases of the following kind:

assez de	enough
beaucoup de	much, many
bien de	many
chacun de	each one of
chaque	each
moins de	less, fewer
peu de	few
pas de	no, not any of
plus de	more
quelques	a few, some
plusieurs	several
trop de	too many
tous	all

Nous n'avons pas assez de temps pour peindre les quatre murs de la pièce.	We haven't enough time to paint the four walls of the room.
Chaque fois qu'il vient, nous nous disputons.	Each time he comes we quarrel.
Tous les jours il commence par faire ses exercices.	Every day he begins by doing his exercises.

▶ When the subject of the sentence is *beaucoup de, bien des, moins de, peu de, plus de* or *trop de* followed by a plural noun, the verb is plural:

Moins de gens viennent ici qu'avant.	Fewer people come here than before.
Peu de gens savent la vérité.	Few people know the truth.

▶ When the quantifier stands on its own as the object of the verb, *en* must precede the verb (see 4.4):

Combien de gens y a-t-il ? Il y en a beaucoup.	How many people are there? There are lots.
Où sont toutes les chaises du jardin ? Il y en a moins qu'hier.	Where are all the garden chairs? There are fewer than yesterday.
Tu as des pansements ? Oui, j'en ai plusieurs.	Have you got any plasters? Yes, I have several.

Note

Quelques becomes *quelques-un(e)s* when standing alone:

Tours est à quelques kilometres d'ici.	Tours is a few kilometres from here.
– Tu connais les films de Godard ?	'Are you familiar with Godard's films?'
– Oui, j'en ai vu quelques-uns.	'Yes, I've seen a few.'

NUMBERS IN CONTEXT

La fin de Bel Ami

Après 5 ans de bons et loyaux services, le cheval le plus médaillé de ces vingt dernières (1) années se retire en pleine gloire. Trois blessures successives auront eu raison de son courage.

À son palmarès, des gains cumulés atteignant les 637 900 euros (2), trente et une (3) courses courues, neuf victoires et sept placés sur le podium, dont cinq victoires de groupe II. À l'âge de six ans et cinq mois, c'est un exploit. Mais après une honorable deuxième (4) place, malgré deux blessures légères, lors de l'avant-dernier critérium d'Enghien, Bel Ami n'aura pu terminer ce qui allait être son ultime challenge.

En tout, deux tendons et cinq muscles abîmés en trois courses. C'est plus qu'il n'en faut pour abattre un champion de cette trempe. Nos derniers (5) espoirs de voir ce grand coureur de nouveau en piste se sont définitivement évanouis lors de cette dernière (5) course, il y a 3 jours à peine. La vilaine blessure que s'est infligée Bel Ami fait suite à une série de deux autres, plus légères mais handicapantes tout de même. L'incident s'est produit alors que Bel Ami avait déjà couru les trois quarts (6) du parcours, en première (7) position. Sur cette course élégante, de 2,6 km de long (8), talonné par le huit (9), Black Beauty, un pur sang de première (7) classe, lui-même suivi en troisième (10) position par le onze (11), Bourguignon, Bel Ami a dû céder sa place de leader.

Le 3 octobre (12), Bel Ami finira ses jours dans un haras, à 1 heure 10 (13) à peine de Paris. Son propriétaire lui a déjà trouvé une douzaine (14) de juments, de quoi faire des dizaines (15) de poulains de son envergure et qui sait, peut-être des centaines (15) de petits enfants.

1 *vingt dernières*	order of numbers [6.3]
2 637 900	cardinal numbers [6.1]
3 *trente et une*	cardinal numbers [6.1]; hyphens [6.1.1]

(continued)

(continued)

4 *deuxième*	ordinal numbers [6.2]
5 *derniers/dernière*	ordinal numbers [6.2]
6 *les trois quarts*	fractions [6.8]
7 *première*	ordinal numbers [6.2; 6.2.2]
8 *2,6 km de long*	measurements [6.7]; decimals [6.8]
9 *le huit*	*le* is not elided before *huit* [6.1.3]
10 *troisième*	ordinal numbers [6.2]
11 *le onze*	*le* is not elided before *onze* [6.1.3]
12 *Le 3 octobre*	dates [6.6]
13 *1 heure 10*	distances in terms of time [6.5]
14 *douzaine*	approximate numbers [6.4]
15 *dizaines, centaines*	approximate numbers [6.4]

EXERCISES

1. **Write the following numbers in words:**
    1. *121 pages*
    2. *380*
    3. *l'an 1800*
    4. *page 400*
    5. *120 pages*
    6. *200 000*
    7. *200 000 000 €*
    8. *tous les 20 ans*
    9. *2 220 300*
    10. *80 000 000*

2. **Write the following numbers in words and make the words in brackets agree where necessary:**
    1. *8 (milliard)*
    2. *6 (mille)*
    3. *1,9 (million)*
    4. *2,1 (million)*
    5. *4 (mile/h)*
    6. *3 (mille nautique)*

7. $9 \div 3 = 3$
8. $8 - 1 = 7$
9. $4 \times 6 = 24$
10. $1 + 1 = 2$

3. **Write the following numbers in words and put the hyphens in the correct place(s):**

   1. *99*
   2. *171*
   3. *172*
   4. *1 286*
   5. *33*
   6. *778*
   7. *180*
   8. *97,62*
   9. *191*
   10. *281*

4. **Write the following numbers in words:**

   1. *page 31*
   2. *31e page*
   3. *page 300*
   4. *ligne 80*
   5. *1er jour*
   6. *21e semaine*
   7. *81e semaine*
   8. *71e semaine*
   9. *91e semaine*
   10. *l'an 800*

Adverbs are invariable words or phrases which modify the meaning of different parts of a sentence, including other adverbs. An adverb can also modify a phrase or a whole sentence.

In the sentence 'We walked slowly', the adverb 'slowly' tells you *how* we walked.

In 'She speaks French very well', the adverb 'very' indicates the *degree* of her proficiency in the language.

In 'Yesterday, we went to the races', the adverb 'yesterday' tells you *when* the action of the sentence happened.

KEY POINTS

✦ In French adverbs function in a similar way as in English. For example, they modify:

○ verbs

Ils aiment **passionnément** la montagne.	They love the mountains **passionately**. [*passionnément* modifies the verb *aiment*]

○ adjectives

| *Cette chemise est* **trop** *grande pour lui.* | That shirt is **too** big for him. [*trop* modifies the adjective *grande*] |

○ adverbs

| *Cette chemise est* **beaucoup** *trop grande pour lui.* | That shirt is **much** too big for him. [*beaucoup* modifies the adverb *trop*] |

○ prepositional phrases

| *Le pont est* **exactement** *derrière ce bâtiment.* | The bridge is **exactly** behind that building [*exactement* modifies the prepositional phrase *derrière ce bâtiment*] |

○ sentences

| **Théoriquement**, *il n'est jamais en retard.* | **In theory**, he is never late. [*théoriquement* applies to the whole sentence] |

✦ A large number of adverbs end in **-ment**, which corresponds roughly to English **-ly**, e.g. *absolument* (absolutely)

✦ Adverbs are classified in various types, for example:

   ○ manner: *heureusement* (happily)

   ○ degree: *beaucoup* (a lot)

   ○ time: *hier* (yesterday)

   ○ place: *dedans* (inside)

   ○ assertion: *bien sûr* (of course)

   ○ negation: *jamais* (never).

7.1 Adverbs and adverbials

Adverbs can be single words or expressions of more than one word:

▶ Examples of one-word adverbs are: *bien* (well), *hier* (yesterday), *loin* (far), *mieux* (better), *plus* (more), *bientôt* (soon), *maintenant* (now).

▶ Examples of adverbials are: *tout de suite* (at once), *en vain* (in vain), *ne . . . rien* (nothing). Adverbials may be linked by a hyphen: *avant-hier* (the day before yesterday).

▶ Adverbial expressions frequently consist of a preposition followed by a noun, adjective or verb: *pour ainsi dire* (so to speak), *à nouveau* (afresh), *au fur et à mesure* (as one goes along, gradually).

▶ Some adjectives can be used as adverbs, without changing their form:

Elles coûtent **cher**.	They cost **a lot** [lit. 'dear'].
Elle s'habille **court**.	She wears her skirts **short**.
Ils ont crié **fort**.	They shouted **loudly**.

Note

Droit (straight) can be used either as an adverb or an adjective: *Elles se tiennent* **droit** or *Elles se tiennent* **droites**. (They stand up straight.)

▶ Some adverbs are borrowed from foreign languages:

payer **cash**	to pay cash down (English)
a priori	a priori (Latin)
Allez-y **piano**.	Go easy. (Italian)

7.2 Formation of adverbs ending in *-ment*

Adverbs ending in *-ment* are very common, and the majority are derived from adjectives.

▶ Adverbs derived from the masculine form of adjectives ending in a consonant, which add *-ment* to the feminine form:

Masculine	Feminine → Adverb	
amoureux	*amoureuse → amoureusement*	loving → lovingly
doux	*douce → doucement*	gentle → gently
faux	*fausse → faussement*	false → falsely
fort	*forte → fortement*	strong → strongly
plein	*pleine → pleinement*	full → fully
sec	*sèche → sèchement*	dry → drily

Exceptions

bref	*brève → brièvement*	brief → briefly
gentil	*gentille → gentiment*	kind → kindly
traître	*traîtresse → traîtreusement*	treacherous → treacherously

Adverbs which carry an acute accent on the *-e* of the feminine ending:

commun	*commune → communément*	common → commonly
confus	*confuse → confusément*	confused → confusedly
obscur	*obscure → obscurément*	obscure → obscurely
précis	*précise → précisément*	precise → precisely
profond	*profonde → profondément*	deep → deeply

Note

It is not always possible to derive an adverb from an adjective. A considerable number of adjectives do not add the ending *-ment*, among them *têtu* (stubborn), *équivalent* (equivalent), *gros* (big, fat) and *mince* (thin). In these cases an adverbial phrase introduced by *de manière* or *de façon* is used, e.g. *de manière têtue*, *de manière équivalente*.

▶ Adverbs derived from the masculine form of adjectives which end in *-ai, -e, -é, -i, -u* add *-ment* to the adjective:

aisé → aisément	easy → easily
poli → poliment	polite → politely
vrai → vraiment	true → truly

Exceptions

▶ The following adverbs ending in *-e, -i*

aveugle → aveuglément	blind → blindly
commode → commodément	comfortable → comfortably
énorme → énormément	enormous → enormously
gai → gaiement (sometimes *gaîment*)	cheerful → cheerfully
impuni → impunément	unpunished → with impunity

▶ Adjectives ending in *-eau, -au*

nouveau → nouvellement	new → newly

Note

▶ *fou* and *mou* also belong to this category, being derived from the masculine form in Old French.

Masculine	Feminine	Adverb
fou [Old French *fol*]	*folle → follement*	mad → madly
mou [Old French *mol*]	*molle → mollement*	soft → softly

▶ A number of adverbs ending in **-ument** add a circumfex accent to the *-u: -ûment:*

assidu → assidûment	assiduous → assiduously
cru → crûment	crude → crudely
incongru → incongrûment	incongruous → incongruously
indu → indûment	inappropriate → inappropriately

(See 17.4 for new spelling rules on the circumflex accent.)

▶ Adverbs derived from the masculine form of adjectives ending in **-ent** or **-ant**:

　▶ *-ant* endings become *-amment*:

constant → constamment	constant → constantly
élégant → élégamment	elegant → elegantly

▶ *-ent* endings become *-emment*:

récent → récemment	recent → recently
évident → évidemment	evident → evidently

The adverb endings **-amment** and **-emment** are pronounced the same (the phonetic symbol for this sound is [-amã]).

Exceptions

lent (slow), *présent* (present) and *véhément* (vehement) follow the general rule for adjectives whose masculine form ends in a consonant: *lentement* (slowly); *présentement* (presently); *véhémentement* (vehemently).

Summary

	Formation	Examples		
		Adjective	**Feminine**	**Adverb**
Masculine adjective ending in a consonant	Feminine form of the adjective + **-ment**	*attentif* *long* *premier*	*attentive* *longue* *première*	*attentivement* *longuement* *premièrement*
		Masculine form of adjective		**Adverb**
Masculine adjective ending in a vowel	Masculine adjective + **-ment**	*modéré* *résolu* *vrai*		*modérément* *résolument* *vraiment*

	Formation	Examples		
		Adjective	**Feminine**	**Adverb**
Masculine adjective ending in **-ant**	Stem + **-amment**	courant → couramment		
		galant → galamment		
Masculine adjective ending in **-ent**	Stem + **-emment**	différent → différemment		
		prudent → prudemment		
		violent → violemment		

Notes

▶ Adverbs cannot be formed from adjectives of colour, except for *vert* (green) in the sense of 'vigorous':

Ils se sont faits vertement réprimandés.	They were sharply rebuked.

▶ A number of adverbs ending in *-ment* are not derived from adjectives:

bigre (= my goodness! exclamation) → *bigrement* (jolly, extremely)

bougre (= fellow, masculine noun) → *bougrement* (damned)

diable (= devil, masculine noun) → *diablement* (devilishly)

vache (= cow, feminine noun) → *vachement* (colloquial: really, very).

7.3 Different types of adverbs

Adverbs are categorized according to their meaning, but it has to be borne in mind that some adverbs can be considered to belong to several categories.

7.3.1 Adverbs of manner

▶ Adverbs which indicate the manner in which something is done, e.g.:

ainsi	thus
bien	well
clairement	clearly
comme	how
comment	how
debout	up(right)
ensemble	together

(continued)

(continued)

facilement	easily
gentiment	kindly
heureusement	happily
lentement	slowly
mal	badly
mieux	better
plutôt	rather
vite	quickly

▶ Most adverbs ending in **-ment** are in this category:

Il a répondu gentiment.	He answered kindly.
Il est clairement ivre.	He's clearly drunk.
Elle avance lentement.	She's moving forward slowly.

7.3.2 Adverbs of degree

▶ Adverbs of this kind indicate a degree of intensity, e.g.:

assez	enough
autant	as much
aussi	as
beaucoup	much
combien	how much
davantage	more
environ	about
fort	greatly
moins	less
peu	little
plus	more
si	so
tant	so much
tellement	so (much)

très	very
trop	too much
Elle est assez forte.	She's quite strong.
Elle est arrivée trop tôt.	She's arrived too early.
Ils s'aiment tant!	They love each other so much!

7.3.3 Adverbs of time

Adverbs of time refer to the time when something happened, how long it took or its frequency, e.g.:

aujourd'hui	today
déjà	already
après	after(wards)
depuis	since
demain	tomorrow
encore	still
enfin	at last
ensuite	then, next
hier	yesterday
longtemps	(for) a long time
maintenant	now
parfois	sometimes
quelquefois	sometimes
soudain	suddenly
souvent	often
tard	late
tôt	soon
toujours	always

Les œufs sont parfois bruns parfois blancs.	Eggs are sometimes brown, sometimes white.
Il arrive souvent tard.	He often arrives late.
Il était polisson mais il a bien changé depuis.	He was very naughty but he's changed a lot since.

7.3.4 Adverbs of place

Adverbs of place refer to where something is or happened:

ailleurs	elsewhere
après	after
autour	around
dedans	inside
dehors	outside
derrière	behind
dessus	on top
dessous	underneath
ici	here
là	there
loin	far
partout	everywhere
près	near

Il a cherché partout son portefeuille.	He's looked everywhere for his wallet.
Il était loin derrière quand on l'a vu la dernière fois.	He was far behind when we saw him last.

7.3.5 Adverbs of assertion

These adverbs indicate the degree of belief or agreement of the speaker in response to a statement. They usually modify a whole sentence:

bien sûr	of course
certainement	certainly
oui	yes
sans doute	probably, no doubt
si	yes (responding to a negative remark)
soit	very well
volontiers	willingly
vraiment	really

Vous ne venez pas avec nous ? Si, je viens.	Aren't you coming with us? Yes, I am.

| Il a sans doute pris le taxi pour aller à l'aéroport. | No doubt he's taken a taxi to the airport. |
| Il ne fait pas la cuisine, mais il fait volontiers la vaisselle. | He's doesn't cook but he happily [lit. willingly] does the washing up. |

7.3.6 Negative adverbs

Negative words, such as *ne . . . pas* and *ne . . . rien*, are classified as adverbs (see Chapter 8):

| Je ne sais pas comment faire avec cet étudiant. | I don't know what to do about that student. |
| On n'a rien sans rien. | You don't have anything without working for it. [lit. you have nothing without anything] |

7.4 Comparison of adverbs

Adverbs of degree (*plus*, *moins*, *aussi*, etc.) are used to make comparisons (see also 5.12).

7.4.1 Relative degree of comparison

▶ The comparative

    ▶ Comparative of superiority (*plus*, *plus . . . que*)

| plus | more |
| plus . . . que | more . . . than |

| L'herbe est **plus** verte ailleurs. | The grass is greener elsewhere. |
| Paul est **plus** grand que Jean. | Paul is taller than Jean. |

    ▶ Comparison of equality

aussi	as
aussi . . . que	as . . . as
pas aussi/pas si . . . que	not as . . . as
autant (with verbs)	as much

Elle n'est **pas si** méchante **qu'**elle en a l'air.	She's not as nasty as she looks.
Il ne boit pas **autant** depuis sa maladie.	He doesn't drink as much since his illness.
Mon ordinateur ne fonctionne pas **aussi** bien **que** le sien.	My computer doesn't work as well as his.

▶ Comparison of inferiority

moins	less
moins ... que	less ... than

| Elle est **moins** méchante **qu'**elle en a l'air. | She's less nasty than she looks |

▶ The superlative

> ▶ The **relative** superlative: the idea of 'the most' or -est after a short adjective ('the most intelligent', 'the greatest', etc.) is rendered by *le plus* + adverb or adjective:

C'est **le plus** beau spectacle de l'année.	It's the most beautiful spectacle of the year.
C'est lui qui court **le plus** vite.	He's the one who runs fastest.
Les longs courriers sont les avions qui volent **le plus** haut.	Long-haul planes are the ones that fly highest.

> ▶ The **absolute** superlative, or superlative of 'high degree': this type of superlative indicates a high degree of a quality without comparing it with anything else. Adverbs like *beaucoup* (with verbs) and *très* (with adjectives and past participles used adjectivally) are examples:

Elle semble **très** à l'aise mais en fait elle est **très** appréhensive.	She looks very much at ease but in fact she is very apprehensive.
Elle a **beaucoup** travaillé et elle ne se plaint pas **trop**.	She has worked a lot and she doesn't complain too much.

Summary

Degree of comparison	**Comparative**	Elle est plus / aussi / moins grande que moi.
		She is taller than / as tall as / less tall than me.
	Relative superlative	C'est elle qui est la plus / la moins heureuse de toutes.
		She is the happiest / least happy of all.
	Absolute superlative	Elle est très / extrêmement heureuse.
		She is very / extremely happy.

7.4.2 Comparative and superlative forms of bien, mal, pis, beaucoup *and* peu

Some adverbs, as well as adjectives, have irregular forms in the comparative and superlative (see 5.12):

▶ *bien*

	Comparative	Superlative
bien (well)	*mieux* (better)	*le mieux* (the best)

Elle conduit bien.	She drives well.
Elle conduit mieux que moi.	She drives better than me.
Elle conduit le mieux.	She drives the best (of all).

▶ *mal* and *pis*

The comparative and superlative of *mal* are regular:

mal (badly)
plus mal (worse)
le plus mal (the worst)

Il conduit mal.	He drives badly.
Il conduit plus mal que moi.	He drives worse than me.
Il conduit le plus mal.	He drives the worst (of all).

The irregular forms *pis* (worse) and *le pis* (the worst) also exist. These forms are used nowadays only in set expressions such as *tant pis* (too bad) and *de mal en pis* (from bad to worse).

▶ *beaucoup*

beaucoup (much, a lot)
plus (more)
le plus (the most)

Il sort beaucoup.	He goes out a lot.
Il sort plus que moi.	He goes out more than me.
Il sort le plus.	He goes out the most (of all).

▶ *peu*

peu (little, not much)
moins (less)
le moins (the least)

(continued)

(continued)

Elle sort peu.	She doesn't go out much.
Elle sort moins que moi.	She goes out less than me.
Elle sort le moins.	She goes out the least (of all).

7.5 Position of adverbs

7.5.1 Adverbs which modify verbs

▶ With simple tenses of the verb, the adverb is usually placed *after* the verb:

Il cherche **désespérément** un emploi.	He's looking desperately for a job.
Il travaille **lentement**.	He works slowly.

Note

Presque may be placed before or after a verb in the infinitive:

Presque arriver à l'heure n'est pas arriver à l'heure / Arriver **presque** à l'heure n'est pas arriver à l'heure.	Arriving almost on time is not the same as arriving on time.

▶ With compound tenses the adverb is usually placed between the auxiliary verb and the past participle:

Il l'avait **instamment** prié d'attendre son tour.	He had asked him insistently to wait his turn.

Note

Adverbs of time and place are often placed after the past participle:

Il a travaillé **hier** et **avant-hier**.	He worked yesterday and the day before.
Il est parti **loin** de chez lui.	He has gone far from home.

7.5.2 Adverbs which modify an adjective, a past participle or another adverb

The adverb is usually placed *before* an adjective, a past participle or another adverb:

Il est **plutôt** patient avec ses élèves.	He's quite patient with his pupils.
Elle est **beaucoup** trop fière pour présenter des excuses.	She's far too proud to make apologies.

7.5.3 Adverbs denoting frequency

With verbs in simple tenses, adverbs of frequency, e.g. *toujours* (always), *parfois* (sometimes), *jamais* (never), *de temps en temps* (now and again), *souvent* (often), are placed *after* the verb in French but *before* the verb in English:

Je pense souvent à elle.	I often think of her.
Il ne répond jamais quand je l'interroge.	He never answers when I question him.

In compound tenses the adverb may be placed *after* the auxiliary verb **or** *after* the past participle, whereas in English the adverb is placed *after* the auxiliary:

J'ai marché **souvent** dans la neige / J'ai **souvent** marché dans la neige.
I have often walked in the snow.

7.5.4 Change of meaning of adverbs according to position

Some adverbs change their meaning according to where they are placed in the sentence.

Compare:

Franchement, Jacques a parlé toute la journée.	**To be frank**, Jacques talked for the entire day. [*franchement* modifies the whole sentence]
with	
Jacques a parlé **franchement** toute la journée.	Jacques talked **with sincerity** for the entire day. [*franchement* modifies the verb only, with the resultant change of meaning of the adverb]
and	
Logiquement, on devrait pouvoir tout faire.	**In principle**, we should be able to do everything. [*logiquement* modifies the whole sentence]
with	
On devrait pouvoir tout faire **logiquement**.	We should be able to do everything **logically**. [*logiquement* modifies the verb only]

7.6 Inversion after certain adverbs

When placed at the beginning of a sentence, some adverbs, for example *peut-être* and *à peine*, require the verb and subject to be inverted (see 4.1.4):

Peut-être sont-ils allés au concert.	Perhaps they've gone to the concert.
À peine étions-nous arrivés qu'il se mit à pleuvoir.	Scarcely had we arrived than it began to rain.

ADVERBS IN CONTEXT

La vraie Tartiflette

– Bonjour Camilla, tu sembles **bien** préoccupée.

– **Ne** m'en parle **pas ! Récemment**, j'ai voulu faire une tartiflette à mes amis, elle était **carrément** sèche.

– Tu n'as peut-être pas mis assez de fromage. Laisse-moi t'expliquer la vraie recette:

Tout d'abord, épluche 500 grammes de pommes de terre et coupe-les **soigneusement** en dés; rince-les bien.

Fais chauffer délicatement deux cuillères à soupe d'huile dans une poêle et verses-y 200g d'ognons finement coupés. Une fois les oignons parfaitement cuits, ajoute les pommes de terre. Fais dorer légèrement toutes les faces des cubes de tes pommes de terre, rajoute 200g de lardons et attends **patiemment** la cuisson.

Simultanément, prends ton reblochon, assure-toi que les côtés soient assez mous, et gratte la croûte superficiellement. Coupe-le en deux.

Maintenant préchauffe le four; ne le mets pas **trop fort**, environ 200°C.

Munis-toi d'un plat à gratin dont tu auras **préalablement** frotté les bords avec de l'ail.

Verses-y une première couche de tes pommes de terre aux lardons; étale une moitié de ton reblochon **par-dessus. Ensuite**, étale le reste des pommes de terre que tu recouvriras avec la deuxième moitié de ton reblochon. . . Attention, la croûte endessous!

Mets au four pendant 20 minutes. Et n'oublie pas de m'inviter.

– D'accord, dès demain!

In this recipe adverbs are used to give more information, telling us how, where, when, etc. actions take place. Adverbs modify other parts of speech such as verbs, adjectives and other adverbs. The following table picks out some of the adverbs in the passage showing their type and their function within the sentence.

Adverb	Type	Function
bien	degree	modifies the adjective *préoccupée* [7.3.2]
ne . . . pas	negation	modifies the verb *parle* [7.3.6]
récemment	time	modifies the clause: *j'ai voulu faire une tartiflette à mes amis* [7.3.3]
carrément	manner	modifies the adjective *sèche* [7.3.1]

Adverb	Type	Function
soigneusement	manner	modifies the verb coupe [7.3.1]
patiemment	manner	modifies the verb attends [7.3.1]
simultanément	time	modifies the sentence: prends ton reblochon, assure-toi que les côtés soient assez mous, et gratte la croûte superficiellement [7.3.3]
maintenant	time	modifies the sentence préchauffe le four [7.3.3]
trop	degree	modifies the adverb fort [7.3.2]
fort	degree	modifies the verb mets; this is an example of an adjective used as adverb [7.3.2]
préalablement	time	modifies the verb [tu] auras frotté [7.3.3]
ensuite	time	modifies the sentence: étale le reste des pommes de terre que tu recouvriras avec la deuxième moitié de ton reblochon ... [7.3.3]
par-dessus	place	modifies the verb étale [7.3.4]

EXERCISES

I. **Turn the adjectives between brackets into adverbs:**

Hier, je me promenais (nonchalant) _____ le long de la plage. Les mouettes planaient (silencieux) _____. Ce morceau de rivage est (général) _____ désert. On y rencontre que (rare) _____ quelques photographes.

J'arpentais donc (tranquille) _____ le pied de la falaise et ne me doutais pas que ce jour-là j'allais tout (simple) _____ faire un bond en arrière de plusieurs millions d'années.

(Habituel) _____ ces choses n'arrivent que dans les livres ou au cinéma.

Je me tenais (parallèle) _____ à la falaise. Je voulais éviter (soigneux) _____ les petites pierres qui tombaient (inévitable) _____ le long de la paroi friable.

Soudain, une vague un peu plus forte m'obligea à me jeter (précipitant) _____ sur la muraille de terre et de cailloux. (Inopiné) _____ mon pied trébucha.

Je sentis une douleur à la main. Je venais de heurter (violent) _____ quelque chose de pointu.

Quelque chose qui ressemblait (étrange) _____ à de la pierre sans être (vrai) _____ de la pierre. En regardant plus (attentif) _____ et en écartant (délicat) _____ la terre, je crus voir comme un morceau d'os pétrifié.

(Rapide) _____, mon esprit se ressaisit. Je compris l'importance de ma découverte.

Je rentrai (hâtif) _____ chez-moi. Je venais tout (bon) _____ de découvrir un fossile rare.

Il ne me restait plus qu'à alerter les autorités et attendre de devenir ce qu' (indubitable) _____ je ne manquerais pas de devenir: un héros.

2. **Match the adverbs in the left-hand column with their opposites in the right-hand column:**

A	souvent	1	peut-être
B	tard	2	beaucoup
C	ailleurs	3	jamais
D	toujours	4	lentement
E	trop	5	rarement
F	sans nul doute	6	méchamment
G	ne … guère	7	tôt
H	environ	8	ici
I	gentiment	9	peu
J	vite	10	précisément

A			B			C			D			E	
F			G			H			I			J	

3. **Complete the questions using the adverbs between brackets:**

Example

Question: *Tu promènes le chien ? Non, je _____ (souvent).*

Answer: *Non, je ne le promène pas souvent.*

1. *Tu as aimé le film ? Oui, je _____ (beaucoup)*
2. *Vas-tu à la bibliothèque ? Non, je n'y _____ (souvent)*
3. *Comment chante Mikaela ? Elle _____ (très bien)*
4. *Sandra attend son ami ? Oui, elle _____ (toujours)*
5. *Vas-tu encore à l'université ? Oui, j'y _____ (quelquefois)*
6. *As-tu lu Camus ? Non, je _____ (vraiment)*
7. *Tu tiens à aller au restaurant ? Oui, je _____ (absolument)*
8. *Jean-Louis est parti ? Oui, il _____ (brusquement)*
9. *Tu manges combien de fruits chaque jour ? J' _____ (assez)*
10. *Est-il toujours fort ? Non, il _____ (aussi… qu'avant)*

Negative words are used to say no, to deny or refuse something. In English, these are words like 'not', 'never' and 'nobody'. In general, a negative sentence in English may be expressed in two ways, e.g. '**I never** eat fish' or, alternatively, 'I **don't ever** eat fish'.

In French negation is expressed generally by using **two** words. The first of these words is invariably *ne*:

ne . . . *aucun*	no, not any, none
ne . . . *guère*	hardly
ne. . . *jamais*	never, not ever
ne. . . *ni* . . . *ni*	neither . . . nor
ne . . . *nul*	no, not any
ne . . . *nullement*	in no way, not in any way
ne . . . *nulle part*	nowhere, not anywhere

(continued)

(continued)

ne ... pas	not
ne ... personne	nobody, not anybody, no one, not anyone
ne ... point*	not
ne ... plus	no more, not any more, no longer, not any longer
ne ... que	only
ne ... rien	nothing, not anything

* ne ... point is hardly used in contemporary French.

KEY POINTS

✦ In simple sentences the first negative element (**ne**) is always placed before the verb and the second one (*pas, jamais,* etc.) after it. **Ne** is elided to **n'** before a vowel:

Je **ne** comprends **pas** ce que tu me dis.	I don't understand what you are saying to me.
Il **n'a pas** beaucoup d'amis.	He hasn't got many friends.

✦ In compound sentences, the first negative element is always placed before the verb. The position of the second element is variable: some are placed before the past participle, others after it:

Il **n'a rien** dit	He said nothing.
Je **n'ai vu personne**.	I haven't seen anyone.

✦ Negative words may stand on their own:

Qu'est-ce que tu as dit ? **Rien.**	What did you say? Nothing.

8.1 Position of negative expressions

▶ With simple tenses *ne* is placed before the verb and any object pronouns; the second element immediately follows the verb:

Il **ne** sera **pas** là avant demain.	He won't be there before tomorrow.
Je **ne** vois **personne**.	I can't see anybody.
Je **ne** m'en souviens **jamais**.	I never remember.
Pourquoi tu **ne** t'y intéresses **pas** ?	Why aren't you interested?

▶ With compound tenses

▶ *guère*, *jamais*, *pas*, *plus* and *rien* are placed after the auxiliary verb:

Elle **ne** *m'a* **jamais** *répondu.*	She has never answered me.
Il **ne** *m'a* **rien** *caché.*	He hasn't hidden anything from me.

▶ in all other negative expressions the second part goes after the past participle:

Depuis deux ans je **n'ai** *connu* **aucun** *succès.*	For two years I've had no success.
Il **n'a** *rencontré* **personne.**	He hasn't met anyone.

▶ The position of the negative expression is the same in questions and imperatives:

N'as-tu **pas** *vu le feu d'artifice ?*	Didn't you see the fireworks?
Ne *vous faites* **pas** *de soucis.*	Don't worry.

▶ With infinitives in the negative

▶ *ne guère*, *ne jamais*, *ne pas*, *ne plus* and *ne rien* precede the infinitive:

Il vaut mieux **ne pas** *le faire.*	It's better not to do it.
J'essaie de **ne jamais** *manger de chocolat.*	I try never to eat chocolate.
J'ai fermé les yeux pour **ne plus** *voir.*	I shut my eyes so as not to see any more.

▶ in all other negative expressions, in general, **ne** precedes the infinitive and the second element follows it:

Il est allé là parce qu'il espère **ne** *voir* **personne.**	He's gone there because he hopes he won't see anybody.
Il souhaite **n'**étudier **ni** *à Paris* **ni** *a Londres.*	He doesn't want to study either in Paris or in London.

8.2 Order of negative expressions

When two or more negative expressions appear in a sentence, the order of the second element is variable. In the most common expressions the following is generally true:

▶ *jamais* normally precedes *rien*, *ni* and *personne*:

Il **ne** *dit* **jamais** *bonjour* **ni** *au revoir.*	He never says either hello or goodbye.
Elle **n'a** **jamais** **rien** *fait de bon.*	She's never done anything good.
Il **n'aimera** **jamais** **personne.**	He'll never like anyone.

▶ *plus* normally precedes *rien* and *personne*:

Il **n'a plus rien** *fait de bon depuis son retour.*	He hasn't done anything good since his return.
Après tant d'années, elle **ne** *reconnaissait* **plus personne.**	After so many years, she didn't recognize anyone any more.

▶ *rien* normally precedes *personne*:

Nous **n'avons rien** *donné à* **personne** *cette année.*	We've given nothing to anybody this year.
Il **n'a rien** *dit à* **personne** *de ses échecs.*	He's said nothing to anyone about his setbacks.

8.3 *de* with a direct object in negative sentences

Where an indefinite or partitive article is used in an affirmative sentence, *de / d'* is used when the sentence is negated (see 3.5):

Il a une carte mémoire.	He's got a memory stick.	*Il* **n'a pas de** *carte mémoire.*	He hasn't got a memory stick.
Elle a des amis.	She has (some) friends.	*Elle* **n'a pas d'amis.**	She hasn't any friends.
Je mange de la viande.	I eat meat.	*Je* **ne** *mange pas* **de** *viande.*	I don't eat meat.

Similarly, in sentences containing *ne . . . jamais*, *ne . . . plus* or *ne . . . guère*, a following direct object is always preceded by the article *de*:

Je **ne** *prend* **jamais de** *sucre.*	I don't ever take sugar.
Il **n'y a plus de** *café.*	There's no more coffee.
Il **n'y avait guère de** *voyageurs.*	There were scarcely any travellers.

Note

This rule does not apply to the verb *être*:

Ce **n'est pas un** *film agréable.*	It's not an enjoyable film.

8.4 *ne . . . aucun* (no, not any, none)

aucun(e) acts as an adjective or pronoun. It is only found in the singular, except for *d'aucuns*, the pronoun equivalent of 'some':

Il **n'**aura **aucun** mal à terminer le travail.	He'll have no difficulty finishing the job.
Aucun de mes collègues **ne** va refuser de t'aider.	None of my colleagues will refuse to help you.
Aucune de ses amies **ne** peut l'oublier.	None of her friends can forget her.

8.5 *ne . . . guère* (hardly)

ne . . . guère is a restrictive rather than a negative expression:

Je **ne** sors **guère** le weekend.	I hardly go out at weekends.
Il **n'**y a **guère** de pain.	There's hardly any bread.

8.6 *ne . . . jamais* (never, not ever)

▶ *ne . . . jamais* is an adverbial expression:

Il **ne** faut **jamais** parler la bouche pleine.	You must never speak with your mouth full.
Elle **ne** s'est **jamais** trompée.	She's never made mistakes.

▶ *jamais* can be placed at the beginning of a sentence, followed by *ne*:

Jamais je **n'**ai vu un tel spectacle !	I've never seen such a spectacle!

▶ *jamais* can stand on its own:

▶ as a single word

Vous allez revenir ? **Jamais**.	You'll come back? Never.

▶ as the equivalent of 'ever'

As-tu **jamais** pensé que tu pourrais avoir tort ?	Have you ever thought you could be wrong?
Après les vacances je me sens mieux que **jamais**.	After the holidays I feel better than ever.

8.7 *ne . . . ni . . . ni* (neither . . . nor)

ne. . . ni. . . ni is a conjunction which can link different elements of a sentence, such as the subject, object pronouns and adjectives:

Ni *l'un ni l'autre* **n'ont** *su quoi faire.*	Neither one nor the other knew what to do.
Je **n'ai** *besoin* **ni** *d'aide* **ni** *de conseil.*	I need neither help nor advice.
Elle **n'était ni** *triste* **ni** *contente.*	She was neither sad nor happy.

Note

The equivalent of *ni* in English is often 'or':

Il **ne** *faut pas donner de conseils* **ni** *à Claude* **ni** *à sa femme.*	You musn't give advice to Claude or his wife.

8.8 *ne . . . nul(le)* (no, not any); *ne . . . nulle part* (nowhere, not anywhere); *ne . . . nullement* (in no way, not in any way)

▶ *ne . . . nul(le)*

Nul has the same meaning as *aucun* and acts as an adjective or a pronoun. It is almost always found in the singular. *ne . . . nul* means the same as *ne . . . aucun*, but is more formal (see 5.1.3).

Je **n'ai nul** *besoin de pratiquer plus de sport.*	I've no need to play more sport.

▶ *ne . . . nulle part*

Je **ne** *l'ai vue* **nulle** *part.*	I haven't seen her anywhere.

▶ *ne . . . nullement*

Je **n'avais nullement** *envie de partir.*	In no way did I want to leave.

8.9 *ne . . . pas* (not)

▶ *pas* can be placed at the beginning of a sentence, followed by *ne*:

Pas *un jour* **ne** *se passe sans qu'il ne me rende visite.*	Not a day goes by without his visiting me.

▶ *pas* can be omitted after the following verbs: *cesser de, oser, savoir, pouvoir*:

Il **n'**a cessé de pleuvoir.	It hasn't stopped raining.
Je **n'**ose lui rappeler l'argent qu'il me doit.	I daren't remind him of the money he owes me.
Tu **ne** sais comment le faire.	You don't know how to do it.
Nous **ne** pouvons aller à Lyon à cause de la grève.	We can't go to Lyons because of the strike.

▶ *pas* is used without *ne* in certain phrases:

C'est pas grave (colloquial).	It's not serious.
Pas de problème !	No problem!
Pas encore.	Not yet.
Pas vrai !	It's not true!
Pas du tout !	Not at all!
Pas grand-chose (colloquial).	Not important / Not much.

8.10 *ne ... personne* (nobody, not anybody, no one, not anyone)

▶ *personne* may act as subject or object of a verb, or appear after a preposition:

Personne n'avait l'air de faire attention à lui.	Nobody seemed to pay attention to him.
En général, en fin de semaine elle **ne** voit personne.	In general, at the weekend she doesn't see anybody.
Je **n'**ai plus besoin de **personne**.	I don't need anyone any more.
Je **n'**ai parlé de lui à **personne**.	I haven't spoken to anyone about him.

▶ *personne*, meaning 'nobody', can stand on its own:

Il y a quelqu'un dehors ? Non, **personne**.	Is there somebody outside? No, nobody.

8.11 *ne ... plus* (no more, not any longer, no longer, not any more)

Depuis quelques mois je **ne** lui donne **plus** grand-chose à faire.	For a few months I haven't given him much to do any more.
Il **ne** sera **plus** comme avant.	He won't be like he was any more.

(continued)

(continued)

| Je n'ai **plus** besoin d'aller chez elle. | I don't need to go to her place any longer. |
| Ça n'existe **plus**. | That doesn't exist any longer. |

Note

non plus is the equivalent of 'neither', 'nor':

| Je ne veux plus y aller. Moi **non plus**. | I don't want to go any more. Neither do I / Nor me. |

8.12 *ne . . . que* (only)

ne . . . que is a restrictive rather than a negative expression:

| Il **ne** me reste **que** 20 euros. | I've only 20 euros left. |
| Il **n'**y a **qu'**une personne qui puisse nous aider. | There's only one person who can help us. |

8.13 *ne . . . rien* (nothing, not anything)

▶ *Rien*, like *personne*, may act as subject or object of a verb, or appear after a preposition:

Rien ne va le changer.	Nothing will change him.
Il **ne** connaissait **rien** au sujet dont on parlait.	He knew nothing about the subject we were discussing.
Elle **ne** croit à **rien**.	She doesn't believe in anything.
Il m'a fait attendre pour **rien**.	He made me wait for nothing.

▶ *rien de* plus an adjective is a frequent construction:

| Il **n'**y avait **rien** de bon dans ce film. | There was nothing good in that film. |
| Il **n'**avait **rien** d'autre à offrir. | He had nothing else to offer. |

▶ *rien* meaning 'nothing' can stand on its own:

| Alors, qu'est-ce que vous voulez ? **Rien**. | Well, what do you want? Nothing. |

▶ expressions with *rien*:

Ça n'a rien à voir avec . . .	That has nothing to do with . . .
Ça ne veut rien dire.	That means nothing.
Ce n'est rien.	It's nothing.

De rien.	You're welcome.
en moins de rien	in no time
mieux que rien	better than nothing
rien du tout	nothing at all
Rien à faire !	It's no use!

8.14 Omission of *ne* in speech

In the expression *ne . . . pas*, **ne** is frequently omitted in colloquial French:

C'est pas moi qui l'ai fait.	It's not me who did it.
Je sais pas.	I don't know.

8.15 Use of *non* and *si*

▶ *non* is frequently used in negative expressions:

Je crois que **non**.	I don't think so.
Mais **non** ! Vous avez tort !	No, you're wrong!
Non loin d'ici il y a les ruines d'une abbaye.	Not far from here there lie the ruins of an abbey.
La crise va changer la vie **non** seulement des pauvres mais aussi des riches.	The crisis will change the lives not only of the poor but also of the rich.

▶ *si* is used to answer 'yes' to a negative question:

Tu n'es pas prêt ? **Si**.	You aren't ready, are you? Yes (I am).

(See 16.1.4.)

8.16 *n'est-ce pas ?*

The English question tags 'isn't it?', 'aren't you?', 'didn't they?' etc. are rendered in French by *n'est-ce pas ?*

Tu viendras demain, **n'est-ce pas** ?	You'll come tomorrow, won't you?
Vous avez manqué le train, **n'est-ce pas** ?	You've missed the train, haven't you?

(See 16.1.2.)

8.17 Use of *ne* without a negative sense

Ne without a negative sense is used optionally in formal French, in the following circumstances:

▶ after verbs of fearing, e.g. *craindre*, *avoir peur que*:

| *J'ai peur qu'il (**ne**) revienne.* | I'm afraid he'll come back. |

▶ after the conjunctions *à moins que*, *avant que* and *sans que*:

| *On voyagera ensemble à moins qu'il (**n'**) ait pris un billet de première classe.* | We'll travel together unless he's bought a first-class ticket. |
| *Rentre le linge avant qu'il (**ne**) pleuve.* | Bring in the washing before it rains. |

▶ in comparative sentences:

| *La Scandinavie, c'était mieux que je **ne** le pensais.* | Scandanavia was better than I thought. |

8.18 Negative words with *sans*

When used with *sans* (without), negative words have positive equivalents in English (*rien* = **anything**, *plus* = **any** longer, etc.):

*sans **aucun** doute*	without any doubt
*sans **rien** demander*	without asking for anything
*sans **jamais** me rendre compte*	without my ever realizing

NEGATION IN CONTEXT

Celui que l'on n'attendait pas !

Ils étaient beaucoup plus nombreux qu'on **ne** (1) l'avait prévu dans ce pub londonien en ce dimanche de juillet. De nombreux jeunes qui **n'**étaient **pas** (2) venus pour boire mais pour assister en direct à l'arrivée du Tour de France, avaient les yeux rivés sur deux écrans de télévision. On **n'**avait **pas** (2) lésiné sur la technologie: un écran géant à l'intérieur et un autre à l'extérieur.

Personne (3) ici **n'**avait imaginé que cette année le Tour serait remporté par un Britannique, et **surtout pas** (4) ces jeunes enthousiastes qui, il y a peu **n'**avaient **jamais** (5) entendu parler **ni** du Tour **ni** (6) de son arrivée sur une des plus belles avenues du monde.

Aujourd'hui, oublie Wimbledon, oublie Roland Garros, **rien n'**est (7) plus beau que ce maillot jaune sur les Champs Elysées.

Pas question (4) de se laisser distraire d'**aucune** (8) manière.

Il est loin l'enfant qui rêvait en regardant les compétitions cyclistes **sans jamais** oser (9) imaginer qu'un jour il serait sur la plus haute marche du podium. Aujourd'hui le champion **n'**est agé **que** (10) de 22 ans, mais il **n'**est **nullement** (11) un inconnu dans le monde du cyclisme. Il a déjà gagné plusieurs médailles lors de courses sur pistes. Malgré ses succès, **notre jeune sportif n'**est **pas** (2) encore une vraie star. Cela **ne** (12) saurait tarder.

Pendant le Tour, il **ne** fut certes **pas** (2) le plus fort dans les étapes de haute montagne, mais il fut suffisamment fort en plaine pour **ne pas perdre** (13) le maillot jaune endossé dès les premiers jours. Alors bravo quand même au vainqueur, et tant pis s'il **n'a pas** (2) revêtu une seule fois le maillot à pois du meilleur grimpeur.

Pour ces téléspectateurs il **ne** fait **aucun** (8) doute qu'ils vivent là un moment historique: la naissance du nouveau roi de la petite reine!*

* *la petite reine* nickname for 'bicycle'

1	*Ils étaient beaucoup plus nombreux qu'on* **ne** *l'avait prévu*	**ne** without a negative meaning [8.17]
2	*De nombreux jeunes qui* **n'**étaient **pas** *venus; on* **n'**avait **pas** *lesiné; notre jeune sportif* **n'**est **pas** *encore une vraie star; il* **ne** *fut certes* **pas**; *s'il* **n'a pas** *revêtu*	**ne . . . pas** [8.9]; with an auxiliary [8.1]
3	**Personne** *ici* **n'**avait imaginé	**ne . . . personne** [8.10]
4	*surtout* **pas** *ces jeunes enthousiastes;* **Pas** *question de se laisser distraire*	**pas** standing alone [8.9]
5	*. . .* **n'**avaient **jamais** *entendu*	**ne . . . jamais** [8.6]
6	*. . .* **n'**avaient jamais entendu parler **ni** du Tour **ni** de son arrivée sur une des plus belles avenues du monde.	**ne . . . ni. . . ni** in the context of two negatives [8.2 and 8.7]
7	**rien n'**est plus beau que ce maillot jaune	**ne . . . rien** [8.13]
8	de se laisser distraire d'**aucune** manière. il **ne** fait **aucun** doute	**aucun** [8.4]
9	**sans jamais** oser imaginer	**sans** followed by an infinitive (jamais = English 'ever') [8.18]

(continued)

(continued)

10 *Aujourd'hui le champion **n'**est âgé **que** de 22 ans,*	***ne . . . que*** [8.12]
11 *mais il **n'**est **nullement** un inconnu dans le monde du cyclisme.*	***ne . . . nullement*** [8.8]
12 *Cela **ne** saurait tarder.*	***ne**: one element only; without **pas** after savoir* [8.9]
13 *pour **ne pas** perdre le maillot jaune*	***ne pas**: both parts of negative before infinitive* [8.1]

EXERCISES

1. Put the following sentences into the negative:

1. *Le jardinier taille les arbres.*
2. *Il a eu le temps d'arroser les fleurs auparavant.*
3. *Il commence toujours sa journée par les fleurs.*
4. *Dans sa cabane, il a tout.*
5. *Il a même une meule pour affûter les lames.*
6. *Doit-il affûter les lames ?*
7. *Les sécateurs, oui.*
8. *Demain il lui restera encore beaucoup à faire.*
9. *Il lui faudra préparer les engrais.*
10. *Répandre les produits aussi.*

2. Put the following sentences into the correct order:

1. *il a personne vu n'*
2. *trois de jours reste ne lui que révision il*
3. *depuis il n' mangé a rien matin ce*
4. *aujourd'hui est n' nulle il part allé*
5. *théâtre cinéma au ni il ni va ne au*
6. *temps, il a n' de dormir guère le*
7. *plaisanter envie il a n' nullement de*
8. *compris n' je à ai discours rien son*
9. *elle en jamais souvient s' ne*
10. *rencontrer nous personne espérons ne*

3. Translate into French:

1. They won't be there before the weekend.
2. For two days I haven't had a single cup of coffee.

3.   I never set foot in either Asia or Africa.
4.   They haven't got any bakers in this village.
5.   It isn't a shop.
6.   They haven't seen any anywhere.
7.   No plant can survive without water.
8.   They made me work for nothing.
9.   They're Irish, aren't they?
10. He left without buying anything.

4.   Put the text into the negative:

Je suis heureux. J'ai des diplômes et ma vie s'annonce bien. J'aurai même une maison, un jardin et une voiture.

Je fumerai toujours des gros cigares. J'aurai des amis sincères. Mes parents seront toujours là pour pour garder les enfants.

J'aurai assez d'argent pour envoyer mes enfants étudier à l'étranger. Ils fréquenteront les plus grandes écoles. Ils voyageront toujours.

Ils connaîtront toutes les grandes cultures du monde. Ils seront souvent épanouis et tout le monde les aimera. Ils auront beaucoup d'amis sur Facebook. Ce sera la fête tous les jours.

9 VERBS I

There is no area of grammar that is more important to understand than the verb. This chapter classifies its features under several headings and explains a number of grammatical concepts and constructions relating to the verb, with the aim of clarifying the way in which it functions in French. Further explanation and exemplification of these concepts are to be found in Chapter 10. For definitions of the terminology used refer to the Glossary on p. xiv.

9.1 The verb

> ### KEY POINTS
>
> ✦ The verb is a word that expresses either an action (*travailler*, *marcher*) or a state (*être*, *paraître*).
>
> ✦ The verb is the core of the sentence, around which the other elements of the sentence (the subject, object, etc.) are arranged.
>
> ✦ All clauses must contain a verb.
>
> ✦ The past participle form of the verb (*parlé*, *vendu*, etc.) can function as an adjective.
>
> ✦ The infinitive form (*parler*, *vendre*) can function as a noun.

Verbs are classified in three groups: (1) -*er* verbs (e.g. *parler* [to speak]), (2) most -*ir* verbs (e.g. *finir* [to finish]) and (3) a third group consisting of -*re* verbs (e.g. *vendre* [to sell]), -*oir* verbs (e.g. *pouvoir* [to be able]) and some -*ir* verbs (e.g. *venir* [to come]) (see 10.2.4).

9.2 Characteristics of the verb

Verbs can be classified and regrouped into linking verbs, transitive verbs, intransitive verbs, pronominal verbs and impersonal verbs, as in the table on the following page.

The different forms that a verb can take are called *conjugations* (see 10.2.1).

Characteristics of the verb

Person	6 persons: *je*, *tu*, *il / elle*, *nous*, *vous*, *ils / elles*	*Je parle anglais.* (1st person) I speak English. *Tu parles français.* (2nd person) You speak French. *Elle parle russe.* (3rd person) She speaks Russian.
Number	Singular: *je*, *tu*, *il / elle* Plural: *nous*, *vous*, *ils / elles*	*Je parle anglais.* (singular) I speak English. *Nous parlons français.* (plural) We speak French.
Mood*	7 moods: – 4 personal: **indicative, imperative, conditional** and **subjunctive** and – 3 impersonal: **infinitive, participles (present** and **past), gerund**	*Vous parlez anglais, je le sais !* (indicative) You speak English, I know it! *Parlez français, S.V.P. !* (imperative) Speak French, please! *Il faut que nous parlions russe.* (subjunctive) We have to speak Russian. *Avec de la pratique tu parlerais mieux.* (conditional) With practice you would speak better. *un candidat parlant trois langues* (present participle) a candidate speaking three languages *Il a peu parlé à la conférence.* (past participle) He did not speak much at the conference. *En parlant tu as dévoilé ton origine.* (gerund) By speaking you revealed your origin.
Tense	**Present, imperfect, compound past, future**, etc.	*Je parle anglais.* (present) I speak English. *Je parlerai français.* (future) I will / shall speak French. *Avant je parlais mieux.* (imperfect) I used to speak better before.
Type	4 types of verb: – **verb (standing on its own)** – **auxiliary and semi-auxiliary** – **transitive and intransitive** – **impersonal**	*J'ai une vieille voiture.* (verb) I have an old car. *J'ai acheté une vieille voiture.* (auxiliary) I've bought an old car. *Elle va parler.* (near future) (semi-auxiliary) She's going to speak. *Tu as gagné un million ? Tu parles !* (intransitive verb) You've won a million? You must be joking ! *Je gagne de l'argent.* (transitive) I earn money. *Il fait beau.* (impersonal) It's fine weather.

(continued)

(continued)

Voice**	3 voices **active, passive** and **pronominal**	*Il **parle** anglais.* (active) He speaks English. *L'anglais **est parlé** partout.* (passive) English is spoken everywhere. *Ils ne **se parlent** plus.* (pronominal) They don't speak to each other any more.
Aspect	Numerous ways of describing an action (e.g. beginning it, finishing it, showing its duration, repeating it, etc.)	*Elle **parle**.* (the simple present = the duration of the action is not indicated) She speaks. *Elle **est en train de parler**.* (the present continuous = the duration of the action is emphasized) She is speaking.

* Note that in English it is usual to speak of three important grammatical moods (i.e., expressions of the speaker's attitude by means of the verb): the indicative, the subjunctive and the imperative.

** Note that English differs from French in specifying that there are two voices only, active and passive.

9.2.1 Linking verbs

A linking verb, or copula, is one which connects the subject to the predicate. This type includes:

▶ *être*

*Steinbeck **était** américain.*	Steinbeck was American.
*Steinbeck **était** un écrivain américain.*	Steinbeck was an American writer.

▶ verbs or verbal expressions of **state**, indicating the idea of:

  ▶ appearance:

apparaître (comme)	to look like
avoir l'air	to look like
être tenu pour	to be considered to be
paraître	to appear, seem
passer pour	to be taken for
sembler	to seem
se trouver	to be

*Des banques américaines **furent tenues pour responsables** de la crise.*	American banks were considered to be responsible for the crisis.

▶ remaining:

demeurer	to remain
rester	to stay

Il **est resté** infirme après son accident.	He remained disabled after his accident.

▶ designation:

être fait	to be made
être élu	to be elected
être choisi pour	to be chosen for
être proclamé	to be proclaimed

Elizabeth II **a été proclamée** Reine en 1952.	Elizabeth II was proclaimed Queen in 1952.
François Hollande **a été élu** Président en mai 2012.	François Hollande was elected President in May 2012.

▶ naming:

être appelé	to be called
être dit	to be said to be
être traité de	to be called
s'appeler	to be called
se nommer	to be called / named

Il **a été traité de** paresseux par son professeur.	He was called lazy by his teacher.

▶ state:

devenir	to become
se faire	to become
tomber	to fall

Il **est tombé** malade.	He fell ill.

9.2.2 Auxiliary verbs: avoir and être

The verbs *avoir* (to have) and *être* (to be) have a meaning in their own right as verbs but their basic meaning is lost when they:

▶ act as auxiliaries to form **compound tenses** of verbs;

▶ are used in the formation of the **passive voice**;

▶ are used to form **pronominal verbs**.

Avoir

As an auxiliary verb, *avoir* is used to form the compound tenses of:

▶ all transitive verbs (followed by a direct or an indirect object) in the active voice, and not pronominal verbs:

Elle **a changé** de style, mais nous l'**avons reconnue** tout de suite.	She's changed her style, but we recognized her straight away.

▶ *avoir* and *être* themselves:

Ils **ont eu** beaucoup de chance à l'oral.	They've had a lot of luck in the oral exam.
Vous **avez été** souvent en retard cet hiver.	You've often been late this winter.
J'**ai été** heureuse de vous rencontrer.	I was happy to meet you.

▶ many intransitive verbs:

Il **a dormi** tout l'après-midi.	He's slept the whole afternoon.

▶ most impersonal verbs:

Il **a fait** chaud en mai mais **il a plu** en juin.	It was hot in May but it rained in June.

Être

As an auxiliary verb *être* is used:

▶ to form the **passive voice** of all tenses:

La ferme **est constituée de** trois bâtiments principaux.	The farm comprises [lit. is composed of] three main buildings.
Les bagages **avaient été mis** dans le coffre.	The luggage had been put in the boot.
Il **est découragé** par le mauvais temps.	He's put off by the bad weather.
Elle **était submergée** de travail.	She was snowed under with work.

▶ to conjugate the compound tenses of all **pronominal verbs**:

Elle **s'est levée** tôt, **s'est douchée** et **s'est précipitée** à l'arrêt d'autobus.	She got up early, had a shower and hurried off to the bus stop.

▶ to conjugate the compound tenses of a number of **intransitive verbs**, which for the most part express movement or a change of state (see 10.5.2):

Il **est entré**.	He came in.
Elle **est tombée** *en cours de route et elle* **est arrivée** *couverte de boue.*	She fell on the way and arrived covered in mud.

Note

When a sequence of verbs has the same compound tense and uses the same auxiliary, the auxiliary can be omitted on the second and subsequent occasions:

Ils **ont** *d'abord* **lu** *puis* **déclamé** *le texte.*	First they read and then declaimed the text.
Nous **avons pris** *place dans l'amphithéâtre,* **ouvert** *nos livres et* **commencé** *à écrire.*	We took our seats in the lecture theatre, opened our books and began to write.

But when the auxiliaries are different, they cannot be omitted:

Ils **sont sortis** *de l'autobus,* **ont crié** *et* **chanté** *à tue-tête et se* **sont enfuis**.	They got off the bus, shouted and sang at the top of their voices and ran off.

9.2.3 Active and passive voices

When the subject of the verb *carries out* the action, the verb is in the **active voice**:

Le lion poursuit la gazelle	The lion hunts the gazelle.
Daniel jouera le rôle.	Daniel will play the part.

When the subject of the verb *receives* the action, the verb is in the **passive voice**.

An active statement, in which the verb has a direct object, may be turned into a passive one, as follows:

Le rôle sera joué par Daniel.	The part will be played by Daniel.

Active sentence: Daniel will play the part.		
1	the auxiliary verb *être* is used in the same tense as the active verb (*jouera*)	*sera* will be
2	the active verb (*jouera*) becomes a past participle	(*sera*) **joué** (will be) played
3	the direct object of the active verb (**le rôle**) becomes the **subject** of the verb *être* in the passive voice	**Le rôle** (*sera joué*) The part (will be played)

(continued)

(continued)

4	the subject of the active voice sentence (*Daniel*) becomes the **agent** and is introduced by *par*, *de* or *à*	(*Le rôle sera joué*) **par Daniel.** (The part will be played) by Daniel.
Passive sentence: The part will be played by Daniel.		

Similarly, *La gazelle est poursuivie par le lion.* (The gazelle is hunted by the lion.)

In theory, all verbs which take a direct object can be used in the passive voice, but in practice French uses the passive far less than English. Two important alternatives to the passive voice exist in French:

▶ *on* plus an active verb as an alternative to the passive:

On dit que les Anglais achètent de plus en plus de maisons en France.	**It is said** that the English are buying more and more houses in France.
De nos jours, **on construit** moins de lignes TGV en France.	Nowadays fewer TGV lines **are being built** in France.

▶ a pronominal verb as an alternative to the passive (see 9.4):

Les abricots **se vendent** au marché à des prix modérés.	Apricots **are sold** at the market at reasonable prices.
La Tour Eiffel **se voit** de loin.	The Eiffel Tower **can be seen** from afar.

9.2.4 Semi-auxiliary verbs

Semi-auxiliary verbs in French, such as *aller* (to go), *devoir* (to have to), *pouvoir* (to be able), *commencer à* (to begin), *venir de* (to have just) are always followed by an infinitive, except for *aller* (to go) which can be followed by the form ending in -*ant*.

Like auxiliary verbs they lose their meaning when they express certain nuances of tense, mood and aspect:

Elle **vient d'arriver** mais elle **va partir** tout de suite.	She has just arrived (recent past), but she is going to leave (near future) at once.

▶ Semi-auxiliaries of tense:

▶ *devoir* can express the future:

Je **dois** partir pour Londres demain.	I am to go to London tomorrow.

▶ *aller*, *être sur le point de* express the near future:

| *L'avion **va** décoller.* | The plane is about to take off. |

▶ *venir de* expresses a recent past:

| *L'avion **vient de** décoller.* | The plane has just taken off. |

▶ Semi-auxiliaries of mood (see also 9.2.5):

▶ *devoir* expresses an action that is obligatory, probable or desirable:

*Un étudiant **doit** apprendre.*	A student has to learn.
*Il **a dû** finir son livre.*	He must have finished his book.
*Il pense qu'on **doit** procéder ainsi.*	He thinks we have to proceed in this way.

▶ *pouvoir* expresses possibility, probability, wishes:

*N'importe qui **peut** se tromper.*	Anyone can make a mistake.
*Il **peut** être dix heures.*	It may be ten o'clock.
***Puisse**-t-il réussir !*	If only he can succeed!

▶ Semi-auxiliaries of aspect:

Different verbs are used for different aspects, for example:

▶ *commencer à*, *se mettre à* for the beginning of an action

▶ *être en train de* (to be in the process of) for duration

▶ *finir de*, *cesser de* (to finish) for the conclusion of an action.

▶ Verbs categorized as semi-auxiliary:

▶ Semi-auxiliary verbs followed by an infinitive:

aller	to go
devoir	to have to, must
faillir	to almost do (impersonal)
faire	to do
falloir	need, must, have to (impersonal)

(continued)

(continued)

laisser	to leave, let
manquer	to miss, lack
pouvoir	to be able, can
paraître	to appear
savoir	to know
sembler	to seem
venir	to come
vouloir	to wish, want

Il **va** partir ce soir.	He's going to leave this evening.
Nous **devons** finir notre travail.	We have to finish our work.
La rivière **a manqué** déborder.	The river almost overflowed.

▶ Semi-auxiliary verbs followed by a preposition plus infinitive:

avoir à	to have to
cesser de	to stop, cease to
commencer à	to begin to
être en train de	to be (busy)
être sur le point de	to be about to
finir de	to stop
se mettre à	to begin
se voir en train de	to see oneself (doing)
sortir de	to come out of
venir de	to have just

Il avait **fini de** pleuvoir.	It had stopped raining.
Il **s'est mis à** geler et j'**ai failli** glisser plusieurs fois.	It began to freeze and I almost slipped several times.
Il **a fallu** rentrer.	It was necessary to go back.

9.2.5 Modal verbs

The term 'modal verb' in English describes a category of semi-auxiliary verbs, which communicate attitude and intention, affecting the meaning of the verb in the infinitive which follows. The English modal verbs, *can*, *may* and *must* express attitudes relating, for example, to ability, probability, permission and obligation. *May I speak French?* expresses permission; *may* is the modal verb and *speak* the infinitive; *must I speak French?* expresses obligation.

French does not have modal verbs. The principal equivalents of English modal verbs in French are *pouvoir* (to be able), *devoir* (to have to), *savoir* (to know), *falloir* (must) and *vouloir* (to wish, want).

Devoir

Devoir expresses three essential ideas:

▶ the future *to be to*

*Il **doit** arriver demain.*	He is to arrive tomorrow.

▶ likelihood

*Cela **doit** coûter très cher !*	That must cost a lot!
*Cette personne **devait** être très belle étant jeune.*	That person must have been beautiful when young.

▶ obligation

Je dois absolument partir dans quelques minutes.	I must leave without fail in a few minutes.

Different meanings according to tense

▶ In the **present** *devoir* expresses:

   ▶ obligation (must, have to, should or ought to)

Je dois absolument m'absenter pour quelques jours.	I absolutely must go away for a few days.

   ▶ when followed by an infinitive it can express a strong probability:

Il doit être 10 heures déjà, non ?	It must be 10 o'clock already, mustn't it?

▶ it is used to correct someone politely:

| *Vous devez faire erreur, Monsieur !* | You must be mistaken, sir! |

▶ In the **compound past,** *devoir* expresses two different meanings:

  ▶ an obligation (*had to*)

| *Il était tellement epuisé qu'il a dû abandonner la course.* | He was so exhausted he had to give up the race. |

  ▶ a probability (*must have*)

| *Il a abandonné la course, il a dû être fatigué.* | He gave up the race; he must have been exhausted. |

▶ In the **imperfect** *devoir* can have four different meanings:

  ▶ a compound conditional meaning (*should have / ought to have*)

| *Nous devions (= nous aurions dû) être à Paris demain, mais pour raisons familiales nous ne sommes pas partis.* | We should have been in Paris tomorrow, but for family reasons we haven't gone. |

  ▶ obligation (*had to*)

| *Nous sommes desolés d'avoir manqué le rendez-vous, mais nous devions aller à Paris de toute urgence.* | We are sorry to have missed the meeting, but we had to go to Paris very urgently. |

  ▶ supposition, speculation (*must have*)

| *Je ne me souviens plus pourquoi nous avons manqué le rendez-vous, nous devions être à Paris.* | I don't remember any more why we missed the meeting; we must have been in Paris. |

▶ It has a **future** meaning:

| *Il était sur le balcon où plus tard de Gaulle devait faire son célèbre discours.* | It was on the balcony where later de Gaulle would make his famous speech. |

▶ In the **conditional** it expresses:

  ▶ a recommendation (*should, ought to*)

| *Tu devrais t'habiller mieux que ça !* | You should dress better than that! |

▶ a politely expressed obligation or a piece of advice

| Vous devriez vous concentrer sur votre travail. | You should concentrate on your work. |

▶ a supposition (*should*, *ought to*)

| Avec de tels résultats, tu devrais trouver un stage intéressant. | With results like that you ought to find interesting internship. |

▶ In the **compound conditional** it expresses:

▶ a regret, reproach or a piece of advice (*should have / ought to have*)

| Tu aurais dû réfléchir avant d'agir. | You ought to have thought before you acted. |
| J'aurais dû prendre une aspirine. | I should have taken an aspirin. |

▶ *Devoir* is also used **pronominally**, expressing a moral obligation:

| Elle se devait d'être à l'heure. | She had to be on time. |

Notes

▶ *Devoir* takes a circumflex accent in the masculine singular of the past participle only: *dû* (but *due*, *dus*, *dues*).

▶ The imperative of *devoir* is rarely used.

Falloir

Falloir, meaning *to have to*, *must*, *should*, *ought to*, is an impersonal verb that is followed by the subjunctive:

| Il faut qu'il apprenne à cuisiner avant de commencer ses études. | He must learn to cook before beginning his studies. |
| Il faudra que tu amènes les billets dès que possible. | You'll have to bring the tickets as soon as possible. |

Pouvoir

Pouvoir expresses:

▶ physical capacity

| Avec ma blessure je ne peux pas faire de sport. | With my injury I can't play sports. |

▶ permission or possibility

| Je ne peux pas sortir, mes parents me l'interdisent. | I can't go out because my parents have forbidden me to. |
| Ici on peut marcher sur les pelouses. | You can walk on the grass here. |

▶ being in a state

| Je ne peux pas dormir. | I can't sleep. |

▶ a hypothesis or eventuality

| En juin il peut encore faire froid ! | In June it can still be cold! |
| Fais attention ! Tu peux te blesser avec cet outil. | Take care! You can hurt yourself with that tool. |

▶ a polite question

| Pouvez-vous m'aider à monter cette valise, s'il vous plaît ? | Can you please help me to take this case up? |

(See *savoir* for the way of expressing 'have the means to', 'know how to' in the meaning of *pouvoir*.)

Different meanings according to tense

▶ In the **compound past**, *pouvoir* often expresses an action completed successfully (= *réussir à*, to succeed, manage to):

| Il a finalement pu résoudre le problème. | He's finally succeeded in solving the problem. |
| Il a pu avoir un billet pour ce soir. | He's been able / managed to get a ticket for this evening. |

▶ In the **conditional**, *pouvoir* expresses future potentiality:

| Il pourrait bien se débrouiller tout seul s'il le voulait. | He could cope by himself if he wanted to. |
| On pourrait changer notre salon, qu'en penses-tu ? | We could change our living room; what do you think? |

▶ In the **compound conditional** *pouvoir* can express a hypothesis or an eventuality:

| *Vous auriez pu manquer votre train !* | You could have missed your train. |

Pouvoir takes a **pronominal form** in the expression *il se peut que*, followed by the subjunctive. It is often translated by 'may':

| *Il se peut qu'il arrive après 18 heures.* | He may arrive after 6 pm. |
| *Il se peut qu'il pleuve.* | It may rain. |

Note

▶ The first person singular of the present indicative of *pouvoir* has two forms:

  ▶ a standard form: *je peux*

  ▶ in more formal language: *je puis*

  Puis is the form used when there is inversion of the verb and subject: *puis-je*.

▶ *Pouvoir* has two *rs* in the future and conditional form: e.g. *je pourrai*, etc., *je pourrais*, etc.

Savoir

Savoir expresses:

▶ acquired knowledge

| *Il sait parler turc et japonais.* | He can speak Turkish and Japanese. |

▶ success in doing something, having the aptitude to do something

| *Je saurai le convaincre.* | I will be able / know how to convince him. |

▶ having the means to do something

| *Il sait parler en public.* | He knows how to speak in public. |

▶ ability, e.g. to play a musical instrument

| *Elle sait jouer du piano.* | She can play the piano. |

Different uses of **savoir**

▶ *Savoir* in the **conditional**, followed by an infinitive, can have the meaning of *pouvoir* in negative utterances (from which *pas* is omitted):

| *Je ne saurais vous dire laquelle je préfère.* | I could not tell you which I prefer. |

▶ An **infinitive clause** after *savoir* can be used as the complement of a direct object:

Il fréquentait un ami qu'il savait être criminel.	He associated with a friend who(m) he knew to be a criminal.
Elle s'engagea sur un sentier qu'elle savait être périlleux.	She started on a path that she knew was dangerous.

▶ *Savoir* is used **pronominally** in the meaning of self-knowledge:

Il se sait malade.	He knows himself to be ill.

Vouloir

Vouloir expresses:

▶ a 'strong' wish

▶ an intention, desire to carry out something and stick to it.

Different uses

▶ In the **present** *vouloir* expresses a determined desire or wish:

Il ne veut pas marcher, il veut être porté.	He won't walk; he wants to be carried.
Le proviseur veut connaitre l'auteur des graffitis.	The headteacher wants to know who wrote the graffiti.

▶ In **interrogative and exclamatory sentences** *vouloir* expresses an order. It is often followed by *bien*:

Voulez-vous bien rester à votre place !	Will you stay in your place!

▶ With **a subject that is not a person**, often in the negative, it indicates persistence:

J'ai un mal de tête qui ne veut pas passer.	I have a headache that won't go away.

▶ In the **imperative or the infinitive** after verbs like *prier* (to beg) and *demander* (to ask), it expresses a desire or a request in a polite way:

Veuillez me suivre, s'il vous plaît !	Kindly follow me.
Je vous prie de vouloir bien me suivre !	Be so kind as to follow me.

▶ In the **compound past** it expresses a wish that is unsatisfied or unsuccessfully completed:

Il a voulu sauter le mur et il s'est cassé la cheville.	He tried to jump over the wall and he broke his ankle.
On dirait que les malfaiteurs ont voulu passer par le jardin.	It seems that the thieves were trying to go through the garden.

► In the **conditional** it expresses a potential wish or a hope:

| Au retour, je voudrais passer par la boulangerie. | On the way back, I would like to call at the baker's. |
| Il voudrait savoir si vous êtes libre. | He'd like to know if you are free. |

► *Vouloir* is used **pronominally**:

| Il se voudrait intègre mais l'est-il vraiment ? | He'd like to think himself honest, but is he really? |

9.3 Transitive and intransitive verbs

9.3.1 *Transitive verbs*

Transitive verbs must be followed by a **direct object** (in French COD = *complément d'objet direct*) or an **indirect object** (in French COI = *complément d'objet indirect*).

► If the object is not introduced by the prepositions *à*, *de* or *en*, the verb affects directly the person or thing that is receiving the action. The object is then **direct**:

| Elle a trouvé un emploi. | She's found a job. |

► If the object is introduced by the prepositions *à* or *de*, it is **indirect**:

Elle pense **à** ses amis.	She thinks about her friends.
Il rêve **d'**une maison au bord de la mer.	He dreams of a house by the sea.
Le tabac nuit **à** la santé.	Smoking damages your health.

Note

In the last example the object is indirect in French but direct in English.

► Some verbs are **double transitive**, i.e. they may be followed by a direct and an indirect object:

| Il offre un verre à son ami. | He offers a drink (direct object) to his friend (indirect object). |
| Elle enseigne l'espagnol à ses collègues. | She teaches Spanish (direct object) to her colleagues (indirect object). |

Note

In the sentence: *Il enseigne l'espagnol à l'université* (He teaches Spanish at the university), *à l'université* is an adverbial phrase of place and not an indirect object.

9.3.2 Intransitive verbs

▶ An intransitive verb is one which is not followed by a direct or an indirect object:

Le chat miaule de façon étrange.	The cat miaows strangely.
Le clown gesticule sur la scène.	The clown gesticulates on stage.
Le cheval trotte allègrement.	The horse trots along cheerfully.

Note

Typically, intransitive verbs are accompanied by an adverbial, as in the examples above.

▶ Most active verbs can be either transitive or intransitive. In some cases, the change from transitive to intransitive is accompanied by a change of meaning, e.g. *arrêter* (to stop), *commencer* (to begin), *habiter* (to live in), *manquer* (to miss, fail, be missing), *servir* (to serve), *rompre* (to break), *retarder* (to delay).

   ▶ verbs without a change of meaning e.g. *habiter* (*à*), *hériter* (*de*):

     ◦ Transitive verb with direct object: *Il habite la campagne.*   He lives in [lit. inhabits] the country.

     ◦ Intransitive verb: *Il habite à la campagne.*   He lives in the country.

   ▶ verbs with a change of meaning:

Transitive verb with direct object	Intransitive verb
Il a manqué la cible. He missed his target.	*J'ai contrôlé, rien ne manque.* I checked, nothing is missing.
Elle entre les données. She enters the data.	*Elle entre dans la pièce.* She goes into the room.
Je monte la valise. I take the case up.	*Je monte.* I go up.
Ils ont fui le danger à temps. They escaped the danger in time.	*Les lâches fuient; les courageux se battent.* Cowards flee; the brave fight on.

▶ Some verbs are always intransitive, e.g. *miauler* (to miaow), *rugir* (to blush), *arriver* (to arrive), *venir* (to come), *voyager* (to travel):

*Il sont en train d'**arriver** à la gare.*	They are arriving at the station.
*Les jeunes **voyagent** de plus en plus.*	Young people travel more and more.

▶ Verbs of state, e.g. *être, paraître, sembler, devenir, avoir l'air, passer pour, rester, demeurer*, are classified as intransitive:

*Ils **paraissent** en forme.*	They look fit.
*Il **a l'air** convenable.*	He seems respectable.

▶ Some verbs are almost always intransitive, e.g. *pleurer* (to cry), *nager* (to swim):

*Il ne **pleure** jamais.*	He never cries. (intransitive)
*Elle **pleure** des larmes de crocodile.*	She weeps crocodile tears. (transitive)
*Vous **nagez** comme un champion !*	You swim like a champion! (intransitive)
*Vous **nagez** mieux le crawl que la brasse.*	You swim the crawl better than the breast-stroke. (transitive)

9.4 Pronominal verbs

Pronominal verbs are verbs in which the subject and the object of the verb are the same person. In these verbs the **reflexive** pronoun (*me / m', te / t', se / s', nous, vous*) always precedes the verb.

In the infinitive the reflexive pronoun is always *se* or *s'*:

s'amuser	to enjoy oneself
s'habituer	to get used to
se réconcilier	to make one's peace
se hasarder	to venture

Note

In *Je me demande* (I wonder) [lit. 'I ask myself'], the verb is reflexive (*se demander*). The reflexive pronoun *me* reflects back on the subject of the sentence 'I', i.e. 'I am asking myself'.

But *demander* can also be used without a reflexive pronoun, as in *Il me demande* (He asks me). In this sentence, the pronoun *me* is not a reflexive pronoun because it does not reflect back on to the subject *il*. The subject, and *me*, the object, are different people.

In compound tenses:

▶ Pronominal verbs are conjugated with the auxiliary verb *être* (see 9.2.1, **Linking verbs**)

▶ The reflexive pronoun is placed before the auxiliary *être*:

| Il s'est trompé. | He made a mistake. |

9.4.1 Verbs which are both pronominal and non-pronominal

Some verbs, such as *(se) laver* (to wash), can be both pronominal and non-pronominal. For example, in *Je me lave* (I wash [myself]) *laver* is used pronominally; in *Je lave la voiture* (I wash the car), *laver* is not used pronominally. Other verbs, such as *s'en aller* (to go away), are always pronominal.

These verbs are of three kinds:

▶ **Reflexive verbs**

    ▶ These verbs express an action which the subject does to itself:

Je me lave.	I wash.
Il s'est surmené.	He worked himself too hard.
Nous nous inquiétons.	We're getting worried.
Taisez-vous !	Keep quiet!

    ▶ In order to know whether a verb is reflexive add *moi-même*, *toi-même*, etc.:

| Je me rase = je rase moi-même. | I shave = I shave myself. |

    ▶ The pronoun that is part of a reflexive verb can have different functions:

| Direct object: | Elles se sont baignées. They bathed. |
| Indirect object: | Elles se sont donné du temps. They gave [to] themselves time. |

▶ A reflexive pronominal verb is often translated into English by an active verb:

Il s'est coupé le doigt.	He cut his finger.
Il se rase tous les matins.	He shaves every morning.
Sa santé s'est dégradée.	His health deteriorated.

▶ **Reciprocal verbs**

   ▶ When the subjects of the verb are doing something to each other the pronominal verb is called *reciprocal*. The action is carried out and received by each one at the same time:

Les enfants se querellent dans la cour.	The children quarrel among themselves in the playground.
Ils s'entraident.	They help one another.
Ils se sont rencontrés dans la rue après s'être cherchés pendant des heures.	They met each other in the street after looking for each other for hours.

   ▶ Sometimes reciprocity is indicated by adding *l'un l'autre* or *les uns les autres* (each other, one another):

Ils se sont encouragés les uns les autres.	They encouraged one another.

   ▶ Some reciprocal verbs can be reinforced by the prefix *entre-*: *s'entraider* (to help each other); *s'entre-déchirer* (to tear each other to pieces); *s'entre-tuer* (to kill one another):

Dans le besoin, il est bon de s'entraider.	When in need it's good to help one another.

   ▶ To know whether a pronominal verb has a reciprocal meaning, complete the sentence by adding *l'un l'autre, les uns les autres*, etc.:

Toutes les élèves se sont averties par téléphone (les unes les autres).	All the pupils informed each other by telephone.

▶ **Verbs with a passive meaning**

   ▶ A pronominal verb can have a passive meaning when the subject receives the action of the verb.

   ▶ In *La cloche s'entend de loin* (The bell is heard from afar), the sense is a passive one: it is clearly not the bell which hears itself, and whoever hears the bell is not identified. In this kind of sentence the agent of the action is often not stated, but understood. Here we can assume that the agent is 'people / us'.

Je m'appelle ...	My name is / I am called ...
Cela s'entend de loin.	That is heard from a distance.
Cela se situe au nord.	That is situated in the north.
Cela se voit rarement.	That is rarely seen.
Cela ne se fait pas.	That is not done.

▶ To know whether a pronominal verb has a passive sense, replace it by a passive:

Cela s'entend de loin = Cela est entendu de loin.	That is heard from a distance.
Cela se voit rarement = Cela est rarement vu.	That is rarely seen.
L'or se vend cher cette année = L'or est vendu cher cette année.	Gold is sold at a high price this year.

9.4.2 Verbs found only in the pronominal form

Some pronominal verbs exist only when accompanied by the reflexive pronoun *me*, *te*, *se*, *nous* or *vous* (see 4.5). The action of the verb is always carried out on the subject itself. Examples of these verbs are:

s'évanouir	to faint, vanish
s'écrier	to cry out
se réfugier	to take refuge
se repentir	to repent
s'en aller	to go away
s'enfuir	to run off
se suicider	to commit suicide
s'envoler	to take off, e.g. aircraft

In general, these verbs do not have a reflexive, reciprocal or passive sense:

Elle **s'est évanouie** dans la nature.	She vanished into thin air.
Le directeur **s'écria**: « Fermez la porte ! »	The director shouted: 'Shut the door!'

9.4.3 Verbs with a non-reflexive and a pronominal form

Some verbs, e.g. *rire / se rire de*, have both a non-reflexive and a pronominal form. The pronominal form differs from the non-reflexive one in meaning, e.g. *se douter de* (to suspect), *se jouer de* (to make light of), *se rire de* (to make light of), *s'apercevoir* (to notice), *s'attendre à* (to expect):

Il **rit** à toutes les blagues qu'on lui raconte.	He laughs at all the jokes we tell him.
Obélix **se rit du** danger.	Obelix makes light of the danger. (He does not laugh at it)

Notes

▶ Some pronominal verbs, like *s'apercevoir*, can have several meanings:

apercevoir (usual form) / s'apercevoir (pronominal form)		
Reflexive meaning	*Le chimpanzé **s'aperçoit** dans le miroir.* The chimpanzee sees himself in the mirror.	The subject sees himself.
Reciprocal meaning	***Nous nous aperçûmes** à travers la vitre.* We saw each other through the window.	The subjects see each other.
Passive meaning	*Le Mont-Blanc **s'aperçoit** de loin.* Mont Blanc can be seen from afar.	The subject is seen in a general way.
Change of meaning	*Joël **s'aperçut** qu'il venait de dire une bourde.* Joël saw that he had made a blunder.	The subject notices.

▶ Some expressions, like *se faire mal* (to hurt oneself), *se rendre compte* (to realize), *se donner rendez-vous* (to arrange a meeting), do not have a direct object:

Elles **se sont rendu compte** du danger.	They realized the danger.
Il **s'est fait mal** au dos.	He hurt his back.

9.5 Impersonal verbs

Impersonal verbs are verbs that are introduced by a subject *il* (the equivalent of English *it*), which does not refer to a specific person or thing. Impersonal verbs are used especially for statements about the weather, for saying the time and with some common expressions like *il y a* (there is / are) and *il s'agit de* (it is a question of) (see 4.1.5):

Il est cinq heures et quart.	It is a quarter past five.
En été, **il y a** trop de touristes ici.	There are too many tourists here in summer.
De quoi **s'agit-il** ?	What's it about?

9.6 Verbal aspect

'Aspect' is a term which defines actions in relation to time, as perceived by the speaker. There are two broad types of action: those which are seen by the speaker as being part of the flow of time and those which do not refer to time passing.

This opposition is shown in two forms of the present tense in English: *I am working* and *I work*. *I am working* describes an action in its duration in time; *I work* expresses a general idea without reference to duration.

Verbal aspect describes an action in its progression and evolution; this action can be of a number of different types: *repetitive*, *instantaneous*, *continuous*, *fulfilled*, *imminent*, *progressive*, etc. It is important to know some of these aspects because they are not expressed in the same way in French as they are in English.

For example, a Frenchman who wishes to help an old lady to lift her suitcase up on to a luggage rack will say: *Laissez, Madame, je vais m'en charger !* [lit. 'Leave (it to me), Madame, I'm going to see to it!'], using the **immediate future** (*aller* + the infinitive), since the action is seen as an imminent one. An Englishman, on the other hand, is likely to say: *I'll see to it!*, using the **simple future** tense.

In the sentence *L'avion est en train de voler* (The aeroplane is flying), the verb expresses the act of flying. Aspect tells us (a) that the action is taking place at the moment the person is speaking, and (b) that it will last for a length of time that is not specified.

Un avion vole (An aeroplane flies): the action described – an aeroplane flying – is the same as in the first example, but aspect does not necessarily indicate the action in its duration. Without a context the action cannot, for example, be seen in its entirety and tell us that an aeroplane *flies* as opposed, say, to a ship, which *sails*.

L'avion a volé (The aeroplane flew): the action is still the same, but aspect tells us that the action was completed at the time of speaking.

L'avion volait (The aeroplane was flying): the action remains the same, but aspect tells us that the action was continuing at the time of speaking.

In English the progressive aspect is very important. Simple forms like *I work*, and continuous forms like *I am working*, are in opposition in all tenses and moods of the verb: *I worked* / *I was working*, *I'll work* / *I'll be working*, etc.

In French, the progressive aspect is rare; it is expressed by phrases such as *être en train de* (to be in the process of) + the infinitive:

| Il est en train de scier du bois. | He is sawing wood. |

or by the archaic construction *aller* + present participle:

| La crise va croissant. | The crisis is growing. |
| Ma douleur va s'estompant. | My pain is easing. |

Many grammarians classify aspects under three headings: *grammatical*, *lexical* and *semantic*.

9.6.1 Grammatical aspect

Grammatical aspect depends on the conjugation of the verb. It can therefore vary according to the intentions of the speaker.

One example of grammatical aspect is the opposition between a verbal action that is in the act of being carried out and one that is completed.

If you say *Elle travaillait* (She was working), the action is in the course of being completed. In *Elle a travaillé* (She worked) the action is completed.

This distinction depends on the **tense** of the verb and not its **meaning**; it is therefore grammatical aspect.

Each simple tense has a corresponding compound form. The compound form, the auxiliary verb *avoir* or *être* plus the past participle, expresses the completed aspect of an action, whereas the simple form expresses the aspect in process.

Whether the aspect is completed or in process is therefore linked to the presence or not of an auxiliary verb: the imperfect, the compound past or the past simple will express different aspects according to whether they are simple or compound tenses:

> *Il dormait* (He was sleeping): expresses a past action which is ongoing and is incomplete at the time of being spoken.

> *Il a dormi* (He slept): expresses a completed past action.

In the sentence *Il jouait quand sa mère l'a appelé* (He was playing when his mother called him), an action has begun but has not yet been completed (*jouait*); it serves as background to another action which is seen in its entirety and has been completed (*a appelé*).

9.6.2 Lexical aspect

Lexical aspect is indicated by a specific verb, adverb, semi-auxiliary, etc.

An example of lexical aspect is the 'iterative' aspect which marks repetition, as opposed to an action which happens once only.

Adverbs like *régulièrement* (regularly), *souvent* (often), *jamais* (never), *toujours* (always), or expressions like *tous les jours* (every day), express frequency. In past time, the tense used in French with these adverbs will generally be the imperfect, the equivalent of English *used to / would* plus the infinitive. In the present, the English equivalent will generally be the simple present and, occasionally, the continuous present.

Tous les matins il lisait le journal.	Every morning he would read the paper.
Tous les matins il lit le journal.	Every morning he reads the paper.

Here are some ways in which French marks certain lexical aspects.

▶ Use of adverbs

Adverb	Aspect	Examples	English
chaque fois (every time) *souvent* (often) *de nouveau / à nouveau* (again) *parfois* (sometimes) *quelquefois* (sometimes) *de temps en temps* (from time to time)	repetition	*Sa voiture cale à **chaque fois qu'il s'arrête**.*	His car stalls every time it stops.
longtemps (for a long time) *toujours* (always) *tout le temps* (all the time) *constamment* (constantly) *sans cesse / sans arrêt* (ceaselessly)	duration	*Elle a attendu **longtemps**.*	She waited for a long time.
bientôt / sous peu (soon) *incessamment* (shortly)	imminence	*Il arrive **bientôt**.*	He'll arrive soon.
peu à peu / petit à petit (bit by bit)	progression	*Il y arrivera **petit à petit**.*	He's managing bit by bit.
enfin / finalement (finally, at last) *juste* (just)	end	*Elle arrive **enfin**.*	She's coming at last.
Use of an expression which reinforces the iterative value. *chaque année* (each year) *tous les mois, ans,* etc. (every month, year, etc.)		*Il **reprend** du paracétamol **toutes les 5 heures**.*	He **takes** paracetamol **again** (iterative) **every** 5 hours (reinforced iterative).

▶ Use of prefixes

Prefix	Aspect	Examples	
re- / ré-	repetition or return	*Il a **repris** du paracétamol.* *Elle est **retournée** chez elle.*	He's taken paracetamol again. She's returned home.

Prefix	Aspect	Examples	
en-	distance or passage from one state to another	*dormir / s'endormir*	to sleep / to fall asleep
		porter / emporter	to carry / to carry away
par-	completion	*faire / parfaire*	to do / to perfect
		venir / parvenir	to come / to reach

▶ Use of suffixes and infixes*

Infixes / suffixes	Examples	Aspect	English
-aill-	*crier / criailler*	frequentatives	to shout / to shriek
	tirer / tirailler	pejoratives	to tug / pull at
-ifier	*solidifier*	action	to solidify
-iser	*pacifier*	change of state	to pacify
	nationaliser / étatiser		to nationalize
-ot-	*voler / voleter*	frequentatives	to fly / to flutter
-et-	*trembler / trembloter*	pejoratives	to shake / to tremble
	pianoter	diminutives	slightly or quiver
	vivre / vivoter		to tinkle, drum
			to live / to struggle along
-on-	*chanter / chantonner*	frequentatives	to sing / to hum
		pejoratives	
		diminutives	
-el-	*harceler*	frequentatives	to pester / harass
		pejoratives	
		diminutives	
-ass-	*rêver / rêvasser*	frequentatives	to dream / to (day) dream
	pleuvoir / pleuvasser	pejoratives	to rain / to drizzle
		diminutives	
-ill-	*mordre / mordiller*	frequentatives	to bite / to nibble at
	sauter / sautiller	pejoratives	to jump / to skip along
		diminutives	

(continued)

(continued)

Infixes / suffixes	Examples	Aspect	English
-ouill-	*gribouiller* *chatouiller*	frequentatives pejoratives diminutives	to scribble to tickle
-oyer	*rudoyer* *guerroyer*	action or state	to bully to wage war
-nich-	*pleurer / pleurnicher*	frequentatives pejoratives diminutives	to cry / to snivel

* infix – an element inserted into the root of a word

9.6.3 Semantic aspect

The perfective / imperfective aspect is an example of a **semantic** opposition. In French this opposition is based simply on the meaning of the verb.

▶ The **perfective** aspect expresses an action that, once it is completed, cannot be prolonged, or an action which only comes into being when it is finished:

In the sentence *Caroline est née à Cambridge* (Caroline was born in Cambridge), the action of being born only comes into being when it is completed; no interruption is possible because this would mean the action ceased to exist. The same is true of verbs like *fermer* (to close), *ouvrir* (to open), *sortir* (to go out), *mourir* (to die), *trouver* (to find), *atteindre* (to reach), whatever the tense or mood. These verbs are not generally used with adverbs of duration. You cannot say: **Il naquit sans cesse / longtemps* (*He was born for a long time).

Note

If the meaning of the verb changes because of the context, the verb can be imperfective, e.g. *mourir d'ennui* (to die of boredom).

▶ The **imperfective** aspect indicates an action that has been carried out even if it is interrupted before its end. The action only has to be started, and it can be stopped at any moment.

In the sentence *Caroline dort au premier étage* (Caroline sleeps on the first floor), if the action of sleeping is interrupted, this changes nothing since the action of sleeping can go on indefinitely. The same is true of verbs like *vivre* (to live), *chanter* (to sing), *marcher* (to walk), *regarder* (to look at), *attendre* (to wait), *aimer* (to love), irrespective of tense or mood.

Some verbs, e.g. *tomber* (to fall) can be both perfective and imperfective:

La neige tombe à gros flocons.	Snow is falling in big flakes. (imperfective)
Le vieillard tombe.	The old man falls. (perfective)

9.6.4 Aspect in auxiliary verbs

▶ Use of the auxiliary verb *être* in certain expressions:

Aspect	Auxiliary / semi-auxiliary expressions	English	Examples
duration (in the act of)	*être en train de* *être occupé à* + infinitive	to be + ing to be busy + ing	*Il est occupé à remplir sa feuille* He is busy filling in his tax form.
imminence, near future	*être sur le point de / en passe de* + infinitive	to be about to	*Les équipes de France et d'Angleterre sont sur le point de jouer.* The French and English teams are about to play.
obligation	*être à* + infinitive	to have to be	*Les règles de jeu sont à corriger ou à revoir entièrement.* The rules of the game have to be corrected or reviewed entirely.

▶ Use of semi-auxiliaries:

Aspect	Semi-auxiliary expressions	English	Examples
immediate or near future	*aller* + infinitive	to be going to	*Laissez ces livres, je vais les ranger dans la bibliothèque.* Leave those books. I'm going to put them back in the library.
progressive evolution / development	*aller* + *-ant* (present participle not preceded by *en*)	to go + present participle	*La crise va croissant; ses réserves vont diminuant.* The crisis is growing; their reserves are dwindling.

(continued)

(continued)

Aspect	Semi-auxiliary expressions	English	Examples
immediate / recent past	*venir de* + infinitive	just + past tense	*On vient de lui annoncer la nouvelle !* They've just told him the news!
beginning	*se mettre à + infinitive, commencer à / de + infinitive*	to start + ing	*Les équipes de France et d'Angleterre ont commencé à jouer.* The French and English teams have begun to play.
end	*finir de / cesser de + infinitive*	to stop + ing	*Les équipes de France et d'Angleterre ont fini de jouer.* The French and English teams have finished playing.

▶ The use of semi-auxiliaries such as *faillir* + infinitive, *manquer de* + infinitive:

Il a failli *rater son train.*	He almost missed his train.
Il a manqué *de tomber sur la voie.*	He almost fell on the line.

VERBS IN CONTEXT

Souvent, quand M. Madeleine **passait** (1) dans une rue, calme, affectueux, entouré des bénédictions de tous, il **arrivait** (2) qu'un homme de haute taille, vêtu d'une redingote gris de fer, armé d'une grosse canne et coiffé d'un chapeau rabattu, **se retournait** (3) brusquement derrière lui, et le **suivait** (4) des yeux jusqu'à ce qu'il **eût disparu** (5), croisant les bras, secouant lentement la tête, et haussant sa lèvre supérieure avec sa lèvre inférieure jusqu'à son nez, sorte de grimace significative qui pourrait se **traduire** (6) par: « Mais qu'est-ce que c'est que cet homme-là?-Pour sûr je l'**ai vu** (7) quelque part. [...] »

Ce personnage, grave d'une gravité presque menaçante, était de ceux qui, même rapidement entrevus, préoccupent l'observateur.

Il **se nommait** (6) Javert, et il était de la police.

Il remplissait à Montreuil-sur-mer les fonctions pénibles, mais utiles, d'inspecteur. Il n'**avait** (8) pas **vu** les commencements de Madeleine. Javert **devait** (9) le poste qu'il occupait à la protection de M. Chabouillet, [...] préfet de police à Paris. Quand Javert **était arrivé** (10) à Montreuil-sur-mer, la fortune du grand manufacturier **était** déjà **faite** (11), et le père Madeleine **était devenu** (10) monsieur Madeleine.

Certains officiers de police ont une physionomie à part et qui **se complique** (6) d'un air de bassesse mêlé à un air d'autorité. Javert avait cette physionomie, moins la bassesse.

Dans notre conviction, si les âmes **étaient** (12) visibles aux yeux, on verrait distinctement cette chose étrange que chacun des individus de l'espèce humaine **correspond** (13) à quelqu'une des espèces de la création animale; et l'on pourrait reconnaître aisément cette vérité à peine entrevue **par le penseur** (14), que, depuis l'huître jusqu'à l'aigle, depuis le porc jusqu'au tigre, tous les animaux sont dans l'homme et que chacun d'eux est dans un homme. Quelquefois même plusieurs d'entre eux à la fois.

[...]

Maintenant, si l'on admet un moment avec nous que dans tout homme il y a une des espèces animales de la création, il nous **sera** (12) facile de dire ce que c'était que l'officier de paix Javert.

Les paysans asturiens sont convaincus que dans toute portée de louve il y a un chien, lequel **est tué** (11) **par la mère** (14), sans quoi en grandissant il dévorerait les autres petits.

Donnez une face humaine à ce chien fils d'une louve, et ce sera Javert.

Extract from *Les Misérables* (part I, book 5, chapter 5) by Victor Hugo

1 *passait*	intransitive verb [9.3.2]; imperfective (of duration) [9.6.1]
2 *il arrivait*	impersonal verb [9.5]
3 *se retournait*	pronominal verb [9.4]
4 *suivait*	uncompleted aspect [9.6.1]
5 *eût disparu*	completed aspect [9.6.1]
6 *se traduire, se nommait, se complique*	pronominal verbs with passive meaning [9.4.1]
7 *ai vu*	transitive verb with direct object [9.3.1]; auxiliary *avoir* [9.2.2]
8 *avait*	auxiliary verb *avoir* [9.2.2]
9 *devait*	double transitive verb [9.3.1]
10 *était arrivé, était devenu*	verbs conjugated with auxiliary *être* [9.2.2]
11 *était faite, est tué*	passive verbs [9.2.2] [9.2.3]
12 *étaient, sera*	*être* as copula [9.2.1]
13 *correspond*	transitive verb followed by indirect object [9.3.1]
14 *par le penseur, par la mère*	agents of passive verbs (*être* understood before *par le penseur*) [9.2.3]

1. **Fill the gaps with the verbs listed below:**

   ▶ Write the verbs in the tenses indicated, not forgetting to use the correct preposition where necessary.

   ▶ Say whether the verbs are (1) transitive with a direct object, (2) transitive with an indirect object, (3) intransitive or (4) double transitive, putting a tick in the appropriate box.

	Verb	Tense	Example	I	2	3	4
I.	aller	present	Ils _____ Londres ce samedi				
2.	penser	present	Nous _____ vacances				
3.	poster	compound past / perfect	Tu _____ la lettre hier ?				
4.	avoir besoin	present	Je _____ rien pour l'instant				
5.	dédicacer	compound past / perfect	Elle_____son livre à sa fille				
6.	voyager	compound past / perfect	Nous _____ dans toute l'Europe				
7.	passer	present	Je _____ mes vacances en France				
8.	jouer	present	Est-ce que tu _____ échecs ?				
9.	jouer	present	Est-ce que vous _____ piano ?				
10.	travailler	present	Il _____ le bois				

2. **Put into the passive voice:**

   1. On a appelé les étudiants par leur nom.
   2. On les a installés dans différentes salles d'examen.
   3. Les surveillants ont contrôlé les identités.
   4. Puis, ils ont décacheté les enveloppes.
   5. et ils ont distribué les sujets.
   6. On a autorisé une bouteille d'eau par table.
   7. On avait mis tous les portables dans une boîte en entrant.
   8. et on avait laissé les vestes aux porte-manteaux.
   9. Le règlement n'autorisait pas les étudiants à sortir avant une heure.
   10. Un étudiant rendit sa copie bien avant les autres.

3. **Complete the sentences using the pronominal verbs in the present or compound past, according to the context:**

Tick in the relevant box to say if the pronominal verbs below are (1) reflexive, (2) reciprocal or (3) passive in meaning:

	Verb	Example	1	2	3
1.	se dégrader	La situation _____			
2.	se saluer	Ils ne … pas _____			
3.	se battre	Ils _____ comme des chiffonniers.*			
4.	se voir	De tels événements _____ rarement.			
5.	se demander	Elle _____ ce qu'elle va faire.			
6.	s'entraider	Elles _____ chaque fois qu'elles le peuvent.			
7.	s'appeler	Nous _____ Claude tous les deux.			
8.	se chercher	Elle _____ un emploi convenable.			

* to fight like cat and dog (*chiffonniers* = scavengers)

10 VERBS 2: TENSES OF THE INDICATIVE

10.1 Tenses

Beneath a verb like *vive* in *Vive la démocratie !* (Long live democracy!) complex elements lie hidden: each of these elements influences the form of the verb. The same is true of all verbs: to conjugate a verb like *vive* is to answer a certain number of questions, such as:

What is the speaker's intention?	the mood	The action is not a reality but a strong wish.	subjunctive
At what moment in time does the action occur?	the tense	the moment the action is uttered	present
What is the subject of the action?	the person	a concept	third person
Are there several subjects or just one?	number	a single subject	singular
Does the subject carry out the action or is the action done to him?	voice	The subject carries out the action.	active voice

In the previous chapter we have seen that it is traditional in France to treat the verb as having seven moods. According to this system, each of these moods includes a number of tenses.

The difference between *je finis* (present indicative) and *(que) je finisse* (present subjunctive) does not lie in the tense – in each case the tense is the same – but in the **intention** of the speaker (the mood).

▶ Mood

The action of the verb is variable: it can, for example, be real, wished for, put in doubt, etc. These different ways of expressing the verbal action are called moods. Moods express the intention or the attitude of the speaker to the action, or to the different ways in which the action may be carried out.

The number of moods in French varies according to different grammarians. Many grammars say that there are seven, four of which are 'personal': the indicative, the subjunctive, the imperative and the conditional, and three 'impersonal': the infinitive, the participle and the gerund.

Other grammarians, however, do not consider the impersonal moods as moods, and treat the conditional as a tense of the indicative rather than a mood.

For our purposes, we will describe the verb according to the latter view and present the verb in French as having three moods: the indicative, the subjunctive and the imperative.

▶ **The infinitive** (see 11.2)

The infinitive is the 'non-inflected' form of the verb, i.e. it is not marked for person or number. It can be recognized by its ending, either *-er, -(o)ir*, or *-re*: *généraliser* (to generalize), *abolir* (to abolish), *naître* (to be born), *concevoir* (to conceive).

▶ **Tenses**

The tenses are the forms that are taken by verbs to situate the action in time. These different forms of the verb are called the **conjugations**.

The verbal action can be situated:

▶ **at the moment** of speaking: the **present** tense

Regarde, regarde ! C'est Catherine ! Elle passe à la télé !	Look, look. It's Catherine. She's on TV!

▶ **before** the moment of speaking: the **past** tenses

Tu as vu Catherine ? Elle est passée à la télé hier !	Did you see Catherine? She was on TV yesterday!

▶ **after** the moment of speaking: the **future** tenses

Catherine passera probablement à la télé demain.	Catherine will probably be on TV tomorrow.

10.1.1 Time and tense

The chart below represents graphically a 'timeline' of tenses which we describe in this chapter. The present tense communicates what is happening now. The past tenses represent different moments before present time: the pluperfect is a 'before-past' tense, the simple and compound past both express a defined moment in past time and the imperfect describes past time in its extension. Beyond the present lies the future, which is preceded in the sequence by the compound future, a tense that conveys the future as a completed action.

The tenses are sometimes used with an auxiliary verb, sometimes not. We speak of simple tenses and compound tenses. For compound tenses, there is a choice between the

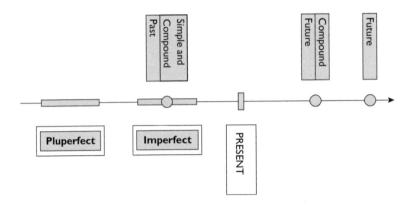

auxiliary verbs *avoir* and *être*. The majority of verbs employ *avoir*; *être* is used for: (a) pronominal verbs; (b) about twenty verbs, principally of movement (*aller* [to go], *venir* [to come], *entrer* [to go in], *sortir* [to go out], etc.); (c) verbs in the passive voice.

For the majority of simple tenses there is a corresponding compound tense:

	Simple tenses		Compound tenses	
Indicative	Present	*tu dors*	Compound past	*tu as dormi*
	Imperfect	*tu dormais*	Pluperfect	*tu avais dormi*
	Future	*tu dormiras*	Compound future perfect	*tu auras dormi*
	Conditional	*tu dormirais*	Compound conditional	*tu aurais dormi*
Subjunctive	Present	*que tu dormes*	Past	*que tu aies dormi*
Imperative	Present	*dors !*	Past	*aie dormi !*
Participle	Present	*dormant*	Past	*dormi*
Infinitive	Present	*dormir*	Past	*avoir dormi*

The compound tenses are used for two meanings:

▶ completion: every compound form shows a completed action.

▶ prior actions: the compound form expresses an action prior to one that is in the process of being carried out.

*Après qu'il **aura fini** son rapport, il le **présentera**.*	After he has finished his report, he will present it.
*Après qu'il **a fini** son rapport, il le **présente**.*	After he has finished his report, he presents it.
*Après qu'il **eut fini** son rapport, il le **présenta**.*	After he had finished his report, he presented it.

10.2 The radical and verb endings

10.2.1 Expression of mood, tense, person, number and voice

The mood, tense, person, number and voice are expressed:

▶ by the endings of the verbs

　▶ In order to conjugate a verb, it has to change its form.

In the following forms: *je parle, nous parlons, vous parliez, tu parlais*
one part of the verb is fixed: *parl-*
one part is variable: *-e, -ons, -iez, -ais*.
The fixed part is the **radical** of the verb and the variable parts are the **endings**. The variable part changes according to the tense, person and mood.

　▶ The radical is the part that carries the meaning of the verb. The majority of verbs have one radical, and this is true in particular for regular verbs of the first and second groups.

chant- is the radical of *chanter*
fin- is the radical of *finir*.

　▶ Certain verbs have irregular radicals in the various tenses:

v-, ir- and *all-* are all radicals used in conjugating *aller,*
sai-, sav-, sach-, saur- are all radicals used in conjugating *savoir.*
Each mood and tense and each of the three groups of verbs have specific endings.

Changes in the form of verbs take place:

▶ when the radical is modified

　▶ by the addition of an insertion called an **infix** between the radical and the ending.

In the following forms:

finir (to finish)	je finis, nous fin**iss**ons
couvrir (to cover)	je couvre, nous couvrons

-iss- appears in the middle of *finissons*, but not in *couvrons*.

　▶ by variation in the spelling of the radical
In the following form:
tenir (to hold): *je tiens, nous tenons*, the spelling of the radical changes from *ten-* to *tien-*.

　▶ by a change in the radical

In the following forms:

aller (to go): *je vais, nous allons, nous irons*: the radical *all-* disappears completely, to be replaced by *v-* or *ir-*, depending on the tense. This type of irregularity can be found in English too, for example: I go, I went; I am, I was.

▶ with the use of auxiliary verbs

The auxiliary verbs *avoir* and *être* are used to form compound tenses, and the auxiliary *être* to form the passive:

J'arrive → Je suis arrivé	I arrive → I (have) arrived
Je choisis → J'ai choisi	I choose → I have chosen / I chose
Il pleut → Il a plu	It's raining → It (has) rained
Elle annonce → Elle est annoncée	She announces → She is announced

10.2.2 Verb endings

-ait is the ending which marks the third person singular of the imperfect tense or of the conditional: *il aimait* (he used to love), *il aimerait* (he would love).

Unlike the radical, verb endings present few irregularities. They vary according to group, from the present indicative to the imperative, but they are the same for all verbs and all groups in, for example, the conditional or the subjunctive.

There are a few verbs which do not have a form in certain tenses or persons. *Clore* (to close), for example, has no form for the simple past, the imperfect indicative or the imperfect subjunctive.

10.2.3 Defective verbs

Verbs such as *bruire* (to buzz), *choir* (to fall), *échoir* (to fall due), *gésir* (to lie, be at rest), *paître* (to graze), *quérir* (to fetch) and *traire* (to milk) are called 'defective' because they do not conjugate in all forms of the verb.

10.2.4 The three groups of verbs

▶ Verbs ending in *-er*

These verbs have a regular conjugation except for certain verbs ending in *-ayer, -cer, -ger, -eler, -eter*, e.g. *payer* (to pay), *commencer* (to begin), *manger* (to eat), *appeler* (to call), *acheter* (to buy). *Aller* is an exception.
The *-er* group of verbs represents 90 per cent of all verbs.

▶ Verbs ending in *-ir* which form their present participle in *-issant*

These verbs have:

▶ an infix *-iss-* between the radical and the ending in certain persons of certain tenses;

▶ a regular and stable radical, with the exception of *haïr* (to hate) and *fleurir* (to bloom);

▶ a past participle that ends in *-i*, with the exception of *maudire* (to curse), which belongs to this group despite ending in *-ire*: past participle, *maudit*.

The verbs in this group have a regular conjugation: *finir* (to finish), *abolir* (to abolish), *choisir* (to choose).

▶ **A group ending in *re*, *-oir* and *-ir* with a present participle ending in *-ant* (not in *-issant*)**

Many of these verbs are irregular, e.g. *faire* (to do), *dire* (to say), *venir* (to come), *pouvoir* (to be able), *exclure* (to exclude).
Aller also belongs to this group.

▶ *Être* and *avoir* do not belong to any group; their conjugation has a number of features which are peculiar to them.

10.3 The indicative mood

The indicative mood presents facts as real or certain: *Il est sûr qu'il viendra à l'heure.* (It's certain that he will come on time.)

It is the mood that presents a fact as it is envisaged by the speaker. In conversation, it is by far the most used of the moods.

In a subordinate clause after *que* the indicative can be used if the action is considered to be certain. If, however, there is doubt or uncertainty in the mind of the speaker the subjunctive must be used (see Chapter 12):

Il est clair qu'il viendra (indicative).	It's clear that he'll come.
Il est possible qu'il vienne (subjunctive).	It's possible that he'll come (perhaps he'll come).

10.3.1 Tenses of the indicative

The following are the indicative tenses:

One **present** tense

Seven **past** tenses:

    2 simple: imperfect, simple past

    3 compound: compound past, pluperfect, past anterior

    2 other compound past tenses: double compound past, compound pluperfect

Two **future** tenses:

  1 simple: future

  1 compound: compound future

Two **conditional** tenses

  1 simple: conditional

  1 compound: the compound conditional

Each compound form expresses a previous action, unfinished in relation to the corresponding simple form. In *Quand elle a (avait, eut, aura) dîné, elle regarde (regardait, regarda, regardera) la télévision.* [lit. When she has (had, had, will have) dined, she watches (watched, watched, will watch) television].

Each double compound form corresponds to an unfinished action in relation to the corresponding compound form, e.g. *Quand elle a eu dîné, elle a regardé la télévision* (When she had dined, she watched the television).

10.4 The present tense

This is the tense that is employed most in the spoken language. It refers to actions that take place in present time. In English there are two forms: 'He speaks' and 'He is speaking'.

The first of these forms is used to talk about actions which are **habitual** or are **generally or always true**:

  'He goes to church on Sundays.' 'The moon goes round the earth.'

The second form, called the progressive or continuous present, is usually for actions **which are happening at the time of speaking**:

  'He's running away.' 'They are not talking sense.'

Unlike English, French does not possess a progressive form; it has only one form to express both of the above ideas.

10.4.1 Formation

1st group: gagner *(to earn, win)*

Number and person		Radical	Endings	Conjugated verb
singular	*je*	*gagn*	**-e**	*je gagne*
	tu	*gagn*	**-es**	*tu gagnes*
	il / elle	*gagn*	**-e**	*il / elle gagne*

Number and person		Radical	Endings	Conjugated verb
plural	*nous*	*gagn*	**-ons**	*nous gagnons*
	vous	*gagn*	**-ez**	*vous gagnez*
	ils / elles	*gagn*	**-ent**	*ils / elles gagnent*

10.4.2 Orthographic and phonetic changes

Some verbs in the 1st group have orthographic and phonetic changes.

Ending	Verb	Change	Example
-cer	*placer* (to place), *prononcer* (to pronounce)	**c → ç** before **a** and **o**	*placer → nous plaçons*
-e*er	*mener* (to lead), *lever* (to raise)	They carry a grave accent on the **e** before a silent **e**.	*je lève → nous levons* *je mène*
-é*er	*espérer* (to hope), *préférer* (to prefer), *sécher* (to dry), *posséder* (to possess), *assiéger* (to besiege)	**e** or **é** in the penultimate syllable changes to **è** when the consonant is followed by a silent **e**.	*posséder → je possède* *nous possédons*
-ger	*interroger* (to question), *bouger* (to move)	Insert **e** before **a** and **o**.	*bouger → nous bougeons*
-eler or **-eter**	*appeler* (to call), *jeter* (to throw)	Double the **l** or the **t** before a silent **e**.	**appeler →** *j'appel**l**e* **jeter →** *je jet**t**e*
	Exceptions *acheter* (to buy), *geler* (to freeze), *congeler* (to freeze), *peler* (to peel), *marteler* (to beat), *modeler* (to model)	These verbs do not double the consonant but they carry a grave accent on the **e** before a silent **e**.	*j'achète* *nous achetons*
-guer **-quer**	*naviguer* (to sail), *fabriquer* (to make, manufacture)	Keep the **u** throughout the conjugation.	*je navigue* *nous naviguons*

(continued)

(continued)

Ending	Verb	Change	Example
-oyer or **-uyer**	*nettoyer* (to clean), *ennuyer* (to bore)	Change the **y** into **i** before a silent **e**.	*je nettoie* *j'essuie*
-ayer	*payer* (to pay)	There are two possibilities. These verbs can either maintain the **y** or change it into **i** before a silent **e**.	*je paye* *je paie*

2nd group: finir *(to finish)*

Number and person		Radical	Infix	Endings	Conjugated verb
singular	*je*	*fin*	—	**-is**	*je finis*
	tu	*fin*	—	**is**	*tu finis*
	il / elle	*fin*	—	**-it**	*il / elle finit*
plural	*nous*	*fin*	**-iss-**	**-ons**	*nous finissons*
	vous	*fin*	**-iss-**	**-ez**	*vous finissez*
	ils / elles	*fin*	**-iss-**	**-ent**	*ils / elles finissent*

Note

Haïr loses its diaeresis in the first three persons of the singular of the present indicative: *je hais, tu hais, il hait, nous haïssons, vous haïssez, ils haïssent.*

3rd group: perdre *(to lose)*

Number and person		Radical	Endings	Conjugated verb
singular	*je*	*perd*	**-s**	*je perds*
	tu	*perd*	**-s**	*tu perds*
	il / elle	*perd*	**-**	*il / elle perd*
plural	*nous*	*perd*	**-ons**	*nous perdons*

Number and person		Radical	Endings	Conjugated verb
	vous	perd	**-ez**	vous perdez
	ils / elles	perd	**-ent**	ils / elles perdent

Auxiliary verb avoir

Number and person		Radical	Endings	Conjugated verb
singular	j'	ai	-	j'ai
	tu	a	**-s**	tu as
	il / elle	a	-	il / elle a
plural	nous	av	**-ons**	nous avons
	vous	av	**-ez**	vous avez
	ils / elles	o	**-nt**	ils / elles ont

Auxiliary verb être

Number and person		Radical	Endings	Conjugated verb
singular	je	sui	**-s**	je suis
	tu	e	**-s**	tu es
	il / elle	es	**-t**	il / elle est
plural	nous	s	**-ommes**	nous sommes
	vous	êt	**-es**	vous êtes
	ils / elles	s	**-ont**	ils / elles sont

Note

(s')asseoir / (s')assoir

S'asseoir (to sit down) is conjugated in two different ways: *je m'assieds*, which is more literary, and more frequent than *je m'assois*. The opposite occurs in Quebec, where the radical *assoi-* is more frequent. The two roots are found in all tenses and moods. *S'assire* also exists, but it has almost disappeared; it can be heard in some regions of France.

je m'assieds	je m'assois
tu t'assieds	tu t'assois
il, elle s'assied	il, elle s'assoit

(continued)

(continued)

nous nous asseyons	*nous nous assoyons*
vous vous asseyez	*vous vous assoyez*
ils, elles s'asseyent	*ils, elles s'assoient*

The orthographic changes of 1990 recommend that this verb is written *s'assoir* (with no change in pronunciation).

10.4.3 Uses of the present tense

KEY POINT

The present tense describes a state of affairs which exists at the time of speaking, and which is held to be true by the speaker.

Tiens ! Ils passent les Beatles à la radio.	Why, the Beatles are on the radio!
Il fait beau aujourd'hui.	The weather's fine today.

The present tense describes:

▶ general truths which have always existed and will always exist, maxims, sayings, definitions:

*Deux et deux **font** quatre.*	Two and two make four.
*L'appétit **vient** en mangeant.*	Eating stimulates the appetite.
*La Terre **tourne** autour du Soleil.*	The Earth goes round the Sun.

▶ repeated actions, accompanied by an adverb:

*Il **joue** souvent au football.*	He often plays football.
*Le samedi il **va** au pub.*	On Saturdays he goes to the pub.

▶ habits or tendencies, without reference to time:

*Son chat **griffe**.*	His cat scratches.
*Il **maltraite** son chien.*	He ill-treats his dog.

▶ a past that is very recent or linked to the present:

| Je le **quitte** à l'instant! | I just left him! |
| Il **est** marié depuis 10 ans. | He has been married for 10 years. [and still is married now] |

▶ a future action:

| Il **joue** au foot samedi. | He's playing football on Saturday. |
| L'an prochain il **commence** un doctorat. | He begins his doctorate next year. |

▶ an event situated entirely in the past. This is called the historical present:

| En 1789, la France **connaît** une révolution importante. | In 1789 France experiences / experienced an important revolution. |

▶ prophetic utterances:

| Au train où vont les choses, dans 50 ans il **n'y a** plus de forêts en Europe. | The way things are going, in 50 years there will be no more forests in Europe. |

10.5 The imperfect tense

When we talk about the past in English we can choose between three different forms of the verb:

▶ if we want to describe what we did last Saturday we might say 'We *swam* in the sea last Saturday'.

▶ if we want to stress the *continuous* nature of this action we might say 'We *were swimming* in the sea'.

▶ in order to convey the idea that the same action was *repeated* or *habitual*, we use the auxiliary verb 'used to' or 'would': 'We *used to / would swim* in the sea'.

The latter two forms can have a different meaning from the first one. In order to express continuous or habitual actions in the past in French the **imperfect tense** is used.

10.5.1 Formation

The same radical and the same endings are used for all verb groups. The endings are: *-ais, -ais, -ait, -ions, -iez, -aient*.

Note that:

▶ there is an *-i-* in the first and second persons plural, which distinguishes the imperfect from the present indicative:

nous traduisions, vous abolissiez, vous veniez, nous avions, vous étiez

▶ the infix *-iss-* appears in all persons plural of verbs in the second group (*-ir*).

The conjugation of the imperfect presents few difficulties. The radical of the verb is the same as that of the first person plural of the present indicative. The only exception is *être*.

1st group: gagner

Number and person		Radical	Endings	Conjugated verb
singular	je	gagn	**-ais**	je gagnais
	tu	gagn	**-ais**	tu gagnais
	il / elle	gagn	**-ait**	il / elle gagnait
plural	nous	gagn	**-ions**	nous gagnions
	vous	gagn	**-iez**	vous gagniez
	ils / elles	gagn	**-aient**	ils / elles gagnaient

2nd group: finir

Number and person		Radical	Infix	Endings	Conjugated verb
singular	je	fin	**-iss-**	**-ais**	je finissais
	tu	fin	**-iss-**	**-ais**	tu finissais
	il / elle	fin	**-iss-**	**-ait**	il / elle finissait
plural	nous	fin	**-iss-**	**-ions**	nous finissions
	vous	fin	**-iss-**	**-iez**	vous finissiez
	ils / elles	fin	**-iss-**	**-aient**	ils / elles finissaient

3rd group: perdre

Number and person		Radical	Endings	Conjugated verb
singular	je	perd	**-ais**	je perdais
	tu	perd	**-ais**	tu perdais
	il / elle	perd	**-ait**	il / elle perdait
plural	nous	perd	**-ions**	nous perdions

Number and person		Radical	Endings	Conjugated verb
	vous	perd	**-iez**	vous perdiez
	ils / elles	perd	**-aient**	ils / elles perdaient

Auxiliary verb avoir

Number and person		Radical	Endings	Conjugated verb
singular	j'	av	**-ais**	j'avais
	tu	av	**-ais**	tu avais
	il / elle	av	**-ait**	il / elle avait
plural	nous	av	**-ions**	nous avions
	vous	av	**-iez**	vous aviez
	ils / elles	av	**-aient**	ils / elles avaient

Auxiliary verb être

Number and person		Radical	Endings	Conjugated verb
singular	j'	ét	**-ais**	j'étais
	tu	ét	**-ais**	tu étais
	il / elle	ét	**-ait**	il / elle était
plural	nous	ét	**-ions**	nous étions
	vous	ét	**-iez**	vous étiez
	ils / elles	ét	**-aient**	ils / elles étaient

10.5.2 Orthographic and phonetic changes

Some verbs in the 1st group have orthographic and phonetic changes:

radical ending in **-i**, **-y**, **-ill** or **-gn**	se *méfier* (to mistrust), *gagner* (to earn, win), *voir* (to see), *habiller* (to dress)	The [i] sound of the first and second persons plural blends with the **-ll-** or **-i** of the end of the radical and is therefore not pronounced. It is important not to forget to write the **i**.	habi**lli**ons / habi**lli**ez vo**yi**ons / vo**yi**ez nous méf**i**ions / vous méf**i**iez ga**gni**ons / ga**gni**ez

(continued)

(continued)

-cer	placer (to place), prononcer (to pronounce)	c → ç before a	placer → elle plaçait
-ger	interroger (to question), bouger (to move)	Insert an e before a.	bouger → il bougeait
-eler or -eter		The l and the t are not doubled in the imperfect (cf. present).	appeler → j'appelais jeter → tu jetais
-guer -quer	naviguer (to sail), fabriquer (to make, manufacture)	Keep the u, even before a.	Je naviguais

10.5.3 Uses of the imperfect

KEY POINTS

The imperfect describes a past action which was taking place; its beginning and end are not clearly defined:

J'allais à la plage tous les jours.	I used to go to the beach every day.

The imperfect describes:

▶ a past action seen in its duration, which is not defined or limited by time:

Il **aimait** se promener avec sa petite fille.	He liked going for a walk with his grand-daughter.
Il **travaillait** pour la SNCF.	He worked for the SNCF.

▶ a scene, a picture or a setting:

C'**était** la fin de l'automne. Il **neigeait**. Au loin, la montagne s'**estompait** derrière le tourbillon incessant des flocons.	It was the end of autumn. It was snowing. In the distance the mountain was becoming blurred in the unceasing whirl of the snowflakes.

▶ a background against which an event occurs:

Il **lisait** quand soudain le téléphone sonna.	He was reading when suddenly the phone rang.
Il **faisait** nuit, les rues **étaient** désertes. Un cri retentit.	It was night, the streets were deserted. A cry rang out.

▶ a habitual action:

Tous les soirs grand-père **fumait** sa pipe au coin du feu pendant que grand-mère **faisait** des mots croisés.	Every evening grandpa used to / would smoke his pipe at the fireside while grandma did the crossword.

The **historical** or **narrative** imperfect describes a series of actions at a precise moment in the past. It could often be replaced by a simple past or a compound past, but the imperfect slows the action and gives it more breadth and presence than the simple past or a compound past. The idea of duration that characterizes the imperfect allows us to glimpse the consequences of an action:

En 1944 les troupes **débarquaient** en Normandie.	In 1944 the troops disembarked in Normandy.
Tout de suite après la guerre ils **émigraient** en France.	Immediately after the war they emigrated to France.

▶ an action which takes place after another moment in the past:

Le lendemain, il **partait** pour les Antilles.	The next day he was leaving for the West Indies.

▶ an action which almost took place but was prevented and therefore did not occur. An alternative would be the compound conditional:

Un point de plus et il **sortait** (serait sorti) major de sa promotion.	One mark more and he would have come first in his year.
Sans votre présence d'esprit, cet élève **se blessait** (se serait blessé) sérieusement.	Without your presence of mind, this pupil would have been seriously injured.

▶ polite utterances which are an alternative for a blunter present tense:

J'**allais** vous demander la permission de m'absenter une heure ou deux.	I was going to ask permission to be absent for an hour or two.

Notes

▶ **The sequence of tenses**

After a verb in the past tense, according to the sequence of tenses, the verb in a subordinate clause is in the imperfect tense:

| Joseph **fit signe** qu'il **partait**. | Joseph motioned that he was leaving. |

▶ **The imperfect in conditional clauses**

The imperfect is used after a hypothetical *si*. It expresses a present or future action:

| Si j'**avais** les moyens je voyagerais en Ire classe. | If I had the means, I'd travel first class. |

▶ **The imperfect with *si* can express:**

> ▶ regret: *S'il pouvait revenir sur sa décision !*   If only he could go back on his decision!
>
> ▶ a wish: *Ah ! Si j'étais riche !*   Ah! If I were rich!
>
> ▶ a suggestion: *Et si nous **allions** nous coucher les enfants !*   How about us going to bed, children!

10.6 The compound past

In the sentence 'She has lost her passport', the verb 'has lost' is in the compound past tense. This tense combines the *auxiliary verb* (has) and the *past participle* of the verb ('lost'). In English this tense is used to describe actions that have begun in the past and carry through to the present. What we are interested in is that the passport isn't here *now* (see 10.2.1).

10.6.1 Formation

Avoir or *être* in the present indicative plus the past participle:

1st group: gagner

Number and person		Auxiliary	Past participle	Conjugated verb
singular	j'	ai	gagné	j'ai gagné
	tu	as	gagné	tu as gagné
	il / elle	a	gagné	il / elle a gagné
plural	nous	avons	gagné	nous avons gagné

Number and person		Auxiliary	Past participle	Conjugated verb
	vous	**avez**	gagn**é**	vous avez gagné
	ils / elles	**ont**	gagn**é**	ils / elles ont gagné

2nd group: finir

Number and person		Auxiliary	Past participle	Conjugated verb
singular	j'	**ai**	fin**i**	j'ai fini
	tu	**as**	fin**i**	tu as fini
	il / elle	**a**	fin**i**	il / elle a fini
plural	nous	**avons**	fin**i**	nous avons fini
	vous	**avez**	fin**i**	vous avez fini
	ils / elles	**ont**	fin**i**	ils / elles ont fini

3rd group: descendre

Number and person		Auxiliary	Past participle	Conjugated verb
singular	je	suis	descend**u(e)**	je suis descendu(e)
	tu	es	descend**u(e)**	tu es descendu(e)
	il / elle	est	descend**u(e)**	il / elle est descendu(e)
plural	nous	sommes	descend**u(e)s**	nous sommes descendu(e)s
	vous	êtes	descend**u(e)(s)**	vous êtes descendu(e)(s)
	ils / elles	sont	descend**u(e)s**	ils / elles sont descendu(e)s

Auxiliary verb avoir

Number and person		Auxiliary	Past participle	Conjugated verb
singular	j'	**ai**	**eu**	j'ai eu
	tu	**as**	**eu**	tu as eu
	il / elle	**a**	**eu**	il / elle a eu
plural	nous	**avons**	**eu**	nous avons eu
	vous	**avez**	**eu**	vous avez eu
	ils / elles	**ont**	**eu**	ils / elles ont eu

Auxiliary verb être

Number and person		Auxiliary	Past participle	Conjugated verb
singular	j'	**ai**	**été**	j'ai été
	tu	**as**	**été**	tu as été
	il / elle	**a**	**été**	il / elle a été
plural	nous	**avons**	**été**	nous avons été
	vous	**avez**	**été**	vous avez été
	ils / elles	**ont**	**été**	ils / elles ont été

10.6.2 Conjugation of verbs with être

▶ Over twenty intransitive verbs as follows:

Verb	Past participle	
aller	allé	to go
apparaître	apparu	to appear
arriver	arrivé	to arrive
décéder	décédé	to die
demeurer	demeuré	to remain
descendre	descendu	to go down
devenir	devenu	to become
entrer	entré	to go in
monter	monté	to go up
mourir	mort	to die
naître	né	to be born
partir	parti	to leave
passer	passé	to pass by
rester	resté	to remain
retourner	retourné	to return
sortir	sorti	to go out
tomber	tombé	to fall
venir	venu	to come

In addition the auxiliary *être* is used with derivatives of the above verbs, like *rentrer* (to go back in), *repartir* (to set off again), *revenir* (to come back), *parvenir* (to reach).

▶ All pronominal verbs (see 9.4).

▶ All verbs in the passive voice (see 9.2.3).

KEY POINTS

In French the compound past tense has two main functions:

✦ it describes past actions which are completed:

De Gaulle a démissionné en 1969 et est mort en 1970.	De Gaulle resigned in 1969 and died in 1970.
Il a travaillé comme postier dans sa jeunesse.	He worked as a postman in his youth.

✦ it also describes past actions which carry through to the present:

Zut ! J'ai perdu mon passeport.	Damn! I've lost my passport.

10.6.3 Uses of the compound past

The compound past expresses:

▶ an action begun in the past which continues into the present:

J'ai déjà ramassé deux paniers de champignons depuis midi.	I've already gathered two baskets of mushrooms since midday.
J'ai acheté un nouvel ordinateur.	I've bought a new computer.

▶ in the spoken language, an action situated entirely in the past which would normally be in the simple past:

Molière et sa troupe ont connu des débuts difficiles.	Molière and his company had a difficult beginning.

▶ an action in the near future that is described as already completed (often with a compound future meaning), with a time reference:

J'ai peint (aurai peint) ce mur dans une heure.	I will have painted this wall in an hour.
J'ai pratiquement fini mon livre.	I've practically finished my book. (I'll have finished it soon)

▶ understatement in negative sentences:

À cette allure, on n'est pas encore rentrés !	At this rate, we won't be back for quite a while yet. (to say that we are still a long way from being back)

Note

The compound past in conditional clauses

The compound past is used after conditional *si* to express a future action which happens before another future action:

Si à 8 heures il n'a pas téléphoné c'est moi qui l'appelle.	If he hasn't phoned by 8 o'clock, I'll be the one to call him.

10.7 The simple past

In English the simple past tense refers to actions that have been completed in the past: e.g. 'France won the World Cup in 1998'. The verb consists of a single word, 'won', and the date given confirms that the event is over and done with.

In French, one of two tenses may be used to express a completed past action: the compound past (see 10.6) or the simple past.

10.7.1 Formation

The simple past is formed from the radical plus the endings below.

1st group: gagner

Number and person		Radical	Endings	Conjugated verb
singular	je	gagn	**-ai**	je gagnai
	tu	gagn	**-as**	tu gagnas
	il / elle	gagn	**-a**	il / elle gagna
plural	nous	gagn	**-âmes**	nous gagnâmes
	vous	gagn	**-âtes**	vous gagnâtes
	ils / elles	gagn	**-èrent**	ils / elles gagnèrent

2nd group: finir

Number and person		Radical	Endings	Conjugated verb
singular	je	fin	**-is**	je finis
	tu	fin	**-is**	tu finis
	il / elle	fin	**-it**	il / elle finit

Number and person		Radical	Endings	Conjugated verb
plural	nous	fin	**-îmes**	nous finîmes
	vous	fin	**-îtes**	vous finîtes
	ils / elles	fin	**-irent**	ils / elles finirent

3rd group: perdre

Number and person		Radical	Endings	Conjugated verb
singular	je	perd	**-is**	je perdis
	tu	perd	**-is**	tu perdis
	il / elle	perd	**-it**	il / elle perdit
plural	nous	perd	**-îmes**	nous perdîmes
	vous	perd	**-îtes**	vous perdîtes
	ils / elles	perd	**-irent**	ils / elles perdirent

Note

For verbs in the third group the vowel of the ending can be either *i* or *u*:

nous conclûmes, vous aperçûtes, ils virent, je dus, etc.

Auxiliary verb avoir (eu- pronounced /y/)

Number and person		Radical	Endings	Conjugated verb
singular	j'	e	**-us**	j'eus
	tu	e	**-us**	tu eus
	il / elle	e	**-ut**	il / elle eut
plural	nous	e	**-ûmes**	nous eûmes
	vous	e	**-ûtes**	vous eûtes
	ils / elles	e	**-urent**	ils / elles eurent

Auxiliary verb être

Number and person		Radical	Endings	Conjugated verb
singular	je	f	**-us**	je fus
	tu	f	**-us**	tu fus
	il / elle	f	**-ut**	il/elle fut
plural	nous	f	**-ûmes**	nous fûmes

(continued)

(continued)

Number and person		Radical	Endings	Conjugated verb
	vous	*f*	**-ûtes**	*vous fûtes*
	ils / elles	*f*	**-urent**	*ils / elles furent*

10.7.2 Uses of the simple past

The simple past is hardly ever employed in the spoken language, where the compound past takes its place. On the other hand, it is used in the written language, especially in the third persons singular and plural.

KEY POINT

The simple past expresses a completed past action, with its beginning and end being clearly defined, and with no relevance to the present:

Hier ils jouèrent un beau match.	Yesterday they played a fine match.
L'avion décolla à 13.30.	The plane took off at 13.30.

The simple past

▶ expresses an action that takes place at a particular moment in the past:

*J'étais plongé dans mes pensées quand soudain on m'**appela** de l'autre coté de la rue.*	I was deep in thought when suddenly somebody called out to me from the other side of the street.

▶ contrasts with the imperfect, in that it describes a past action without reference to its duration:

*Hier il **fit** des courses.*	Yesterday he did some shopping.

▶ is the tense used for narrating the past (e.g. in folk tales). It is ideal for describing a succession of actions, whereas the imperfect describes a number of simultaneous actions in the past (see 10.8):

*À la lecture de la lettre mon sang ne **fit** qu'un tour. Je **pris** la plume et lui **répondis** sur le champ !*	On reading the letter my heart missed a beat. I took up my pen and replied on the spot!
*« Nous **partîmes** cinq cents; mais par un prompt renfort*	'Five hundred of us departed but, soon reinforced,
*Nous nous **vîmes** trois mille en arrivant au port. »* (Corneille, *Le Cid*, acte IV, scène 3)	We were three thousand strong when we reached the port.'

10.8 The imperfect and the simple past contrasted

The imperfect and the simple past are the tenses most used in narrative texts, but they contrast fundamentally in their uses.

Imperfect		Simple past	
Habit / repetition / simultaneity		**Successive actions**	
Repeated, habitual actions.		A succession of actions which build up the narrative.	
J'allais volontiers chez grand-père car tous les soirs il me montrait ses vieilles photographies.	I used to go willingly to my grandfather's because every evening he would show me his old photos.	*Elle prit l'aspirateur, le présenta à mon père, et dit: « À toi maintenant ! »*	She took the vacuum cleaner, handed it to my father and said: 'It's your turn now'.
Duration		**Suddenness, exactitude**	
Actions which last, are drawn out in time.		A succession of sudden actions which build up the narrative.	
J'aimais ces journées d'automne où la nature prenait des couleurs étonnantes.	I used to like those autumn days when nature took on astonishing colours.	*En début d'après-midi une explosion se produisit et tout le monde se mit à courir dans tous les sens.*	At the beginning of the afternoon there was an explosion and everyone began to run in all directions.

(continued)

(continued)

Imperfect		Simple past	
Background		**Foreground**	
Evokes a 'background' action which continues in the past, serving as a framework for a foreground action which does not last.		Evokes a single action in the foreground situated within the background.	
		*Je dormais quand le chien **aboya**.*	I was asleep when the dog barked.
*Je **dormais** profondément quand il entra en claquant la porte.*	I was fast asleep when he came in slamming the door.		
Unlimited		**Limited**	
A past action which is evolving, without time limits.		A past action with a beginning and an end, happening at a precise moment.	
*Je **profitais** de la gentillesse de grand-mère pour avoir des bonbons que maman me **refusait**.*	I would take advantage of my grandmother's kindness to have sweets that mummy wouldn't give me.	*Elle **eut** juste le temps d'aller acheter les billets quand il **commença à** pleuvoir.*	She had just enough time to go and buy the tickets when it began to rain.

10.9 The pluperfect tense

This tense is used to indicate an action which occurred *before another action in the past*. The English equivalent is 'I *had* (spoken, etc.)'.

10.9.1 Formation

Avoir or *être* in the imperfect tense plus the past participle:

1st group: gagner

Number and person		Auxiliary	Past participle	Conjugated verb
singular	*j'*	**avais**	*gagné*	*j'avais gagné*
	tu	**avais**	*gagné*	*tu avais gagné*
	il / elle	**avait**	*gagné*	*il / elle avait gagné*
plural	*nous*	**avions**	*gagné*	*nous avions gagné*
	vous	**aviez**	*gagné*	*vous aviez gagné*
	ils / elles	**avaient**	*gagné*	*ils / elles avaient gagné*

2nd group: finir

Number and person		Auxiliary	Past participle	Conjugated verb
singular	j'	**avais**	fini	j'avais fini
	tu	**avais**	fini	tu avais fini
	il / elle	**avait**	fini	il / elle avait fini
plural	nous	**avions**	fini	nous avions fini
	vous	**aviez**	fini	vous aviez fini
	ils / elles	**avaient**	fini	ils / elles avaient fini

3rd group: descendre

Number and person		Auxiliary	Past participle	Conjugated verb
singular	j'	**étais**	descend**u(e)**	j'étais descendu(e)
	tu	**étais**	descend**u(e)**	tu étais descendu(e)
	il / elle	**était**	descend**u(e)**	il / elle était descendu(e)
plural	nous	**étions**	descend**u(e)s**	nous étions descendu(e)s
	vous	**étiez**	descend**u(e)(s)**	vous étiez descendu(e)(s)
	ils / elles	**étaient**	descend**u(e)s**	ils / elles étaient descendu(e)s

Auxiliary verb avoir

Number and person		Auxiliary	Past participle	Conjugated verb
singular	j'	**avais**	**eu**	j'avais eu
	tu	**avais**	**eu**	tu avais eu
	il / elle	**avait**	**eu**	il / elle avait eu
plural	nous	**avions**	**eu**	nous avions eu
	vous	**aviez**	**eu**	vous aviez eu
	ils / elles	**avaient**	**eu**	ils / elles avaient eu

Auxiliary verb être

Number and person		Auxiliary	Past participle	Conjugated verb
singular	*j'*	***avais***	***été***	*j'avais été*
	tu	***avais***	***été***	*tu avais été*
	il / elle	***avait***	***été***	*il / elle avait été*
plural	*nous*	***avions***	***été***	*nous avions été*
	vous	***aviez***	***été***	*vous aviez été*
	ils / elles	***avaient***	***été***	*ils / elles avaient été*

KEY POINT

The pluperfect expresses an indeterminate past which took place before another event in the past:

*Il a visité l'Ecosse cette année et il **avait** **visité** l'Irlande l'an dernier.*	He visited Scotland this year and he had visited Ireland the previous year.
*Il ne pouvait pas marcher car il s'**était** **blessé** au genou.*	He could not walk because he had injured his knee.

10.9.2 Uses of the pluperfect

▶ Like the imperfect, the pluperfect is used for description:

*Il **avait plu**. On **avait plié** les parasols et on **avait rentré** les tables et les chaises.*	It had rained. They had folded the umbrellas and taken in the tables and chairs.

▶ The pluperfect can refer to a present action that is expressed as if it was in the past:

*Bonjour Monsieur le directeur, j'**étais venu** vous demander s'il était possible d'avoir une journée de congé.*	lit. Hello, Director, I had come to ask you if it would be possible to have a day's leave.

▶ Sequence of tenses:

If the main verb is in a past tense, the verb of the subordinate clause can be in the pluperfect:

| Il a avoué qu'il **avait renversé** le café sur la moquette. | He admitted that he had spilt the coffee on the carpet. |
| Elle croyait que j'**avais menti**. | She thought that I had lied. |

▶ The pluperfect in conditional clauses:

when the subordinate clause introduced by *si* is in the pluperfect the main clause is in the conditional perfect:

| Si j'**avais connu** le prix avant j'aurais réfléchi à deux fois. | If I had know the price beforehand I'd have thought twice about it. |

10.10 The past anterior

10.10.1 Formation

Avoir or *être* in the simple past plus the past participle:

1st group: gagner

Number and person		Auxiliary	Past participle	Conjugated verb
singular	j'	**eus**	gagn**é**	j'eus gagné
	tu	**eus**	gagn**é**	tu eus gagné
	il / elle	**eut**	gagn**é**	il / elle eut gagné
plural	nous	**eûmes**	gagn**é**	nous eûmes gagné
	vous	**eûtes**	gagn**é**	vous eûtes gagné
	ils / elles	**eurent**	gagn**é**	ils / elles eurent gagné

2nd group: finir

Number and person		Auxiliary	Past participle	Conjugated verb
singular	j'	**eus**	fin**i**	j'eus fini
	tu	**eus**	fin**i**	tu eus fini
	il / elle	**eut**	fin**i**	il / elle eut fini
plural	nous	**eûmes**	fin**i**	nous eûmes fini
	vous	**eûtes**	fin**i**	vous eûtes fini
	ils / elles	**eurent**	fin**i**	ils / elles eurent fini

3rd group: descendre

Number and person		Auxiliary	Past participle	Conjugated verb
singular	je	**fus**	descend**u(e)**	je fus descendu(e)
	tu	**fus**	descend**u(e)**	tu fus descendu(e)
	il / elle	**fut**	descend**u(e)**	il / elle fut descendu(e)
plural	nous	**fûmes**	descend**u(e)s**	nous fûmes descendu(e)s
	vous	**fûtes**	descend**u(e)(s)**	vous fûtes descendu(e)(s)
	ils / elles	**furent**	descend**u(e)s**	ils / elles furent descendu(e)s

Auxiliary verb avoir

Number and person		Auxiliary	Past participle	Conjugated verb
singular	j'	**eus**	**eu**	j'eus eu
	tu	**eus**	**eu**	tu eus eu
	il / elle	**eut**	**eu**	il / elle eut eu
plural	nous	**eûmes**	**eu**	nous eûmes eu
	vous	**eûtes**	**eu**	vous eûtes eu
	ils / elles	**eurent**	**eu**	ils / elles eurent eu

Auxiliary verb être

Number and person		Auxiliary	Past participle	Conjugated verb
singular	j'	**eus**	**été**	j'eus été
	tu	**eus**	**été**	tu eus été
	il / elle	**eut**	**été**	il / elle eut été
plural	nous	**eûmes**	**été**	nous eûmes été
	vous	**eûtes**	**été**	vous eûtes été
	ils / elles	**eurent**	**été**	ils / elles eurent été

KEY POINT

The past anterior, like the pluperfect, is a pre-past tense: it describes a single action happening before another past action which is usually in the simple past tense. This tense occurs only in formal French:

Dès qu'il se **fut changé**, il se servit un verre et s'installa devant la télévision.	As soon as he had got changed he poured himself a drink and sat in front of the television.

10.10.2 Use

Like the simple past with which it is generally associated, the past anterior is used less and less in modern French.

The past anterior is frequently used after time conjunctions like *quand* (when), *dès que* (as soon as), *lorsque* (when), *après que* (after), with a verb in the main clause in the simple past, but also, less frequently, in another past tense:

*Après qu'il **eut** soigneusement **fermé** la porte, il se dirigea vers l'arrêt de bus.*	After he had shut the door carefully, he went to the bus stop.
*Dès que le public **se fut installé**, il prit la parole.*	As soon as the audience was settled he spoke.

10.11 The future tense

We use the future tense to express future actions. In English we place the auxiliary verb 'will' or 'shall' before the verb to form the future, as in 'It *will* / It'*ll* be hot today' and 'We *will* / We'*ll* arrive at 7.30'. Future actions can also be expressed by the progressive form of 'to go' plus the infinitive of the verb, as in 'It'*s going to* be hot today' and 'We *are going to* arrive at 7.30'.

10.11.1 Formation

The infinitive plus the endings of *avoir* in the present indicative, except for irregular verbs (see 'Verb tables', p. 422).

1st group: gagner

Number and person		Infinitive	Endings	Conjugated verb
singular	*je*	*gagner*	**-ai**	*je gagnerai*
	tu	*gagner*	**-as**	*tu gagneras*
	il / elle	*gagner*	**-a**	*il / elle gagnera*
plural	*nous*	*gagner*	**-ons**	*nous gagnerons*
	vous	*gagner*	**-ez**	*vous gagnerez*
	ils / elles	*gagner*	**-ont**	*ils / elles gagneront*

2nd group: finir

Number and person		Infinitive	Endings	Conjugated verb
singular	*je*	*finir*	**-ai**	*je finirai*
	tu	*finir*	**-as**	*tu finiras*

(continued)

(continued)

Number and person		Infinitive	Endings	Conjugated verb
	il / elle	finir	**-a**	il / elle finira
plural	nous	finir	**-ons**	nous finirons
	vous	finir	**-ez**	vous finirez
	ils / elles	finir	**-ont**	ils / elles finiront

3rd group: perdre

Number and person		Infinitive	Endings	Conjugated verb
singular	je	perdr	**-ai**	je perdrai
	tu	perdr	**-as**	tu perdras
	il / elle	perdr	**-a**	il / elle perdra
plural	nous	perdr	**-ons**	nous perdrons
	vous	perdr	**-ez**	vous perdrez
	ils / elles	perdr	**-ont**	ils / elles perdront

Auxiliary verb avoir

Number and person		Radical	Endings	Conjugated verb
singular	j'	aur	**-ai**	j'aurai
	tu	aur	**-as**	tu auras
	il / elle	aur	**-a**	il / elle aura
plural	nous	aur	**-ons**	nous aurons
	vous	aur	**-ez**	vous aurez
	ils / elles	aur	**-ont**	ils / elles auront

Auxiliary verb être

Number and person		Radical	Endings	Conjugated verb
singular	je	ser	**-ai**	je serai
	tu	ser	**-as**	tu seras

Number and person		Radical	Endings	Conjugated verb
	il / elle	ser	**-a**	il / elle sera
plural	nous	ser	**-ons**	nous serons
	vous	ser	**-ez**	vous serez
	ils / elles	ser	**-ont**	ils / elles seront

KEY POINT

The simple future describes an action which takes place after the moment that it is spoken about:

Il viendra demain.	He will come tomorrow.

10.11.2 Uses

The future tense:

▶ describes a general truth, outside of time, and is frequently seen in maxims:

Le menteur sera toujours démasqué.	The liar will always be revealed.
Rira bien qui rira le dernier.	He who laughs last laughs [lit. will laugh] loudest.
Qui vivra verra.	What will be will be.

▶ can be used to describe historical events. In a sequence of historical events the future can describe a past event which comes after another event:

Childéric Ier, chassé par son peuple, se refugia en Thuringe où il connut Basine qu'il épousa. De ce mariage **naîtra** Clovis en 466, premier roi de France.	Childeric I, pursued by his own people, took refuge in Thuringia where he met Basine, whom he married. From this union was born [lit. will be born], in 466, Clovis the first king of France.

▶ expresses politeness. The future can replace the present to avoid brusqueness and so soften the impact of the verb:

Maintenant je vous **demanderai** de vous taire et d'ouvrir vos livres à la page 24.	Now I shall ask you to be quiet and to open your books at page 24.

▶ can be used as an imperative, to express a command, a prayer or a wish:

Tenez ! Vous **rangerez** ce livre dans la bibliothèque !	Right! You will put that book back in the library.
Vous **voudrez** bien me remplir ce document et me le signer, s'il vous plaît !	You will fill in this document and sign it for me, please!

▶ can replace the present in some exclamative phrases which express indignation or irony:

Comment ! Ces gens m'insulteront et je ne dirai rien !	What! These people [lit. will] insult me and I don't [lit. won't] say anything!
Quel être prétentieux ! Il connaîtra la philosophie plus que moi !	What a pretentious person! He knows [lit. will know] philosophy better than me!

▶ can express a probability, in familiar language, giving a plausible explanation to an action:

J'entends un bruit au grenier, ce sera un chat qui se sera égaré.	I can hear a noise in the loft; it will be a stray cat.

▶ can be expressed by the verb *devoir* followed by an infinitive:

Je dois partir pour le Canada samedi.	I'm to go to Canada on Saturday.

Notes

▶ Sequence of tenses

When a subordinate clause introduced by *si* is in the present indicative, the verb in the main clause is in the present, the future or the imperative:

Si tu apprends bien ton texte, tu **pourras** tenir le rôle dans la pièce.	If you learn the part well you will be able to play the role in the play.

▶ The immediate future

The immediate future is expressed by the verb *aller* in the present tense followed by the infinitive:

J'ai soif ! Je vais me servir un jus de fruit.	I'm thirsty. I'm going to get myself a fruit juice.
On va prendre le train dans à peine deux heures.	We're going to catch the train in barely two hours.

▶ The future after conjunctions of time

▶ In clauses introduced by a conjunction of time, like *après que* (after), *aussitôt que / dès que* (as soon as), *quand / lorsque* (when), when the meaning is a future one, the verb is in the future. Note the use of the present tense in English (see 14.3.3).

Example:

*Dès qu'elle **arrivera**, donne-lui les billets.*	As soon as she **arrives**, give her the tickets.

10.12 The compound future

10.12.1 Formation

Avoir or *être* in the simple future plus the past participle.

1st group: gagner

Number and person		Auxiliary	Past participle	Conjugated verb
singular	j'	**aurai**	gagné	j'aurai gagné
	tu	**auras**	gagné	tu auras gagné
	il / elle	**aura**	gagné	il / elle aura gagné
plural	nous	**aurons**	gagné	nous aurons gagné
	vous	**aurez**	gagné	vous aurez gagné
	ils / elles	**auront**	gagné	ils / elles auront gagné

2nd group: finir

Number and person		Auxiliary	Past participle	Conjugated verb
singular	j'	**aurai**	fini	j'aurai fini
	tu	**auras**	fini	tu auras fini
	il / elle	**aura**	fini	il / elle aura fini
plural	nous	**aurons**	fini	nous aurons fini
	vous	**aurez**	fini	vous aurez fini
	ils / elles	**auront**	fini	ils / elles auront fini

3rd group: descendre

Number and person		Auxiliary	Past participle	Conjugated verb
singular	je	serai	descendu(e)	je serai descendu(e)
	tu	seras	descendu(e)	tu seras descendu(e)
	il / elle	sera	descendu(e)	il / elle sera descendu(e)
plural	nous	serons	descendu(e)s	nous serons descendu(e)s
	vous	serez	descendu(e)(s)	vous serez descendu(e)(s)
	ils / elles	seront	descendu(e)s	ils / elles seront descendu(e)s

Auxiliary verb avoir

Number and person		Auxiliary	Past participle	Conjugated verb
singular	j'	aurai	eu	j'aurai eu
	tu	auras	eu	tu auras eu
	il / elle	aura	eu	il / elle aura eu
plural	nous	aurons	eu	nous aurons eu
	vous	aurez	eu	vous aurez eu
	ils / elles	auront	eu	ils / elles auront eu

Auxiliary verb être

Number and person		Auxiliary	Past participle	Conjugated verb
singular	j'	aurai	été	j aurai été
	tu	auras	été	tu auras été
	il / elle	aura	été	il / elle aura été
plural	nous	aurons	été	nous aurons été
	vous	aurez	été	vous aurez été
	ils / elles	auront	été	ils / elles auront été

KEY POINT

The compound future describes a completed future action which comes before another future action or date:

Demain à 10 heures il aura pris connaissance de ses résultats.	Tomorrow at 10 o'clock he will have got to know his results.
Quand il aura passé tous ses examens, on parlera des vacances.	When he has taken all his exams, we'll talk about holidays.

10.12.2 Uses

The compound future:

▶ can express speculation or a supposition:

Elle **aura pris** froid en sortant de la piscine.	She'll have got cold getting out of the swimming pool.
C'est sans doute ses parents qui **auront été** trop sévères.	It's certainly her parents who will have been too strict.

▶ can express a judgement or assessment of a past event:

| Finalement, l'année 2008 **aura** surtout **été** l'année de la crise. | In the end, 2008 will have been the year of the crisis. |

▶ can be used to play down a past action, in a polite manner:

| Ce n'est pas grave. Vous **aurez oublié**, c'est tout ! | It's not serious. You'll have forgotten, that's all. |

Note

The compound future after conjunctions of time

The compound future is used in clauses introduced by a conjunction of time, like *après que* (after), *aussitôt que / dès que* (as soon as), *quand / lorsque* (when). Note the use of the perfect tense in English (see 14.3.3):

| Quand il **aura fini** ses études il pourra enfin voyager. | When he **has finished** his studies, he will be able to travel at last. |

10.13 The conditional tense

The conditional tense (see 10.1 for the conditional as a mood in French), as its name suggests, is mainly used to describe events which would only take place if specific conditions were met. In the sentence 'If she went to Paris she *would get* a better job', the verb 'would get' is in the conditional tense. In this case the girl's job prospects are conditional on the move to Paris. The conditional is also used when expressing oneself politely, as in 'Would you like a drink?', and for expressing the future as seen from the past, as in 'He said he would leave'. In English we place the auxiliary verb 'would' or 'should' before the infinitive to form the conditional.

10.13.1 Formation

The conditional is formed from the infinitive of the verb plus the endings of the imperfect indicative, except for irregular verbs. The formation of the conditional is therefore similar to that of the future: *Je couperais, il remplirait, vous tendriez . . .*

1st group: gagner

Number and person		Infinitive	Endings	Conjugated verb
singular	je	gagner	**-ais**	je gagnerais
	tu	gagner	**-ais**	tu gagnerais
	il / elle	gagner	**-ait**	il / elle gagnerait
plural	nous	gagner	**-ions**	nous gagnerions
	vous	gagner	**-iez**	vous gagneriez
	ils / elles	gagner	**-aient**	ils / elles gagneraient

2nd group: finir

Number and person		Infinitive	Endings	Conjugated verb
singular	je	finir	**-ais**	je finirais
	tu	finir	**-ais**	tu finirais
	il / elle	finir	**-ait**	il / elle finirait
plural	nous	finir	**-ions**	nous finirions
	vous	finir	**-iez**	vous finiriez
	ils / elles	finir	**-aient**	ils / elles finiraient

3rd group: perdre

Number and person		Infinitive	Endings	Conjugated verb
singular	je	perdr	**-ais**	je perdrais
	tu	perdr	**-ais**	tu perdrais
	il / elle	perdr	**-ait**	il / elle perdrait
plural	nous	perdr	**-ions**	nous perdrions
	vous	perdr	**-iez**	vous perdriez
	ils / elles	perdr	**-aient**	ils / elles perdraient

Auxiliary verb avoir

Number and person		Radical	Endings	Conjugated verb
singular	j'	aur	**-ais**	j'aurais
	tu	aur	**-ais**	tu aurais

Number and person		Radical	Endings	Conjugated verb
	il / elle	aur	**-ait**	il / elle aurait
plural	nous	aur	**-ions**	nous aurions
	vous	aur	**-iez**	vous auriez
	ils / elles	aur	**-aient**	ils / elles auraient

Auxiliary verb être

Number and person		Radical	Endings	Conjugated verb
singular	je	ser	**-ais**	je serais
	tu	ser	**-ais**	tu serais
	il / elle	ser	**-ait**	il / elle serait
plural	nous	ser	**-ions**	nous serions
	vous	ser	**-iez**	vous seriez
	ils / elles	ser	**-aient**	ils / elles seraient

KEY POINT

The conditional describes a future action from the perspective of the past:

Elle pensait sincèrement que ses poèmes la **rendraient** célèbre.	She sincerely thought that her poems would make her famous.

10.13.2 Uses

The conditional:

▶ is used in indirect speech when the main verb is in the past; in direct speech the future would be employed.

Direct speech	Indirect speech
Il **pensa**: « Ce **sera** plus simple de prendre le train. »	Il **pensait** que ce **serait** plus simple de prendre le train.
He thought: 'It will be simpler to take the train.'	He thought that it would be simpler to take the train.

▶ has a future sense when related to a verb in a past tense, i.e., it is a 'future in the past':

Le professeur montrait les exercices que les étudiants **auraient** à résoudre la semaine suivante.	The teacher showed the exercises that the students would have to work out the following week.

▶ expresses politeness, as in English:

Je **voudrais** vous parler un instant, **auriez-vous** l'obligeance de m'attendre après la réunion ?	I'd like to speak to you for a moment; would you please wait for me after the meeting?

▶ expresses what would happen if a condition is met:

J'accepterais volontiers ce travail si j'étais mieux payé.	I'd accept this work willingly if I was better paid.

▶ expresses an unsubstantiated statement (often in the media):

Les premières estimations montrent que l'opposition **perdrait** 200 sièges à l'issue de ce second tour.	The first estimates indicate that the opposition would lose 200 seats at the end of the second round.

▶ is used in sentences where the conjunction joining two statements is omitted. Both clauses may be in the conditional:

Il **présenterait** ses excuses, je ne l'**écouterais** pas.	He would give his apologies, I wouldn't listen to him.

In this sense it resembles the following type of structure:

Même s'il présentait ses excuses, je ne l'**écouterais** pas.	Even if he gave his excuses I wouldn't listen to him.

10.13.3 Sequence of tenses

When a conditional clause introduced by *si* is in the past, the conditional can be used in the main clause:

S'il faisait beau j'**irais** à la plage.	If it was fine I'd go to the beach.

10.14 The compound conditional

10.14.1 Formation

The auxiliary *avoir* or *être* in the conditional + the past participle.

1st group: gagner

Number and person		Auxiliary	Past participle	Conjugated verb
singular	j'	**aurais**	gagné	j'aurais gagné
	tu	**aurais**	gagné	tu aurais gagné
	il / elle	**aurait**	gagné	il / elle aurait gagné
plural	nous	**aurions**	gagné	nous aurions gagné
	vous	**auriez**	gagné	vous auriez gagné
	ils / elles	**auraient**	gagné	ils / elles auraient gagné

2nd group: finir

Number and person		Auxiliary	Past participle	Conjugated verb
singular	j'	**aurais**	fini	j'aurais fini
	tu	**aurais**	fini	tu aurais fini
	il / elle	**aurait**	fini	il / elle aurait fini
plural	nous	**aurions**	fini	nous aurions fini
	vous	**auriez**	fini	vous auriez fini
	ils / elles	**auraient**	fini	ils / elles auraient fini

3rd group: descendre

Number and person		Auxiliary	Past participle	Conjugated verb
singular	je	**serais**	descend**u(e)**	je serais descendu(e)
	tu	**serais**	descend**u(e)**	tu serais descendu(e)
	il / elle	**serait**	descend**u(e)**	il / elle serait descendu(e)
plural	nous	**serions**	descend**u(e)s**	nous serions descendu(e)s
	vous	**seriez**	descend**u(e)(s)**	vous seriez descendu(e)(s)
	ils / elles	**seraient**	descend**u(e)s**	ils / elles seraient descendu(e)s

Auxiliary verb avoir

Number and person		Auxiliary	Past participle	Conjugated verb
singular	j'	**aurais**	**eu**	j'aurais eu
	tu	**aurais**	**eu**	tu aurais eu
	il / elle	**aurait**	**eu**	il / elle aurait eu
plural	nous	**aurions**	**eu**	nous aurions eu
	vous	**auriez**	**eu**	vous auriez eu
	ils / elles	**auraient**	**eu**	ils / elles auraient eu

Auxiliary verb être

Number and person		Auxiliary	Past participle	Conjugated verb
singular	j'	**aurais**	**été**	j'aurais été
	tu	**aurais**	**été**	tu aurais été
	il / elle	**aurait**	**été**	il / elle aurait été
plural	nous	**aurions**	**été**	nous aurions été
	vous	**auriez**	**été**	vous auriez été
	ils / elles	**auraient**	**été**	ils / elles auraient été

KEY POINT

The compound conditional expresses a hypothetical situation, referring to an event which would have taken place:

J'**aurais pu** marcher avec eux mais je m'étais blessé le genou la veille.	I would have been able to walk with them but I had injured my knee the day before.

10.14.2 Use of the compound conditional

The compound conditional:

▶ describes past events which could not be fulfilled, unlike the conditional:

▶ regret or remorse: *J'aurais aimé être plus grand.*   I would have loved to be taller.

▶ a reproach: *Tu aurais dû y penser plus tôt !*   You should have thought about it sooner!

▶ a condition: *Si j'avais sauvegardé régulièrement mes documents je n'aurais pas perdu deux mois de recherche.*   If I had saved my documents regularly I wouldn't have lost two months of research.

▶ a hypothesis: *Si j'avais étudié correctement les mathématiques j'aurais pu travailler à la City.*   If I had studied maths properly I'd have been able to work in the City.

▶ expresses possibility or uncertainty:

▶ in an unsubstantiated statement (often in the media) about a past fact: *Les bombes auraient causé la mort de plus de 100 personnes.*   The bombs would have caused the deaths of 100 people.

▶ is used in indirect speech, when the main verb is in the past. In this case, in direct speech the compound future would be used.

Direct speech	Indirect speech
Il pensa: « j'aurai fini mon rapport avant la nuit. »	*Il pensait qu'il aurait fini son rapport avant la nuit.*
He thought: 'I'll have finished my report before nightfall.'	He thought that he would have finished his report before nightfall.

Notes

▶ The compound conditional in conditional clauses

In these clauses, the compound conditional combines with the pluperfect and describes a condition that has not been fulfilled:

Si j'avais su j'aurais suivi un cours d'informatique.	If I'd known I would have followed a course on computing.
Si tu étais venu à l'heure tu aurais eu une place assise.	If you'd come on time you would have had a seat.

▶ A second form of the compound conditional also exists but is rarely used (mostly in written French). It is used in practically the same way as the compound conditional described above. It is formed from the auxiliary *avoir* or *être* in the imperfect subjunctive plus the past participle: *j'eusse gagné, fini, descendu,* etc.

10.15 Summary of the sequence of tenses in conditional clauses

	Subordinate clause	Main clause	Meaning	Example
1	*Si* + present	simple future	certainty	*S'il fait beau, j'irai me promener.* If the weather's good I'll go for a walk.
2	*Si* + imperfect	conditional	present action impossible future action possible	*S'il faisait beau, j'irais me promener.* If the weather were good I'd go for a walk.
3	*Si* + pluperfect	compound conditional	past action impossible	*S'il avait fait beau hier, je serais allé me promener.* If the weather had been good yesterday, I'd have gone for a walk.

INDICATIVE TENSES IN CONTEXT

"Ils **sont apparus**, comme dans un rêve, au sommet de la dune, à demi cachés par la brume de sable que leurs pieds **soulevaient**. Lentement, ils **sont descendus** dans la vallée, en suivant la piste presque invisible."

Cet extrait est tiré de *Désert*, de J.M.G Le Clézio, un livre qui **combine** deux histoires tragiques de l'Afrique du Nord. Le livre **a obtenu** le prix Renaudot en 1980. Mais dès son premier roman Le Clézio **frappait** fort puisqu'il **obtenait** déjà le prix Renaudot pour *Le Procès verbal*. Il **était passé** très près du prix Goncourt. Il n'**avait** alors que 23 ans. En effet, Le Clézio **naquit** en avril 1940, à Nice, d'un père britannique et d'une mère bretonne. En 2008 il **obtiendra** le prix Nobel de littérature.

Mais qu'**aurait été** la littérature française si ce livre remarquable que **fut** *Désert* n'**avait vu** le jour? Que **serait** le monde littéraire francophone aujourd'hui si Le Clézio n'**avait fait** tache d'huile sur nombre de jeunes auteurs? Car il s'**agit** bien là d'un livre universel qui **a voulu** faire la part belle aux cultures du monde. Un livre singulier qui **marie** classicisme et modernisme. Le Clézio s'**était** déjà **écarté** du formalisme du roman avec *Le Procès verbal*, mais avec *Désert* nous entrons dans la littérature des contrastes et de la tension créatrice. *Désert* **est** à la fois roman merveilleux et roman noir, à la fois poème et tragédie.

sont apparus, sont descendus	compound past of verbs conjugated with *être* [10.6.2]
soulevaient, frappait, obtenait, avait	imperfect tense [10.5.1]
combine, s'agit de, marie, entrons, est	present tense [10.4]
a obtenu, a voulu	compound past of verbs conjugated with *avoir* [10.6.1]
était passé	pluperfect of verb conjugated with *être* [10.9.1]
naquit, fut	simple past tense of *naître* and *être* [10.7]
obtiendra	irregular future tense of *obtenir* [10.11]
aurait été	compound conditional tense of *être* [10.14.1]
avait vu, avait fait	pluperfect tense of *voir* and *faire*, with irregular past participles [10.9.1]
serait	irregular conditional of *être* [10.13]
s'était écarté	pluperfect tense of pronominal verb, conjugated with *être* [10.9]

EXERCISES

1. **Fill the blanks using the tense in brackets:**

    1. *Hier (je — prendre) _____ le train pour le sud* (compound past).
    2. *(Je — retourner) _____ la semaine suivante* (compound past).
    3. *Dans un mois (nous — reprendre) _____ les cours* (compound future).
    4. *Mais avant (je — repartir) _____ bien _____ une semaine* (compound conditional, first form).
    5. *Hélas, pour cela (il — falloir) _____ de l'argent* (present).
    6. *(Je — pouvoir) _____ en demander à mes parents* (conditional).
    7. *(Je — demander) _____ leur / déjà / beaucoup* (compound past).
    8. *(Il — être) _____ un temps* (simple past) *où (je — demander) _____ sans vergogne* (imperfect).

9. *Maintenant (je — préférer)* _____ *me débrouiller seul (conditional).*
10. *(On — voir)* _____ *(future) ! D'ici là (je — trouver)* _____ *une solution (compound future).*

2. **Put the verbs in brackets in the appropriate tense, either the imperfect or the compound past:**

    1. *Ce café (être) trop mauvais, je ne le (boire) pas.*
    2. *On (rire) bien hier, mais il (ne pas faire) beau de toute la journée.*
    3. *En quelle année vous (se marier) ?*
    4. *Vous (arriver) pendant que je (dormir).*
    5. *Je (ne pas entendre) le téléphone, je (dormir) toute la matinée.*
    6. *Nous (aller) la voir trois fois mais elle (n'être jamais) là.*
    7. *Je (vouloir) bavarder avec lui mais il (partir) trop vite.*
    8. *Où vous (aller) hier pendant que je (écrire) mes lettres ?*
    9. *Hier il (emprunter) la voiture de ses parents car ses amis l'(attendre) depuis une heure.*
    10. *Je (aimer) bien lire le journal les matins au petit déjeuner quand je (être) en stage.*

3. **Put the verbs in brackets in the appropriate tense, either the imperfect or the past simple:**

    1. *Je (dormir)* _____ *quand soudain le téléphone (sonner)* _____ *.*
    2. *Ils (arriver)* _____ *au moment où je (se laver)* _____ *les mains pour passer à table.*
    3. *Nous (avoir)* _____ *l'habitude de lui rendre visite souvent.*
    4. *En entendant le bruit, le chat (prendre)* _____ *la fuite.*
    5. *Dès que je (sortir)* _____ *sur le balcon, l'oiseau (s'envoler)* _____ *dans un éclair.*
    6. *Tous les matins en sortant je (faire)* _____ *attention à bien fermer la porte.*
    7. *En un instant les nuages (s'accumuler)* _____ *et il (se mettre)* _____ *à pleuvoir. Nous (devoir)* _____ *courir nous abriter.*
    8. *Ils (rentrer)* _____ *chaque jour en autobus.*
    9. *Grand-père (s'arrêter)* _____ *toutes les demi-heures pour reprendre son souffle.*
    10. *Il (se coucher)* _____ *tard tous les soirs, mais il (comprendre)* _____ *très vite qu'à ce rythme son travail en pâtirait.*

11 VERBS 3: THE IMPERATIVE, THE INFINITIVE, PARTICIPLES

11.1 The imperative

The imperative mood of the verb is used to express commands, warnings, advice, requests, etc. 'Come on!', 'Don't be foolish!', 'Light the touch paper and stand back', 'Let's see' are all examples of imperatives.

KEY POINTS

✦ In French the imperative is used in a similar way as in English, but the verb forms which express the imperative are more complex.

✦ Object pronouns are placed *after* the verb in affirmative imperatives, but *before* the verb in negative imperatives:

Donne-lui *les bonbons !*	Give him the sweets!
*Ne **lui donne** pas les bonbons !*	Don't give him the sweets!

11.1.1 Formation

▶ There are two forms of the imperative, **present** and **past**.

▶ The imperative is conjugated in three persons:

Second person singular	*Regarde !*	Look! (informal)
First person plural	*Regardons !*	Let's look!
Second person plural	*Regardez !*	Look! (formal singular or plural)

▶ There is no subject pronoun before the verb.

The present imperative

The present imperative is formed from the radical of the present indicative, adding the following endings:

the second person singular: *-e* or *-s*

the first person plural: *-ons*

the second person plural: *-ez*

Person	**-er** verbs *parler* (to speak)	**-ir** verbs *finir* (to finish)	**-re** verbs *descendre* (to go down)	Auxiliary verb *avoir*	Auxiliary verb *être*
2nd sing.	*Parle !*	*Finis !*	*Descends !*	*Aie !*	*Sois !*
1st pl.	*Parlons !*	*Finissons !*	*Descendons !*	*Ayons !*	*Soyons !*
2nd pl.	*Parlez !*	*Finissez !*	*Descendez !*	*Ayez !*	*Soyez !*

Notes

▶ The *-er* group of verbs, *aller*, *avoir* and all verbs ending in a silent syllable (/ə/) in the second person singular of the present indicative (verbs like *cueillir* [to pick], *offrir* [to offer] and *savoir* [to know]) do not add *-s* in the imperative singular: *Cherche !* (Look!), *Aie !* (Have!), *Va !* (Go!), *Sache !* (Know!), *Offre !* (Offer!), *Cueille !* (Pick!).

▶ When, however, these verbs are followed by the pronouns *y* or *en* they add *-s*, and are linked to the pronoun by a hyphen.

Parles-en à ton père !	Talk to your father about it!
Vas-y !	Go on!
Cueilles-en plusieurs !	Pick several (of them)!
Accompagnes-y tes enfants !	Go there with your children!

▶ Verbs like *s'en aller* (to go away) become *Va-t'en !* (Go away!), *Ne t'en va pas !* (Don't go away!) in the informal imperative (see irregular verbs below).

Position and order of pronouns with the imperative

▶ In the affirmative:

  ▶ pronouns follow the verb and are linked to it by a hyphen;

  ▶ the direct object pronouns *me*, *m'*, *te*, *t'*, become the stressed pronouns *moi*, *toi*, **except** when *moi* and *toi* are followed by **en** or **y**; when this happens they revert to *m'* and *t'*: *m'en*, *t'en*; *m'y*, *t'y*.

– *J'ai trouvé des macarons.*	I've found some macaroons.
– *Ah! Donne-**m'en** quelques-uns.*	Ah! Give me some.
*Mets-**t'y**, mais fais attention.*	Go [lit. place yourself] there, but pay attention.

▶ In the **negative**, object pronouns are placed before the verb, between **ne** and the verb, without a hyphen.

▶ In **pronominal verbs**, *te*, *t'*, *nous*, *vous* follow the same rules.

	Affirmative imperative	Negative imperative
Puis-je finir les frites ? May I finish the chips?	*Finissez-les !* Finish them!	*Ne les finissez pas !* Don't finish them!
Devrai-je être à la gare aussi ? Will I have to be at the station too?	*Allez-y !* Go there!	*N'y allez pas !* Don't go there!
Dois-je faire de la publicité sur cette affaire ? Must I tell everybody about that business?	*Parlez-en partout !* Spread it everywhere!	*N'en parlez à personne.* Don't speak about it to anyone.
Dois-je t'attendre ? Must I wait for you?	*Attends-moi !* Wait for me!	*Ne m'attends pas !* Don't wait for me!
Dois-je me lever ? Do I have to get up?	*Lève-toi!* Get up!	*Ne te lève pas.* Don't get up.

▶ When the affirmative imperative is followed by two pronouns, the direct object pronoun is placed before the other pronoun. The pronouns are linked to the verb by hyphens.

▶ In the negative, object pronouns are placed before the verb, in the same order but without a hyphen.

▶ If the object is *en*, it will always be in second position.

	Affirmative imperative	Negative imperative
Dois-je lire l'histoire aux enfants ? Must I read the story to the children?	*Lisez-la-leur !* Read it to them!	*Ne la leur lisez pas!* Don't read it to them!
Dois-je lire des histoires à cet enfant ? Must I read stories to that child?	*Lisez-lui-en !* Read some to him!	*Ne lui en lisez pas !* Don't read any to him!
Dois-je m'en aller ? Must I go away?	*Allez-vous-en !* Go away!	*Ne vous en allez pas !* Don't go away!

Past imperative

Formation

Avoir or *être* in the present imperative plus the past participle of the verb:

Person	*-er* verbs *parler*	*-ir* verbs *finir*	*-re* verbs *descendre*	*avoir*	*être*
2nd sing.	*aie parlé !*	*aie fini !*	*sois descendu(e) !*	*aie eu*	*aie été*
1st pl.	*ayons parlé !*	*ayons fini !*	*soyons descendu(e)s !*	*ayons eu*	*ayons été*
2nd pl.	*ayez parlé !*	*ayez fini !*	*soyez descendu(e)(s) !*	*ayez eu*	*ayez été*

Note

Pronominal verbs have no past imperative.

The past imperative is little used. It functions in the same way as the present imperative, but it expresses the prior nature of the action in relation to a date, fact or another future action:

Aie fini ton devoir avant d'aller au lit !	Have your homework finished before going to bed!
Soyez revenus avant 8 heures !	Be back before 8 o'clock!

Some imperatives of irregular verbs

	2nd person singular	**1st person plural**	**2nd person plural**
aller (to go)	*va !*	*allons !*	*allez !*
faire (to do, make)	*fais !*	*faisons !*	*faites !*
savoir (to know)	*sache !*	*sachons !*	*sachez !*
venir (to come)	*viens !*	*venons !*	*venez !*
vouloir (to wish)	*veuille !*	–	*veuillez !*
Verbs of the *s'en aller* type			
s'en aller (to go away)	*va-t'en !*	*allons-nous-en !*	*allez-vous-en !*
s'en faire (to worry)	*fais-t'en !*	*faisons-nous-en !*	*faites-vous-en !*
s'en remettre (à quelqu'un / quelque chose) (to leave it to someone/thing)	*remets-t'en !*	*remettons-nous-en !*	*remettez-vous-en !*
s'en sortir (to cope)	*sors-t'en !*	*sortons-nous-en !*	*sortez-vous-en !*

(See also 'Verb tables' on p. 422.)

11.1.2 Uses

The imperative is used to express:

▶ an order

Sortez *immédiatement de là !*	Come out of there at once!
Veuillez *montrer vos passeports, s'il vous plaît !*	Show your passports, please!

▶ a prohibition

Ne piétinez pas *les plates-bandes !*	Don't walk on the flower-beds!

▶ a piece of advice

N'oublie *pas ton écharpe, il risque de faire froid.*	Don't forget your scarf; it might get cold.

▶ a prayer

Laissez*-moi, je vous prie, un peu plus de temps !*	Let me have a little more time, I beg you!

▶ instructions

Sortez la carte SIM de votre ancien portable et **insérez**-la dans le nouvel appareil. **Appuyez** ensuite sur la touche dièse en bas, à droite.	Take out the SIM card from your old mobile and insert it into the new one. Then press the hash key, bottom right.

▶ a suggestion disguised as an order

Change de compagnie de téléphone, mon cher, cela te coûtera moins cher.	Change your phone company, dear; it will be cheaper for you.

▶ a polite formula

Veuillez agréer, Monsieur / Madame, l'expression de mes sentiments les meilleurs …	Yours sincerely

▶ a condition in statements like:

Travaille et tu seras récompensé.	lit. Work and you will be rewarded.
Aide-toi et le ciel t'aidera.	God helps those who help themselves.

Note

A few verbs, such as *devoir* and *pouvoir*, do not have an imperative.

11.2 The infinitive

The infinitive is the form of the verb which is not inflected, and the one always given in the dictionary. In English the infinitive consists of two words, the first of which is always 'to' and the second of which is the verb, e.g. 'to smile', 'to remain'.

KEY POINTS

In French the infinitive form of the verb:

✦ consists of one word

✦ ends in either -er, -(o)ir or -re:

chanter (to sing), finir (to finish), vivre (to live)

✦ is invariable

✦ is impersonal

✦ can also function as a noun.

11.2.1 The infinitive and the past infinitive

▶ The infinitive can express both present and past time:

Cela fait deux heures qu'il cherche à te **joindre**.	He's been trying to get hold of you for two hours.

▶ The past infinitive expresses a completed action:

Après **avoir marché** toute la nuit, il aspirait à un repos bien mérité.	Having walked the whole night, he was looking forward to a well-earned rest.

▶ Unlike verb tenses, the infinitive:

▶ has no inflections;

▶ does not have a subject except in particular circumstances.

11.2.2 Forms

The infinitive

There are three groups. Note that group 3 verbs have three possible endings.

Group	Ending	Examples
1 about 90% of all verbs	-er except *aller* (to go)	*arriver* (to arrive)
2	-ir (with -issant as the ending of the present participle) + *maudire* (to curse)	*rajeunir* (to make young), *vieillir* (to grow old), *définir* (to define)
3	-re, -oir, -ir (with -ant as the ending of the present participle)	*devenir* (to become), *prévoir* (to foresee), *asseoir* (to sit), *conduire* (to drive), *faire* (to do, make), *éteindre* (to switch off), *inclure* (to include), *dissoudre* (to dissolve)

The past infinitive

Formation

The infinitive of *avoir* or *être* plus the past participle. The past participle follows the rules for the agreement of the past participle (see 11.6.4):

Pour l'avoir lavée très souvent sa voiture est comme neuve.	His car is like new because he's washed it so often.

Group	Auxiliary	Past participle	Conjugated verb
-er	*avoir*	gagné	*avoir gagné*
-ir (-iss-)	*avoir*	fini	*avoir fini*
-re	*être*	descendu	être descendu
avoir	*avoir*	eu	*avoir eu*
être	*avoir*	été	*avoir été*

The past infinitive, which expresses a completed action, can indicate a prior temporal relationship with any past period. It is often associated with the preposition *après*:

Après avoir cherché partout, il a enfin trouvé ses clés.	After having looked everywhere, he finally found his keys.

The compound past infinitive

If the idea of completion is to be insisted on, the verb can be put in the compound past infinitive. The auxiliary of the past infinitive is then itself put into the past, giving a double auxiliary:

Après avoir eu marché longtemps il atteignait enfin la ville.	After having walked for a long time he finally reached the village. [lit. After having had walked . . .]

11.2.3 Uses of the infinitive

▶ In instructions, explanatory notices and recipes it can replace the imperative:

Voir page 26.	See page 26.
Agiter le flacon avant de s'en servir.	Shake the bottle before use.
Couper les avocats en dés, ajouter quelques gouttes de citron et servir avec quelques feuilles de salade.	Dice the avocados, add a few drops of lemon juice and serve with a few salad leaves.

▶ For 'polite commands' it replaces the imperative:

Ne pas fumer, s'il vous plaît.	Please do not smoke.
Ne pas se garer devant le portail !	Do not park in front of the gate.

▶ After modal verbs such as *vouloir* (to wish), *pouvoir* (to be able), *devoir* (to have to), *savoir* (to know):

J'ai su jouer au poker très jeune.	I knew how to play poker when I was very young.
Je voudrais **pouvoir être** un génie des mathématiques plus tard.	I would like to be able to be a mathematical genius when I grow up.

▶ After verbs such as *aimer* (to like), *adorer* (to love):

Elles adorent faire du sport.	They love playing sport.

▶ After prepositions, except *en*:

À vendre.	For sale.
Ils s'efforcent de faire le bien.	They try hard to do good.

▶ The infinitive of narration, or historical infinitive, is used to make a narrative more vivid and more rapid. It is always used in the present and almost always linked to a past event. The structure employed is: *et* + subject + de + the infinitive:

Le politicien prit le micro. Et les partisans d'applaudir et l'opposition de narguer.	The politician took the microphone. The supporters applauded and the opposition taunted him.

▶ The exclamative infinitive expresses a keenly felt sentiment, a surprise, a reaction:

Moi, **traverser** ce courant à la nage !	Me, swim across against that current! (subjunctive equivalent: *que je traverse ce courant !*)
Me **dire** ça après ce que j'ai fait pour toi !	To say that to me after all I've done for you! (present indicative meaning: You tell me that. . .)

▶ In questions which do not have a subject the infinitive expresses uncertainty or a 'false' question:

Que penser de tout cela ?	What should we think about all that?
Que lui conseiller ?	What shall I advise him/her?
À quoi bon insister ?	What's the point of insisting?

▶ In complex sentences, the infinitive is generally compulsory when the subject of the main clause and that of the infinitive are the same:

Elle cherche à se rapprocher du centre ville.	She is trying to move nearer to the town centre.
Dites-lui de fermer les portes et les fenêtres.	Tell him / her to shut the doors and windows.

▶ With verbs that have two objects such as *dire* (to say), *demander* (to ask), *offrir* (to offer), *souhaiter* (to wish), followed by *quelque chose à quelqu'un* (something to somebody). The object of these verbs can be the subject of the infinitive verb in the subordinate clause. (This also occurs in English: in 'I told him to come early', 'him' is the subject of the infinitive 'to come' and the object of 'told'.)

| *J'ai dit aux membres du comité d'arriver plus tôt.* | I told the members of the committee to arrive earlier. |

▶ In indirect questions:

| *Je lui ai dit où trouver la nappe.* | I told him where to find the tablecloth. |

▶ In subordinate clauses with main clauses containing:

▶ *verbs of perception*: *voir* (to see), *regarder* (to look at), *entendre* (to hear), *écouter* (to listen to), *sentir* (to feel), etc., the order of the infinitive and its subject is interchangeable:

| *Ils regardent impuissants monter les eaux / les eaux monter.* | Powerless, they watch the waters rising. |
| *J'entends un chat miauler / miauler un chat.* | I hear a cat meowing. |

▶ causative verbs of movement such as *emmener* (to take), *envoyer* (to send), *conduire* (to drive):

| *Elle **envoya** son fils **faire** les courses.* | She sent her son to do the shopping. |

▶ after *faire* and *laisser*:

| *Elle a **fait construire** une belle maison.* | She's had a beautiful house built. |

▶ In relative clauses introduced by *où*:

| *Il a oublié l'endroit où prendre le bus.* | He's forgotten where to catch the bus. |

11.2.4 The infinitive as a noun

Some infinitives exist independently as masculine nouns and are accompanied by a determiner.

infinitive as a verb	infinitive as a noun	example
devenir = to become	le devenir = future	*Le devenir de l'Union européenne dépendra de sa capacité à résoudre la crise.* The future of the European Union will depend on its capacity to resolve the crisis.

infinitive as a verb	infinitive as a noun	example
devoir = to have to	*le devoir* = duty / homework	*Il n'a fait que son devoir.* He only did his duty. *Le professeur de français nous donne beaucoup de devoirs.* The French teacher gives us a lot of homework.
manger et boire = to eat and drink	*le boire et le manger* = food and drink	*Ce qui préoccupe l'être vivant c'est bien le boire et le manger.* Food and drink are indeed what concern living beings.
pouvoir = to be able to	*le pouvoir* = power	*Pleins pouvoirs et démocratie sont incompatibles.* Total power and democracy are incompatible.
rire = to laugh	*le rire* = laughter	*Le rire est le propre de l'homme.* Laughter is peculiar to mankind.
savoir = to know	*le savoir* = knowledge	*Les hommes se transmettent leur savoir de génération en génération.* Mankind transmits its knowledge from generation to generation.

11.2.5 Functions of the infinitive as a noun

Infinitives can have all the functions of a noun. Note that the English equivalent is frequently the present participle (see 11.4.1):

▶ Subject:

Escalader des parois abruptes est une activité grisante.	Scaling steep rock faces is an exhilarating activity.

▶ Direct object:

*Elles aiment **voyager**.*	They like travelling.

▶ Indirect object:

*Je rêve de **faire** le tour du monde.*	I dream of travelling around the world.

▶ Second object:

*Il les a laissés **se débrouiller** seuls.*	He let them get along by themselves.

▶ Noun complement:

*Elle a eu le courage de **résister**.*	She had the courage to resist.

▶ Adjective complement:

Tu n'es pas gentil de la **traiter** de la sorte.	It's not nice of you to treat her in that way.

▶ Pronoun complement:

Son seul défaut c'est celui de **manquer** d'humour.	Her only fault is that she lacks a sense of humour.

▶ Adverbial complement

  ▶ of purpose:

Elle a baissé le thermostat pour **faire** des économies.	She's lowered the thermostat to save money.

  ▶ of cause:

Il a perdu trois points sur son permis de conduire pour **avoir refusé** une priorité.	He's lost three points on his driving licence for having ignored a right of way.

  ▶ of manner:

Elle passa devant sans même **regarder**.	She went past without even looking.

  ▶ of time:

Avant d'**arriver**, il savait déjà ce qui l'attendait.	Before arriving he already knew what to expect.

▶ Apposition to a noun:

Je ne souhaite qu'une chose, **trouver** un grand appartement.	I wish for only one thing, to find a big apartment.

11.2.6 Verbs followed by a preposition plus an infinitive

▶ Numerous verbs can be followed by a preposition:

penser à l'été	to think of summer

  ▶ There are often no logical rules for these structures and so it is necessary to learn which preposition goes with which verb. For example:

venir de (faire quelque chose)	to have just (done something)
s'occuper de	to take care of
avoir besoin de	to need

▶ Most French prepositions are followed by a verb in the infinitive:

sans rire !	seriously!
pour se changer	to change (clothes)
afin de comprendre	so as to understand

▶ Some prepositions cannot be followed by verbs, e.g. *avec, sur*.

▶ *en* may be followed by a verb ending in *-ant*, e.g. *en marchant* (while walking):

en venant	while coming

▶ *après* may be followed by the past infinitive:

après avoir fait les calculs	after making the calculations
après être allé à la mairie	after going to the town hall
après s'être baigné	after bathing

▶ Some verbs are followed directly by the infinitive:

  ▶ verbs expressing desire, wishes, will, necessity

vouloir marcher	to want to walk
devoir travailler	to have to work
Il faut chercher . . .	It is necessary to look for . . .

  ▶ verbs of feeling and opinion

aimer danser	to love to dance
préférer nager	to prefer to swim

  ▶ verbs of movement

sortir chercher le pain	to go and fetch the bread
courir prendre le bus	to run to catch the bus

  ▶ verbs of perception

entendre frapper	to hear (something) strike
voir arriver	to see (someone / -thing) arrive

In French, as in English, many verbs are followed by a preposition + infinitive.

*Elle a choisi **de** passer ses vacances à la montagne.*	She chose to spend her holidays in the mountains.
*Il a enfin réussi **à** réparer son vélo.*	He finally succeeded in repairing his bike.

▶ Verbs followed by *à* and *de* + infinitive

The most common prepositions after French verbs are *à* and *de*. Listed below is a selection of commonly used verbs which require a preposition.

Note

In many cases the English equivalent of the French infinitive in these constructions ends in *-ing*.

▶ Verbs followed by *à* + infinitive

arriver à	to manage, to succeed in
avoir à	to have to, must
avoir du mal à	to find it hard to
avoir tendance à	to tend to
chercher à	to seek to, to attempt to
commencer à	to begin to / to begin + -ing
consister à	to consist of (+ -ing)
continuer à (or de)	to continue to / to continue + -ing
décider (quelqu'un) à	to convince (someone) to
être décidé à	to be determined to
hésiter à	to hesitate to
mettre (du temps) à	to take time to
obliger à (or de)	to oblige to
passer (du temps) à	to spend (time) (+ -ing)
penser à	to think about (+ -ing)
renoncer à	to give up (+ -ing)
réussir à	to succeed in (+ -ing)
s'attendre à	to expect
se décider à	to make up one's mind to
s'habituer à	to get used to (+ -ing)

s'intéresser à	to be interested in (+ -ing)
se mettre à	to start (+ -ing)
tarder à	to take a long time to
tenir à	to care about (+ -ing)

*Ce travail **consiste à** classer des dossiers.*	This job consists of filing documents.
*Elle a **appris à** conduire.*	She has learned to drive.
*Il **continue à** (or **de**) chercher encore un peu.*	He's continuing to search for a little longer.
*Elles **se préparent à** sortir.*	They are getting ready to go out.

▶ Verbs followed by *de* + infinitive

accepter de	to accept, agree to
s'agir de	it's a question of (+ -ing)
arrêter de	to finish (+ -ing)
avoir besoin de	to need
avoir envie de	to feel like (+ -ing)
avoir l'intention de	to intend (+ -ing)
avoir peur de	to be afraid (of + -ing)
avoir le temps de	to have the time to
choisir de	to choose to
se contenter de	to be happy (+ -ing)
continuer de (or à)	to continue to / to continue + -ing
décider de	to decide to
défendre de	to forbid to
dire (à quelqu'un) de	to tell (someone) to do
empêcher (quelque chose or quelqu'un) de	to stop (someone or something) from (+ -ing)
essayer de	to try to
être désolé de	to be sorry for (+ -ing)
être obligé de	to be obliged to
s'excuser de	to apologize for (+ -ing)
faire bien de	to be right to do

(continued)

(continued)

finir de	to finish (+ -ing)
interdire de	to forbid to
s'occuper de	to take responsibility for + -ing
oublier de	to forget to
permettre à (quelqu'un) de	to permit (someone) to
prier (quelqu'un) de	to beg (someone) to
rappeler à quelqu'un de	to remind someone to
refuser de	to refuse to
regretter de	to be sorry for (+ -ing)
remercier quelqu'un de	to thank someone for (+ -ing)
se souvenir de	to remember
venir de	to have just

*Il **s'agit de** bien comprendre la situation.*	It is a question of understanding the situation properly.
*Je te **souhaite de** passer de bonnes vacances.*	I hope you have a good holiday.
*Ils **ont fini de** semer.*	They've finished sowing.
*Elle **se souvient d'**avoir visité Venise quand elle était enfant.*	She remembers having visited Venice when she was a child.
*Il **a essayé de** changer le filtre à air.*	He tried to change the air filter.
*Je vous **remercie de** vous occuper aussi bien de mes enfants.*	Thank you for looking after my children so well.
*Mon père ne m'**a pas permis de** voyager seul.*	My father has not allowed me to travel alone.

Note

Some verbs can be followed by à and *de* without any change of meaning; others change their meaning.

Without a change of meaning:

*Il **continue à** travailler / il **continue de** travailler.*	He continues to work / working.

With a change of meaning:

*Je **tiens à** cette bague, elle me vient de ma grand-mère.*	That ring means a lot to me; it was my grandmother's.

Elle **tient de** sa mère.	She takes after her mother.

▶ Other prepositions

　▶ Prepositions other than à or *de* are used to a lesser extent:

Il a **fini par** comprendre.	He has finally understood. [lit. finished by understanding]
Il a **commencé par** faire ce qu'on lui avait dit.	He began by doing what he had been told.
Il **passe pour** être le meilleur de sa catégorie.	He is considered [lit. passes for] the best in his group.

▶ Alternation of *à* and *de*

　▶ Certain verbs have a different structure according to whether they have a direct object or not and according to whether the subject of the infinitive is the same as that of the main clause.

Same subject: Il a **demandé à** rester un peu plus.	He asked to stay a little longer. (permission)
Different subject: Il lui a **demandé de** rester un peu plus.	He asked him to stay a little longer. (order)
Il m'**a obligé à** partir.	He obliged me to leave.
Je **suis obligé de** partir.	I am obliged to leave.

　▶ With neutral or impersonal verbs, *il est* or *c'est* + adjective + infinitive (see 4.1.5), the preposition can be either *à* or **de**:

　　○ When the subject is neutral, i.e., it refers to something previously mentioned, and the infinitive has a passive meaning, *à* is used:

Un problème comme celui-là, c'est toujours difficile **à** resoudre.	A problem like that is always difficult to resolve.

　　○ When the subject is impersonal, i.e., not related to anything previously mentioned or understood, *de* is used:

Il est essentiel **de** connaître sa version des faits.	It is essential to know her version of the facts.
Il est honteux **de** mentir.	It is shameful to lie.

▶ Similarly, the following neutral or impersonal expressions are followed by either *à* or **de:**

Il est difficile / C'est difficile (à / de ...)	It's difficult (to ...)
Il est facile / C'est facile (à /de ...)	It's easy (to ...)
Il est impossible / C'est impossible (à / de ...)	It's impossible (to ...)
Il est possible / C'est possible (à / de ...)	It's possible (to ...)

11.3 Participles

KEY POINTS

The participle is a verb which takes the form of an adjective.

✦ It functions as a **verb**, followed by the direct and indirect objects and by adverbial phrases, and

✦ as a **verbal adjective**, having all the characteristics of an adjective, including agreement in number and gender.

There are three forms:

Present participle	*chantant* singing
Past participle	*chanté* sung
Compound past participle	*ayant chanté* having sung

Present participle		
verb plus direct object	*Je l'ai vu **cherchant** partout ses lunettes.*	I saw him looking everywhere for his glasses.
adjective	*des histoires **amusantes***	amusing stories
Past participle		
adjective	*une langue parlée*	a spoken language
verb	*Je lui ai parlé déjà.*	I've already spoken to her.

11.4 The present participle

The form of the verb ending in *-ing* in English (talking, drinking, etc.) is called the present participle. This form of the verb is frequently used and very versatile: it can act as part of a verb, 'you're *dreaming*', as an adjective, 'a *sinking* ship' or as a noun, '*swimming* is good exercise'.

In French the part of the verb ending in *-ant* is the equivalent of the present participle. There are some similarities between English and French in the use of the present participle, but important differences also exist.

11.4.1 Formation

Replace the ending *-ons* or *-ez* of the present indicative by the ending *-ant* of the present participle:

Infinitive	1st person plural present indicative	Ending of the present participle	Present participle
parler (to speak)	*nous parl**ons***	*-ant*	*parlant*
réagir (to react)	*nous réagiss**ons***	*-ant*	*réagissant*
voir (to see)	*nous voy**ons***	*-ant*	*voyant*
dire (to say)	*nous dis**ons***	*-ant*	*disant*

The auxiliary verbs *être*, *avoir* and *savoir* have an irregular present participle:

Infinitive	1st person plural present indicative	Ending of the present participle	Present participle
être (to be)	*nous somm**es***	*-ant*	*étant*
avoir (to have)	*nous av**ons***	*-ant*	*ayant*
savoir (to know)	*nous sav**ons***	*-ant*	*sachant*

Notes

▶ The present participle is invariable:

Je l'ai vue sortant du bateau / Je les ai vues sortant du bateau.	I saw her coming off the boat / I saw them coming off the boat.

But in legal language, which has kept some archaic expressions, the present participle is variable: *les ayants droit* (legal claimants), *toute(s) affaire(s) cessante(s)* (forthwith).

▶ The English *-ing* form of the verb ('seeing', 'believing', etc.) often corresponds to an infinitive rather than a present participle:

Avant d'envoyer la lettre n'oublie pas de l'affranchir.	Before sending the letter don't forget to stick a stamp on it.

11.4.2 Meaning and uses

▶ **As a verb,** the present participle expresses **an action** which is **simultaneous** with that of the main verb.

▶ When placed at the beginning of a sentence, the present participle is only possible if it is related to the subject of the main verb:

Prenant son courage à deux mains, il alla parler au directeur.	Taking his courage in both hands, he went to speak to the director. (the same person plucks up courage)

But you cannot say **Prenant son courage à deux mains, je le vis aller parler au directeur.* *Taking his courage in both hands, I saw him go to speak to the director.

▶ The present participle always has an active meaning as a verb; it expresses the present, past or future, depending on the tense of the main verb:

  ▶ Present: *Il arrive **tenant** son journal à la main.* He arrives holding his newspaper in his hand.

  ▶ Past: *Je le vis **tenant** son journal (qui tenait son journal).* I saw him holding his newspaper (i.e., I saw him who was holding . . .)

  ▶ Future: *Je le verrai encore demain **tenant** son journal à la main.* I'll see him tomorrow holding his newspaper in his hand.

▶ It expresses a continuing action but one which is limited in its duration:

*Il lit tranquillement, **fumant** une cigarette.*	He's reading calmly (a continuing action), smoking a cigarette (an action of more limited duration).

▶ The present participle can replace a subordinate relative clause introduced by **qui**:

*Seuls les étudiants **qui ont** la moyenne réussiront.*	Only the students who have (achieved) the average mark will succeed.
*Seuls les étudiants **ayant** la moyenne réussiront.*	Only the students having the average mark will succeed.

▶ The present participle can replace a causal subordinate clause introduced by *puisque* (since), *étant donné que* (in view of the fact that), *parce que* (because), *comme* (as):

Etant donné que sa télévision est en panne il n'a pas pu voir le match.	*Sa télévision étant en panne, il n'a pas pu voir le match.*
In view of the fact that his televison isn't working, he couldn't watch the match.	As his television was not working, he couldn't watch the match.
Il n'est pas allé à l'école parce qu'il était malade. He didn't go to school because he was ill.	*Étant malade, il n'est pas allé à l'école.* Being ill, he didn't go to school.

▶ It can be used with the semi-auxiliary verb *aller* to express the idea of progression or continuity:

Les statistiques montrent que le chômage va croissant.	The statistics show that unemployment goes on growing.

▶ As a verbal adjective

> ▶ It keeps the *-ant* ending of the present participle but with the occasional small change in spelling. The verbal adjective can therefore be spelled differently from the present participle used as a verb:

*Leurs ambitions **différant** (invariable present participle) des nôtres, nous avons rédigé deux projets **différents** (adjective in agreement with plural noun).*	Their ambitions differing from ours, we have drafted two different projects.

> ▶ It functions fully as an adjective and agrees in gender and number:

*Ces tempêtes fréquentes sont **décourageantes**.*	These frequent storms are depressing.
*Il a d'**importantes** informations à nous communiquer.*	He has some important information to tell us.

11.4.3 *The present participle and the verbal adjective contrasted*

Present participle	Verbal adjective
As a **verb**: – it expresses an action and behaves like a verb – its form is invariable. *Je les ai vu **encourageant** leurs équipes.* I've seen them encouraging their teams.	As an **adjective**, formed from the present participle of a verb: – it agrees in gender and number with the noun it qualifies. *J'aime ces attitudes **encourageantes**.* I like these encouraging [i.e., positive] attitudes.

(continued)

(continued)

It can be followed by an object complement:	It can function either as an attributive or predicative adjective (see Chapter 5, Key points):
Je les ai vues **encourageant leurs équipes favorites**. I've seen them encouraging their favourite teams.	*C'étaient des gens* **exigeants**. They were demanding people.
	Ils étaient **exigeants**. They were demanding.
It can be modified by an adverb of manner, time, etc. (except *ne*) placed after it:	It can be modified by a preceding adverb (of degree or other) placed before it:
Je les ai vues **chantant joyeusement**. I've seen them singing cheerfully.	*Elles sont* **souvent perturbantes**. They are often troubling.
It can be replaced by a relative subordinate clause:	It can be replaced by another adjective.
Je les ai vues **chantant** (*qui chantaient*). I've seen them singing.	*Elles sont* **excellentes** (*très bonnes*). They are excellent (very good).
It can be preceded by a reflexive pronoun:	
Il marchait, **se depêchant** *du mieux qu'il pouvait*. They walked, hurrying as best they could.	

Present participles and verbal adjectives with variations in spelling (see 5.13)

▶ Verbs ending in *-ger* form their present participle in *-geant* and their verbal adjective in *-geant* or *-gent*.

▶ Verbs ending in *-guer* form their present participle in *-guant* and their verbal adjective in *-gant*:

Le cyclisme est un sport **fatiguant** *surtout les muscles des mollets.*	Cycling is a sport which tires the calf muscles especially.
Le cyclisme est un sport **fatigant**.	Cycling is a tiring sport.

▶ Verbs ending in *-quer* and *convaincre* form their present participle in *-quant* but some verbal adjectives end in *-cant*:

Les groupes **communiquant** *les informations auront du retard.*	The groups communicating the news will be delayed.
les vases **communicants**	connected vessels

▶ Verbal adjectives ending in *-ent*

    ▷ A number of verbal adjectives end in *-ent* instead of *-ant*. The present participle of these verbs, however, always ends in *-ant:*

*Les pneus d'aujourd'hui sont incontestablement plus **adhérents** que jadis.*	Tyres today have undoubtably got a better grip than in the past.
*Pour votre sécurité il vaut mieux choisir des pneus **adhérant** solidement à la route.*	For your safety it's best to choose tyres which grip the road well.

    ▷ Examples of spelling differences

Present participle	Verbal adjective	Present participle	Verbal adjective
adhérant (becoming a member, gripping)	*adhérent* (binding)	*expédiant* (sending, dispatching)	*expédient* (expedient)
communiquant (communicating)	*communicant* (en suite)	*fatiguant* (making someone tired)	*fatigant* (tiresome, arduous, tiring)
convainquant (persuading, convincing)	*convaincant* (persuasive, convincing)	*influant* (having an influence on)	*influent* (influential)
différant (differing)	*différent* (different)	*négligeant* (neglecting, ignoring)	*négligent* (negligent, careless)
divergeant (diverging, differing)	*divergent* (divergent)	*précédant* (being in front/ahead of)	*précédent* (previous)
équivalant (amounting, being equivalent to)	*équivalent* (identical, equivalent)	*provoquant* (causing, provoking)	*provocant* (provocative)
excellant (excelling in)	*excellent* (excellent, great)		

11.4.4 The compound present participle

Formation

▶ *être* or *avoir* with the present participle plus the past participle of the verb:

*Le prix du gaz **ayant augmenté**, ils réduisirent leur consommation.*	The price of gas having increased they reduced their consumption.

▶ It has roughly the same uses as the present participle.

▶ It expresses an action completed prior to another action:

Ayant ecouté *les informations, il alla se coucher.*	Having listened to the news he went to bed.

11.4.5 Nouns and prepositions derived from the present participle

As a noun	*les tenants et les aboutissants* (the ins and outs)
	un(e) assistant(e) (assistant)
	un(e) débutant(e) (beginner)
	un(e) participant(e) (participant)
	un(e) passant(e) (passer-by)
As a preposition	*pendant le jour* (during the day)
	suivant le cas (as is the case)

11.5 The gerund

11.5.1 Formation

en + the present participle of the verb. The gerund corresponds to 'while (doing)' / 'by (doing)' in English. The subject of both verbs is the same (see 13.5.29):

*Il s'est cogné la tête **en se baissant**.*	He hit his head while ducking.

11.5.2 Uses

The gerund expresses:

▶ Simultaneous or connected actions ('at the moment when'):

*Il a appris la nouvelle **en écoutant** la radio.*	He learned the news while listening to the radio.
*Je me suis blessé(e) **en descendant** du train.*	I injured myself while getting off the train.

▶ Manner or means:

*C'est **en forgeant** qu'on devient forgeron.*	Practice makes perfect.
***En respectant** les autres tu seras respecté.*	By respecting others you will be respected.

▶ Time:

En laçant *ses chaussures il vit le billet sous la table.*	While lacing his shoes he saw the ticket under the table.

▶ Cause:

C'est ce qui arrive **en voulant** *n'en faire qu'à sa tête !*	That's what happens when you want your own way!

▶ Condition:

En arrivant *en avance tu auras la meilleure place.*	By arriving in advance you will get the best seat.

11.5.3 Tout + *gerund*

Tout + *en* + present participle is used to insist on:

▶ Two simultaneous actions:

Elle téléphonait à une amie **tout en cherchant** *à se garer.*	She was telephoning a friend while looking for a parking place.

▶ Two opposing ideas:

Il essaie l'examen **tout en sachant** *qu'il ne réussira pas.*	He is attempting the exam while knowing that he will not succeed.

11.5.4 *The gerund in the negative*

The gerund can be used negatively as follows:

▶ In the usual way, *ne . . . pas* around the present participle:

En **n'arrivant pas** *en avance, il court le risque d'avoir la plus mauvaise place.*	In failing to arrive in advance, he runs the risk of getting the worst seat.

▶ *Sans* + infinitive:

Il a traversé **sans regarder**.	He crossed without looking.

11.5.5 Equivalents in French of the English form of the verb ending in -ing

The form of the verb ending in *-ing* in English is frequently translated by the infinitive or a noun, and not the present participle:

*Il passe son temps à **jouer** aux jeux vidéo.*	He spends his time **playing** computer games.
*Je n'ai aucune intention d'**aller** voir ce film.*	I've no intention of **going** to see that film.
***L'aviron** est le sport que j'aime mieux.*	**Rowing** is the sport I like best.

11.6 The past participle

The past participle is a special form of the verb which can act as an adjective, part of a compound verb and a noun. The past participle in English is usually formed by adding -(e)d to the verb: *look → looked*, etc. but there are many irregular past participles: *find → found, go → gone, make → made*, etc.

The past participle is an *adjective*, as in the phrase 'a lost cause', where 'lost' is the past participle, describing the noun.

The same word acts as a *verb* in the sentence 'We've lost the match'. Here the auxiliary verb 'have' combines with 'lost' to form the perfect tense.

A few *nouns*, such as 'a drunk' and 'the damned' are derived from past participles.

11.6.1 Formation

The past participle of regular verbs is formed by replacing the endings *-er, -ir* and *-re* of the infinitive by *-é, -i* and *-u* respectively:

Infinitive	Radical	Ending	Past participle ending	Past participle
travailler (to work)	*travaill-*	*-er*	*-é*	*travaillé*
bâtir (to build)	*bât-*	*-ir*	*-i*	*bâti*
rendre (to give back)	*rend-*	*-re*	*u*	*rendu*

Most irregular verbs have an irregular past participle. There are no clear rules for their formation but irregular verbs can be grouped according to their endings.

11.6.2 Irregular past participles

▶ Past participle ending in *-é*

Verbs ending in *-er* do not have irregular past participles. The irregular verbs *être* and *naître* are the only verbs which do not belong to this group to have a past participle ending in *-é*.

Infinitive		Past participle	
être	to be	été	been
naitre	to be born	né	born

▶ Past participle ending in -*u*

These verbs form the majority of verbs in the *-re* group, and many verbs ending in -*(o)ir*:

Irregular verb	Past participle	
avoir	eu	had
boire	bu	drunk
connaître	connu	known
courir	couru	run
croire	cru	believed
paraître, apparaître	paru, apparu	seemed, appeared
tenir	tenu	held
apercevoir	aperçu	perceived
vouloir	voulu	wanted
savoir	su	known
pouvoir	pu	been able

▶ Past participle ending in -*is*

Irregular verb	Past participle	
mettre, permettre, commettre	mis, permis, commis	put, allowed, committed
prendre, comprendre, surprendre	pris, compris, surpris	took, understood, surprised

▶ Past participle ending in -*it*

Irregular verb	Past participle	
dire	dit	said, told
conduire	conduit	driven
écrire	écrit	written
instruire	instruit	taught

▶ Past participle ending in *-ert*

Irregular verb	Past participle	
ouvrir	*ouvert*	open, opened
offrir	*offert*	offered
souffrir	*souffert*	suffered

▶ Other irregular verbs

Irregular verb	Past participle	
suivre	*suivi*	followed
faire	*fait*	done, made
atteindre	*atteint*	reached
joindre	*joint*	joined

11.6.3 Nouns derived from past participles

As with the present participle, nouns are frequently derived from past participles:

produire (to produce)	*un produit* (product)
permettre (to permit)	*un permis* (permit)
faire (to do, make)	*un fait* (deed)
vivre (to live)	*un vécu* (personal experiences)
se tenir (to stand)	*une tenue* (clothes)
suivre (to follow)	*un suivi* (follow-up, monitoring)
devoir (to have to)	*un dû* (due)
découvrir (to discover)	*un découvert* (overdraft)
acquérir (to acquire)	*un acquis* (gain)

▶ Uses

   ▶ to form compound tenses with the auxiliaries *avoir* and *être*:

J'ai parlé devant un large public.	I spoke to a large audience.

   ▶ to form the passive voice with the auxiliary *être*:

Ce livre est très apprécié par ses lecteurs.	This book is much loved by its readers.

Note

In the passive the past participle agrees in gender and number with the subject of the verb:

Ces livres sont très *appréciés* par leurs lecteurs.	These books are much loved by their readers.

▶ the past participle can act as an adjective:

J'ai vu un homme **assis** qui observait des passants **pressés**.	I saw a man sitting down, observing people who were hurrying past.

11.6.4 Agreement of the past participle

In compound tenses such as the compound past, the pluperfect, etc. agreement with the past participle follows certain rules.

▶ Used without an auxiliary verb, the past participle acts as an adjective and agrees in gender and number with the noun or pronoun it qualifies:

l'année **passée**	last year
le participe **passé**	the past participle
Dans notre société nous avons trois voitures **louées** et une **achetée**.	In our company we have three hired cars and one bought car.

▶ When conjugated with *être*, the past participle agrees in number and gender with the subject of the sentence:

Le sort en est **jeté**.	The die is cast.
« Quand la bise fut **venue**, la cigale se trouva fort **dépourvue**. » (La Fontaine)	When the north wind came, the cicada was without food. [lit. deprived]

▶ When conjugated with *avoir*, the past participle does not agree with the subject but with the direct object if, **and only if**, the direct object is placed before the past participle:

  ▶ Direct object after, no agreement: *Nous avons **écrit** cette lettre ensemble.* We wrote this letter together.

  ▶ Direct object before, agreement: *Cette lettre, nous l'avons **écrite** ensemble.* This letter, we wrote it together.

  ▶ Indirect object, no agreement: *Nous leur avons **parlé** nous-mêmes.* We have spoken to them ourselves.

▶ If the past participle is connected with several subjects or objects that are placed before it, agreement is made according to whether they are linked or not by:

  ▶ *et* or a comma: the elements are combined and the participle is in the plural:

Son père et sa mère furent récompens**és** par l'État.	Her father and mother were rewarded by the State.

  ▶ *ou* or *ni*: the elements can be combined or not. When they are, the past participle is in the plural. When they are not, the past participle agrees with the last element:

Ni le père ni la mère ne seront récompens**és**.	Neither the father nor the mother will be rewarded.
Le père ou la mère sera récompens**ée**.	The father or the mother will be rewarded.

▶ With conjunctions of comparison like *comme* (as), *autant que* (as much as), *ainsi que* (as well as), etc. the past participle is in the plural if the elements are combined:

La voiture comme le train sont appréci**és** par les voyageurs.	The car as well as the train are liked by travellers.
C'est Marie autant que Pierre que j'ai appréci**és**.	It's Marie as well as Pierre that I liked.

▶ The past participle agrees with the first element if the elements are not closely linked:

La voiture, comme le train, est appréci**ée** par les voyageurs.	The car, as well as the train, is liked by travellers.
C'est Marie plutôt que Pierre que j'ai appréci**ée**.	It's Marie rather than Pierre that I liked.

Special cases

In certain cases the above general rules do not apply.

▶ Invariable expressions

▶ *Ci-joint*, *ci-inclus* (enclosed, attached) behave like adverbs when they are placed before the noun or pronoun, and so are invariable. They vary in gender and number when placed after the noun or pronoun:

Ci-joint les documents que vous avez sollicités. / Les documents **ci-joints** sont ceux que vous avez sollicités.	The documents that you requested are enclosed. / The enclosed documents are the ones that you requested.
Ci-inclus les lettres demandées / les lettres **ci-incluses**.	Enclosed the letters requested / the enclosed letters.

▶ *Étant donné* (given [that]), *mis à part* (excepting) and *passé* (after) may be either variable or invariable when they are placed before a noun:

Passé *cette date ... /* **Passée** *cette date ...*	Once the date has passed ...
Etant donnés *les faits ... /* **Étant donné** *les faits.*	Given the facts ...

▶ *Attendu* (considering), *compris* (including), *non-compris* (excluding), *y compris* (including), *entendu* (agreed / heard), *excepté* (except), *supposé* (alleged), *vu* (given / considering) are considered as prepositions, and are therefore invariable, when placed before the noun or pronoun. When placed after the noun or pronoun they are variable:

Vu *ses résultats, elle ne sera pas promue.*	Given her results, she won't be promoted.
Tout le monde l'a critiquée, **excepté** *ses amies. / Tout le monde l'a critiquée, ses amies* **exceptées**.	Everyone criticized her except her friends.
Entendu *les témoins, il devrait etre acquitté. / Les témoins* **entendus**, *il devrait être acquitté.*	The witnesses having been heard, he should be acquitted.

▶ The participles *cru* (believed), *dit* (said), *dû* (owed), *pensé* (thought), *permis* (permitted), *prévu* (planned), *pu* (been able), *su* (known), *voulu* (wanted), etc., are invariable when used in a relative subordinate clause, with an infinitive or other clause understood as a direct object. The relative pronoun *que* is then the object of the verb that is understood and not the verb containing the past participle:

Elle a accompli toutes les tâches qu'elle avait **prévu**.	She's carried out all the tasks that she had planned. ([*prévu*] *de faire* is understood).
Il a tenu toutes les promesses qu'il avait **dit**.	He kept all the promises that he had made. ([*qu'il avait dit*] *qu'il tiendrait* is understood).

▶ Agreement of the past participle between *que* and *que* or *que* and *qui* (see 15.1)

　▶ The past participle is invariable when it is preceded by the conjunction *que* and followed by the relative pronoun *qui*:

Les touristes que j'avais prévu qui arriveraient dimanche sont arrivés samedi.	The tourists that I had anticipated would arrive on Sunday arrived on Saturday.

▶ The past participle is invariable when it is preceded by the relative pronoun *que* and followed by the conjunction que:

Les fleurs qu'elle aurait **voulu** *qu'on lui offre ...*	The flowers that she would have wished to be given to her ...

Note

If the first relative pronoun *que* is the direct object complement of the participle, agreement is made in the normal way:

Les personnes que tu as prévenues que je viendrais ...	The people you forewarned that I would come ...

▶ Participles related to measures or estimates such as *coûté* (cost), *valu* (valued), *mesuré* (measured), *marché* (walked), *couru* (ran), *pesé* (weighed), *vécu* (lived), *dormi* (slept), *régné* (reigned), *duré* (lasted) are invariable when they are used intransitively with an adverbial phrase of measurement:

- ▶ *Les 10 ans qu'aura **régné** le roi.* The ten years that the King will have reigned ... (*Les 10 ans* is an adverbial phrase of time, i.e., it answers the question: How long has the King reigned?)

- ▶ *Les 50 livres que ça m'a **coûté**.* The £50 that that cost me. (*Les 50 livres* is an adverbial phrase of degree, i.e., it answers the question: How much did that cost me?)

- ▶ *Les 8 km que j'ai **couru**.* The 8 km that I ran. (*8 km* is not the direct object but an adverbial phrase of **degree**, i.e., it answers the question: How many kilometres have I run?, and not What?)

  But *Les risques que j'ai **courus**.* The risks that I have taken. (There is agreement because *risques* is the direct object and so *courir* is employed transitively.)

  In the same way in: *Les 90 ans qu'elle a **vécu**.* (The 90 years that she has lived), *Les 90 ans* is an adverbial phrase, and so there is no agreement, but in *La vie qu'elle a **vécue*** (The life that she has lived), *La vie* is the direct object and so there is agreement.

▶ *Laisser* and *faire* followed by an infinitive

- ▶ The past participles of *faire* and *laisser* followed by an infinitive are invariable. They are considered as semi-auxiliary verbs:

La maison qu'elle a fait construire.	The house that she has had built.
Il les ont laissé fuir.	He let them run away.

▶ The past participle followed by an infinitive

- ▶ The past participle conjugated with *avoir* and followed by the infinitive agrees with a direct object that precedes the verb, provided it is related to the participle. If the infinitive itself has a direct object the participle also agrees:

*Ces gens, je les ai **vus** peindre ce mur.*	I have seen those people painting that wall.
*Je les ai entend**us** dire des mensonges.*	I have heard them tell lies.

▷ If the direct object relates to the infinitive the past participle is invariable:

| Je les ai prié d'arrêter. | I've pleaded to stop them. |

▷ If the direct object carries out an action expressed by the infinitive, in an active meaning, the past participle agrees. If it 'receives' the action, in a passive meaning, the participle does not agree. In the latter case the sentence could continue by adding an agent, preceded by *par*:

| Les gens que j'ai **vus** peindre. | The people I saw painting. |
| Les murs que j'ai **vu** peindre (par les gens). | The walls I saw being painted (by the people). |

▶ The past participle of impersonal verbs

The past participle of impersonal verbs is invariable:

| La quantité d'eau qu'il a fall**u** | The amount of water that was necessary |

▶ Agreement with *en*

▷ When the object is *en* the past participle is usually invariable, but it can agree with *en*, according to the speaker's intention:

| Des livres, j'**en** ai **lus** des dizaines cet été. | Books, I've read dozens of them this summer. (The focus is on the numbers of books that have been read, therefore plural) |
| Des livres, j'**en** ai cherch**é** partout. | Books, I've looked everywhere for them. (The focus is on the idea of looking for books, therefore singular) |

▶ Agreement with collective nouns

▷ When the antecedent of a relative pronoun is a collective noun, e.g. *groupe* (group), *foule* (crowd), *les trois quarts des* (three quarters of), *la moitié des* (half of), *le tiers des* (a third of), etc., followed by a complement that represents the parts of the collective entity (e.g. young folk, sheep, people, etc.) the past participle agrees either with the collective noun (singular) or with the things represented (plural), according to the intention of the speaker (see 2.1.3):

| un troupeau de moutons que le chien avait poussé vers la bergerie | a flock of sheep that the sheepdog had driven towards the sheepfold (the **flock** is driven towards the sheepfold) |
| un troupeau de moutons qu'on avait tondus | a flock of **sheep** that had been shorn (the **sheep** are shorn) |

Similarly,

La moitié des élèves était restée.	Half the pupils had remained.
La moitié des élèves étaient restés.	Half the pupils had remained.

▶ When the collective noun is *dizaine* (about ten), *douzaine* (a dozen), *centaine* (about a hundred), *une infinité de* (an infinite number of), *un grand nombre de* (a great number of), *la plupart de* (most of), etc., agreement is with the complement:

Une douzaine d'individus que j'avais attendus sur le quai...	A dozen individuals that I had waited for on the platform . . .
Une infinité de lettres que j'ai écrites . . .	An infinite number of letters that I have written . . .

▶ With adverbs of quantity or degree like *peu* (few), *trop* (too much / many), *combien* (how much / many), the past participle agrees in general with the complement (see 7.3.2):

Peu d'élèves sont restés.	Few pupils have remained.
Trop de verres se sont cassés.	Too many glasses were broken.

▶ Agreement with the past participle of pronominal verbs (see 9.4)

All pronominal verbs are conjugated with the auxiliary verb *être* but not all participles agree in the same way.

▶ Verbs that are essentially pronominal like *s'enfuir* (to run away), *se repentir* (to repent) etc., behave like verbs conjugated with *être*, and so the participle agrees with the subject of the verb:

Elles se sont enfuies.	They ran away.

▶ Verbs that are occasionally pronominal behave like verbs conjugated with *avoir* and the participle follows the rule for agreement for all verbs conjugated with *avoir*.

   ▶ If there is no direct object the participle agrees with the reflexive pronoun which refers to the subject:

Elle s'est baignée.	She bathed.

   ▶ If the direct object is placed after the verb, there is no agreement:

Elle s'est lavé les mains.	She washed her hands.

   ▶ If the direct object comes before the verb, the participle agrees:

La patte qu'il s'est cassée . . .	The paw that it broke . . .

▶ Agreement of past participles with double compound tenses

   ▶ Double compound tenses are conjugated with a double auxiliary. These tenses express actions already completed in relation to other actions, themselves carried out previously, for which compound tenses are used:

Quand j'ai enfin eu fini mon travail, j'ai couru voir mon copain.	lit. When I have had finished my work, I ran to see my friend.

   ▶ In the double compound tenses agreement is, in general, only with the last past participle:

Ces injures que soi-disant j'aurais eu proférées.	lit. These insults that I supposedly would have had uttered.

Agreement is, however, permitted with two participles: *Ces injures que soi-disant j'aurais eues proférées.*

▶ Agreement of the past participle with *on*

   ▶ When *on* is the equivalent of *nous* in speech a following past participle with *être* is in the plural (see 4.1.3):

Bien sûr qu'on est pressés.	Of course we're in a hurry!

IMPERATIVES, INFINITIVES AND PARTICIPLES IN CONTEXT

En famille

Mère: Qu'**avez**-vous **fait** à l'école les enfants ?

Pierre: On **s'est ennuyés** terriblement.

Mère: **Allons ! Arrête** de dire des bêtises !

Pierre: Parce que **s'ennuyer** et le **dire**, c'est une bêtise ?

Paul: Nous, on a **ri** au contraire. **Avant d'entrer**, quelqu'un avait **fait** une caricature **très ressemblante** du prof au tableau. Le prof est **entré en regardant** le tableau, et **devinez** ce qui s'est passé !

Mathieu: Il n'a **pu** que se **casser** la figure.

Paul: **Excellente** réponse, mon cher ! En effet, le prof a **trébuché** sur un cartable qui traînait; il a **voulu se retenir** au bureau mais il était trop loin et il n'**a** pas **pu l'atteindre**.

   Remarque bien ! C'est un prof sympa d'habitude, mais **pour avoir perturbé** la classe, il nous a **donné** 30 problèmes de maths **à résoudre**. J'ai **dit** que je n'avais rien fait, mais je n'ai pas **été entendu**. Il n'a rien **voulu savoir**. C'est ce qui arrive quand on veut **jouer** au plus fin, a-t-il **dit**. J'ai donc **dû faire** les exercices en question.

Mère: Bon, les enfants, **éteignez** vos portables, **rangez** vos consoles et **mettons-nous** à table ! Votre père **va arriver** d'un instant à l'autre.

Pierre: **En attendant** je **vais me laver** les mains.

Mère: **Descends sans courir** dans les escaliers ! Et **n'oublie pas d'éteindre** la lumière !

Qu'**avez**-vous **fait** . . . ?	irregular past participle [11.6.2]
On **s'est ennuyés** terriblement.	past participle agreement with **on** = **nous** [11.6.4]
Allons ! Arrête de dire des bêtises !	imperatives in first person plural and second person singular [11.1.1]
Parce que **s'ennuyer** et le **dire** c'est une bêtise ?	infinitives [11.2.5]
Nous, on a **ri** au contraire.	regular past participle -**ir** verb [11.6.1]
Avant d'**entrer** . . .	infinitive after a preposition [11.2.3]
une caricature **très ressemblante**	present participle, verbal adjective [11.4.2/3]
Le prof est **entré en regardant** le tableau,	regular past participle -**er** verb [11.6.1] gerund [11.5.2]
. . . **devinez** ce qui s'est passé !	imperative second person plural [11.1.1]
Il n'a **pu** que **se casser** la figure.	irregular past participle [11.6.2] infinitive after a modal verb [11.2.3]
Excellente réponse,	present participle, verbal adjective [11.4.2/3]
le prof a **trébuché** sur un cartable qui traînait	regular past participle of -**er** verb [11.6.1]
il a **voulu se retenir** au bureau	irregular past participle [11.6.2] infinitive after a modal verb [11.2.3]
il n'**a** pas **pu** l'**atteindre**.	irregular past participle [11.6.2] infinitive after a modal verb [11.2.3]
pour avoir perturbé la classe	past infinitive [11.2.2]
il nous a **donné** 30 problèmes de maths **à résoudre**.	regular past participle of -**er** verb [11.6.1] followed by infinitive preceded by **à** [11.2.6]
J'ai **dit** que . . .	irregular past participle [11.6.2]

je n'ai pas **été entendu**.	past participle of *être* in passive verb [11.6.2]
	regular past participle of **-re** verb [11.6.1]
Il n'a rien **voulu savoir**.	irregular past participle [11.6.2]
	infinitive after a modal verb [11.2.3]
J'ai donc **dû faire** les exercices en question.	irregular past participle [11.6.2]
	infinitive after a modal verb [11.2.3]
Bon, les enfants, **éteignez** vos portables, **rangez** vos consoles et **mettons-nous** à table !	imperatives in second person plural (-ez) and first person plural (-ons) [11.1.1]
Votre père **va arriver** d'un instant à l'autre.	*aller*, verb followed by infinitive [11.2.6]
En attendant je **vais me laver** les mains.	gerund [11.5.2]
	aller, verb followed by infinitive [11.2.6]
Descends sans courir dans les escaliers !	imperative in second person singular [11.1.1] infinitive after *sans* [11.5.4]
Et **n'oublie pas d'éteindre** la lumière !	negative imperative second person singular [11.1.1]
	oublier + *de* + infinitive [11.2.6]

1. The infinitive

Put the sentences into indirect speech:

Example: *Je lui ai dit: « calme-toi ! » Je lui ai dit de se calmer.*

1. *Je lui ai dit: « dépêche-toi ! »*
2. *On nous a dit: « laissez-tomber les sucreries ! »*
3. *Ils nous ont recommandé: « faites vos courses après 18 heures ! »*
4. *Le médecin nous a recommandé: « mangez des fruits et des légumes ! »*
5. *Le médecin m'a conseillé: « pesez-vous régulièrement ! »*
6. *Le médecin m'a conseillé: « prenez votre pouls tous les matins ! »*
7. *Le médecin m'a dit: « ne maigrissez pas trop vite ! »*
8. *Le médecin m'a répété: « ne vous faites pas de soucis ! Reposez-vous ! »*
9. *Mon mari m'a dit: « ne crois pas tout ce que disent les médecins ! »*
10. *J'ai dit à mon mari: « occupe-toi de tes affaires ! »*

2. **The imperative**

    Put the sentences into direct speech:

    Example: *Il nous a dit de nous dépêcher. Il nous a dit: « dépêchez-vous ! »*

    1. *Le professeur nous a demandé de ne pas oublier les livres.*
    2. *Il nous a conseillé de ne pas boire trop de café.*
    3. *Le professeur nous a conseillé de bien réviser le cours.*
    4. *Il nous a suggéré de laisser de côté les trois premiers chapitres.*
    5. *Il nous a précisé de bien penser à apporter une pièce d'identité.*
    6. *Il a répété de ne pas commettre la même faute que l'an dernier.*
    7. *Il a dit d'apporter un dictionnaire.*
    8. *Il a dit d'éviter tout appareil électronique à l'examen.*
    9. *Il a dit ne pas être surpris par le sujet d'examen.*
    10. *Il a dit nous souhaiter bonne chance.*

3. **Present participle and verbal adjective**

    Make the underlined words agree when necessary:

    1. *Les jeunes <u>courant</u> _____ dans la forêt étaient nombreux.*
    2. *Ce sont de bons pneus <u>adhérent</u> _____.*
    3. *En tant que membres <u>adhérant</u> _____ au club, ils ont droit aux réductions.*
    4. *C'est une position <u>fatigant</u> _____ pour les jambes.*
    5. *Ils sont arrivés <u>brûlant</u> _____ de fièvre.*
    6. *Ils sont arrivés <u>parcourant</u> _____ les allées par petts groupes.*
    7. *Les jours <u>précédant</u> _____ son mariage furent moins <u>reposant</u> _____ que les jours le*
        <u>suivant</u> _____.
    8. *Elles ont eu des débuts <u>encourageant</u> _____*
    9. *Ces derniers jours furent plus <u>fatigant</u> _____ que les <u>précédent</u> _____.*
    10. *Elles sont arrivées en <u>chantant</u> _____ à tue-tête.*

12 VERBS 4: THE SUBJUNCTIVE

The subjunctive is one of the *moods* of the verb. It is important to distinguish between moods and tenses, which are sometimes confused. In order to understand the subjunctive mood it is useful to compare it with two other moods, the *indicative* and the *imperative*. Each of these three moods corresponds to a **distinctive attitude in the mind of the speaker** (see 10.1).

Broadly speaking, the indicative is used when the speaker wishes to state a fact or a certainty:

> I know that he is here.

The imperative is for commands:

> Come here!

The subjunctive is for unreality, doubt or hypothesis:

> I wish that Simon were here.

> If I were you I'd apply for the job.

In the last two examples, which show two of the few surviving subjunctive uses in English, the speaker is clearly addressing an unreality (Simon isn't here; I am not you). In both cases the subjunctive form 'were', rather than 'was', is used. It is essential to understand that, unlike in English, the subjunctive is used extensively in French, and **must** be employed in certain circumstances.

KEY POINTS

The fundamental idea that underlies the subjunctive in French is that, in the mind of the speaker, the action of the verb is not a reality. It is therefore the mood of *subjectivity*. Note especially that:

✦ The subjunctive is used, for the most part, in subordinate clauses. The attitude of the subject of the main clause determines whether the verb in the subordinate clause is subjunctive or not.

(continued)

(continued)

✦ The subjunctive is normally used if the action in the subordinate clause is considered to be *doubtful*, *unlikely*, *unreal*, or if a *personal feeling* (such as a wish, fear or order) is expressed towards the action.

✦ For practical purposes it is useful to learn certain expressions and conjunctions after which the subjunctive has to be used.

✦ The subjunctive is not used in all tenses, and there are some differences between its use in writing and speaking.

The following examples compare indicative and subjunctive uses:

Indicative	Subjunctive
Je sais qu'il sera là plus tôt la prochaine fois. I know he will be there earlier next time. (indicative because considered to be a fact by the speaker)	*Je veux qu'il soit là plus tôt la prochaine fois.* I want him to be there earlier next time. (subjunctive because the speaker wishes something to happen)
Les nuits je rêve que nous sommes amis. At night I dream that we are friends. (this actually happens)	*Je doute que vous m'aimiez un jour.* I doubt that you will ever love me. (the speaker is uncertain that something will happen)
Je cache les cadeaux parce qu'il vient. I'm hiding the presents because he's coming. (his coming is a reality)	*Cache les cadeaux de peur qu'il ne vienne !* Hide the presents in case he comes! (the speaker is afraid that something might happen)

Tenses in which the subjunctive is used

There is a marked difference between the use of the subjunctive in speech and in writing:

▶ In **written** French the subjunctive is used in four tenses: the present, the past, the imperfect and the pluperfect.

▶ In **spoken** French, although officially three tenses may be used – the present, the past and double compound past – in fact it is rare for any tense other than the present and past to be heard.

The subjunctive has no future tense.

12.1 The present subjunctive

12.1.1 Formation

The endings of the present subjunctive are as follows for all groups of verbs, except for *avoir* and *être:*

je	**-e**	nous	**-ions**
tu	**-es**	vous	**-iez**
il / elle	**-e**	ils / elles	**-ent**

Note

In the first and second persons plural of the verb, the present indicative of -er verbs and subjunctive are differentiated by the insertion of -*i*- in the subjunctive form. This -*i*- is to be found in all tenses and all verbs of the subjunctive.

▶ **Regular verbs**

  ▶ To form the present subjunctive it is essential to know the *radical* of the verb. For regular verbs:

    1. take the third person plural of the present indicative;
    2. remove the ending, leaving the radical;
    3. conjugate the verb adding the subjunctive endings to the radical.

	Infinitive	3rd person plural of the present indicative	Radical	Examples of endings	Example of subjunctive
-er verbs	*parl-er*	*parl-ent*	*parl-*	-ions	que nous parl**ions**
-ir verbs	*fin-ir*	*finiss-ent*	*finiss-*	-iez	que vous finiss**iez**
-re verbs	*craind-re*	*craign-ent*	*craign-*	-es	que tu craign**es**

▶ Irregular verbs

Some irregular verbs, e.g. *aller*, *savoir*, *tenir*, have irregular radicals (see 10.2). *Avoir* and *être* form the present subjunctive as follows:

		être	**avoir**
que	*je / j'*	*soi-s*	*ai-e*
que	*tu*	*soi-s*	*ai-es*
qu'	*il / elle*	*soi-t*	*ai-t*
que	*nous*	*soy-ons*	*ay-ons*
que	*vous*	*soy-ez*	*ay-ez*
qu–	*ils / elles*	*soi-ent*	*ai-ent*

12.2 The compound past subjunctive

12.2.1 Formation

The compound past subjunctive is formed from the auxiliary verb *avoir* or *être* in the present subjunctive plus the past participle of the verb in question. The formation of the compound past subjunctive is the same for all verbs.

	Infinitive	Perfect indicative	Present subjunctive of *avoir* or *être*	Past participle of the verb	Compound past subjunctive
-er verbs	*march-er*	*j'ai march-é*	*que j'ai-e*	*march-é*	*que j'**aie** marché*
-ir verbs	*atterr-ir*	*j'ai atterr-i*	*que j'ai-e*	*atterr-i*	*que j'**aie** atterri*
-re verbs	*attend-re*	*j'ai attend-u*	*que j'ai-e*	*attend-u*	*que j'**aie** attendu*
verbs conjugated with *être*	*venir*	*je suis ven-u / e*	*que je soi **-s***	*ven-u / e*	*que je **sois** venu / e*

12.3 The imperfect subjunctive

12.3.1 Formation

To conjugate the imperfect subjunctive, it is important to know the simple past form. There are three steps:

1. take the 2nd person singular of the simple past of any verb, regular or irregular
2. take off the -s ending of the 2nd person singular of the simple past
3. add the following endings: -sse, -sses, -^t, -ssions, -ssiez, -ssent

In the third person singular, the circumflex accent will go over the vowel that precedes the 't' ending, e.g *qu'il parlât, qu'il vînt.*

Note

For *–er* verbs, the third person singular of the simple past is distinguished from third person singular of the imperfect subjunctive by the addition of a circumflex accent plus -*t*: *il marcha* → *qu'il marchât*. For all other verbs, the third person singular of the simple past is distinguished from the third person singular of the imperfect subjunctive only by the circumflex accent: *il connut* (he knew) → *qu'il connût*; *il vit* (he saw) → *qu'il vît.*

	Infinitive	2nd person singular of the simple past indicative	Examples of endings	Example of subjunctive
-er verbs	*parl-er*	*parlas*	*-ssions*	*que nous parlassions*
-ir verbs	*fin-ir*	*finis*	*-^t*	*qu'il finît*
-re verbs	*craind-re*	*craignis*	*-sses*	*que tu craignisses*

Auxiliaries être and *avoir*

		être	**avoir**
que	je / j'	*fu-sse*	*eu-sse*
que	tu	*fu -sses*	*eu-sses*
qu'	il / elle / on	*fû-t*	*eû-t*
que	nous	*fu-ssions*	*eu-ssions*
que	vous	*fu-ssiez*	*eu-ssiez*
qu'	ils / elles	*fu-ssent*	*eu-ssent*

12.3.2 Uses

The imperfect subjunctive is used for actions that are simultaneous with or take place after the action of a main verb:

*Depuis son doctorat, elle appréciait qu'on la **considérât** avec autant de respect* (simultaneous)	After her doctorate she was pleased that she was considered with so much respect.
*La prochaine fois, elle souhaiterait qu'on la **considérât** avec plus de respect.* (after)	The next time she would wish to be considered with more respect.

12.4 The pluperfect subjunctive

12.4.1 Formation

The pluperfect subjunctive is a compound tense which is formed by the auxiliary *avoir* or *être* in the imperfect subjunctive followed by the past participle of the verb.

	Infinitive	Imperfect subjunctive of *avoir or être*	Past participle of the verb	Past subjunctive
-er verbs	march-er	que j'eusse	march-é	que j'**eusse** marché
-ir verbs	atterr-ir	qu'il eût	atterr-i	qu'il **eût** atterri
-re verbs	attend-re	que nous eussions	attend-u	que nous **eussions** attendu
verbs conjugated with être	venir	que je fusse	ven-u / e	que je **fusse** venu / e

Pour réussir, il aurait fallu qu'il **eût travaillé** dès le début.	To succeed it would have been necessary for him to work from the beginning.
Pour avoir du bon temps, il fallait qu'elles **fussent venues** plus tôt.	To get good weather, it was necessary for them to have come earlier.

12.4.2 Uses

The pluperfect subjunctive is only found in very formal or literary discourse. It is used when the main clause is in the past and the action of the subordinate clause takes place before that of the main clause:

Elle souhaitait tellement qu'il eût vu des photos de son enfance.	She wished so much that he had seen the photos of her childhood.

12.5 The double compound past subjunctive

12.5.1 Formation

This tense is not used in the written language and scarcely used in the spoken language. The double compound form of verbs applies to almost all compound tenses. It is a compound tense whose auxiliary verb is itself a compound ('double compound').

In the subjunctive, the double compound form is derived from the past subjunctive and the pluperfect subjunctive.

The double compound form is obtained by adding the auxiliary *avoir* in a compound form, its own past participle being followed by the past participle of the verb. There are therefore two consecutive past participles.

Infinitive	Past subjunctive	Auxiliary *avoir* followed by its past participle	Double compound past subjunctive
travailler	*que j'aie travaillé*	*... aie eu ...*	*que j'aie eu travaillé*

Infinitive	Pluperfect subjunctive	Auxiliary *avoir* followed by its past participle	Double compound pluperfect subjunctive
travailler	*que j'eusse travaillé*	*... eusse eu ...*	*que j'eusse eu travaillé*

12.5.2 Uses

Double compound tenses are used mostly in the southern half of France.

These tenses are used to describe completed actions that take place prior to actions that have themselves taken place already before other actions. This is especially true of subordinate clauses of time:

Il fallait qu'il ait eu terminé son essai en moins d'une heure.	lit. He must have had finished his essay in less than half an hour.

Double compound tenses are also used as a form of insistence and they underline the fact that the action took place at a remote time in the past: *Je l'ai eu appris* (lit. I had had learned it) (what is understood is 'I did learn it a long time ago and I've now forgotten it'):

Il fallait que j'eusse eu fini à temps.	lit. It was necessary that I had had finished on time. (What is understood is: It was necessary to have finished on time, now it's too late.)

12.6 Examples of the five subjunctive tenses

Subjunctive tense	Examples
Present	*Je pense qu'il quittera le pays avant qu'on finisse son procès.* I think he'll leave the country before his trial finishes.
Past	*S'il ne veut pas être jugé, il faut qu'il ait quitté le pays avant son procès.* If he doesn't want to be judged he'll have to leave the country before his trial.

(continued)

(continued)

Subjunctive tense	Examples
Imperfect	*Pour éviter le procès, il fallait qu'il quittât le pays avant.* To avoid the trial, it was necessary for him to leave the country beforehand.
Pluperfect	*Il aurait fallu qu'il eût quitté le pays avant son arrestation.* He would have had to leave the country before his arrest.
Double compound past	*Il était hors du pays bien avant qu'on ait eu fini son procès.* He was out of the country well before his trial had finished.

12.7 Uses of the subjunctive

12.7.1 *The subjunctive in subordinate clauses dependent on certain verbs*

Wishes, expectation, orders, permission, prohibition, advice

Wishes, desires, expectation	
vouloir / désirer / souhaiter to wish, want *tenir à** to insist *attendre* to wait *s'attendre à** to expect *avoir envie que* to want, feel like *avoir besoin que* to need	*Je veux qu'il soit plus rapide la prochaine fois.* I want him to be quicker next time. *Il attend que nous nous décidions.* He is waiting for us to make a decision. *Elle s'attend à ce qu'ils finissent les travaux d'un moment à l'autre.* She expects them to finish the work any time now. *Cet enfant a besoin que vous le réconfortiez.* That child needs you to comfort him.

Orders, permission, prohibition	
exiger to demand *ordonner* to order, command *permettre* to allow *admettre* to admit *accepter / consentir à** to accept, agree to *empêcher* to prevent *s'opposer à** / *défendre* / *interdire* to oppose *refuser* to refuse	*J'exige que tu me dises ce qui s'est vraiment passé.* I insist that you tell me what really happened. *Ils consentent à ce que vous preniez la parole . . . Mais ils s'opposent à ce que vous parliez longtemps.* They agree that you should speak . . . But they are against you speaking for a long time. *Je n'accepte pas qu'on nous fasse travailler le dimanche.* I don't agree that we should be made to work on Sundays.

* In the case of verbs and expressions followed by *à*, *que* is preceded by **ce**:

| - *consentir à* **ce** *qu'il l'accompagne.* | to agree that he accompanies them. |
| - *s'attendre à* **ce** *qu'il l'accompagne.* | to expect that he accompanies them. |

Recommendation, advice	
conseiller to advise *recommander* to recommend *suggérer* to suggest *déconseiller* to advise against *recommander* to recommend	*Je suggère que vous changiez toutes les cartouches de votre imprimante.* I suggest that you change all your printer cartridges. *Les dentistes déconseillent que vous donniez trop de bonbons aux enfants.* Dentists advise against giving too many sweets to children.

Note

The verb *espérer* (to hope, expect) is followed by the indicative when used in the affirmative:

| *J'espère qu'il tiendra sa promesse.* | I hope that he will keep his promise. |

It can however be followed by the subjunctive when used in the negative:

| *Je n'ai jamais espéré qu'elle fût si brillante dans ses études.* | I never expected that she would be such a brilliant student. |

▶ Feelings such as love, hate, anger, surprise; judgement

Love, hate, sadness, anger, distress	
aimer to love *détester* to hate *apprécier* to like, appreciate *être impatient que* . . . to be impatient that *être content / heureux / fier que* . . . to be happy / content / proud that *cela fait plaisir que* (I'm) pleased that *être triste / désolé que* . . . to be sad / sorry that *être furieux / fâché / mécontent / déçu que* . . . to be furious / angry / displeased / disappointed that *trouver absurde que / avoir honte que* to find (it) absurd that / to be ashamed that *ne pas avoir le sentiment / l'impression que* not to have the feeling / impression that	*Je suis désolé que vous preniez les choses si mal.* I am sorry that you take things so badly. *Il est fâché que vous ayez échoué au concours.* He's annoyed that you have failed the exam. *Je suis impatient qu'on se mette à table.* I'm eager to sit down to eat.

Surprise, astonishment	
s'étonner to be surprised être étonné / surpris / choqué que . . . to be astonished / surprised / shocked that	*Je suis agréablement surpris que les musées soient gratuits au Royaume-Uni.* I'm agreeably surprised that museum entry is free in the UK.

Appreciation, judgement	
préférer to prefer *il est préférable que* it is preferable that *déplorer* to deplore *regretter* to regret *ne pas être sûr que* not to be sure that *trouver normal / anormal / juste que* to find (it) normal / abnormal / just that	*Je déplore que les trains soient si chers !* I deplore the high cost of rail fares [lit. that trains are so expensive]. *Elles préfèrent qu'on passe par l'autoroute.* They prefer us to take the motorway. *Je trouve anormal qu'il soit si nerveux.* I find it unusual that he's so nervous.

Doubt, fear

Doubt	
douter to doubt	*Je doute qu'ils soient de gauche.* I doubt if they are left-wingers.

Fear	
avoir peur to be afraid *craindre* to fear *redouter* to dread *trembler* to be terrified	*J'ai bien peur qu'il ne* soit encore bloqué dans les embouteillages.* I'm afraid that he may still be held up by traffic jams.

* After verbs of fearing, the verb in the subordinate clause is normally preceded by *ne*. In this case *ne* is redundant and the verb does not have a negative sense.

12.7.2 The subjunctive used after verbs which express a degree of doubt on the part of the speaker.

Verbs like *croire* (to believe), *penser* (to think), *trouver* (to find), *être certain* (to be certain), *être sûr* (to be sure), *se souvenir* (to remember) are followed by the indicative when expressing a fact in the affirmative. However, when these verbs are used in the negative or interrogative in the inverted form they can be followed either by the indicative or (more usually) by the subjunctive, to reflect the additional degree of doubt.

Affirmative	Negative	Interrogative with inversion of the subject
Je trouve qu'ils ont trop dépensé ce mois-ci. I think that they have spent too much this month.	*Je ne trouve pas qu'ils ont trop dépensé ce mois-ci.* (the speaker is sure of his facts) *Je ne trouve pas qu'ils aient trop dépensé ce mois-ci.* (the speaker lacks certainty) I don't think that they have spent too much this month.	*Trouves-tu qu'ils ont trop dépensé ce mois-ci ?* *Trouves-tu qu'ils aient trop dépensé ce mois-ci ?* Do you think that they have spent too much this month?
Il est certain qu'il a fait faillite. It's certain that he has gone bankrupt.	*Il n'est pas certain qu'il a fait faillite.* *Il n'est pas certain qu'il ait fait faillite.* It's not certain that he has gone bankrupt.	*Est-il certain qu'il a fait faillite ?* *Est-il certain qu'il ait fait faillite ?* Is it certain that he has gone bankrupt?
Je me souviens qu'elle a le teint mat. I remember that she has an olive complexion.	*Je ne me souviens pas qu'elle a le teint mat.* I don't remember that she has an olive complexion. (a comment on my memory) *Je ne me souviens pas qu'elle ait le teint mat.* I don't remember that she has a dark complexion. (the speaker has a doubt about the colour of her skin)	*Se souvient-il qu'elle a le teint mat ?* Does he remember that she has an olive complexion? (a question about his memory) *Te souviens-tu qu'elle ait le teint mat ?* Do you remember that she has a dark complexion? (the speaker queries the colour of her skin)
Je crois que le monde va mieux. I think the world is getting better.	*Je ne crois pas que le monde va mieux.* (the speaker contradicts an interlocutor and is sure of his view) *Je ne crois pas que le monde aille mieux.* (the speaker is not very sure of his view) I don't believe the world is getting better.	*Crois-tu que le monde va mieux ?* (the speaker is sure that it is not) *Crois-tu que le monde aille mieux ?* (the speaker is unsure of his view) Do you believe the world is getting better?

The subjunctive is used in the same way after verbs of saying and thinking, such as *dire* (to say), *affirmer* (to assert), *déclarer* (to state), *prétendre* (to maintain), *nier* (to deny).

Affirmative	Negative	Interrogative form with inversion of the subject
Je dis que vous cherchez à m'intimider. I am saying that you are trying to intimidate me.	*Je ne dis pas que vous cherchez à m'intimider.* *Je ne dis pas que vous cherchiez à m'intimider.* I am not saying that you are trying to intimidate me.	*Dis-tu que nous cherchons à t'intimider ?* (Is this your belief?) *Dis-tu que nous cherchions à t'intimider ?* (Is this what you are saying?) Are you saying that we are trying to intimidate you?

12.7.3 The subjunctive after certain conjunctions

▶ Time

avant que + redundant *ne* before the verb *jusqu'à ce que* up to, until *en attendant que* while	*Je dois partir avant qu'il (ne) soit trop tard.* I must leave before it is too late.

Note

après que (after) is followed by the indicative.

▶ Purpose

afin que so that *pour que* so that *de façon que* in such a way as to *de manière que* in such a way as to *de sorte que* (expressing a purpose not a consequence) so that	*Prête-lui un dictionnaire pour qu'il puisse traduire.* Lend him a dictionary so that he can do the translation. *Il prendra le bus de sorte qu'il vienne plus tôt* (synonym of *afin qu'il* – purpose). He'll catch the bus so that he can arrive earlier.[*]

[*] Compare with: *Il prit le bus, de sorte qu'il est arrivé plus tôt* (synonym of *et ainsi il* – consequence). He caught the bus, so he arrived earlier.

▶ Condition

à condition que on condition that *à supposer que* supposing that *pourvu que* provided that	*J'accepte n'importe quel travail pourvu qu'il soit bien rémunéré.* I accept whatever the work provided it is well paid.

▶ Concession

bien que although, though quoique although, though	Elle veut faire sa marche quotidienne bien qu'il pleuve. She wants to go on her daily walk although it's raining.

▶ Restriction

à moins que + redundant ne unless	Je veux bien marcher avec vous, à moins qu'il ne pleuve. I'd like to walk with you, unless it rains.

▶ Fear

de peur que + redundant ne* for fear that de crainte que + redundant ne* for fear that	Ferme ta porte à clé de peur qu'il ne revienne. Lock the door in case (i.e., for fear that) he returns.

* After this conjunction the verb in the subordinate clause is normally preceded by ne. In this case ne is redundant and the verb does not have a negative sense.

12.7.4 The subjunctive after impersonal expressions beginning with il

These express necessity, judgement, sorrow, surprise, doubt, probability and possibility.

il faut que it's necessary that il est nécessaire que it's necessary that il est bon que it's good that il est utile que it's useful that il est juste que it's right that il est important que it's important that il est normal que it's normal that il est dommage que it's a pity that il est étonnant que it's surprising that il est temps que it's time that il vaut mieux que it's better that il importe que it's important that il est douteux que it's doubtful that il est peu probable que it's not likely that	Il faut que vous rendiez la clé au concierge. You must give back the key to the porter. Il est juste qu'à travail égal les femmes aient le même salaire que les hommes. It is right that for the same work women have the same salary as men. Il est dommage qu'il soit si susceptible. It's a pity that he's so sensitive. Il est bon qu'il pleuve de temps en temps. It's no bad thing that it rains now and again. Il vaudrait mieux que nous déménagions au plus vite. It would be best for us to move (house) as quickly as possible.

(continued)

(continued)

il est improbable que it's unlikely that *il est possible que* it's possible that *il se peut que* it may be that *il n'est pas possible que* it's not possible that *il est impossible que* it's impossible that	*Il est temps qu'ils se mettent enfin au travail.* It's time that they finally get down to work. *Il est possible qu'elle soit membre du parti socialiste.* It's possible that she's a member of the socialist party.

12.7.5 The subjunctive after the superlative and indefinite antecedents

▶ superlative or a word preceded by a superlative

le seul only *l'unique* only, sole *le premier* first *le dernier* last *le meilleur* best	*Elles sont les seules qui aient réussi* avec tant de facilité.* They are the only ones to have succeeded so easily.

* Note that the indicative may also be used in this construction.

▶ 'indeterminate': the person or thing on which the subordinate clause depends is hypothetical or 'unreal'

personne nobody *quelqu'un* somebody *quelque chose* something *peu de* few, not much / many *rien* nothing	*Il y a peu de gens qui aient réussi* avec autant de facilité.* There are few people who have succeeded so easily. *Il n'y a personne qui ait eu* autant de problèmes avec sa voiture.* There's nobody who has had so many problems with his car.

* Note that the indicative may also be used in this construction.

▶ preceded by an indefinite adjective or article

un / une (. . .) a / an (. . .) *tout* any, all	*Je voudrais une étudiante qui puisse résoudre cette équation.* I'm looking for a student who can solve this equation. *Y a-t-il une personne qui soit capable de m'expliquer ce mode d'emploi ?* Is there anyone who is able to explain these instructions to me?

12.7.6 The subjunctive in subordinate clauses which appear at the beginning of a sentence

Que . . . that, whether	Que vous aimiez la bonne cuisine, cela est clair (**but** Il est clair que vous aimez la bonne cuisine). lit. That you like good cooking, that is clear.

Que followed by the subjunctive may be placed before the verb in a main clause, as a replacement for the 'missing persons' of the imperative (English *let me*, *let him*, etc.).

> The imperative in French is in three persons only (see 10.1):
>
> 2nd person singular: *Entre dans la pièce !* Go into the room!
>
> 1st person plural: *Entrons dans la pièce !* Let's go into the room!
>
> 2nd person plural and polite form: *Entrez dans la pièce !* Go into the room!
>
> The 1st person singular and 3rd persons singular and plural are therefore 'missing' and can be supplied by using this construction.
>
> *Que je sois mille fois puni, si je vous ai menti !* May I be punished a thousand times over if I have lied to you!
>
> *Que personne n'entre dans la pièce !* Let no one enter the room!

THE SUBJUNCTIVE IN CONTEXT

Le banquier, le philosophe et la crise

B: **J'ai bien peur** que les orientations actuelles ne **soient** pas les bonnes. Il faut se mobiliser pour une politique en faveur de l'économie réelle. **Refusons** que les banques **s'affaiblissent.**

Ph: Ne **trouvez-vous pas normal** que vous, les responsables de la crise, **payiez** les pots cassés ?

B: Je ne peux pas vous laisser dire cela. **S'il est vrai** que la crise **ait été causée** par quelques banques américaines, **que** trop de prêts immobilers **aient été mal gérés**, il est aussi vrai que les banques françaises ont mené une politique de crédit responsable.

Ph: **Je m'étonne** que vous **disculpiez** les banques avec autant de légèreté. Vous êtes bien le **premier qui fassiez** de telles affirmations à l'encontre du bon sens le plus élémentaire. N'est-il pas temps de voir la réalité en face ? **Il se peut que** vous, banquiers français, **ayiez généré** moins de mauvais crédits, soit, je vous l'accorde. Mais, ne bénéficiez-vous pas de taux de refinancement avantageux de la BCE et des États ? Et **n'est-il pas vrai** que vous **prêtiez** à des taux excessifs qui mettent sur la paille des peuples entiers ? Et n'**éprouvez-vous point de honte** que tant de maisons **soient saisies** par vos soins, que tant d'imprudents qui vous avaient fait confiance se **trouvent** maintenant à la rue ?

B: **Il est injuste que** les banques **soient** unanimement **attaquées** quand elles sont elles-mêmes fragilisées. **Il est nécessaire** que nous **ayions** une économie dynamique **pour que** les banques **puissent** à nouveau prêter, et cette fois plus sainement. **Il faut que** les banques **soient** fortes **afin que** l'économie **reparte**.

J'ai bien peur que les orientations actuelles ne **soient** *pas les bonnes*	subjunctive after verb of fearing *J'ai bien peur* [12.7.1]
Refusons que les banques **s'affaiblissent.**	subjunctive after verb expressing prohibition *Refusons* [12.7.1]
Ne trouvez-vous pas normal que vous, les responsables de la crise, **payiez** *les pots cassés ?*	subjunctive after verbs expressing judgement *Ne trouvez-vous pas normal* [12.7.1]
S'il est vrai que la crise **ait été causée** . . . *que trop de prêts immobilers* **aient été mal gérés** . . .	subjunctive after impersonal expression of doubt *S'il est vrai que* [12.7.4], intention of the writer unconvinced about the crisis
Je m'étonne que vous **disculpiez** *les banques avec autant de légèreté*	subjunctive after verb expressing surprise *Je m'étonne* [12.7.1]
Vous êtes bien le premier qui **fassiez** *de telles affirmations*	subjunctive after antecedent *le premier* [12.7.5]
Il se peut que vous, banquiers français, **ayiez généré** *moins de mauvais crédits*	subjunctive after impersonal expression *Il se peut que* [12.7.4]
Et n'est-il pas vrai que vous **prêtiez** *à des taux excessifs . . . ?*	subjunctive after negative statement expressing doubt *n'est-il pas vrai* [12.7.2]
Et n'éprouvez-vous point de honte que tant de maisons **soient saisies** *par vos soins . . . que tant d'imprudents . . . se* **trouvent** *maintenant à la rue*	subjunctives after verb of feeling (*avoir*) *honte que* [12.7.1]
Il est injuste que les banques **soient** *unanimement* **attaquées**	subjunctive after impersonal expression of judgement *Il est injuste que* [12.7.1]
Il est nécessaire que nous **ayions** *une économie dynamique . . .*	subjunctive after impersonal expression of necessity *Il est necéssaire* [12.7.4]
pour que les banques **puissent** *à nouveau prêter,*	subjunctive after conjunction of purpose *pour que* [12.7.3]

Il faut que les banques **soient** fortes …	subjunctive after impersonal expression *il faut que* [12.7.4]
afin que l'économie **reparte**.	subjunctive after conjunction of purpose *afin que* [12.7.3]

EXERCISES

1. Fill the gaps with the correct form of the present subjunctive:

infinitive	je / j'	tu	il / elle	nous	vous	ils / elles
jouer	joue			jouions		jouent
finir	finisse		finisse			finissent
rendre		rendes	rende		rendiez	
avoir		aies		ayons		aient
être	sois		soit		soyez	
dormir		dormes			dormiez	dorment
recevoir		reçoives	reçoive		receviez	
construire			construise	construisions		construisent
écrire		écrives			écriviez	écrivent
aller	aille		aille			aillent

2. Complete the sentences using the present subjunctive:

    a. *Ils ont déménagé à Lyon pour que leur fille _____ (aller) à l'école de danse.*
    b. *Il faut que tu _____ (venir) avec moi à la gendarmerie.*
    c. *Je doute que ton frère _____ (comprendre) ce qu'il faut faire.*
    d. *Marc est le seul qui n' _____ (avoir) pas envie de m'accompagner.*
    e. *Je veux que vous me _____ (permettre) d'aller voir le match.*
    f. *Il insiste que nous _____ (partir) avant minuit.*
    g. *Allez-vous-en avant qu'il _____ (être) trop tard !*
    h. *Il est dommage que vous ne _____ (pouvoir) pas vivre près de votre fille.*

3. Choose which of the two verbs in bold is correct:

    a. *Il est nécessaire que ton ami* **vient / vienne** *sans délai.*
    b. *Dites-moi si vous l'***avez / ayez** *vu la semaine dernière.*
    c. *Il a l'intention de terminer le travail avant que vous* **arrivez / arriviez**.
    d. *Je crois que le gouvernement* **va / aille** *réformer la loi sur l'avortement.*
    e. *Faut-il que nous vous* **racontons / racontions** *toute l'histoire?*

f. *Nous avons peur que cela ne / n'est / soit pas vrai.*
g. *Cela m'agace qu'ils **ont / aient** oublié d'apporter l'argent.*
h. *Cet homme est le plus grand menteur que j'**ai / aie** jamais connu.*

4. **Three people are waiting for Claude at the airport arrivals gate. Each one has a different reason to be anxious:**

Francine, his girlfriend, had a row with him over the phone and is frightened that he is going to split up with her.

Agnès, his mother, is annoyed with him because he hasn't been in touch for three weeks.

Georges, his younger brother, is preparing an apology for betting some money borrowed from Claude on a horse which lost.

Write two sentences order to express their feelings containing subjunctives that each one says to him- / herself (or to each other!) as they wait.

13 PREPOSITIONS

Prepositions are invariable words which connect parts of a sentence, showing the relation between them. In English, prepositions govern nouns, noun phrases or pronouns.

In 'After the picnic the children ran to the top of the hill shouting with delight', the words **after, to, of** and **with** are prepositions. They make prepositional phrases with the words that follow them.

▶ '*After* the picnic' links the time this happened with the children's running up the hill.

▶ '*to* the top' links the running with where they went.

▶ '*of* the hill' links 'top' with the noun 'hill', clarifying exactly where on the hill they went.

▶ '*with* delight' links with 'shouting', describing the manner in which they celebrated.

In French, prepositions have the same function as in English but there are some specific differences in the way they work.

KEY POINTS

✦ French prepositions may consist of one word:

à (at, to, in), **de** (of, from, with, in, by), **en** (in, on, at), **sans** (without), etc.

or they may be phrases of more than one word:

à côté de (next to), **au dessous de** (below), **près de** (near to), etc.

✦ Prepositions may be followed by different elements of the sentence:

- **a noun:** *Le capot* **de la voiture** the car bonnet
- **a pronoun:** *Je pense* **à eux.** I think of them.
- **an infinitive:** *Il lui reste trois pages* **à écrire.** He has three pages left to write.
- **an adverb of place or time:** *Il vaut mieux passer* **par derrière.** It's best to go in by the back way.
- **a phrase:** *C'est* **pour encourager la recherche contre le sida**. It's to encourage research into AIDS.

✦ Prepositions in French are followed by the element they introduce and in general do not become detached from it, as often happens in English:

| *Je ne sais pas* **de quel garçon** *tu parles.* | I don't know which boy you're talking about. |

✦ The form of the verb that is used after prepositions is the infinitive. In this respect French differs from English, where the gerund (a kind of verbal noun consisting of the infinitive + -ing) is frequently used for this construction:

Il l'a fait **sans réfléchir**.	He did it without thinking.
Pour réussir *il faudra travailler plus.*	To succeed it is necessary to work harder.
Avant d'éteindre *ton ordinateur commence* **par fermer** *tous tes documents.*	Before turning off your computer first of all close all your documents.

Exception

The preposition **en** + the gerund (the form of the French verb ending in **-ant**) is used for actions that take place simultaneously (see 11.5):

| *Il aime regarder la télévision e**n mangeant**.* | He likes watching the television while eating. |
| *Il chante toujours* **en prenant** *sa douche.* | He always sings when he's having a shower. |

✦ In many cases a French preposition may be translated by the direct English equivalent, but with the most frequently used prepositions the English translation is often unpredictable:

| *la fin* **de** *la leçon* | the end **of** the lesson |

but

d'une façon ou **d'une** autre ...	**in** one way or another ...
un roman **de** Jean-Paul Sartre	a novel **by** Jean-Paul Sartre
boire **dans** un verre	to drink **from** a glass
être **dans** le train	to be **on** the train
voir un film **à** la télévision	to watch a film **on** the television

It is therefore important to learn the particular uses of prepositions.

13.1 Coordination of prepositions

If two prepositions introduce the same element, that element is not repeated:

Il a tondu la pelouse **devant et derrière** la maison.	He cut the lawn in front of and behind the house.

▶ *à*, *de* and *en*

If *à*, *de* or *en* precede more than one element, they are usually repeated before each one:

Cet été il ira **en** Italie, **en** Croatie et **en** Grèce.	This summer he will go to Italy, Croatia and Greece.
Dans son cours il fait des allusions **à** la politique, **à** la religion et **à** la sociologie.	In his lecture he refers to politics, religion and sociology.
Son cours comprend des éléments **de** politique, **de** religion et **de** sociologie.	His lecture contains elements of politics, religion and sociology.

▶ Special cases

▶ In the following cases *à*, *de* and *en* are not repeated:

   ▶ set expressions:

condamné à des dommages et intérêts	sentenced to pay damages
L'École nationale des ponts et chaussées	[A civil engineering school, literally 'National School of Bridges and Roads']
en son âme et conscience	in all honesty

   ▶ when both elements refer to the same being or object:

Je m'adresse au voisin et ami que vous avez toujours été.	I'm speaking to you as the neighbour and friend you have always been.

▶ when the elements are beings or ideas that are closely linked:

L'état des cérisiers, abricotiers et pommiers me préoccupe.	The state of cherry, apricot and apple trees worries me.

▶ when the elements are numbers connected by *ou*:

Il est arrivé avec deux ou trois minutes de retard.	He arrived two or three minutes late [lit. 'with . . . of delay'].

▶ Other prepositions

▶ All other prepositions can be repeated or not, depending on the speaker.

13.2 Verb + preposition constructions

Certain verbs are followed by a specific preposition, for example:

jouer **à** la belote	to play belote (a card game)
jouer **du** piano	to play the piano
penser **à** l'avenir	to think about the future
tenir **à** ses bijoux	to prize one's jewels
se souvenir **de** son enfance	to remember one's childhood

Many verbs are followed by a preposition and an infinitive. For example, *commencer à (faire)* (to begin [to do]), *oublier de (faire)* (to forget [to do]). (These constructions are covered fully in 11.2.6.)

13.3 Adjectives and adverbs + prepositions

Certain adjectives and adverbs are followed by a specific preposition:

bon en	good at (academic subject)
content de	pleased about / to / with
prêt à	ready to
ravi de	delighted to
beaucoup de (qqch)	much / many, a lot of (+ something)
trop de (qqch)	too much / many of (something)
Il est bon **en** mathématiques mais pas **en** chimie.	He's good at maths but not at chemistry.
Elle est plutôt contente **de** ses résultats.	She's rather pleased about her results.
Il fait trop **de** fautes d'orthographe.	He makes too many spelling mistakes.

But with an infinitive *beaucoup* and *trop* are followed by *à*:

beaucoup à (faire)	much / many, a lot of (+ to do)
trop à (faire)	too much / many (to do)
Elle a encore beaucoup **à** apprendre.	She has a lot to learn.

13.4 Differentiating between prepositions and adverbs

▶ A number of prepositions can also act as adverbs, e.g. *après, avant, depuis, derrière, devant, entre, sans, selon.* When these words function as adverbs they do not introduce a following noun, pronoun or noun phrase. The use of adverbs instead of prepositions is commonplace in familiar language (see Chapter 7):

Après la réunion je suis allé chez moi.	After the meeting I went home (*après* is a preposition governing *la réunion*).
Je suis allé chez moi **après**.	I went home afterwards. (*après* an adverb of time)
Que penses-tu de la nouvelle réforme ? Je n'ai rien **contre**.	What do you think of the new reform? I've nothing against it. (*contre* acts as an adverb)
Il a voté **contre** la réforme.	He voted against the reform. (*contre* acts as a preposition)
Penses-tu que c'est une bonne idée ? C'est **selon** !	Do you think it's a good idea? It all depends! (*selon* acts as an adverb)
Selon moi, ils voteront avec les autres partis.	In my view [lit. according to me], they will vote with the other parties. (*selon* acts as a preposition)

▶ A number of prepositions are differentiated from adverbs by the addition of *de*:

autour	around (adverb)
autour de	around (preposition)
près	near (adverb)
près de	near (preposition)
en face	opposite (adverb)
en face de	opposite (preposition)

| Magali habite tout **près**. | Magali lives quite near. |
| Magali habite **près de** sa famille. | Magali lives quite near her family. |

13.5 Prepositions and their uses

Certain common prepositions, especially *à*, *de*, *dans*, *en* and *par*, have a variety of equivalents in English and are best learnt in the context in which they are used. For example, the equivalent of *dans* is 'in' but the idea of 'in' can be translated by other prepositions according to the context.

▶ *dans*

  ▶ In the sense of 'living in a street' *dans* is used:

| Mes parents habitent **dans*** la rue Molière. | My parents live in Molière Street. |

* It is also possible to express this idea without a preposition at all: *Mes parents habitent rue Molière.*

▶ *à*

  ▶ In the sense of '(out) in the street' *à* is used:

| Depuis qu'il est au chômage, il se retrouve **à** la rue. | Since he lost his job he's on the streets. |

▶ *en plein*

  ▶ In the sense of 'in the middle of' *en plein* is used:

| Ils se sont disputés **en pleine** rue. | They had an argument in (the middle of) the street. |

The list of the most common prepositions which follows gives a range of equivalents and exemplifies their use.

13.5.1 à

> **Reminder (see 3.3):**
> *à* + *le* = *au*
> *à* + *les* = *aux*

à is used to express:

▶ place, location: *at, in, on*

à la dernière minute	at the last minute
au commissariat	at the police station
Ils attendent à la gare.	They are waiting at the station.

*Elle vit **à** Londres.*	She lives in London.
***au** palais royal*	in / at the royal palace
à la télévision	on television
***au** volant pas de portable*	no mobiles at the wheel

▶ destination: *to*

*Nous allons **à** Vienne.*	We are going to Vienna.
*Pour l'église vous tournez **à** gauche.*	You turn left for the church.

▶ location and destination with masculine countries, e.g. *le Canada, les États-Unis, le Japon, le Portugal: in, to, into*

***Aux** États-Unis l'espagnol est la première langue étrangère.*	In the United States Spanish is the first foreign language.
*L'année dernière il est allé **au** Portugal.*	Last year he went to Portugal.

▶ a moment in time: *at, in, on, until*

***au** début*	at the beginning
à trois heures	at 3 o'clock
***au** final*	in the end
***au** 19e siècle*	in the 19th century
à la fois	at a time / at the same time
à la mort de mon oncle	at / on my uncle's death
à son arrivée à la maison	on his arrival at the house
*du matin **au** soir*	from morning until night

▶ manner, means or method: *in, on, by, with*

à voix basse	in a low voice
à pied	on foot
à cheval	on horseback
à bicyclette	by bicycle
*cuisiner **au** beurre*	to cook with butter
*des pâtes **aux** champignons et **à la** crème*	pasta with mushrooms and cream
*mariage **à** l'italienne*	marriage Italian-style

▶ noun complements

   ▶ In the English equivalent the complement is frequently turned into an adjective and placed before the noun:

un croissant **au** beurre	a butter croissant
peinture **à** l'huile	oil painting
un sandwich **au** saucisson	a sausage sandwich
une tarte **aux** pommes	an apple tart
du beurre **à** l'ail	garlic butter

▶ prices: *at*

des tomates **à** 3 euros le kilo	tomatoes at 3 euros a kilo
des interrupteurs **à** 5 euros pièce	switches at 5 euros each

▶ distance and speed:

Le pont est **à** dix kilomètres.	The bridge is ten kilometres away.
La nouvelle Peugeot roule **à** 140 kilomètres **à** l'heure.	The new Peugeot travels at 140 kilometres an hour.

▶ possession:

C'est **à** moi, ce ballon !	That ball is mine [lit: to me]!
Ce livre est **à** Daniel.	This book belongs to Daniel.
une façon bien **à** lui d'écrire	a way of writing that is all his own

Notes

à is used:

▶ in prepositional expressions e.g. *aux mains de* (in the hands of), *à l'exception de* (except), *à partir de* (from):

Nous sommes **aux mains des** politiques et des banquiers.	We are in the hands of politicians and bankers.
Ils étaient tous là, **à l'exception** de Georges.	They were all there except George.
Le restaurant sera fermé **à partir de** demain.	The restaurant will be closed from tomorrow.

▶ to describe features:

la fille **aux** *cheveux noirs*	the girl with black hair
l'homme **à la** *barbe blanche*	the man with the white beard
une tasse **à** *thé*	a tea cup
un moulin **à** *vent*	a windmill
une cuiller **à** *café*	a tea / coffee spoon

▶ in certain verb constructions (see 11.2.6):

Il pense **à** *ses amis.*	He thinks of his friends.

▶ with pronouns

à *plusieurs*	several (people) together
Ils ont fait ce travail **à** *plusieurs.*	Several of them did the work together.
À *moi !*	Help!

13.5.2 à cause de: *because of*

Ils ont annulé la fête **à cause de** *la pluie.*	They've cancelled the festival because of the rain.

13.5.3 à côté de: *beside, next to*

Tu ne peux pas le rater, c'est **à côté de** *la boulangerie.*	You can't miss it, it's next to the baker's.

13.5.4 afin de: *so as to*

Elle a pris un taxi **afin de** *ne pas être en retard.*	She took a taxi so as not to be late.

13.5.5 à l'exception de: *except for*

Ils sont tous venus **à l'exception de** *Marie, qui est malade.*	They've all come except for Marie, who is ill.

13.5.6 à moins de: *unless*

À moins de *partir tout de suite nous allons rater le train.*	Unless we leave straight away we'll miss the train.

13.5.7 à partir de: *from*

à partir de *mercredi prochain*	from next Wednesday

13.5.8 après: *after*

après *la révolution*	after the revolution
Après *le petit déjeuner nous sommes partis pour Paris.*	After breakfast we left for Paris.

13.5.9 à travers: *across, through*

Ils ont réussi à passer **à travers** *les mailles du filet.*	They managed to slip through the net.

13.5.10 au delà de: *beyond*

Au delà d'une certaine limite les billets ne sont plus valables.*	Beyond a certain point tickets are not valid any more.
De cet endroit, on pouvait voir **au-delà de** *la frontière.*	From this place we could see beyond the border.

13.5.11 au-dessous de: *below*

au-dessous de *la fenêtre*	below the window
Au-dessous d'un certain âge les enfants peuvent entrer gratuitement.*	Under a certain age, children can go in free of charge.

13.5.12 au-dessus de: *over, above*

J'aime quand en avion je me trouve **au-dessus des** *nuages.*	I like it when I'm up above the clouds in a plane.

Le drapeau tricolore flottait **au-dessus du porche de la mairie**.	The tricolour floated above the porch of the town hall.

13.5.13 au lieu de: *instead of*

Pourquoi tu n'irais pas, **au lieu de** moi ?	Why wouldn't you go instead of me?
Nous avons préféré faire une marche **au lieu d'**aller nous enfermer au cinéma.	We preferred to go for a walk instead of being shut in the cinema.

13.5.14 auprès de: *beside, with*

La politique du Président n'a pas eu beaucoup de succès **auprès des** électeurs.	The President's policy hasn't been very successful with the electorate.

13.5.15 autour de: *around*

Je regardais **autour de** moi avec précaution.	I looked around me carefully.
Soudain, **autour de** lui il n'y avait que des gens ivres.	Suddenly, there were only drunken people around him.

13.5.16 avant: *before*

avant la guerre	before the war
avant le départ	before leaving

Note

When an infinitive follows *avant*, *de* is always placed before the infinitive:

avant de commencer	before starting

13.5.17 avec: *with*

Ils sont venus **avec** leurs enfants.	They came with their children.
Avec ceci ?	(in shops) Anything else? [lit: With this?]

Note

avec often translates by the *-ly* form of adverbs:

avec curiosité	inquisitively
*Il a fait ses devoirs **avec** soin.*	He did his homework carefully.

13.5.18 chez: at the place / house / home of, with

Chez is used both literally and figuratively:

*Je vais **chez** mon amie.*	I'm going to my girlfriend's place.
*Fais comme **chez** toi !*	Make yourself at home.
*La critique de la société est courante **chez** Molière.*	Social criticism is common in Molière.
*Comment ça va **chez** les Martin ?*	How are things with the Martins?

13.5.19 contre: against

*Le match le plus dur, c'est l'Angleterre **contre** la France.*	The hardest match is England against France.

13.5.20 dans

dans is used to express:

▶ place: *in, on*

*Nous prenons le petit déjeuner **dans** la cuisine.*	We have our breakfast in the kitchen.
*Mon passeport est **dans** le tiroir.*	My passport is in the drawer.
***dans** l'avion*	on the plane

▶ movement to a place: *into*

*J'ai mis les billets **dans** une enveloppe scellée.*	I put the tickets into a sealed envelope.
*Elle a glissé la lettre **dans** la poche de son jean.*	She slipped the letter into the pocket of her jeans.
*Nous allons pénétrer **dans** la forêt.*	We are going to go deep into the forest.

▶ *from, out of*

*Il prend l'argent **dans** un tiroir.*	He takes the money from a drawer.
*Je l'ai appris **dans** un livre.*	I learnt it from a book.
*Pas tous les peuples mangent **dans** des assiettes et boivent **dans** des verres.*	Not all peoples eat from plates and drink out of glasses.

▶ time:

   ▶ in, *during*

dans *les années 1970 . . .*	in / during the seventies . . .
*J'ai voyagé beaucoup **dans** ma jeunesse.*	I travelled a lot in my youth.

   ▶ after a period of time has gone by: *in*

*Je commence mon nouvel emploi **dans** une semaine.*	I begin my new job in a week's time.

13.5.21 d'après: according to, based on

d'après *mes recherches . . .*	according to my research . . .
d'après *lui . . .*	according to him . . .
*Ce film a été fait **d'après** un roman de Dalton Trumbo.*	This film was made based on a novel by Dalton Trumbo.

13.5.22 de

> **Reminder (see 3.3):**
> **de** + **le** = **du**
> **de** + **les** = **des**

de is used:

▶ for origin, provenance, distance: *from*

*Il vient **de** Norvège.*	He comes from Norway.
*Elle habite à quelques kilomètres **de** là.*	She lives a few kilometres from there.
*Il part **de** la mairie tous les jours à 5 heures.*	He departs from the town hall every day at 5 o'clock.
de *temps à autre*	from time to time
de *la tête aux pieds*	from head to foot

▶ for possession: *of*, possessive *'s* or *s'*

*le roi **d'**Espagne*	the King of Spain
*le bateau **de** mon père*	my father's boat
*les contrats **des** ouvriers*	the workers' contracts

▶ for a noun complement: *of*

Note that in the English equivalent the complement is frequently placed before the noun:

*une tasse **de** thé*	a cup of tea
*l'année **de** naissance*	the year of birth
*un bol **de** café*	a bowl of coffee
*le bureau **de** poste*	the post office
*le mal **de** mer*	sea sickness
*une ligne de chemin **de** fer*	a railway line
*du fromage **de** brebis*	ewe's cheese
*le café **du** village*	the village café

▶ for an agent: *by*, *with*, *of*

*un roman **d'**Albert Camus*	a novel by Albert Camus
*Il m'a salué **de** la main.*	He waved to me [lit: He greeted me with the hand].
*mourir **de** froid*	to die of cold
*un exercice rempli **de** fautes*	an exercise full of mistakes

▶ as the complement of a past participle or adjective: *with*, *of*, *in*, *by*

*Le béton est composé **d'**eau, **de** sable et **de** ciment.*	Concrete is made of water, sand and cement.
*Il est fier **de** ses élèves.*	He is proud of his pupils.
*une montagne couverte **de** neige*	a mountain covered with snow
*Elle était accompagnée **de** deux amis.*	She was accompanied by two friends.
*Elle était vêtue **d'**un pantalon noir.*	She was wearing black trousers [lit. dressed with].

▶ after quantifiers

*trop **de** problèmes*	too many problems
*beaucoup **d'**amis*	lots of friends
*un seau plein **d'**eau*	a bucket full of water

▶ in expressions of manner: *with, in*

de *la même manière*	in the same way
de *toute façon*	in any case
d'une certaine manière	in a way
d'un air triste	with a sad face

▶ after superlatives: *in*

la montagne la plus haute **d'**Europe	the highest mountain in Europe
Elle est la plus habile gymnaste **de** *son club.*	She's the most skilful gymnast in her club.

▶ after *quelqu'un, quelque chose, rien*:

quelque chose **d'**intéressant	something interesting
quelqu'un **d'**autre	someone else
rien **de** *neuf*	nothing new

Notes

▶ *de* is omitted in old expressions such as: *l'hôtel-Dieu* (ancient hospital in Paris), *fête-Dieu* (Corpus Christi), and also in some modern expressions such as: *le gouvernement Jospin* (the government of Prime Minister Jospin).

▶ It is important not to confuse the preposition *de* with the partitive article *de* (see 3.5.1):

— Tu veux chercher **du** *pain ?*	'Will you get **some** bread?' (partitive article)
*— **De** la boulangerie **du** village ou **du** supermarché ?*	**'From** the baker **in** the village or **from** the supermarket?' (preposition)

▶ *de* is used in certain verb constructions, e.g. *se souvenir de* (see 11.2.6):

Je me souviens **de** *la visite du Président.*	I remember the President's visit.

13.5.23 de façon à: *in order to, in such a way as to*

Il utilise le vérificateur d'orthographe **de façon à** *ne pas faire de fautes.*	He uses the spell-check so as not to make mistakes.

13.5.24 de manière à: *in order to, in such a way as to*

Il fit un discours lénifiant **de manière à** apaiser le publique.	He made a soothing speech so as to placate the audience.

Note

de manière à and *de façon à* have the same meaning.

13.5.25 depuis: *for, since*

Depuis hier c'est un homme nouveau.	Since yesterday he's (been) a new man.

depuis meaning 'for' is used of a period of time which has not yet finished (see also 13.5.46 and 13.5.47).

C'est une vraie folie **depuis** quinze jours.	Everything has gone crazy for two weeks. [and it hasn't stopped]
Je travaille sur le problème **depuis** une vingtaine d'années.	I've been working on the problem for twenty-odd years. [and I'm still working on it]

13.5.26 derrière: *behind*

Il y avait un beau jardin **derrière** la maison.	There was a beautiful garden behind the house.

13.5.27 dès: *from*

Dès demain les conditions météo sont plus favorables.	From tomorrow weather conditions are more favourable.

13.5.28 devant: *in front of*

Il se trouvait **devant** l'entrée du parc.	He was in front of the park entrance.
Je me suis arrêté **devant** le stade.	I stopped in front of the stadium.

13.5.29 en

en is used for:

▶ location: *in*

| Nous vivons **en** Avignon. | We live in Avignon. |

▶ destination: *to*, *into*

| On va **en** ville demain? | Shall we go to town tomorrow? |

▶ location and destination with feminine countries: *in*, *to*, *into*

| Nous avons beaucoup voyagé **en** France. | We've travelled a lot in France. |
| Elle va **en** Allemagne pour deux ou trois jours. | She's going to Germany for two or three days. |

▶ transformation: *to*, *into*

| traduire **en** français | to translate into French |
| changer des livres **en** euros | to change pounds into euros |

▶ time: *in*

en janvier, **en** février, etc.	in January, in February etc.
en semaine	during the week
en ce moment	at the moment
en (l'an) 2016	in 2016
en été, **en** automne, **en** hiver	in summer, in autumn, in winter
but	
au printemps	in spring

▶ transport: *by*

| aller **en** voiture, avion, train | to go by car, plane, train |

▶ materials: *made of*

une chaise **en** bois	a wooden chair
une casserole **en** aluminium	an aluminium saucepan
des murs **en** pisé	adobe walls

Notes

▶ *en* is used in many common expressions without being followed by a definite or indefinite article:

en *même temps*	at the same time
en *théorie / pratique*	in theory / practice
être *en* *colère*	to be angry
en *plein air*	in the open air
en *tout cas*	in any case
en *quelques minutes*	in a few minutes

▶ *en* followed by the gerund means *while, as, on, by* (see 11.5.1):

En *sortant du magasin je suis allé directement au collège.*	On leaving the shop I went straight to school.
En *voulant trop plaire il s'est rendu ridicule.*	He looked ridiculous when he tried too hard to please.

13.5.30 en deçà de: *on this side*

En *deçà de* *70 dollars le baril, le pétrole ne serait plus rentable.*	This side of 70 dollars a barrel, crude oil will not be profitable.
« *Vérité en* *deçà des* *Pyrénées, erreur au-delà.* » (Pascal, *Pensées*).	'What is right in one place can be wrong in another place.'

13.5.31 en dehors de: *outside*

Nous avons passé une semaine *en dehors du* *pays.*	We've spent a week out of the country.

Note

En dehors de and *hors de* have the same meaning.

13.5.32 en dépit de: *despite, in spite of*

en dépit de *tout*	in spite of everything
Il agit *en dépit du* *bon sens.*	He acts contrary to common sense.

Note

En dépit de and *malgré* have the same meaning.

13.5.33 en face de: *opposite*

*Il s'était assis **en face de** moi.*	He was sitting opposite me.

13.5.34 en plus de: *on top of*

*Ce mois j'ai reçu 1000 euros **en plus de** mon salaire.*	This month I've received 1,000 euros on top of my salary.

13.5.35 entre: *between*

*Ils s'aident **entre** eux.*	They help each other.
*Il va arriver **entre** trois heures et quatre heures et demie.*	He'll get here between 3 o'clock and 4.30.

13.5.36 envers: *towards*

*Elle est respectueuse **envers** l'autorité.*	She's respectful towards authority.
*Elle montre peu de respect **envers** ses parents.*	She shows scant respect for her parents.
*Il est tellement exigeant **envers** lui-même.*	He puts such demands on himself.

13.5.37 grâce à: *thanks to*

***Grâce à** ton aide j'ai réussi à trouver un emploi.*	Thanks to you, I've succeeded in finding a job.
***Grâce à** Dieu.*	Thanks be to God.

13.5.38 hors de: *out of*

*Nous avons passé une semaine **hors du** pays.*	We've spent a week out of the country.
*Elle a passé tout le weekend **hors de** chez elle.*	She spent the whole weekend away from home.
*Il était **hors** d'haleine sur la ligne d'arrivée.*	He was out of breath on the finishing line.

13.5.39 jusqu'à: *until, (up) to, as far as*

Jusqu'à is used of time and place:

jusqu'à lundi / hier	until Monday / yesterday
*Ils ont marché **jusqu'au** bord du lac.*	They walked (up) to the side of the lake.

13.5.40 loin de: *far from*

*Je veux m'échapper et m'installer **loin d'**ici.*	I want to break away and settle far from here.
*Ils sont **loin d'**avoir signé le contrat.*	They are a long way from signing the contract.
***Loin des** yeux, **loin du** cœur.*	Out of sight, out of mind.

13.5.41 lors de: *at the time of*

***Lors de** son voyage il s'est fait de nouveaux amis.*	At the time of / During his journey he met some new friends.
***Lors du** dépouillement du scrutin il a constaté quelques irrégularités.*	When the votes were being counted he noted some irregularities.

13.5.42 malgré: *in spite of, despite*

***malgré** tout*	in spite of everything
*Je peux t'entendre sans difficulté, **malgré** le bruit.*	I can hear you without difficulty, despite the noise.
*C'est un homme plein d'humour **malgré** les apparences.*	He is a witty man in spite of appearances.

Note

Malgré and *en dépit de* have the same meaning.

13.5.43 par

par is used to express:

▶ means: *by, via*

*Le colis fut envoyé **par** la poste.*	The parcel was sent by post.
*payer **par** carte de crédit*	to pay by credit card

| J'ai reçu les DVDs **par** mon frère. | I got the DVDs via my brother. |
| Les achats **par** smartphone représentent 20% des billets vendus. | Smartphone purchases make up 20% of tickets sold. |

▶ the agent after the passive voice: *by*

La vitre a été cassée **par** le ballon.	The window was broken by the ball.
L'équipe du Brésil a été battue **par** l'Argentine.	The Brazilian team was beaten by the Argentinian one.
Son discours a été couvert **par** les cris.	His speech was drowned out by the shouting.

▶ movement through: *out of, by, through, via*

Nous allons **par** ici ou **par** là ?	Do we go this way or that way?
Regardez **par** la fenêtre !	Look out of the window!
Elle est entrée **par** derrière.	She came in through the back.
Par la porte je voyais un pommier fleuri.	Through the door I could see an apple tree in blossom.
Je suis passé **par** Toulouse.	I went via Toulouse.
être toujours **par** monts et **par** vaux	to be always on the move

▶ distribution in time or space: *per, through*

Je suis venu deux fois **par** semaine.	I came twice a week.
Elle gagne 2000 euros **par** mois.	She earns 2,000 euros per month.
Les Français achètent en moyenne deux kilos d'huîtres **par** an et **par** habitant.	The French buy on average two kilos of oysters per year per inhabitant.
Ils furent répartis **par** groupes de trois.	They were divided up in groups of three.

▶ a moment or period of time: *during, on*

| **par** temps de guerre | in wartime |
| **par** une belle matinée de printemps | on a beautiful spring morning |

▶ a cause: *out of, from*

Il a agi **par** devoir.	He acted out of duty.
Nous sommes venu(e)s **par** curiosité.	We came out of curiosity.
L'incident s'est produit **par** sa faute.	It was his fault that the incident happened.

▶ 'by' after the verbs *commencer* and *finir*:

*Il a fini **par** m'énerver.*	He ended up by getting on my nerves.
***Par** où vais-je commencer?*	Where shall I start?

13.5.44 parmi: *among*

***Parmi** les personnalités se trouvait Miss France.*	Among the personalities was Miss France.

13.5.45 par rapport à: *compared with, with regard to*

*La valeur de la livre a augmenté **par rapport** à celle de l'euro.*	The value of the pound has increased against ('compared with') the euro.
*L'attitude des gens **par rapport à** l'immigration est ambigüe.*	The attitude of people with regard to immigration is ambiguous.

13.5.46 pendant: *during, for*

Pendant is normally used to refer to events that took place within a specific period of time (see also 13.5.25 and 13.5.47):

*J'ai suivi un régime **pendant** deux années.*	I followed a diet for two years.
*Nous avons attendu **pendant** des heures mais personne n'est venu.*	We waited for hours but nobody came.
*Il devra prendre de l'aspirine **pendant** tout le mois de juillet.*	He'll have to take aspirin for the whole of July.

Note

Durant has the same meaning as *pendant*.

13.5.47 pour

pour is used to express:

▶ aim: *for, in order to*

*Il a pris le métro **pour** gagner du temps.*	He took the undergound to gain time.
*Faire un régime, ce n'est pas **pour** moi.*	Going on a diet isn't for me.
*Je n'ai pas de pitié **pour** ces gens-là.*	I've no pity for those people.

▶ cause: *for*

*On l'a récompensé **pour** avoir sauvé l'entreprise.*	He was rewarded for having saved the business.
***Pour** avoir lu toute la journée, il a maintenant les yeux fatigués.*	His eyes are tired now because he's been reading all day.

▶ referring to a future period of time: *for* (see also 13.5.25 and 13.5.46)

*Ils vont à Marseilles **pour** quelques jours.*	They're going to Marseilles for a few days.
*Qu'est-ce que tu fais **pour** les vacances de Noël ?*	What are you doing for the Christmas holidays?

▶ *passer pour / prendre pour* = to be taken for:

*Elle le prend **pour** ce qu'il n'est pas.*	She takes him for what he is not.
*Il passe **pour** un expert.*	He's supposed to be an expert.

13.5.48 près de: *near (to)*

*Elle s'assit **près de** lui.*	She sat down near to him.
*La cathédrale est **près du** château, à deux kilomètres.*	The cathedral is near the castle, two kilometres away.

13.5.49 quant à: *as for, regarding*

***Quant aux** risques de malaria en France, je pense que c'est exagéré.*	As for the risks of catching malaria in France, I think this is exaggerated.
*L'expert, **quant à** lui, préfère réserver son diagnostic.*	As for the expert, he prefers to reserve his diagnosis.

13.5.50 sans: *without*

*Je bois du café **sans** sucre.*	I drink coffee without sugar.
*Elle est **sans** souci.*	She has no worries.

13.5.51 sauf: *except (for)*

*Pas de soleil aujourd'hui **sauf** sur le littoral méditerranéen.*	No sun today except on the Mediterranean coast.

13.5.52 selon: according to

Selon vous, qui a été le meilleur candidat?	According to you, who was the best candidate?
Son jugement varie selon son humeur.	His judgement varies according to his mood.

13.5.53 sous: under

Je vais m'abriter de la pluie sous les arbres.	I'm going to shelter from the rain under the trees.

13.5.54 sur: on, in, out of

Sur is the equivalent of:

▶ *on*

un spectacle sur glace	a show on ice
Il fait toujours un beau sourire sur les photos.	He always has a nice smile on photos.
Tu rêves ! Descends un peu sur Terre !	You're dreaming! Come down to earth a little!

▶ *in*

Elle avait laissé la clé sur la porte.	She'd left the key in the door.
Il est sur une affaire douteuse.	He is in a dubious business deal.

▶ *out of*

quatorze sur vingt	fourteen out of twenty
Neuf personnes sur dix possèdent un portable.	Nine out of ten people possess a mobile.

13.5.55 sur le point de: about to, on the point of

J'étais sur le point de t'appeler quand tu es arrivé.	I was about to call you when you arrived.
Il est malheureusement sur le point de faire faillite.	Unfortunately, he is about to go bankrupt.

13.5.56 vers: towards, about

Il se tourna **vers** moi en souriant.	He turned towards me, smiling.
Ils sont revenus **vers** 6 heures du soir.	They returned at about six in the evening.

13.6 Prepositions meaning 'in' and 'to' before geographical names

Preposition	Before ...	examples	
en	the names of countries, regions, states and provinces in the feminine	**en** Grande Bretagne	in Great Britain
		en France	in France
		en Bourgogne	in Burgundy
		Je vais **en** Grande Bretagne.	I'm going to Great Britain.
	all names of countries, whether masculine or feminine, which begin with a vowel or silent h	**en** Afghanistan	in Afghanistan
		en Ouzbekistan	in Uzbekistan
		en Haïti	in Haiti
		Je vais **en** Haïti (or à Haïti).	I'm going to Haiti.
	names of continents	**en** Europe	in Europe
		en Afrique	in Africa
au	names of countries in the masculine	**au** Brésil	in Brazil
		Je vis **au** Maroc.	I live in Morocco.
		Je vais **au** Maroc.	I'm going to Morocco.
à, à la / au	towns, small islands, large islands far from Europe	**à** Londres	in London
		à Chypre	in Cyprus
		à Madagascar	in Madagascar
		à la Martinique	in Martinique
		Je vais **à** Londres, Chypre, etc.	I'm going to London, Cyprus, etc.

(continued)

(continued)

Preposition	Before . . .	examples	
aux	the names of countries in the plural	**aux** *États-Unis*	in the United States
		*Je vais **aux** États-Unis.*	I'm going to the USA.
dans le / la / l' / les	the names of masculine regions, the names of certain islands and archipelagos, all British counties, the names of mountain ranges	**dans le** *Yorkshire*	in Yorkshire
		dans le *Berry*	in the Berry (region of France)
		dans les *Caraïbes*	in the Caribbean
		dans les *Alpes*	in the Alps
		*Je vais **dans les** Alpes / le Berry / le Yorkshire, etc.*	I'm going to the Alps, the Berry region, Yorkshire, etc.

Note

Islands considered as a country follow the rule for countries: *en Irlande* (in Ireland), *en Australie* (in Australia).

PREPOSITIONS IN CONTEXT

La drôle de cigarette

Nous étions **dans** les Alpes, **à** Saint Véran, le village le plus haut **de** France. Mon ami Georges était là qui fumait. Il fume **depuis** toujours, **malgré** les reproches **de** son entourage. **À moins** d'un miracle, il n'arrêtera pas.

Or, dimanche **vers** 11 heures **du** matin, alors que j'étais **sur le point de** l'appeler **pour** l'inviter **à** déjeuner, il arriva **en** me soufflant une bouffée **de** fumée blanche **comme** neige **en** plein visage.

Surpris, je lui demandai d'aller fumer **en dehors de** la maison ou sur le balcon. **Pour** avoir fréquenté Georges **durant** des années, je savais que cette attitude ne lui ressemblait pas.

En fait, j'étais **loin de** me douter **de** la surprise qui m'attendait. Ce qu'il tenait **sur** les lèvres était bien une cigarette, **en** tout cas cela en avait la forme, et le bout rougissait **à** chaque fois que Georges tirait **sur** celle-ci. Cependant la cigarette brûlait **sans** se consumer.

Georges expliqua qu'il s'agissait **d'**une cigarette électronique. Cette cigarette révolutionnaire, inventée **par** un Japonais **au début des** années 2000, venait **de** faire son apparition **en** France. Georges était tout fier **d'**être **parmi** les premiers **à** l'expérimenter.

Pour l'occasion on a créé un nouveau verbe: « vapoter ».

Cette nouvelle cigarette n'est pas bourrée **de** chimie mais **d'**électronique. Elle contient aussi une cartouche aromatisée **avec** recharge et bouchon **de** protection. **En** aspirant, le microprocesseur met **en** marche une batterie. Celle-ci chauffe et transforme le liquide **en** vapeur **d'**eau **à** une température **de** 50 **à** 60 degrés C.

Le fumeur a l'impression **de** fumer **sans** vraiment fumer. Reste **à** savoir si les produits **dans** la recharge sont inoffensifs !

Preposition		Comment
à		[13.5.1]
1 *à Saint Véran*	in Saint Véran	*à* normally = 'in' of towns [13.6]
2 *pour l'inviter **à** déjeuner*	to invite him to have lunch	*inviter* is followed by *à*
3 *parmi les premiers **à** l'expérimenter*	among the first to try it out	*premier* followed by *à* = the first to (do)
4 *à une température de 50 **à** 60 degrés C*	at a temperature from 50 to 60 degrees Celsius	*à* = at, to
5 *Reste **à** savoir.*	It remains to be seen.	idiom
à moins de		[13.5.6]
à moins d'un miracle	short of a miracle / unless there's a miracle	
au début de		
au début des années 2000	at the beginning of the twenty-first century	
avec		[13.5.17]
avec recharge	rechargeable	
dans		[13.5.20] [13.6]
dans les Alpes	in the Alps	
de		[13.5.22]
1 *le village le plus haut **de** France*	the highest village in France	*de* after a superlative = 'in'
2 *vers 11 heures **du** matin*	towards 11 in the morning / am	for times of day and following clock time *de* = in
3 *une bouffée **de** fumée blanche*	a puff of white smoke	noun complement

(continued)

(continued)

Preposition		Comment
4 *j'étais loin de me douter* **de** *la surprise*	I was far from suspecting the surprise that awaited me	*douter* **de** = to doubt
5 *s'agissait* **d'**une	it was (a matter of)	*il s'agit* **de** impersonal verb
6 *venait* **de** *faire son apparition en France*	had just appeared in France	*venir* **de** = to have just. Note imperfect tense in French = pluperfect in English
7 *(pas) bourrée* **de** *chimie mais* **d'**électronique	(not) crammed with chemistry but with electronics	**de** = with
depuis *Il fume* **depuis** *toujours.*	 He has always smoked.	[13.5.25] **depuis** with present tense in French = past tense in English
durant **durant** *des années*	 for years	[13.5.46] **durant** (and **pendant**) refer to events that take place within a specific period of time
en 1 **en** *me soufflant*	 while blowing at me	[13.5.29] **en** + gerund construction = while
2 **en** *plein visage*	right in my face	idiom
3 **en** *tout cas*	in any case	idiom
4 *le microprocesseur met* **en** *marche la batterie*	the microprocessor switches the battery on	*mettre* **en** *marche* = to turn / switch on
5 *transforme le liquide* **en** *vapeur d'eau*	turns the liquid **into** water vapour	*transformer* **en** = to turn into
en dehors de **en dehors de** *la maison*	 outside the house	[13.5.31]
loin de *j'étais* **loin de** *me douter de la surprise*	 I was far from suspecting the surprise	[13.5.40]
malgré		[13.5.42]

Preposition		Comment
malgré les reproches de son entourage	despite the criticism of those around him	
par inventée **par** un Japonais	invented by a Japanese man	[13.5.43] with agent after past participle
parmi **parmi** les premiers à l'expérimenter	among the first to try it out	[13.5.44]
pour **pour** l'inviter à déjeuner	(in order) to invite him to lunch	[13.5.47] **pour** + infinitive expressing aim
sans La cigarette brûlait **sans** se consumer	the cigarette burned without being used up	[13.5.50] **sans** + infinitive (present participle in English)
sur **sur** le balcon	on the balcony	[13.5.54]
sur le point de que j'étais **sur le point de** l'appeler	I was about to call him	[13.5.55]
vers **vers** 11 heures du matin	towards 11 am	[13.5.56]

EXERCISES

I. **Fill the gaps with a suitable preposition:**

1. *Robert a perdu ses clés; elles ne sont ni _____ ses poches ni _____ son sac _____ -dos.*

2. *Réfléchissons ! dit Robert, je suis sorti _____ _____ moi _____ quatre heures _____ l'après-midi.*

3. *Les clés ne se trouvant pas _____ la porte, je les avais donc _____ moi _____ mon départ.*

4. *Puis, je suis allé _____ voiture _____ Cambridge, _____ mon ami Christian.*

5. *Je suis entré* _____ *la maison.* _____ *le hall, j'ai accroché ma veste* _____ *porte-manteau.*

6. *Je suis allé* _____ *salon en passant* _____ *la salle* _____ *manger.*

7. *J'ai joué un moment* _____ *Jeremy, le fils* _____ *Christian.*

8. *Jeremy a voulu jouer* _____ *cheval; je me suis mis* _____ *quatre pattes et il est monté* _____ *mon dos.*

9. *J'ai tourné trois fois* _____ *du canapé.*

10. *Mais bien sûr! Les clés sont tombées* _____ *terre. Elles sont certainement restées* _____ *le canapé.*

2. **Fill the gaps with one of the following: *à, à l' / à la* or *chez*:**

I. *Il va* _____ *(le dentiste)*

2. *Ils travaillent* _____ *(Renault)*

3. *Elle est* _____ *(université)*

4. *Il est* _____ *(le doyen de l'université)*

5. *Elle est* _____ *(église)*

6. *Il est* _____ *(l'imam)*

7. *Il a rendez-vous* _____ *(poste)*

8. *Vous travaillez* _____ *(Carrefour) ?*

9. *Elle est* _____ *(discothèque)*

10. *Elle vient de* _____ *(la coiffeuse)*

3. **Taking note of the word in the first box (*être*, *aller*, etc.) place each word in the box beneath the appropriate preposition:**

1. *Paris – la rue – le dentiste – avance – le trottoir*

	à	dans	chez	en	sur
être					

2. *Normandie – pied – le sud – mon oncle - sa chambre*

	à	dans	chez	en	vers
aller					

3. *la semaine prochaine – le déjeuner – 2 et 3 heures – récupérer les enfants – jeudi après-midi*

	à compter de	à l'exception du	entre	après	avant de
Quand?					

4. *un avare – Marseille – sixième – l'aspirateur – choses sérieuses*

	pour	en		aux	par
passer					

5. *l'apprendre – s'excuser – loin – grec – son chef*

	à	du	après	pour	de
venir					

14 CONJUNCTIONS

The word 'conjunction' means 'joining together'. Typical conjunctions are 'and', 'but' and 'because', and they have the function of connecting two words, phrases, clauses or sentences.

Conjunctions have an important role in communicating meaning. When they connect words, phrases or clauses, conjunctions create sentences of greater complexity. For example, a conjunction can be used to join the two statements 'He complained bitterly' and 'No one took any notice', turning them into a single, more complex one. Linking the sentences with the conjunction 'but' gives one meaning: 'He complained bitterly **but** no one took any notice'; connecting them with 'because' gives a quite different one: 'He complained bitterly **because** no one took any notice'.

KEY POINTS

French conjunctions work in a similar way to English ones. There are two types, **coordinating** and **subordinating**.

✦ **Coordinating conjunctions**, such as **et** (and), **ou** (or) and **mais** (but), are so-called because they make a simple link between two equivalent words or clauses; there is no relation of *dependency* between the two components that are linked:

*Jean **et** Magalie se sont mariés.*	Jean **and** Magalie got married.
*C'est maintenant **ou** jamais.*	It's now **or** never.
*J'essaie de faire un peu de sport **mais**, hélas, je n'ai pas vraiment le temps.*	I try to play a little sport **but** unfortunately I don't really have the time.

✦ **Subordinating conjunctions**, such as ***comme*** (as), ***parce que*** (because), and ***quand*** (when), introduce a subordinate clause which is dependent on (i.e., 'subordinate to') a main clause.

Main clause	Subordinate clause introduced by a conjunction
Il ne parlait pas beaucoup	***parce qu'**il préférait écouter.*
He didn't speak much	because he preferred to listen.
J'irai les voir	***quand** j'aurai terminé mon travail.*
I'll go and see them	when I've finished my work.
Fais	***comme** il te plaît.*
Do	as you like.

14.1 Coordinating conjunctions

Coordinating conjunctions are few in number but they are among the most used words in the language. The principal coordinating conjunctions are:

car	for, since, because
donc	so
et	and
mais	but
or	so, now, and yet
ou	or
ni	neither, nor, or
puis	then, next

Note

et, ou and *ni* can join words (including pronouns), phrases, clauses and sentences. The remaining coordinating conjunctions join two phrases, clauses and sentences, but, for the most part not two words.

351

14.1.1 car

Car is used to link two clauses and does not normally appear at the beginning of a sentence. It is used mostly in written French and has an explanatory sense:

Son frère est resté, **car** il doit étudier.	His brother has remained, for he has to study.
Elle va échouer l'examen, **car** elle n'a pas fait assez de travail.	She'll fail the exam because she's not done enough work.
Il prend toujours ses congés en juillet **car** il tient à voir le Tour de France.	He always takes his holidays in July for he's keen to see the Tour de France.
Il est devenu un vrai expert en cinéma **car** il a lu de nombreux livres sur le sujet.	He's become a real expert on cinema because he's read lots of books about it.

14.1.2 donc

Donc has the function of linking two clauses or sentences, indicating a result. This conjunction is used typically in logical syllogisms, as in Descartes' famous statement « je pense, donc je suis » (I think, therefore I am). The placing of **donc** is variable; it may be situated at the beginning of the clause or after the verb:

Je suis venu ici pour me détendre, **donc** je ne veux pas d'ordinateur.	I've come here to relax, so I don't want a computer.
Nous n'avons pas de financement pour le projet. Il s'agit **donc** d'en trouver.	We haven't enough finance for the project. So it's a question of finding it.

14.1.3 et

▶ Et can be placed between words, phrases and clauses and at the beginning of a sentence:

une photo en noir **et** blanc	a black and white photo
Nous avons pris la clé **et** nous sommes montés au sixième par l'ascenseur.	We took the key and we went up to the sixth floor in the lift.
Et toi ? Qu'est-ce que tu en penses ?	And you? What do you think about it?

▶ both . . . and may be expressed by et . . . et:

Et mon père **et** ma mère sont algériens.	Both my father and my mother are Algerian.

14.1.4 mais

Mais expresses a contrast or a limitation and may be placed at the beginning of a sentence:

Elle s'est couchée de bonne heure **mais** *elle ne dormait pas.*	She went to bed early but she couldn't sleep.
Il est bon en anglais **mais** *médiocre en mathématiques.*	He's good at English but weak in mathematics.
Je voulais répondre **mais** *je ne savais pas quoi dire.*	I wanted to answer but I didn't know what to say.
Mais *que vais-je faire ce soir ? Aucune de mes amies ne veut sortir.*	But what am I going to do tonight? None of my friends wants to go out.

14.1.5 ni

▶ *Ni* can link words, phrases or clauses and is almost always used in tandem with a second *ni* (see 8.7):

Quel livre préférez-vous? **Ni** *l'un* **ni** *l'autre.*	Which book do you prefer? Neither one nor the other.

▶ *ne . . . ni (. . . ni)*:

Je ne sais pas si elle vient, **ni** *même si on l'a invitée.*	I don't know if she's coming or even if she's been invited.
Vous **ne** *pouvez pas m'empêcher de m'en aller,* **ni** *vous* **ni** *personne.*	You can't stop me going, neither you nor anyone else.
Il **n'**a *dit* **ni** *« oui »* **ni** *« non ».*	He said neither 'yes' nor 'no'.

14.1.6 or

Or is normally followed by a comma and serves to link a statement with a previous one. This conjunction is normally placed at the beginning of the sentence or clause:

Il n'aimait pas sa vie d'oisif. **Or**, *un jour, un ami de son père lui a proposé de travailler dans son restaurant.*	He wasn't happy with his idle life. Now, one day, a friend of his father offered him work in his restaurant.
Il disait ne pas aimer les femmes, **or** *il avait une fille et une mère qu'il adorait.*	He said he didn't like women and yet he had a daughter and a mother that he loved.
Tous les Italiens sont bavards; **or** *Giacomo est italien, donc Giacomo devrait être bavard.*	All Italians are talkative; now Giacomo is Italian, so he should be talkative.

14.1.7 ou

▶ *Ou* links words, phrases and clauses and can be placed at the beginning of a sentence. This conjunction states alternatives, which can express the same thing in other words or a genuine alternative choice:

Il travaillait dans une compagnie d'assurances **ou** *quelque chose de ce genre.*	He worked for an insurance company or something of the kind.
Vous pouvez aller au cinéma **ou** *rester chez vous.*	You can go to the cinema or stay at home.

▶ *ou . . . ou* means *either . . . or*:

Ou *la jalousie* **ou** *l'égoïsme l'a fait réagir de cette manière.*	Either jealousy or selfishness made him react that way.

14.1.8 puis

Puis is used for relating a sequence of events:

J'ai pris mon petit déjeuner, **puis** *je suis allé voir ma copine.*	I had breakfast and then I went to see my girlfriend.
Ils ont dansé toute la nut. **Puis**, *épuisés, ils sont allés se coucher.*	They danced the whole night. Then, exhausted, they went to bed.

14.2 Subordinating conjunctions

Subordinating conjunctions connect a main clause with a subordinate clause. The conjunction employed may be:

▶ a single word, such as *que* (that), *quand* (when), *si* (if, whether) and *comme* (as)

▶ a phrase ending in *que* or *si*, such as *parce que* (because), *avant que* (before), *bien que* (although), *à condition que* (provided that), *comme si* (as if).

Subordinate clauses may express a variety of meanings, relating mainly to time, cause, consequence, aim, condition or concession. The subordinate clause may be in the indicative or the subjunctive: certain conjunctions, such as *parce que*, are always followed by the indicative; others, such as *bien que*, are followed by the subjunctive.

There are some important differences of tense between French and English, notably with conjunctions of time (*quand, depuis que* [since], etc.).

14.3 Subordinating conjunctions followed by the indicative

These conjunctions fall into several categories.

14.3.1 que

Que (that), introducing a noun clause, is the most common subordinating conjunction. Note that its equivalent in English is frequently omitted:

| Tu ne m'avais pas dit **que** tu avais un frère. | You hadn't told me (that) you'd got a brother. |
| Je crois **que** ça change tout. | I think (that) that changes everything. |

Note that *que* may also be followed by the subjunctive:

| Je ne crois pas **qu'**elle vienne. | I don't think she's coming. |

14.3.2 Other conjunctions

A variety of conjunctions relating to cause, preference, exception, etc. are followed by the indicative. The most common of these are:

à mesure que	as
ainsi que	just as
alors que	while
autant que	as far as
comme	as
comme si	as if
parce que	because
plutôt que	rather than
puisque	since (= because)
sauf que	except that
sinon que	except that
tandis que	while, whereas
vu que	seeing that

| **À mesure qu'**approchait l'heure elle devenait de plus en plus nerveuse. | As the hour approached she became more and more nervous. |

(continued)

(continued)

*Nous y allons le matin **parce qu'**il y aura moins de monde.*	We'll go there in the morning because there will be fewer people.
*Il n'y a rien d'extraordinaire à ce qu'ils se ressemblent **puisqu'**ils sont cousins.*	It's not surprising that they look alike since they are cousins.
*Je préfère prendre le taxi **plutôt que** d'arriver en retard.*	I prefer to take a taxi rather than arrive late.
*Il a fait ses ablutions avant le repas, **ainsi qu'**il est de coutume dans ce pays.*	He performed his ablutions before the meal, as is the custom in this country.
*Il est passé sans me saluer, **comme s'**il ne m'avait pas vu.*	He went by without greeting me as if he hadn't seen me.

14.3.3 Subordinating conjunctions of time

The most common conjunctions relating to time are:

après que	after
aussitôt que	as soon as
dès que	as soon as
depuis que	since (of time)
maintenant que	now
lorsque	when
pendant que	while
quand	when

***Quand** le printemps arrive, le jardin s'éveille.*	When spring arrives the garden wakes up.
*De quoi avez-vous parlé **lorsque** vous étiez seuls ?*	What did you talk about when you were all on your own?
***Pendant que** tu voyageais en Chine j'étudiais pour mes examens.*	While you were travelling in China I was studying for my exams.
***Maintenant qu'**elle connaît les règles, elle ne commettra plus la faute.*	Now that she knows the rules she won't make the mistake any more.
***Depuis qu'**il a obtenu son diplôme, il semble plus confiant.*	Since he got his degree he seems more confident.

▶ **Time clauses with future and conditional tenses** When the verb in the main clause is in a future or conditional tense, the verb in the subordinate clause must also be in the future, compound future, conditional or compound conditional. Note that in English the verb in the subordinate clause would be in the present or a past tense (see also 10.10–10.13).

*Quand la guerre **sera** terminée il sera possible de visiter le pays.*	When the war **is** over it will be possible to visit the country.
*On leur enverra un texto dès qu'elles **arriveront**.*	We'll send them a text message as soon as they **arrive**.
*Je viendrai aussitôt que j'**aurai** fini.*	I'll come as soon as I**'ve** finished.
*Je pense qu'elle quittera la maison dès qu'elle **aura** 18 ans.*	I think she will leave home as soon as she **is** 18.
*Lorsqu'il **sera** un peu plus riche, il fera des travaux dans la maison.*	When he**'s** a little better off he'll do some work in the house.
*Pendant que lui **sera** tranquille en train de boire une bière, moi je serai chez le dentiste.*	While he**'s** calmly drinking a beer, I'll be at the dentist.

▶ *depuis que* **clauses** After *depuis que* the tense is the same as in English if the action that is being described *has been completed*:

***Depuis qu'**elle est allée vivre en France, j'ai perdu contact avec elle.*	Since she went to live in France, I've lost touch with her.

But if the action *is / was continuing* at the time the speaker is describing it, the English *perfect tense* is conveyed by the *present tense* in French and the English *pluperfect tense* is conveyed by the *imperfect tense* in French:

*Depuis qu'elle **vit** en France je lui écris regulièrement.*	Since she **has been living** in France I write to her regularly. [She's living there now and I'm writing letters to her.]
*Depuis qu'elle **vivait** en France, je lui écrivais regulièrement.*	Since she **had been living** in France I wrote to her regularly. [She was still living in France at the time when I was writing letters to her.]

Note

The same difference between English and French in the use of tenses occurs with *il y a* and *cela fait* or *ça fait* (colloquial) referring to a period of time that is not yet completed:

***Il y a / Ça fait** deux ans que je travaille chez Renault.*	I've been working for Renault for two years.
***Il y avait** deux ans que je travaillais chez Renault.*	I had been working for Renault for two years.

14.3.4 Conditional conjunctions

même si	even if
si	if

Si can mean both 'if' and 'whether' in English.

▶ when *si* is part of a conditional sentence the English equivalent is always 'if'. In these sentences future or conditional tenses cannot be used in the *si* clause:

Si *j'ai bien compris il a raté son examen.*	If I've understood him correctly he's failed his exam.
Si *la météo le permet, ils joueront la finale cet après-midi.*	Weather permitting, they will play the final this afternoon.
*Il ne viendra pas, même **s'**il a le temps.*	He won't come even if he has the time.
*J'aurais pu vous prêter mon portable **si** j'avais su que le vôtre ne marchait pas.*	I could have lent you my laptop if I'd known that yours wasn't working.
Si *j'avais du talent je me mettrais à peindre.*	If I was talented I'd take up painting.
Si *j'avais su j'aurais étudié l'informatique.*	If I'd known I'd have studied computer science.

▶ When *si* is used in an indirect question its equivalent is 'if' or 'whether'. In these constructions any appropriate tense may be used in the *si* clause:

*Je ne sais pas **si** vous avez rencontré mon ami, Charles.*	I don't know if / whether you have met my friend Charles.
*Je me demande **s'**il pleuvra ce soir.*	I wonder if / whether it will rain this evening.
*À l'époque je m'étais demandé **si** cela valait la peine de faire un doctorat.*	At the time I had wondered if it was worthwhile doing a doctorate.

14.4 Subordinating conjunctions followed by the subjunctive

à condition que	provided that
à moins que	unless
afin que	so that

avant que	before
de peur que	for fear that
jusqu'à ce que	until
bien que	although
pour que	so that
pourvu que	provided that
quoique	although
sans que	without

*L'orage a commencé **avant qu'**ils aient pu retourner chez eux.*	The storm began before they were able to get back home.
*Il entre dans la chambre **sans que** personne ne s'en rende compte.*	He goes into the room without anybody realizing.
*Il est parti **avant qu'**elle n'ait eu le temps de répondre.*	He went off before she had had a chance to reply.
***Bien qu'**elle lui ait dit trois fois d'aller se coucher, l'enfant a refusé.*	Even though she told him to go to bed three times the child refused.
*J'accepterai n'importe quel emploi **pourvu qu'**il soit bien rémunéré.*	I'll accept any old job provided it's well paid.
*Attends ici, **jusqu'à ce que** le réservoir soit plein !*	Wait here until the tank is full!

(See also 12.7.)

14.5 Subordinating conjunctions followed by the indicative or the subjunctive, depending on meaning

The following conjunctions can be followed either by the indicative or the subjunctive, depending on meaning:

de façon que	in such a way that, so that
de manière que	in such a way that, so that
de sorte que	in such a way that, so that
si bien que	in such a way that, so that

When these conjunctions describe an action that has taken place, i.e., there has been a result, the indicative is used; when the action intended or desired has not taken place, the subjunctive is used:

Le politicien a parlé de façon que tout le monde **a pu** le comprendre.	The politician spoke in such a way that everyone was able to understand him.
Le politicien parle de façon que tout le monde **puisse** le comprendre.	The politician speaks in such a way that every one can understand him.
La star s'est placée de façon que tout le monde **a pu** la prendre en photo.	The star positioned herself so that everyone was able to take her photo.
La star s'est placée de façon que tout le monde **puisse** la voir.	The star has positioned herself so that everyone can see her.
Puis la crise est arrivée, de sorte que les prix des maisons **sont devenus** de nouveau abordables.	Then the crisis came, so house prices became affordable again.
Il a préféré retirer son argent de la banque, de sorte qu'il **puisse investir** dans la pierre.	He preferred to withdraw his money from the bank so that he can invest in property.

14.6 Conjunctions with more than one meaning

Students often encounter problems with the translation of certain English conjunctions into French because their meanings vary according to their function in the sentence.

14.6.1 'as'

▶ 'at the same time as', 'in the same way as' = *comme*

Il est arrivé comme je m'apprêtais à sortir.	He turned up as (i.e. at the same time as) I was getting ready to go out.
Comme l'an dernier, le Paris Saint-Germain n'est pas arrivé en finale.	As (in the same way as) last year, Paris Saint-Germain failed to reach the final.

▶ 'during the time which' = *à mesure que*

À mesure que les jours passent je deviens de plus en plus frustré.	As the days go by I become more and more frustrated.

14.6.2 'since'

▶ 'from a time in the past until now' = *depuis que*

Depuis que nous vivons à Paris nous avons rarement eu besoin d'utiliser la voiture.	Since we have lived in Paris we have rarely needed to use the car.

▶ 'for the reason that', 'because' = *puisque*, *comme*

Comme je serai en vacances je ne pourrai pas assister à la conférence. / Je ne pourrai pas assister à la conférence puisque je serai en vacances.	I won't be able to go to the conference since I shall be on holiday.

14.6.3 'while'

▶ 'during the time that' = *pendant que*

Je l'ai rencontré trois fois pendant que j'étais à Lyon.	I met him three times while I was staying in Lyons.

▶ 'whereas', 'in spite of the fact that' = *tandis que*

Elle a l'air jeune tandis que son amie a l'air âgée.	She looks young, while her friend looks old.

14.7 Repeated clauses introduced by subordinating conjunctions

When the same subordinating conjunction introduces more than one clause, the repeated conjunction is replaced by *que*. Note that in English the second conjunction is usually omitted.

Quand je suis allé au consulat et que j'eus expliqué la perte de mon passeport, les officiels m'ont beaucoup aidé.	When I went to the Consulate and (when) I explained that I had lost my passport, the officials were very helpful.
Bien que j'aime voyager en train et qu'Eurostar soit très rapide, pour Paris je préfère prendre l'avion.	Although I like train travel and (although) Eurostar is very fast, to Paris I prefer to fly.

But when a clause introduced by *si* is repeated, the *que* clause is in the subjunctive:

Si vous pouvez venir dimanche et qu'il fasse beau, nous ferons un barbecue.	If you can come on Sunday and (if) the weather is good, we'll have a barbecue.

CONJUNCTIONS IN CONTEXT

Aussi rapide que l'éclair . . .

Quand le 3 avril 2007 la société Alstom décida de faire connaître au monde les capacités de son nouveau train AGV (pour Automotrice à Grande Vitesse) **et qu'**elle annonça le chiffre record de 574,8 km/h, ce fut l'ébahissement général . . . **bien que** ce chiffre ne représentât pas le record absolu en la matière, **puisque** le Shinkansen japonais avait atteint, lui, la vitesse époustouflante de 581 km/h en 2003. **Mais** la prouesse résidait dans le fait que l'AGV avait accompli sa performance sur des rails classiques **et** avec un pantographe et des caténaires. **Alors que** le Shinkansen, voulant éviter les frictions, avait opté pour le système maglev à sustentation magnétique.

Qu'on ne s'y trompe pas ! **Tandis que** la performance japonaise est excellente et **qu'**elle est promise à un meilleur avenir encore, la performance française est remarquable à plus d'un titre.

D'abord, **pour qu'**un pantographe puisse résister dans de telles conditions, **sans qu'**il soit sectionné par un câble de caténaire défilant à près de 600 km/h, il a fallu inventer un matériau exceptionnel. **Puis, quoique** la voie soit solidement assise sur le ballast, il a fallu penser à la violence des chocs des roues contre les rails. Là encore, je ne crois pas **que** l'invention d'un métal particulièrement résistant **ait été** chose facile. **Et puis, même si** un train n'est pas un avion, à une telle vitesse, le nez de l'AGV ne peut que piquer vers le haut, **à moins qu'**une aérodynamique appropriée ne soit trouvée.

Avant qu'il soit un symbole de vitesse, l'AGV est d'abord un concentré de technologies de pointe.

Quand *le 3 avril 2007 la société Alstom décida . . .*	*quand*: subordinating conjunction of time with past tense [14.3.3]
et qu'*elle annonça . . .*	*et*: coordinating conjunction [14.1] *qu'*: repeated subordinating conjunction of time (*qu'* = *quand*)
bien que *ce chiffre ne représentât pas le record absolu . . .*	*bien que*: subordinating conjunction followed by subjunctive [14.4]
puisque *le Shinkansen japonais avait atteint . . .*	*puisque*: subordinating conjunction followed by the indicative [14.3.2]
Mais *la prouesse résidait dans le fait que l'AGV . . .*	*mais*: coordinating conjunction [14.1]
Alors que *le Shinkansen, . . .*	*alors que*: subordinating conjunction followed by the indicative [14.3.2]

Tandis que la performance japonaise est... *et qu'*elle est promise à un meilleur avenir encore ...	*tandis que*: subordinating conjunction followed by the indicative [14.3.2] *et*: coordinating conjunction [14.1] followed by *que* (*tandis* repeated is understood)
*pour qu'*un pantographe puisse résister ...	*pour que*: subordinating conjunction followed by subjunctive [14.4]
*sans qu'*il soit sectionné ...	*sans que*: subordinating conjunction followed by subjunctive [14.4]
Puis, quoique la voie soit solidement assise sur le ballast, ...	*puis*: coordinating conjunction [14.1] *quoique*: subordinating conjunction followed by subjunctive [14.4]
je ne crois pas **que** *l'invention d'un métal particulièrement résistant ait été chose facile.*	*que*: subordinating conjunction followed by the subjunctive [14.4]
Et puis, même si un train n'est pas un avion,	*et puis*: coordinating conjunctions [14.1] *même si*: conditional conjunction [14.3.4]
*... à moins qu'*une aérodynamique appropriée ne soit trouvée.	*à moins que*: subordinating conjunction followed by subjunctive [14.4]
*Avant qu'*il soit un symbole de vitesse, l'AGV	*avant que*: subordinating conjunction followed by subjunctive [14.4]

EXERCISES

1. **Fill the gaps with the correct coordinating conjunction: *mais, ou, et, donc, or, ni, car* or *puis*:**

   1. Je suis arrivé après la réunion _____ mon train a eu du retard.
   2. Je n'aime _____ la viande _____ le poisson.
   3. J'aime à la fois les légumes _____ les fruits.
   4. J'aime les matières littéraires _____ pas trop les matières scientifiques.
   5. J'aime la musique _____ elle me détend.
   6. J'étais fort en maths _____ j'ai passé un bac scientifique.
   7. Cela m'est égal, café _____ thé, je n'ai pas de préférence.
   8. La religion _____ la politique sont des sujets délicats.
   9. Tous les hommes ont des défauts, _____ tu es un homme, _____ tu as des défauts.
   10. Il a commencé par apprendre l'espagnol _____ il a continué avec l'allemand.

2. **Fill the gaps with the correct subordinating conjunction:** *à mesure que, bien que, parce que, plutôt que, pour que, que, quand, selon que* **or** *tant que*:

1. *Je viendrai te voir _____ il fera beau.*
2. *_____ on m'a bien expliqué, j'ai pu trouver sans problème.*
3. *_____ de rester devant la télévision tu ferais mieux de bouger un peu.*
4. *Il a pu s'acheter un voilier _____ il a un bon salaire.*
5. *Je vais m'assurer _____ vous avez bien compris.*
6. *La population s'inquiétait _____ l'eau de la rivière montait.*
7. *_____ il soit de grande taille, il n'est pas excellent en basket-ball.*
8. *je vous répète mes conditions _____ tout soit clair entre nous.*
9. *Tu ne pourras pas aller te coucher _____ tu ne te seras pas brossé les dents.*
10. *« _____ vous serez puissant ou misérable, les jugements de cour vous rendront blanc ou noir. »* (Les Animaux malades de la peste – Jean de la Fontaine)

3. **Fill the gaps with a suitable coordinating or subordinating conjunction:**

1. *Ses résultats ont été bons _____ il aurait pu mieux faire.*
2. *Vous n'auriez pas 5 euros à me prêter _____ je puisse m'acheter un ticket de train ?*
3. *Je te prêterai mon livre _____ j'aurai fini de le lire.*
4. *Je n'ai _____ parapluie _____ imperméable.*
5. *Qu'est-ce que tu prends, une bière _____ un cidre ?*
6. *J'aurais bien pris une bière _____ je n'avais pas dû conduire.*
7. *Faites _____ je n'étais pas là.*
8. *_____ j'ai fini d'écrire ce courriel, je m'occupe de toi.*
9. *Tu pourras insister _____ tu voudras, je ne cèderai pas.*
10. *J'ai travaillé tout l'été, _____ maintenant je fais la grasse matinée tous les jours.*

Each of the following sentences contains a relative clause:

> The man *who* answered the phone was very rude.

> The bird (*that*) you saw yesterday was a golden eagle.

> Her house, *which* was built in the eighteenth century, is being restored.

Relative clauses are clauses introduced by words like *who*, *that* and *which*. These words are **relative pronouns**. They have two important functions:

▶ As pronouns, they refer back to a previous element in the sentence. In the above sentences the noun that is referred to ('man', 'bird', 'house') stands immediately before the relative pronoun, and is called the **antecedent**.

▶ They link two clauses together. The clause which is introduced by the relative pronoun is called a **subordinate clause**.

KEY POINTS

Relative pronouns have two functions in French:

✦ as pronouns, they refer to an element that comes before it, known as the **antecedent**. The antecedent can be:

○ a noun: *Le médecin qui l'a soignée.* The doctor who looked after her.

○ a pronoun: *C'est lui qui l'a soignée.* It's him who looked after her.

(continued)

(continued)

- ○ an adjective or a past participle: ***Imprudents*** *que vous êtes.* lit. Foolhardy that you are.

- ○ an adverb: ***Là*** *où elle va n'est un secret pour personne.* Where she's going is not a secret to anyone.

- ○ a clause: ***Elle a fait un beau voyage***, *ce dont je l'envie.* She has had a nice journey, for which I envy her.

- ○ a verb (in set expressions): ***Coûte*** *que coûte !* Whatever the cost!

✦ as subordinating conjunctions, they link a main clause, which usually includes its antecedent, with a subordinate clause. This is called a **relative clause**.

*Un robot **qui** parle.*	A robot that talks.

Unlike in English, in French the relative pronoun is **never omitted**:

*Les livres **que** j'ai lus.*	The books I've read.

15.1 Agreement with the past participle

(see also 11.6.4)

▶ A past participle that follows the relative pronoun agrees in gender and number with it, since the latter refers to its antecedent. The sentence ***Les olives que j'ai achetées viennent de Sicile*** (The olives [that] I bought come from Sicily) consists of:

▶ a main clause: *les olives . . . viennent de Sicile*

▶ a relative clause: *que j'ai achetées*

que	is the relative pronoun which stands in the place of *olives* and which therefore agrees in gender and number.
	is also the direct object of *ai achetées* and is placed before the past participle *achetées*.
olives	the antecedent, is a feminine plural noun.
achetées	is a past participle related to *que*, feminine plural, and agreeing with it.

Note

In old expressions, proverbs and sayings, the antecedent is understood:

Qui cherche trouve !	He who seeks shall find!

15.2 The invariable relatives, *qui, que, quoi, dont, où*

These relatives may be combined with the demonstrative *ce*:

*Je sais **ce qui** compte.*	I know what counts.
*Je sais **ce que** je dis.*	I know what I'm saying.
*Je sais **ce à quoi** vous faites allusion.*	I know what you're referring to.

In French, as in English, the relative pronouns take on a different form according to their function in the sentence:

Function	Pronoun	Antecedent	Example
subject	*qui*	person or thing	*Le médecin **qui** vous a examiné.* The doctor who has examined you.
direct object	*que, qu'*	person or thing	*L'ordonnance **que** vous avez reçue.* The prescription you have received.
indirect object	*quoi*	thing	*Voilà ce **à quoi** vous tenez tant !* That's the thing you're most fond of!
noun complement	*dont*	person or thing	*L'ordonnance **dont** il est question.* The prescription we're talking about.
adverbial expression	*où*	thing	*La pharmacie **où** je vais.* The chemist's I'm going to.

Note

Care should be taken not to confuse the relative pronouns *qui, que, quoi, où* with the interrogative pronouns *qui? que? quoi? où?*

Relative:	*Quel est cet inconnu **qui** approche ?*	Who is that stranger who's approaching?
Interrogative:	***Qui** va là ?*	Who goes there?

15.3 *Qui* (who, which, that)

▶ *Qui* is a subject pronoun, unless it is preceded by a preposition:

*Voilà le technicien **qui** a réparé l'aspirateur.*	There is the engineer **who** repaired the vacuum cleaner.
*L'homme **qui** est venu est notre voisin.*	The man **who** came is our neighbour.
*Le chien **qui** était dans le jardin appartenait à notre voisin.*	The dog **which / that** was in the garden belonged to our neighbour.

▶ *Qui* can stand for people, animals or things:

*C'est l'enfant **qui** a éteint la bougie.*	It's the child who put out the candle.
*C'est la bougie **qui** s'est éteinte.*	It's the candle that blew out.

▶ *Qui* may be preceded by a preposition.

▶ If the antecedent is an animal or a thing it must be replaced by the relative pronoun *lequel* (see 15.8):

*L'ami **à qui** j'ai écrit.*	The friend I wrote to.
*Le chat **auquel** j'ai donné du lait.*	The cat I gave some milk to.

▶ *ce qui* (which, what) is a combination of the demonstrative *ce* + *qui*:

On a decidé d'aller à la Martinique, ce qui est fantastique !	We've decided to go to Martinique, which is fantastic!

15.4 *Que / qu'* (who[m], which, that, what)

que is a direct object pronoun, which is elided to *qu'* before a vowel and silent **h**. It can refer to people or things:

*Il a des moyens **que** je n'ai pas.*	He has means that / which I haven't got.
*Elle a des amis **que** j'apprécie.*	She has friends that I like.
*Les arbres **qu'**on a plantés sont des arbres fruitiers.*	The trees that have been planted are fruit trees.

▶ *ce que* (which, what), a combination of the demonstrative *ce* + *que*,

▶ introduces an idea (what):

| *Ce que je sais, c'est qu'il travaille à Lyon.* | What I know is that he works in Lyons. |

▶ stands for a previous clause (*which*):

| *Il travaille à Lyon, ce que je sais depuis longtemps.* | He works in Lyons, which I have known for a long time. |

▶ *celui / celle / ceux / celles que*

    ▶ The demonstrative pronouns *celui*, *celle*, *ceux* and *celles* are used to introduce relative clauses (see 4.9.1):

| *Celle que tu as rencontrée hier n'est pas ma sœur.* | The person you met yesterday is not my sister. |
| *Ceux que j'ai corrigés, taisez-vous, s'il vous plaît !* | Those whose work I've corrected be quiet, please! |

15.5 *Quoi* (which, what)

Quoi can only refer to things.

Quoi is always preceded by a preposition when referring to an indirect object or an adverbial:

| *Prenez un papier sur quoi écrire.* | Take a piece of paper to write on. [lit. on which to write] |

Its antecedent can be a determiner, an adverb like *rien* or pronouns such as *ce*, *quelque chose*:

| *Il lui faudrait quelque chose **à quoi** se raccrocher.* | He would need something to cling on to. |
| *Demandez-lui **ce à quoi** il pensait quand il a pris une telle décision.* | Ask him what he was thinking about when he took such a decision. |

Quoi can introduce an infinitive clause with *avoir* (to have), *acheter* (to buy), *chercher* (to look for), *trouver* (to find), and after *voici* and *voilà*:

| *Je voulais acheter **de quoi** faire un gâteau, mais je n'avais pas **de quoi** payer.* | I wanted to buy something to bake a cake with, but I didn't have any money to pay for it. |

Note

Care should be taken not to confuse *quoi que* (whatever), the pronoun, with *quoique* (although), the conjunction. In the spoken language this difference can only be understood from the context:

***Quoi que** je fasse* . . .	Whatever I do . . .
***Quoique** je me sois entrainé, je suis arrivé dans les derniers.*	Although I trained, I was among the last to finish.

15.6 *Dont* (whose, of / about whom, of which)

Dont is used for a complement introduced by the preposition *de*. It can be the complement to a noun, adjective or indirect object.

- ▶ Noun complement: *la montagne **dont** je vois le sommet* — the mountain, whose summit I can see (*le sommet **de la montagne***)
- ▶ Adjective complement: *Le sport, **dont** il est fervent, lui fait beaucoup de bien.* — Sport, which he is very keen on, does him a lot of good. (*fervent **de sport***)
- ▶ Indirect object complement: *le grimpeur **dont** j'ai parlé* — the climber I spoke about (*parler **du** / **au** sujet **du** / à propos **du** grimpeur*)

Dont can be used for people or things:

*l'homme **dont** on voit le chapeau*	the man whose hat can be seen
*la forêt **dont** on a coupé les arbres*	the forest whose trees have been cut
*le dentiste **dont** je vous ai parlé*	the dentist (who[m]) I told you about

If *dont* is separated from its antecedent by a preposition, it **must** be replaced by *duquel, de laquelle, desquels, desquelles* (see 15.8):

*L'ami, à la mère **duquel** j'ai téléphoné, sera là ce soir.*	The friend whose mother I phoned will be there this evening. (You cannot say here *dont à la mere.)

15.7 *Où* (where, in / to which, when)

Où as a relative pronoun can only be used for things. It expresses:

- ▶ an adverbial of place:

*la ville **où** j'habite*	the town where I live

▶ an adverbial of time, unlike in English, where 'when' is used:

à l'époque **où** elle travaillait comme infirmière	at the time when she worked as a nurse

▶ *où* can be preceded by a preposition, e.g. *d', par, vers, jusqu'*:

le pays **d'où** il vient	the country he comes from
Voilà le sentier par **où** ils sont passés.	There's the path they went along.

▶ *où* can have an adverb of place as its antecedent:

Là **où** ils vont.	lit. There where they are going.

15.8 *Lequel* ([that] which, who[m])

Lequel as a relative pronoun:

▶ agrees in gender and number with its antecedent;

▶ can have a person or a thing as its antecedent;

▶ combines with the prepositions *à* and *de*.

	Masculine		Feminine	
	Singular	Plural	Singular	Plural
without a preposition	lequel	lesquels	laquelle	lesquelles
à	auquel	auxquels	à laquelle	auxquelles
de	duquel	desquels	de laquelle	desquelles

la personne à laquelle je pense	the person I'm thinking of
les personnes auxquelles je pense	the people I'm thinking of

▶ *Lequel, laquelle, lesquels, lesquelles*

▶ This pronoun is generally preceded by prepositions such as *avec, dans, pour, par, à l'intérieur de, à propos de, au milieu de, au sujet de, au-dessous de, au-dessus de, chez, d'après, en face de, entre, parmi, près de, sans, selon*:

la piscine **dans laquelle** nous nous sommes baignés	the swimming pool in which we bathed
le concept **à propos duquel** il y eut débat	the concept about which there was a debate

▶ If the antecedent is a person, *lequel* can be replaced by *qui*:

*les amis chez **lesquels** nous avons passé l'été*	the friends with whom we spent the summer
*les amis chez **qui** nous avons passé l'été*	the friends with whom we spent the summer

▶ *Lequel* can be used as a subject (*who* in English), but this usage is mainly literary and (especially) administrative, to avoid ambiguities with the antecedent:

*La police a interrogé deux suspects, **lesquels** ont déclaré avoir un alibi.*	The police inteviewed two suspects, who stated that they had alibis.

▶ *Lequel* must replace *qui*:

  ▶ after the prepositions *parmi* and *entre*:

*Ce pays compte cinq millions d'habitants **parmi lesquels** 400 000 suédophones.*	This country has 5 million inhabitants, of whom 400,000 are Swedish-speaking.

  ▶ after all prepositions if the antecedent is not a person:

*le village **auquel** je pense*	the village I'm thinking of
*la femme **à qui** je pense*	the woman I'm thinking of

▶ ***Duquel, de laquelle, desquels, desquelles*** (of / from which, whose)

  ▶ This pronoun replaces *dont* when it is separated from its antecedent by a preposition:

*C'est le professeur dans la classe **duquel** on a trouvé des graffiti.*	It's the teacher in whose classroom graffiti were found.

15.9 Restrictive and non-restrictive relative clauses

The sentences:

Les élèves, qui ont bien travaillé, ont eu d'excellentes notes. (1)	The pupils, who have worked well, have had excellent marks.
Les élèves qui ont bien travaillé ont eu d'excellentes notes. (2)	The pupils who have worked well have had excellent marks.

differ only by the presence of two commas, yet their meaning is quite different: the number of pupils being given excellent marks is not the same in each case. In sentence (1) all the pupils have worked well and been given excellent marks. In sentence (2) only those pupils who have worked well have been given excellent marks.

Sentence (1) is non-restrictive.

Sentence (2) is restrictive.

Non-restrictive clauses give extra information about the antecedent, which is inserted in the sentence. This information can be removed without the meaning of the rest of the sentence being affected. The two commas correspond to a pause when speaking.

Restrictive clauses are essential to the meaning of the sentence and cannot therefore be removed without loss of meaning.

RELATIVE PRONOUNS IN CONTEXT

Que coûtent les guerres?

L'Europe est le continent **où** les conflits furent incessants. **Ce qui** a poussé les nations à tant de barbarie ? La conquête de nouveaux territoires **qui** seuls garantissaient puissance et prestige ! Nous avons lu sur les affrontements entre Espagnols et Français, **lesquels** se ruinaient régulièrement pour s'arracher des bribes de territoires. On nous a tout dit **sur ce que** tel général avait développé de stratégie, **ce à quoi** il avait dû faire face, l'idéal **pour lequel** il s'était battu, et les mille raisons **pour lesquelles** il n'aurait pas dû perdre.

Mais **ce dont** on n'entend jamais parler, **là où** le bât blesse* en quelque sorte, c'est le prix **qu'**ont coûté ces campagnes militaires. Deux pays se mettent soudain à titiller l'histoire: **ce à propos de quoi** on se chamaille est surprenant, car c'est un litige vieux de 400 ans **dont** il est question.

Notre histoire débute au XVIe siècle. À une époque **où** l'Espagne était au sommet de sa gloire. Philippe II, en guerre contre la France, dût emprunter de l'argent. C'est vers la Pologne **qu'**il se tourne, **de laquelle** il reçoit 430 000 ducats en or.

Il pensait que la suprématie **dont** jouissait son pays sur le plan diplomatique lui permettait quelques prérogatives **dont** celle notamment de ne pas rembourser sa dette.

Voilà de quoi irriter aujourd'hui un jeune député polonais, **dont** personne n'avait entendu parler auparavant. Ce dernier adresse une réclamation **par laquelle** il exige un remboursement immédiat.

Aujourd'hui les temps sont durs et notre député a fait des calculs. Ce serait de près de 57 millions d'euros **que** serait redevable l'Espagne, sans compter les intérêts **qui** pourraient s'élever à des centaines de millions.

* *là où le bât blesse* that's where it hurts

. . . *le continent* **où** *les conflits furent incessants.*	**où** [15.7]
. . . *de nouveaux territoires* **qui** *seuls garantissaient puissance et prestige*	**qui** as subject pronoun [15.3]
. . . *les affrontements entre Espagnols et Français,* **lesquels** *se ruinaient régulièrement* . . .	**lequel** [15.8]
On nous a tout dit **sur ce que** *tel général avait développé de stratégie*	**ce que** [15.4]
ce à quoi *il avait dû faire face,*	**quoi** [15.5]
. . . *l'idéal* **pour lequel** *il s'était battu*	**lequel** [15.8]
. . . *les mille raisons* **pour lesquelles** *il n'aurait pas dû perdre*	**lequel** [15.8]
Mais **ce dont** *on n'entend jamais parler*	**dont** [15.6]
là **où** *le bât blesse*	**où** [15.7]
. . . *le prix* **qu'**ont coûté ces campagnes	**que** as object pronoun, elided to **qu'** [15.4]
c'est un litige vieux de 400 ans **dont** *il est question*	**dont** [15.6]
À une époque **où** *l'Espagne était au sommet de sa gloire.*	**où** [15.7]
C'est vers la Pologne **qu'**il se tourne,	**que** as object pronoun, elided to **qu'** [15.4]
. . . **de laquelle** *il reçoit 430 000 ducats en or.*	**lequel** [15.8]
. . . *la suprématie* **dont** *jouissait son pays*	**dont** [15.6]
. . . *quelques prérogatives* **dont** *celle notamment de ne pas rembourser sa dette.*	**dont** [15.6]
Voilà de quoi *irriter un jeune député polonais*	**quoi** [15.5] after *voilà de* followed by an infinitive
. . . **dont** *personne n'avait entendu parler auparavant*	**dont** [15.6]
. . . *une réclamation* **par laquelle** *il exige un remboursement immédiat.*	**lequel** [15.8]
Ce serait de près de 57 millions d'euros **que** *serait redevable l'Espagne*	**que** as object pronoun [15.4]
. . . *sans compter les intérêts* **qui** *pourraient s'élever à des centaines de millions.*	**qui** as subject pronoun [15.3]

1. Choose the correct relative pronoun between *qui*, *que*, *qu'* and *dont*:

La voiture

1. *C'est un objet _____ le prestige est grand.*
2. *C'est un objet _____ on porte au pinacle.*
3. *C'est un objet _____ a quatre roues.*
4. *C'est un objet _____ tout le monde aimerait avoir.*
5. *C'est un objet _____ vous permet de gagner du temps.*
6. *C'est un objet _____ transporte toute la famille.*
7. *C'est l'objet _____ il est nécessaire d'avoir aujourd'hui.*
8. *C'est un objet _____ il faut utiliser avec prudence.*
9. *C'est un objet _____, pour des raisons environnementales, il faut utiliser avec modération.*
10. *C'est un objet _____ l'usage se mondialise.*

2. Choose the correct relative pronoun to fill the gap after the preposition:

1. *C'est l'homme pour _____ il a voté.*
2. *Contre _____ jouez-vous dimanche ?*
3. *C'est la fille avec _____ il sort.*
4. *Le débat à _____ il a pris part la semaine dernière est maintenant sur YouTube.*
5. *C'est le lit sous _____ il a trouvé la bague.*
6. *La chaise sur _____ il veut monter pour son discours est bancale.*
7. *Montre-nous de _____ tu es capable.*
8. *Mais à _____ pensais-tu quand tu as écrit ce mél ?*
9. *À _____ de ces deux personnages t'identifies-tu ?*
10. *De _____ est-elle la fille ?*

3. Relative pronouns combined with ce.

Fill the gaps with the appropriate relative pronoun, preceded by a preposition when necessary.

1. *Ce _____ je me souviens c'est la balançoire du jardin.*
2. *Ce _____ il aspire c'est une maison au bord d'un lac.*
3. *Il a gagné une médaille d'or, ce _____ est incroyable.*
4. *Je n'achète que ce _____ j'ai besoin.*
5. *Généralement je ne lis pas ce _____ m'ennuie.*
6. *Il n'a pas eu son baccalauréat, ce _____ on s'attendait.*
7. *Ce _____ compte pour lui c'est de réussir sa vie sociale.*
8. *Ce _____ elle souhaite réussir c'est sa vie professionnelle.*
9. *Manger sainement, c'est ce _____ j'aime.*
10. *Ce _____ il a peur c'est de ne pas trouver de travail.*

QUESTIONS AND EXCLAMATIONS

16.1 Questions

Introduction

Direct questions are of two kinds: those that ask for information, in which case a question word like *What?*, *When?* or *Why?* introduces the question, as in: **What** *are you doing this evening?*, and those that expect the answer 'yes' or 'no', as in *Are you going out this evening?* Questions may also be indirect: *Ask her* **what** *she's doing this evening*.

KEY POINTS

✦ In French, yes / no questions can be formulated in one of three ways:

Are you going out this evening? can be rendered by:

• turning a statement into question, adding a question mark:

Tu sors ce soir. → *Tu sors ce soir?*

- inverting the verb and the subject pronoun:

Sors-tu ce soir?

- placing *Est-ce que* before the statement, adding a question mark:

Est-ce que *tu sors ce soir?*

✦ A formula may be used, in the spoken language especially, for certain question words, for example:

- questions beginning with *Who?* may be introduced by *Qui est-ce qui?* or *Qui est-ce que?*

| **Qui est-ce qui** *le dit ?* | Who says so? |
| **Qui est-ce qu'***elle a vu hier ?* | Who did she see yesterday? |

- questions beginning with *What?* may be introduced by *Qu'est-ce qui?* and *Qu'est-ce que?*

| **Qu'est-ce qui** *se passe ?* | What's going on? |
| **Qu'est-ce que** *tu as acheté ?* | What did you buy? |

16.1.1   Direct questions: yes / no answers

▶ Questions expressed by intonation

When a statement is turned into a question, the speaker employs a rising intonation at the end of the sentence:

| *Tu reviens demain ?* | Are you coming back tomorrow? |
| *Tu me prêtes ton magazine ?* | Will you lend me your magazine? |

This way of formulating questions is mainly used in the spoken language.

▶ Inversion of the subject pronoun and the verb

When the subject is a pronoun, a question is created by inverting the verb and the pronoun and joining them by a hyphen:

| **Voulez-vous** *m'accompagner au commissariat ?* | Will you go with me to the police station? |
| **Avez-vous** *toujours votre belle voiture ?* | Have you still got your beautiful car? |

With the first person, inversion of this kind is not usual except for a few verbs, such as *pouvoir* and *avoir*:

| **Puis-je** *vous donner la clé ?* | Can I give you the key? |
| **Ai-je** *bien compris vos propos ?* | Have I understood your comments properly? |

Where necessary, *-t-* is inserted between the verb and the pronoun to avoid a clash of two vowels:

| **A-t-elle** *dit ce qu'elle va faire ?* | Has she said what she's going to do? |
| **Chanta-t-il** *sans orchestre ou avec orchestre ?* | Did he sing with or without an orchestra? |

When the subject of the sentence is a noun, inversion can still take place, but the noun is placed at the beginning of the question and 'duplicated' by a subject pronoun after the verb:

| *Claude,* **as-tu** *apporté les disques ?* | Have you brought the disks, Claude? |
| *Marie et Michel,* **viendront-ils** *cet été ?* | Will Marie and Michel come this summer? |

▶ *Est-ce que?*

Est-ce que is placed at the beginning of the statement and a question mark added:

| **Est-ce que** *tu as apporté les disques, Claude ?* | Have you brought the disks, Claude? |
| **Est-ce que** *toutes les portes ont été fermées ?* | Have all the doors been shut? |

16.1.2 Question tags: n'est-ce pas? non?

▶ Question tags in English, like 'isn't it', 'don't they', 'aren't you', 'didn't it' may be rendered in French by *n'est-ce pas?*:

| *Ils sont allés faire des courses, n'est-ce pas ?* | They've gone shopping, haven't they? |
| *C'est vous qui avez laissé les lumières allumées, n'est-ce pas ?* | It's you who left the lights on, isn't it? |

▶ In spoken French the tag *non?* is also used very frequently:

| *Tu as fermé les fenêtres,* **non** *?* | You've closed the windows, haven't you? |
| *On s'est déjà rencontrés,* **non** *?* | We've met before, haven't we? |

16.1.3 Direct questions

Note

A number of question words, or interrogative pronouns, such as *que, qui, lequel* and *où* are also relative pronouns, and should not be confused with the latter (see 15.2).

▶ Using question words

   ▶ Question words can be placed at the beginning or at the end of a question. If they are at the beginning, the verb and subject pronoun are inverted:

Où est-il allé ?	Where has he gone?
Combien de fois as-tu vu ce film ?	How many times have you seen that film?
Lequel des deux est Bertrand ?	Which of the two is Bertrand?

If the question word is at the end of the word there is no inversion:

*Il est allé **où** ?*	Where has he gone?
*Vous avez vu ce film **combien** de fois ?*	How many times have you seen that film?
*Mais ce dessin, ça ressemble à **quoi** ?*	What kind of drawing is that?

The latter construction is colloquial, and the speaker employs a rising intonation at the end of the question.

If there is a noun subject it is placed after the question word and 'duplicated' by a subject pronoun after the verb:

Où Marianne est-elle allée ?	Where has Marianne gone?
Comment tes amis ont-ils voyagé, en train ou en voiture ?	How did your friends travel, by train or by car?
Pourquoi ton frère ne vient-il plus à la gymnastique ?	Why doesn't your brother come to gymnastics any more?

▶ Question words are frequently followed by *est-ce que*, without inversion:

Où est-ce qu'il est allé ?	Where has he gone?
Quand est-ce que tu vas quitter l'université ?	When are you going to leave university?
Pourquoi est-ce qu'elle est venue ce matin ?	Why did she come this morning?
Comment est-ce que tu t'appelles ?	What is your name?
Depuis combien de temps est-ce que tu étudies ?	How long have you studied for?

▶ *Combien?* How much? How many?

Combien may be used alone or followed by a complement:

*Ça t'a coûté **combien** ?*	How much did that cost you?
Combien de gens y a-t-il dans le stade ?	How many people are there in the stadium?
*Cela prend **combien** de jours pour traverser la Sibérie en train ?*	How many days does it take to cross Siberia by train?
*Dans cette pièce vous vivez à **combien** ?*	How many of you live in this room?

▶ *Comment?* How? What?

Comment *vas-tu ?*	How are you?
Comment *trouvez-vous la ville ?*	How do you find / What do you think of the town?
Comment *est ton nouveau portable ?*	What is your new mobile like?
Comment est-ce que *ça marche ?*	How does it work?

▶ *Lequel / laquelle / lesquels / lesquelles?* Which (ones[s])?

  ▶ *lequel*, etc. is used when referring to a choice between options. It agrees in number and gender with the thing referred to:

Lesquels *de ces chocolats préférez-vous, les blancs ou les noirs ?*	Which of these chocolates do you prefer, the white or the dark ones?
– Regarde cette voiture !	'Look at that car!'
– **Laquelle** *?*	'Which one?'

  ▶ In combination with *à*, *lequel*, etc. become: *auquel, à laquelle, auxquels, auxquelles*:

Auquel *des tes collègues as-tu donné les billets ?*	Which of your colleagues did you give the tickets to?

  ▶ In combination with *de*, *lequel*, etc. become: *duquel, de laquelle, desquels, desquelles*:

De laquelle *de ces villes es-tu originaire ?*	Which of these towns do you come from?

▶ *Où?* Where?

Où *est la piscine ?*	Where is the swimming pool?
Où est-ce qu'on peut trouver des magasins de chaussures ?*	Where can we find shoe shops?
Où *Marie va-t-elle avec sa copine ?*	Where is Marie going with her friend?

▶ *Pourquoi?* Why?

Pourquoi *n'est-elle pas revenue ?*	Why hasn't she come back?
Pourquoi *ne veut-il pas nous accompagner ?*	Why doesn't he want to come with us?
Pourquoi *est-ce qu'ils ont pris le train ?*	Why did they take the train?

▶ *Quand?* When?

Quand *reviendrez-vous ?*	When will you come back?
Quand *l'avion arrivera-t-il à Paris ?*	When will the plane get to Paris?
Quand *est-ce que nous pourrons nous promener ?*	When can we go for a walk?

▶ *Que?* and *Qu'est-ce qui / que?* What?

Qu'est -ce qui? is used when referring to things, as **subject**.

Que or *Qu'est-ce que?* are alternatives when referring to things, as **object**.

▶ *Que?* What?

☐ *Que?* **cannot** be used as a subject pronoun. *Qu'est-ce qui?* has to be used.

What comes afterwards? **Qu'est-ce qui** *vient après ?* and not **Que vient après ?*

☐ *Que?* may be used as an object pronoun, and is placed at the beginning of a sentence. *Que?* is elided to *Qu'?* before a vowel or silent *h*:

Que *voulez-vous dire ?*	What do you mean?
Que *fait-il ?*	What's he doing?
Qu'ont dit tes voisins ?	What did your neighbours say?

☐ Colloquially, at the end of a sentence and before a preposition *que?* becomes *quoi?*

Ils parlent **de quoi** ?	What are they talking about?
Il fait **quoi** ?	What's he doing?

☐ *Que?* may be used before an infinitive to ask a question:

Que *faire ?*	What shall we do?
Que *dire ?*	What's to be said?
Que *penser de tout ce gaspillage ?*	What should we think about all this waste?

▶ *Qu'est-ce qui?* What?

Qu'est-ce qui? is the only possibility for *What?* as subject of a sentence:

Qu'est-ce qui *s'est passé ?*	What happened?
Qu'est-ce qui *a changé notre société ainsi ?*	What has changed our society in this way?

▶ *Qu'est-ce que?* What?

Qu'est-ce que? is an alternative to *que* as object of a sentence:

Qu'est-ce que *tu as dit?*	What did you say?
Qu'est-ce que *vous cachez dans vos poches?*	What are you hiding in your pockets?
Qu'est-ce qu'ils attendent?	What are they waiting for?

▶ *Quel / quelle / quels / quelles?* What? Which?

Quel / quelle / quels / quelles, etc. are adjectives that agree with the noun they qualify in number and gender:

À **quelle** *heure tu reviendras ?*	What time will you come back?
Quelle *région de France préférez-vous ?*	Which region of France do you prefer?
Dans **quel** *pays êtes-vous né ?*	In which country were you born?
Quelles *sont les erreurs à ne pas commettre dans ton pays ?*	What are the mistakes that should be avoided in your country?

▶ *Qui?* and *Qui est-ce qui / que?* Who? Whom?

    Qui? and *Qui est-ce qui?* are alternatives, when referring to people, as **subject**.

    Qui? or *Qui est-ce que?* are alternatives, when referring to people, as **object**.

    ▶ *Qui?* Who? Whom?

        ☐ *Qui?* can be used as the subject of a sentence:

Qui *est là ?*	Who's there?
Qui *amènera la voiture chez le garagiste ?*	Who will take the car to the garage?

        ☐ *Qui?* is used, with inversion, as the object of a sentence and after prepositions:

Qui *Monique a-t-elle vu à Marseille ?*	Who did Monique see in Marseilles?
Avec **qui** *est-il venu ?*	Who did he come with?
Qui *Chiara épouse-t-elle ?*	Who is Chiara going to marry?
Par qui *s'est-il fait insulter ?*	Who has he been insulted by?
Pour qui *travaille-t-il ?*	Who does he work for?

▶ *Qui est-ce qui?* Who?

Qui est-ce qui *a crié ?*	Who shouted?
Qui est-ce qui *remplacera notre prof de maths ?*	Who will replace our maths teacher?
Qui est-ce qui *s'est servi de mon savon ?*	Who's been using my soap?

▶ *Qui est-ce que?* Who? Whom?

Qui est-ce qu'*ils ont rencontré à Cannes ?*	Who(m) did they meet in Cannes?
Qui est-ce que *vous avez croisé à Londres, hier ?*	Who did you meet in London yesterday?
Qui est-ce que *vous avez examiné, docteur ?*	Who did you examine, doctor?

▶ *Quoi?* What?

Quoi? replaces *que?* after prepositions and at the end of a sentence, as a direct object:

De quoi *s'agit-il ?*	What's it about?
À quoi *penses-tu ?*	What are you thinking about?
Il a demandé **quoi** *?*	What did he ask for?
Avec quoi *as-tu payé ?*	What did you pay with?
Contre quoi *était-il appuyé ?*	What was he leaning against?

Expressions with *quoi?*

Quoi de neuf ?	What's new?
Quoi encore ?	What now?
Pour quoi faire ?	What for?

16.1.4 Si *in response to negative questions*

When a question which anticipates a negative answer is answered in the affirmative, *si,* and not *oui,* is the response (see 8.15):

| *– Tu ne me crois pas ? – Si.* | You don't believe me. Yes (I do). |

16.1.5 Indirect questions

▶ There is no inversion of the subject pronoun and verb in indirect questions:

Il ne m'a pas dit **quand** il viendra.	He hasn't told me when he's coming.
Elle m'a demandé **quel** temps il faisait.	She asked me what the weather was like.
Il m'a expliqué **comment** cela fonctionnait.	He explained to me how that worked.
Elle demande **qui** viendra la chercher à la gare.	She's asking who will come to get her at the station.

▶ *si* (if, whether) is used when a direct yes / no question becomes an indirect one:

Je me demande **s'**il fait attention.	I wonder if he's paying attention.
Ils ne savent pas **si** leur fils se trouve en France ou en Belgique.	They don't know whether their son is in France or Belgium.

▶ *ce que* and *ce qui*

In indirect questions, the equivalents of *what?* (*qu'est-ce qui?* [subject] and *que / qu'est ce que?* [object]) are *ce qui* and *ce que* respectively:

Je ne sais pas **ce qui** vous gêne.	I don't know what's bothering you.
Il ne comprend pas **ce que** vous avez dit.	He doesn't understand what you said.
Je ne vois pas **ce qui** vous chagrine.	I can't see what's worrying you.
Elle veut savoir **ce que** vous faites dans ce jardin.	She wants to know what you are doing in this garden.

16.2 Exclamations

We use exclamations to express a whole range of emotions: surprise, joy, disgust, horror, relief, shock, etc.

KEY POINTS

✦ Exclamatory expressions in French are frequently introduced by words like *quel(le)!*, *quoi!* and *comment!*

Quel dommage !	What a pity!

✦ The subjunctive is used occasionally for exclamations, in set expressions:

Vive le Président !	Long live the President!

16.2.1 Exclamatory words

▶ *Comme !* (how)

Comme il se vante !	How he boasts!
Comme le temps est clément aujourd'hui !	How mild the weather is today!

▶ *Que !* (how)

Qu'elle est belle, la France !	How beautiful France is!
Qu'il est haut, ce gratte-ciel !	How high that skyscraper is!

▶ *Quel / quelle / quels / quelles !* (how, what)

Quel / quelle / quels / quelles ! agree in number and gender with the noun they qualify:

Quel froid !	How cold it is!
Quelle horreur !	How awful!

▶ *Qu'est-ce que . . . !*

Qu'est-ce qu'il fait chaud !	How hot it is!

▶ *Quoi ! Comment !*

These two words are often used on their own to express disbelief:

Quoi *! Nous avons perdu !*	What! We've lost!
Comment *! Ça, c'est incroyable !*	What! That's unbelievable!
Comment *! Vous arrivez d'Asie et vous ne me dites rien !*	What! You've come back from Asia and you're not saying anything to me!

16.2.2 The subjunctive used in exclamations

Que! followed by the subjunctive has an exclamatory force:

Que *Dieu vous bénisse !*	May God bless you!
Que *ta vie soit pleine de bonheur !*	May your life be full of happiness!

16.2.3 Interjections

As in all languages, interjections are used to express emotion. Here are some common ones:

Aïe !	Ouch!
Hein !	What!
Zut !	Damn!
Allez !	Come on!
Mon Dieu !	My goodness!

QUESTIONS AND EXCLAMATIONS IN CONTEXT

La mère et l'enfant

A – Maman ! C'est quoi que tu regardes ?

B – Quel langage ! Veux-tu bien parler correctement ?

A – Que re-gar-des-tu, ma-man, ché-rie ?

B – Ah ! Mais c'est mieux ainsi, n'est-ce pas ?

A – Oui, mais je me demande si on ne va pas se moquer de moi à l'école. Qu'est-ce que tu regardes ?

B – Ce que je regarde ? Tu vois bien ? Ce sont de vieilles photos de grand-père. Tiens ! Qui est ce jeune homme avec une belle moustache ?

A – Je ne sais pas. Est-ce que je suis censé le connaître ?

B – C'est justement mon grand-père. Ton arrière-grand-père.

A – Mais c'est lequel de tes grand-pères ? De quand date cette photo ? Quel âge avait-il ?

B – Tu ne devines pas son âge ? Qu'est-ce que tu vois derrière ?

A – Ouaou ! Que d'eau ! Comment font les gens pour marcher dans cette eau ?

B – Ce sont les inondations de 1938. Ton grand-père avait donc . . . ?

A – Attends ! Il avait . . . il avait . . . 20 ans ?

B – Presque. Il avait 18 ans.

A – Où il est mort ton grand-père ?

B – Où est-il mort grand-père ! Pas « Où il est mort ?». Combien de fois faudra-t-il que je te le répète ?

A – Comment il est mort, grand-père ?

B – Il est mort à la guerre. Que Dieu ait son âme ! Aux côtés des Anglais à El-Alamein.

A – C'est là-bas qu'il a été tué ? Mais il n'était pas avec les Anglais ?

B – Mais si !

A – Et ça fait combien de temps ?

B – Attends ! . . . Quel jour sommes-nous ? Qu'est-ce que tu as fait du calendrier ? . . . C'était en 1942 . . . Cela va faire . . .

A – Mais est-ce que tu étais née ?

B – Non ! Quelle question !

C'est quoi que tu regardes ?	quoi? [16.1.3]
Quel langage !	exclamatory quel! [16.2.1]
Veux-tu bien parler correctement ?	direct question: yes / no answer [16.1.1]
n'est-ce pas ?	question tag [16.1.2]
je me demande si on ne va pas se moquer de moi . . .	indirect question using si [16.1.5]
Qu'est-ce que tu regardes ?	qu'est-ce que ? [16.1.3]
Qui est ce jeune homme avec une belle moustache ?	qui? [16.1.3]

(continued)

(continued)

Est-ce que je suis censé le connaître ?	direct question: yes / no answer [16.1.1]
Mais c'est lequel de tes grand-pères ?	*lequel?* [16.1.3]
De quand date cette photo ?	*quand?* [16.1.3]
Quel âge avait-il ?	*quel?* [16.1.3]
Ouaou ! Que d'eau !	exclamations [16.2.1 and 16.2.3]
Comment font les gens pour marcher dans cette eau ?	*comment?* [16.1.3]
Où il est mort ton grand-père ?	colloquial for '*Où est-il mort grand-père?*' [16.1.3]
Que Dieu ait son âme !	exclamation using subjunctive [16.2.2]
Mais il n'était pas avec les Anglais ?	direct question: yes / no answer [16.1.1]
Mais si !	*si* in response to a negative question [16.1.4]
Et ça fait combien de temps ?	*combien?* [16.1.3]
Quelle question !	exclamatory *quelle!* [16.2.1]

EXERCISES

1. **Match the questions in the left-hand column with the answers in the right-hand column:**

	Questions		Responses
1	*Où Camilla est-elle née ?*	A	*Elle s'appelle Mikaela*
2	*Qui est sa sœur ?*	B	*L'avion*
3	*Est-ce que sa sœur est plus âgée ?*	C	*Le train*
4	*Laquelle des deux est plus sportive ?*	D	*Oui, à partir du Canada*
5	*Comment ira-t-elle aux Etats-Unis ?*	E	*Si, mais c'est plus cher*
6	*Est-ce qu'il est possible d'aller aux Etats-Unis en bus ?*	F	*La cadette*
7	*N'y a-t-il pas de train ?*	G	*En Suède*
8	*Qu'est-ce qui est plus confortable ?*	H	*Si sa sœur l'accompagnera*
9	*Quel est le moyen le plus rapide ?*	I	*Non, elle a 2 ans de moins*
10	*Que se demande Camilla ?*	J	*En bus*

2. Fill the gap with the correct question word:

1. _____ est cet homme ?
   C'est mon ami.
2. _____ fait-il dans la vie ?
   Il est comédien.
3. *Et tes parents ?* _____ sont-ils ?
   Ils sont plutôt cool.
4. _____ as-tu de frères et sœurs ?
   Deux sœurs et un frère.
5. _____ âge a ton frère ?
   Il a 17 ans.
6. _____ il fait ?
   Il est écolier.
7. _____ vont tes sœurs ?
   À l'école primaire.
8. _____ passe son bac cette année ?
   L'aînée.
9. _____ elle voudra étudier plus tard ?
   La géographie.
10. _____ de ces métiers envisage-t-elle ?
    Le professorat.

3. Isabel's biography

Ask a suitable question for each answer using *est-ce que* …

	Questions	Responses
1. *naissance*		*En mai 1989.*
2. *naissance*		*À Helsinki.*
3. *langue*		*À la maison ? Le suédois !*
4. *éducation*		*Oui, une très bonne élève.*
5. *études*		*Oui, le droit.*
6. *études*		*À l'université de Helsinki.*
7. *études*		*Pour encore 3 ans.*
8. *vie sociale*		*Oui, Camilla est sa meilleure amie.*
9. *vie sociale*		*Des amis ? Au moins trois.*
10. *carrière*		*Après sa licence ? Elle voudra faire un master.*

17 PUNCTUATION, ACCENTS, SPELLING AND SPECIFIC SOUNDS IN FRENCH

17.1 Punctuation

17.1.1 Main punctuation marks

There are 10 main punctuation marks in French:

Punctuation mark	Name		Space (in print)	
			Before	After
.	*le point*	full stop, period, dot	no	yes
,	*la virgule*	comma	no	yes
:	*le / les deux points*	colon	yes	yes
;	*le point-virgule*	semicolon	yes	yes
!	*le point d'exclamation*	exclamation mark	yes	yes
?	*le point d'interrogation*	question mark	yes	yes
. . .	*les points de suspension*	ellipsis (three dots)	no	–
—	*le tiret long*	em-dash (long)	yes	yes
–	*le tiret moyen*	en-dash (medium)	yes	yes
-	*le trait d'union* (or *tiret court*)	hyphen	no	no
« »	*les guillemets* (m)	quotation marks	yes (closing one)	yes (opening one)

To the above can be added the following related punctuation marks:

( )	*les parenthèses* (f)	brackets	yes (closing one)	yes (opening one)
[ ]	*les crochets (droits)* (m)	(square) brackets	no (closing one)	no (opening one)
'	*l'apostrophe* (f)	apostrophe	no	no
*	*l'astérisque* (f)	asterisk	no (depending on position)	no (depending on position)

17.1.2 Other punctuation marks

/	*la barre oblique, le slash*	forward slash	yes	yes
\	*la barre oblique inverse, l'anti-slash*	backslash	yes	yes
@	*l'arobase (f)*	'at' sign	no	no
{}	*les accolades (f)*	curly brackets	yes (closing one)	yes (opening one)

▶ Punctuation marks which consist of several elements such as *le point-virgule* (;), *les deux points* (:), *les guillemets* (« »), *le point d'exclamation* (!), *le point d'interrogation* (?), *le signe de pourcentage* (the percentage sign: %) and *les tirets* (–), *les devises* (currencies: £, €), are all **preceded and followed by a space in French**. However, the rule is less strict for *le point-virgule*, for which the first space may be omitted. In English there is no space before these punctuation marks but there is one after them.

French: Il dit : « *Si nous allions à New York cet été ? »*

English: He says: 'How about going to New York this summer?'

Some of these signs are used in sciences, especially mathematics and physics.

Although punctuation in French and English is very similar, some differences in its use and its written form exist. We have listed below those punctuation marks which have significant differences.

17.1.3 Full stop (.)

▶ The full stop is placed after an abbreviation whose last letter is not the same as that of the word.

Monsieur: M.

But, *Madame*: *Mme* (without a full stop)

▶ With figures

In decimals, French uses a comma where English employs a full stop.

For the figure *mille* and components of larger figures with *mille*, French uses a space or a full stop where English uses a comma as in the example below.

	French	English
Decimals	*108,7 (cent huit* **virgule** *sept)*	108.7 (a hundred and eight **point** seven)
Components of a larger figure than a thousand	*126.322.985* (the full stop is not pronounced) *126 322 985*	126,322,985

▶ Shortened forms of measurements do not have a full stop, even if the abbreviation does not end in the last letter of the word:

36 km

100 m

30 min

17.1.4 Comma (,)

The comma is used when listing words or clauses of the same nature and function (see also full stop above). The last term of the list is linked to the rest by the conjunctions *et* or *ou*. One of these conjunctions is compulsory in French whereas in English a comma is possible instead of *and*:

Deux tranches de pain, un bol de céréales, un pot de confiture **et** du beurre.	Two slices of bread, a bowl of cereal, a pot of jam, **and** butter.

17.1.5 Question mark (?)

The two differences from English are:

▶ the use of the double question mark

▶ the use of the question mark and exclamation mark together, for emphasis or irony intention:

Comment ? La langue chinoise ne serait pas difficile ?!	What? The Chinese language is not difficult?

17.1.6 Exclamation mark (!)

▶ The use of the double or triple exclamation mark, or of the question mark and exclamation mark together, to intensify the emotion:

Vous êtes complètement fou !!!	You're completely crazy!
C'est un Italien et il n'aime pas les pâtes ?!	He's Italian and he doesn't like pasta!

17.1.7 Quotation marks (« . . . »)

▶ Quotation marks take the form of chevrons:

« Approchez, SVP ! »	'Come close, please!'

▶ They are used to mark the beginning and end of dialogue. They are used for all quotations or speechmarks:

« Et ainsi ne pouvant faire que ce qui est juste fût fort, on a fait que ce qui est fort fût juste. » (Blaise Pascal, *Les Pensées*, Raison des effets n° 137)	'And so, not being able to ensure that what is just was strong, we ensured that what is strong was just.'
Il répète souvent « n'est-ce pas ? », c'est agaçant !	He often says 'n'est-ce pas?', it's annoying!

▶ They frame a word or an expression that the speaker recognizes is not his or her own:

Je serais donc « idiot » et je ne comprendrais « rien à rien » d'après lui !	So I'm an 'idiot' and I understand 'nothing about anything', according to him!

▶ They frame foreign words or expressions:

Il a une attitude très « british ».	He has a very 'British' attitude.

▶ English inverted commas may be used for a quotation within another quotation:

« Mesdames et Messieurs, lorsque Descartes dut expliquer que "Cogito, ergo sum" ne signifiait pas simplement que … »	'Ladies and Gentlemen, when Descartes had to explain that "Cogito, ergo sum" did not just mean that …'

▶ Unlike in English, quotations marks in French include short phrases, e.g. *dit-il* (said he), *suggéra Monsieur Untel* … (Mr So-and-so suggested …).

For longer phrases it is preferable to interrupt the quotation marks and to begin again:

« Je n'ai pas trouvé les ingredients », dit mon ami, la mine déconfite et le regard coupable, « j'ai fait pourtant plusieurs magasins ».	'I haven't found the ingredients', said my friend, crestfallen and with a guilty look. 'Yet I've tried several shops'.

17.1.8 The em-dash (long) (—)

The em-dash is used in a dialogue to indicate a change of speaker:

« — Bonjour Mikaela! dit Rose. Comment vas-tu?	'Hello Mikaela!' Rose says. 'How are you?'
— Ah, bonjour Tante! Excellent! s'écria Mikaela, joviale, je viens d'emménager à Paris.	'Oh, hello Auntie! I'm very well', shouted Mikaela jovially. 'I've just moved to Paris.'
— Génial! Dans quel quartier?	'Fantastic! Whereabouts in Paris?'
— Près de la Tour Eiffel, répond-elle.	'Near the Eiffel Tower,' she replies.
— Quelle chance ! ».	'How lucky you are!'

▶ The em-dash in French is never used to indicate that speech has tailed off. Only ellipsis may be used. In English, on the other hand, either ellipsis or the em-dash may be used.

17.1.9 The en-dash (medium) (–)

The en-dash (*tiret d'incise*) may be used instead of brackets to add an explanation, a commentary, etc.:

Le TGV – mon train préféré – fut inauguré en 1986.	The TGV – my favourite train – was inaugurated in 1986.

17.1.10 The hyphen (-)

▶ The hyphen is used to mark:

   ▶ a link between one or more words

   ▶ compound words like *un porte-avions* (aircraft carrier)

   ▶ connections between grammatical terms: *allez-vous-en !* (Go away!) *Qu'y a-t-il dans la soupe ?* (What's in the soup?)

   ▶ words which are broken when they are too long for the line

   ▶ isolating one part of a word, such as a verb ending: the ending *-ais* of the verb.

17.1.11 The apostrophe (')

The apostrophe is used to replace a vowel that is elided in order to avoid contact with another vowel:

si + il → s'il

que + il → qu'il

Care must be taken with *qui* followed by a vowel, which is **not** elided: *qui il.*

17.1.12 The asterisk

Three asterisks indicate a surname which is reduced to an initial:

Mme de T*** ne pourra pas assister au repas de ce soir.	Mme de T. will not be able to attend the meal this evening.

17.1.13 The forward slash

The forward slash is used:

▶ in fractions: ¾, ⅝

▶ for measuring speed, etc. *100 km/h* ('kilometres per hour' understood)

▶ occasionally to replace a dash: *le TGV Paris/Lyon*

▶ to indicate an alternative word or expression: *et / ou.*

17.2 Accents

There are **four** accents in French, which are placed on vowels, and **one** cedilla, which is placed under the letter *c*: *ç.*

17.2.1 The acute and grave accents

▶ The **acute** accent can only be placed on *e* to indicate the closed sound /e/: *été.*

▶ The **grave** accent is placed on *e* to indicate the open sound /ɛ/: *crème*

Note

The following are pronounced /ɛ/ and have a grave accent *è*:

▶ *e* followed by silent *e*: *collège, Irène, chèrement*

Exception

médecin, médecine; the prefixes *dé-* and *pré-*; initial *é-*

▶ *e* followed by a final *-s* when it is not a plural: *près* (compare with *des prés*), *congrès, abcès*

▶ A grave accent is placed on *a* and *u* (*à, ù*) to differentiate between two homographs:

à (at) versus *a* (has); *là* (there) versus *la* (the or her); *où* (where) versus *ou* (or)

Notes

▶ *Ça* is written without an accent, except in the expression *çà et là* (here and there).

▶ *Deçà, delà, au-delà, voilà* are written with an accent; only *cela* is written without an accent.

▶ *ù* with an accent is only found in the word *où.*

▶ A grave accent on a vowel other than *e* does not change the pronunciation: *ou* is pronounced the same as *où*, and *a* as *à*.

17.2.2 The circumflex accent

▶ is found on the vowels *a, e, i, o, u* (*â, ê, î, ô, û*).

▶ indicates an *s* (or, unusually, another letter) that has been lost:

forêt (forest), *hôpital* (hospital), *maître* (master)

▶ The circumflex accent does not change the pronunciation: *un mur* /myʁ/ (wall) *mûr* / myʁ/ (ripe), *sur* (on) / *sûr* (sure), *un atome* (atom) / *un diplôme* (diploma).

▶ With the *Rectifications de l'orthographe de 1990* (see 17.5), the circumflex accent on *u* and *i* disappears: e.g. *couter* (to cost), *paraitre* (to appear), *il parait*, but remains in the following three cases:

    ▶ to differentiate two homographs: *du* (*de + le*) versus *dû* (past participle of *devoir*)

    ▶ 1st and 2nd person plural of past simple: *vous fûtes; nous fîmes*

    ▶ 3rd person singular of the subjunctive: *Que voulez-vous qu'il fît contre trois ? Qu'il mourût !* (P. Corneille, *Horace*)

17.2.3 The diaeresis

▶ is found on the vowels *e, i, u* (*ë, ï, ü*). It indicates two consecutive vowels that must be pronounced separately: *Noël* (Christmas), *naïf* (innocent), *aigüe* (acute)

▶ With the *Rectifications de l'orthographe de 1990* (see 17.5), words which used to contain *-güe-* and *-guï-* and be pronounced /gy/ such as *ambigüe* /ãbigy/, *ambiguïtés* / ãbigɥite/, *aiguë* /egy/, are now written *ambigüe, ambigüité, aigüe*.

17.2.4 The cedilla (ç)

The cedilla is placed beneath a *c* followed by *a, o, u*, to indicate that it must be pronounced /s/ (*c* followed by *e, i, œ* is always pronounced /s/):

Il commença la leçon.	He began the lesson.
Il est déçu.	He's disappointed.
cœliaque	coeliac

17.2.5 Use of the acute and grave accents

▶ When an accent is added to the letter *e* a change in pronunciation follows: compare *un modelé* (contours), *un modèle* (model).

▶ The general rule is as follows:

    ▶ The vowel *e* pronounced /e/ or /ɛ/ only uses an acute or grave accent if it is at the end of an open syllable. An *e* pronounced /e/ which is at the end of a word always uses an acute accent:

    un côté (side), *un pré* (meadow), *amusé* (amused), *parlé* (spoken), *le café* (coffee)

▶ If a syllable ends in a consonant (a closed syllable), the letter *e* never uses an accent:

un pro-jet, per-dre, fo-res-tier

Open syllable	Closed syllable	Mixture of open and closed syllables
clé (key)	jet (jet)	é-ti-quet-te (etiquette)
dé-cé-dé (deceased)	ef-fet (effect)	é-lec-tri-ci-té (electricity)
dé-mé-ri-té (proved unworthy)	er-got (sprocket)	des-hé-ri-té (disinherited)

▶ The *-e* of the feminine and / or the *-s* of the plural do not influence the rules of accentuation, and so every open syllable in the plural will keep its accent before either of these letters: *une clé* (key), *des clés*; *chanté, chantés, chantée, chantées* (sung). By analogy, masculine words ending in *-ée* act similarly e.g. *le musée* (museum).

▶ When *e* is followed by two consonants or a double consonant, it never uses an accent because the syllable is always closed:

un ef-fet (effect), *bel-li-gé-rant* (belligerant), *bes-tial* (brutish)

▶ When *e* is followed by *-x* it never uses an accent since *x* counts as two consonants, /gz/ or /ks/:

exécuter (to carry out), *exister* (to exist), *exact* (exact)

▶ When *e* is followed by a consonant + *r* or *l* (-cr, -gr, -cl, -gl, -tr, etc.), it always uses an accent because the syllable break is made before these consonants, not between them:

é-gli-se (church), *é-cri-tu-re* (handwriting)

▶ But if *r-* or *l-* precedes the consonant (-rb-, -lg, -rt, etc.) it will not use an accent; the syllable break is made between *r-* or *l-* and the consonant, and so the syllable will be closed:

her-be (grass), *el-lip-se* (ellipse), *er-go-no-mie* (ergonomics), etc.

17.3 The tonic accent

In French an accent is placed on:

▶ the last syllable of a word of several syllables which does not end in a silent *e*: *l'ordina'teur*.

▶ the penultimate syllable of a word that ends in a silent *e*: *l'informa'tique*.

▶ the last syllable of a group of words linked by meaning, e.g. *J'ai lu trois livres en une semaine,* which can be pronounced in one go, without a pause. There is only one stress, which will be on *-mai-* in *se'maine*.

Thus, in French there is only one tonic accent per group of words, whereas in English the stress can be on any word in a sentence, according to the emphasis given by the speaker; in French, other ways of stressing parts of a sentence are employed, as seen in the following comparison:

English	French
I bought this book.	*C'est moi qui ai acheté ce livre.*
I bought this book.	*Ce livre, je l'ai acheté.*
I bought this book.	*C'est ce livre que j'ai acheté.*
	J'ai acheté ce livre-ci.

French sometimes exaggerates the stress on the first syllable of a word that the speaker wants to emphasize: e.g. *C'est 'incroyable !* It's incredible!

17.4 Spelling

17.4.1 Summary of the new orthographic rules of 1990

In 1990 the Académie française approved new, simplified rules for spelling. These new rules were not mandatory, but their use was recommended. Around 2,000 words were affected. The rules proved to be contentious: such was the opposition to them that they appeared to have been dropped by the end of the century. In the early 21st century, however, they were revived: publications increasingly adopted them in France, Quebec and Belgium. The Robert and Larousse dictionaries incorporated the new rules, in 2009 and 2011 respectively. From 2016, they were implemented in school books and dictionaries in France, a change that caused outrage. The new spellings, however, remain optional.

The following is a summary of the principal changes:

1. Compound numbers are systematically linked by hyphens:

   vingt-et-un, deux-cent-dix-huit (formerly: *vingt et un, deux cents dix-huit*), *vingt-et-unième*

2. In compound nouns composed of verb + noun (*garde-boue, pèse-lettre*), or preposition + noun (*après-midi, sans-abri*), the second element can no longer have a plural *-s* when singular (e.g. *un porte-avions*) and can no longer have the singular form when plural (e.g. *des après-midi*).

   un porte-avion, des porte-avions; un compte-goutte, des compte-gouttes; un après-midi, des après-midis

3. The grave accent is used rather than the acute accent on a certain number of words (in order to regularize their spelling), in the future and conditional of verbs which are conjugated like *céder*:

   évènement, règlementaire, il cèdera, ils règleraient (previously *événement, réglementaire, il cédera, ils régleraient*).

4. The circumflex accent disappears on *i* and *u* because it cannot be justified phonetically:

cout; entrainer, nous entrainons; il parait (previously *coût, entraîner, entraînons, paraît*)

But it is kept on:

▶ verb endings of the simple past and the subjunctive:

qu'elle fût, qu'il finît, nous reçûmes, vous prîtes

▶ the five cases of masculine singular adjectives which run the risk of ambiguity with homophones:

dû, mûr and *sûr, jeûne(s)* and the forms of *croitre* which might otherwise be confused with forms of *croire* (*je croîs, tu croîs*, etc.)

5. Verbs ending in *-eler* or *-eter* are conjugated like *peler* or *acheter*. Derivatives of these verbs follow suit:

j'amoncèle, amoncèlement, tu époussèteras (previously *j'amoncelle, amoncellement*)

Exceptions

appeler, jeter and their derivatives, including *interpeler*.

6. Words borrowed from foreign languages form their plural in the same way as French words and use accents according to the rules which apply to French words:

des matchs, des révolvers (previously *des matches, des revolvers*)

7. A certain number of words which previously consisted of two words linked by a hyphen become one word. This is applied in particular to compound words beginning with *contr(e)-* and *entr(e)-*, with *extra-, infra-, intra-, ultra-*, with *hydro-, socio-, agro-*, onomatopaeic words and words of foreign origin:

contrepouvoir, entretemps, tictac, weekend, portemonnaie (previously *contre-pouvoir, entre-temps, tic-tac, week-end, porte-monnaie*).

8. Words ending in *-olle* and verbs ending in *-otter* and their derivatives are written with only one consonant respectively:

corole, frisoter (*corolle, frisotter*)

Exceptions

colle, folle, molle and words of the same family as a noun ending in *-otte* (e.g. *botter*, from *botte*).

9. The diaeresis is moved to the letter *u* in *-güe-* and *-güi-* (previously *-guë-* and *-guï-*), and is added to *u* in a few words ending in *-geure* and *-guer*, like the verb *arguer*:

aigüe, ambigüe, ambigüité, argüer, gageüre (previously: *aiguë, ambiguë, ambiguïté, arguer, gageure*)

10. The past participle of *laisser*, like that of *faire*, is invariable when followed by an infinitive:

Je les ai laissé partir (previously *Je les ai laissés partir*).

Elle s'est laissé prendre par la police (previously *Elle s'est laissée prendre par la police*).

A number of anomalies have been removed:

▶ *assoir, sursoir*, etc. (formerly *asseoir, surseoir*, etc.)

▶ *boursouffler, boursoufflure* (*boursoufler, boursouflure*)

▶ *charriot* (*chariot*)

▶ *combattif, combattivité* (*combatif*, etc.)

▶ *dissout, dissoute* (*dissous, dissoute*)

▶ *imbécilité* (*imbécillité*)

▶ *interpeler* (*interpeller*)

▶ *lunetier* (*lunettier*)

▶ *ognon* (*oignon*)

▶ *persifflage* (*persiflage*)

▶ *relai* (*relais*)

▶ *saccarine* (*saccharine*)

Accents are placed on a few words where they had previously been omitted, or whose pronunciation has changed: e.g. *papèterie* (*papeterie*).

Words which were formerly written **-illier**, where the *i* which follows the consonant is not sounded, are written **-iller**: *joailler* (*joaillier*), *serpillère* (*serpillière*).

Exception

The names of trees and bushes, e.g. *groseillier* (redcurrant bush).

Finally, where there is a clash in usage, priority is given to:

▶ the most gallicized form (*leadeur*, not *leader*)

▶ the form without a circumflex accent (*allo*, not *allô*)

▶ the regular plural form.

17.4.2 Contractions

In English **elision**, where the final vowel is replaced by an apostrophe when it is followed by another vowel, is not compulsory: I'll / I shall; we've / we have; you're / you are

In French, by contrast, contractions and elisions, before another vowel or a silent *h*, are compulsory:

▶ *à + le → au ; à + les → aux; de + le → du*

▶ *je, me, le, la, ne, de*, followed by words beginning with a vowel or silent *h* → elision: *j'étais*; *je n'arrive pas à imiter l'accent d'Auvergne.*

17.4.3 The use of the apostrophe

A number of words end in silent *-e* and occasionally in *-a* or *-i*. In these cases, the final vowel is replaced by an apostrophe when it is followed by another vowel or a silent *h*. Here are some examples:

▶ Words of one syllable that contain a silent *-e*, such as *de, le, que, je, me, se, ce, ne*, as well as *la*, always elide before a vowel: *Sois à l'heure, j'y tiens ! Je n'ai eu qu'une minute d'avance.*

▶ *Si* only elides before *il(s)*: *On lui a demandé s'il venait, il a répondu : « Oui, si Irène vient aussi et si elle vient seule ».*

▶ There are, however, some exceptions:

    ▶ Pronouns *le, la, je* and *ce* do not elide when they are attached to the end of the verb by a hyphen, but they do elide before a verb begining with a vowel: *Ta fille, tu l'encourages; ton fils, encourage-le aussi ! Est-ce ainsi qu'on t'a éduqué ? Ai-je été assez clair ?*

    ▶ The adverb *là* never elides: *là encore tu t'es trompée !*

    ▶ The contraction *au* and *du* disappear when there is elision: *C'est de l'avocat ? Je préfère les radis à l'avocat.*

    ▶ There is no elision before numbers: *C'est la huitième fois que le un et le onze se trouvent en tête ! Le matin, je lis rapidement la une du journal.*

▶ Elision takes place before:

    ▶ *un* as an article or an indefinite pronoun, *L'une est blonde, l'autre châtain. Il but sa bière d'un trait !*

▶ There is no elision before:

    ▶ *oui, ouistiti*: *Le oui franc et massif des dernières élections l'a surpris.*

    ▶ words beginning with *y*: *Je ne connais pas le Yémen.*

17.4.4 Capital letters

Capital letters are much less frequent in French than in English

Capital letters in English but not in French:

1.   I versus *je*:

    Soudain, je la vis.   Suddenly, I saw her.

2. Days of the week, months

    C'est arrivé le mardi 20 juillet exactement.   It happened on Tuesday 20th July
    exactly.

3. Addresses: the words *rue, avenue, impasse,* etc.

    Il habite dans la rue Victor Hugo, de   He lives in Victor Hugo Street, just
    suite après l'allée Montaigne.   after Montaigne Alley.

4. Geography

    L'océan Atlantique et le mont Blanc sont   The Atlantic Ocean and Mont Blanc
    les deux extrémités est–ouest de la France.   are the two extreme points of the
    north-east and south-west of France.

5. Adjectives related to nationality, regions, cities and towns can also be nouns
    (German / a German). In French, when these words are nouns or name people, they
    take a capital letter: *un Américain, un Lyonnais,* but when they are adjectives or
    name a language, they do not.

    En Europe, le français est parlé par les   In Europe, French is spoken by the
    Français, les Belges et les Suisses.   French, the Belgians and the Swiss.

    la République française   the French Republic

6. In the titles of works only the first word and proper nouns take capital letters. If
    the first word is an article, the word that follows it immediately will also have a
    capital letter.

    Le Rouge et le noir; Les Fleurs du mal; Voyage au bout de la nuit.

7. In official documents all the letters of the names of families are often capitalised:

    Madame Jeanne, Marie DUPONT, demeurant à Montpellier, lègue à sa fille Marie-
    Christine MARTIN, née DUPONT, la totalité de ses biens.

17.4.5 Useful spelling rules

(i)   Plurals of certain endings, plus exceptions

Words ending in	Plurals in	Examples	Exceptions
-ou	**-ous**	*tabous, verrous*	*bijoux, choux, genoux . . .*
-au, -eau	**-aux, -eaux**	*bureaux, tuyaux*	*landaus*
-eu	**-eux**	*lieux* (place), *vœux*	*pneus, bleus, lieus* (pollock)
-al	**-aux**	*animaux, chevaux*	*bals, carnavals . . .*
-ail	**-ails**	*gouvernails, rails*	*travaux, vitraux . . .*

(ii)   Spellings of specific endings

Nouns ending in				
Sound	Gender	Ending	Examples	Exceptions

/e/	m	-é
		
		-er,
		
		-ier
			– degré, blé, fossé
			
			– jobs: épicier, boulanger
			
			– derived from past participle:
			   employé, marché
			
			– danger, papier
				– apogée, athée,
				   lycée, musée,
				   pygmée, scarabée
				
				– pied, nez,
				   rez(-de-chaussée)

	f	-ée	– allée, cheminée, vallée, donnée – duration or content: bouchée, cuillerée, journée, année, poignée	acné, psyché, clé, mémé

/ɛ/	m	-et, -êt, -ai(s),
		   -ait, -ès,
		   -ect
			– objet, billet, intérêt, essai, quai
			
			– rabais, Anglais, fait, lait, accès,
			   succès, aspect, respect
				– poney, est (= is)
				
				– /-ɛs/: faciès, herpès,
				   hermès, palmarès

	f	-aie	paie, roseraie	forêt, paix
/te/, /tje/	m	-té, -tié	été, côté, comté, doigté, pâté	
	f	-té -tié	– beauté, quantité, égalité, liberté, santé, cité – amitié, moitié, inimitié, rapidité	dictée, montée, jetée, butée
	f	-tée	quantity or content: pelletée, charretée, potée, fourchetée, assiettée, portée	
/i/	m	-i, -ie, -il, -is, -it	merci [= thank you], défi, épi, oubli, cri, ennemi, génie, parapluie, outil, paradis, permis, fruit, esprit, appétit	
	f	-ie	boulangerie, pluie, copie, envie, mairie, philosophie, thérapie	brebis, fourmi, nuit, perdrix, souris, merci [= mercy]
/u/	m	-ou	cou, clou, matou, écrou, genou, hibou, tabou, chou	coup, loup, égout, joug, houx, caoutchouc
	f	-oue	joue, boue, houe, moue, roue, proue	toux

(continued)

403

(continued)

Nouns ending in				
Sound	Gender	Ending	Examples	Exceptions
/o/	m	-eau, -au, -o, -aut, -aud, -aux, -op, -os, -o/ôt	bateau, assaut, tuyau, saut, crapaud, studio, galop, robot, dos, impôt	
	f	-o	virago + shortened words: photo, moto, vidéo, diapo, météo, sono, stéréo, radio	eau, peau, (cerise) bigarreau
/y/	m	-u, -ut -us, -ux	menu, dû, tissu, individu, flux, jus, abus, salut, tribut	
	f	-ue	vue, rue, issue, revue, avenue	vertu, tribu, bru, glu
/aʁ/	m	-ard -ar -are -art -ars	— -ard, the most numerous: regard, placard, guépard, retard, canard — -ar, mostly loan words: bazar, caviar, jaguar, cauchemar — -are: cigare, hectare, phare, square, curare — -art: départ, écart, faire-part, quart, rempart — -ars, very rare: /ar/ jars, /ars/ mars, /a/ gars	
	f	-are —arre	— gare, fanfare, guitare, tare, tiare -arre, rare: amarre, bagarre, barre, jarre	tintamarre
/yʁ/	m	-ure	a few masculine words only: murmure, parjure, silure, mercure, cyanure, chlorure, carbure, bromure, sulfure	futur, azur, fémur, mur
	f	-ure	the majority: mesure, voiture, structure, blessure	mûre, piqûre
/uʁ/	m	-our -ours	— tour, jour, four, séjour — velours, cours, discours, secours	— bourg, faubourg — /yʁs/ ours (bear)
	f	all masculine except: cour (yard), basse-cour; amour (feminine in the plural)			

Nouns ending in				
Sound	Gender	Ending	Examples	Exceptions
/œʁ/	m	-eur	– ordinateur, moteur, bonheur – activities: porteur, explorateur, professeur, chercheur, docteur	beurre, leurre, chœur, cœur, heurt monsieur /məsjø/, messieurs /mesjø/
	f	-eur	– erreur, valeur, terreur, couleur, fleur, hauteur – qualities: rigueur, blancheur, candeur	heure, demeure, sœur
/wa/	m	-oi	roi, emploi, envoi, désarroi, convoi, émoi	bois, toit, foie, doigt, poids, le froid
	f	-oie	joie, voie, soie, proie	fois, croix, voix, noix, loi, foi, paroi
/waʁ/	m	-oire (80%) -oir	– réfectoire, laboratoire, répertoire – comptoir, devoir, couloir, rasoir, trottoir, réservoir, espoir	masculine words derived from verbs → -oir except le boire, déboire, pourboire not derived from verbs → -oire except dortoir, soir, terroir, loir
	f	-oire	armoire, bouilloire, mémoire, gloire, histoire, écumoire, poire, trajectoire, victoire	no exceptions
	adj.	-oire	aléatoire, dérisoire, compensatoire, respiratoire	noir (m), noire (f)
	verb	-oir	voir, apercevoir, devoir, concevoir, pleuvoir	boire, croire, accroire
/itwaʁ/ / atwaʁ/	nouns adj. m	-oire	conservatoire, territoire, observatoire, auditoire, réquisitoire	a few rare feminine words: écritoire, échappatoire
/aj/, /ɛj/, /œj/	m	-il	travail, portail, rail, soleil, conseil, écureuil, fauteuil, cerfeuil	portefeuille, chèvrefeuille, millefeuille
	m /kœj// gœj/	-ueil	accueil, orgueil, recueil	to keep the sound /k/ /g/ before -e, -i, you write -ueil and not -euil
	f	-ille	feuille (only f in /œj/), paille, muraille, abeille, oreille, merveille	

(iii) Adverbs ending in *-ment*

▶ Most adverbs ending in *-ment* are formed from the feminine of the adjective: *froidement, lentement, vivement, heureusement*.

▶ If the adjective ends in *-ent*, the adverb will end in *-emment*, prononced /amã/: *intelligemment, récemment, violemment*.

▶ If the adjective ends in *-ant*, the adverb will end in *-amment*: *brillamment, bruyamment, savamment*.

▶ If the adjective ends in a vowel the feminine is not used: *vraiment, joliment, poliment*, but *gai → gaiement* or *gaîment*.

▶ Adjectives ending in *-u* sometimes make *-ûment*: *crûment, dûment, assidûment*; sometimes *-ument*: *absolument, résolument, éperdument*.

▶ Special spellings: *précisément, gentiment, brièvement, précipitamment*.

(iv) *tout / tous / toute / toutes*

▶ *Tout* as a **determiner** (every, each, all) agrees in gender and number with the noun it is related to:

tous les jours (every day); *toute l'année* (all year); *toutes les fois* (every time)

▶ *Tout* as a **pronoun** (all of) agrees in gender and number with the noun it stands for:

Ils ont tous la grippe.	They all have flu.
Toutes sont restées à la maison.	They all stayed at home.

Note

The *-s* in *tous* as a pronoun is pronounced /tus/.

▶ *Tout* as a **pronoun** can be neuter:

C'est tout ce qui compte.	It's all that matters.

▶ *Tout* as an **adverb** (totally, wholly) is invariable:

Ils sont tout mouillés.	They are wet through.
la chevelure tout ébouriffée	hair all dishevelled

However, for reasons of euphony, when *tout* as an adverb is followed by a feminine noun beginning with a consonant or aspirated *h,* it agrees with the noun:

des fleurs toutes fanées	flowers all withered
Elle se sentait toute honteuse.	She felt quite ashamed.

(v) Numbers

▶ According to the 1990 spelling rules all cardinal numbers that are in one group must be hyphenated:

deux-cent-mille-sept-cent-neuf (200 709)

▶ Cardinal numbers as adjectives are invariable, except *vingt* and *cent*:

les quatre points cardinaux	the four points of the compass
trois mille habitants	three thousand inhabitants

When *vingt* and *cent* are **not** followed by another number, they are put into the plural form:

quatre-vingts (80) **but** *quatre-vingt-trois* (83)

six-cents (600) **but** *six-cent-huit* (608)

Million, milliard, trillion, etc. are nouns. They can be put into the plural, preceded by a determiner or the number *un*, and are followed by the preposition *de*:

trois millions d'habitants	three million inhabitants
un million d'euros	a million euros

(vi) *leur / leurs*

Leur can be either a **determiner** or a **pronoun**. It does not have a feminine form.

▶ *Leur* as a **possessive adjective** is used when there are several possessors. It agrees, in number only, with the thing possessed.

Leur frère, leurs frères	their brother, their brothers
Leur sœur, leurs sœurs	their sister, their sisters

▶ *Leur* as a **personal pronoun** is the plural of *lui*, and is invariable.

*Danielle et Michelle n'ont pas d'argent sur elles, prête-**leur** cinq euros !*	Danielle and Michelle have no money with them; lend **them** some euros!
*Eric et Paul n'ont pas d'argent sur eux, je **leur** ai prêté cinq euros.*	Eric and Paul have no money with them; I've lent **them** 5 euros.

▶ *Leur* as a **possessive pronoun** is preceded by a determiner and agrees in number only.

Tu as recopié les idées de tes amies, ce sont les leurs, non les tiennes !	You've copied the ideas of your friends; these are theirs not yours!

(vii) *vu, excepté, ci-joint, ci-inclus, ci-annexé, étant donné . . .*

▶ When these adjectival phrases are placed at the beginning of a sentence, before a noun phrase with or without a determiner, they are invariable (like the adverbial phrases *ci-dessus* and *ci-après*).

ci-joint les attestations demandées	the required certificates enclosed
Vous trouverez ci-joint photocopie des documents.	You will find enclosed a photocopy of the documents.
ci-inclus copie du rapport	copy of the report enclosed

▶ When they follow a noun phrase they agree in gender and number:

| *les attestations ci-jointes* | the enclosed certificates |
| *les trois premières notes exceptées* | apart from the first three notes |

▶ When they are within a sentence, with a noun phrase, agreement is optional:

| *Vous trouverez ci-joint / ci-joints deux exemplaires du rapport.* | You will find enclosed two copies of the report. |

17.5 Specific sounds in French

17.5.1 *The phonetic alphabet in French*

Vowels

/a/	*image, il parla*
/ɑ/	*vase, âne*
/e/	*été, aimer*
/ɛ/	*bête, il aime, Angleterre*
/i/	*ami, ville*
/ɔ/	*idiote, Paul, donne*
/o/	*beau, idiot, pôle*
/u/	*tout, pour, coût*
/y/	*vue, connu*
/œ/	*peuple, œuf, jeune*
/ø/	*œufs, deux, vieux*
/ə/	*me, Angleterre*
/ɛ̃/	*pain, vin*
/ɑ̃/	*camp, anglais, en*
/ɔ̃/	*rond, mon, ils font*
/œ̃/	*un, aucun, brun*

Semi-vowels (or semi-consonants)

/j/	*y*eux, gri*ll*er, m*i*eux
/ɥ/	l*ui*, h*ui*t, n*ui*t
/w/	*w*eekend, *ou*est, l*oi*

Consonants

/b/	*b*u, a*bb*é
/p/	*p*a*p*a
/d/	*d*oré
/t/	*t*ê*t*e
/g/	*g*ala, *g*arder
/k/	*c*o*q*, *qu*aker, *k*ilo
/f/	*f*ermer, *ph*ilosophie
/v/	*v*allée, vi*v*re
/s/	*S*uède, fa*ç*on
/z/	*z*èbre, ré*s*eau
/ʒ/	*J*apon, *j*our
/ʃ/	*ch*aque, *ch*ic
/l/	*l*e, *l*abour
/ʁ/	*r*obot, ra*r*e
/m/	*m*acadam, *m*aman
/n/	*N*aples, *n*aturel
/ɲ/	lig*n*e, gag*n*er

17.5.2 Combinations of vowels

/ɛ/	ai, ei	lait /lɛ/, peine /pɛn/
/o/ /ɔ/	au, eau	beau /bo/, chaud /ʃo/, Paul /pɔl/
/ø/ /œ/	eu, œu	œuf /œf/, eux /ø/
/wa/	oi	quoi /kwa/
/wɛ̃/	oin	loin /lwɛ̃/
/u/	ou	couteau /kuto/
/ɥ/	ui	huit /ɥit/, conduire /kɔ̃dɥiʁ/
/wi/	oui	Louis /lwi/, oui /wi/

17.5.3 Final consonants

These are sometimes pronounced, sometimes silent.

Silent consonants are useful in writing because:

▶ they tell you a little about the etymology of the word, e.g. *corps* from the Latin *corpus*

▶ they can help to differentiate homophones, e.g. *ver* (worm), *verres* (glasses), *vert* (green), *vers* (towards; verse), *vair* (vair).

The following chart gives examples of the pronunciation of final consonants, as well as some important exceptions (S = silent; P = pronunciation):

	S/P	Examples	Exceptions	Special cases / comments
c	P	arc, bac, échec, sec	clerc, blanc, tabac	
d, t	S	– verb endings -ent, -t: travaillent, peut, fut – -ompt, /ɔ̃/, -empt /ɑ̃/: prompt, exempt – bientôt, part, nord, sport, lourd, court, attend, excellent, second, long, quand, chaud, haut, froid, voit, argot, pied	– /pt/, /kt/: concept, abrupt, strict, abject, correct, affect – /t/, /d/: sud, ouest, est, sept, huit, brut + loan words: spot, exit, apartheid, lord, basket, yaourt	– in the feminine, the t of prompte, exempte is heard but not the p: /pʁɔ̃t/, /ɛgzɑ̃t/ – à Dieu vat ! (it's in God's hands): vat with final -t is unusual and pronounced. – the t in Montréal is silent.
f	P	vif, surf, œuf, neuf, bœuf, bref, tarif, récif, rétif, motif	– cerf, nerf, clef – œufs, bœufs	
g	S	bourg, rang, long, poing, shampooing, seing	loan words: airbag, shopping, all words ending in -ing and gang, blog, boomerang, gag, gong, iceberg, hashtag	
p, b	S	champ, camp, drap, plomb, galop, trop, beaucoup	loan words: jeep, stop, scalp, scoop, handicap, pub, club, snob, kebab	– sept [pron. /sɛt/] but: septembre /sɛptɑ̃bʁ/ – the p in compter is silent

	S/P	Examples	Exceptions	Special cases / comments
l	P	*-il /il/, -el /ɛl/: profil, civil, avril, Brésil, miel, ciel, sel, conditionnel, tunnel* *-al /al/, -ol /ɔl/: idéal, génial, légal, total, espagnol, alcool* *-ul /yl/, -oul /ul/, -oil / wal/: nul, calcul, consul, gasoil, poil* *-ail / -aille /aj/: rail, détail* *-eil / -eille /ɛj/: sommeil, réveil, soleil* *-euil /œj/: œil, fauteuil*	*fusil, gentil, cul-de-sac*	pronounced or silent, e.g. *sourcil* /suʁsil/, / suʁsi/; *saoul, soûl,* / su/, /sul/
m, n	–	*nom /nɔ̃/, non /nɔ̃/, brun /bʁœ̃/*		nasalized after a vowel (see 17.5.6). – silent *m* in *automne* /otɔn/
r1	S /-e/, /-ie/	– infinitives, names of trees, names of jobs and some words ending in -er or -ier: *clignoter, électrifier, pommier, boulanger, cuisinier* – others: *léger, acier, étranger, dernier, entier*		the combination *-er / -ier*, <r> is not pronounced
r2	P /ɛʁ/, /œʁ/, /uʁ/, / waʁ/	– words ending in: *-eur /-œʁ/: professeur, fleur, sœur, extérieur, meilleur* – words ending in: *-our /uʁ/: amour, jour, bonjour, autour, tour, humour*		the combination *-eur, -our, -oir, -er*

(continued)

(continued)

	S/P	Examples	Exceptions	Special cases / comments
		— words ending in: -*oir* /-waʁ/: *apercevoir, avoir, assoir* — words ending in: -*er* /-ɛʁ/: *cher, hiver, mer, hier, fer, fier, enfer, laser, setter, geyser*		
final h	S	after vowels: — interjections: *oh !, ah !, eh !, euh !, Hourrah !* — borrowings: *maharajah, shah, torah* after consonants: — *th* → /t/: *maths, zénith, mammouth* — -*ch* → /k/: *loch, almanach, mach, sheikh*	— /o/ *Goth, Wisigoth, Ostrogoth* — *ph* → /f/: *Joseph, périph*	combined with — *c, s, sc* give the sound /ʃ/ or /tʃ/ *Bakchich, British, clash, goulasch, coach, putsch, sandwich, speech*
s	S	— *alors, bras, tapis, parcours, progrès, pays, anglais, temps, cas, poids, bois, dessus, propos, univers* — plural nouns: *enfants, Américains, os* (plur. bones)	— *fils* /fis/ (= son); *ours, sas, vis, lys, os* (sing. bone), *cassis, myosotis* — words from Latin: *virus, cactus, campus, bonus / malus* — loan words: *atlas, bus, blues, houmous, couscous* — *ss* → /s/: *express, stress, (moto)cross*	— in liaisons where *s* is pronounced /z/ e.g. *les États-Unis* /lezetazyni/ — *plus* and *tous* have specific rules of pronunciation (see 17.5.8) — *fils* /fil/ is the plural of *fil* — *os* sing. /os/ plur. /o/
x	S	grammar marker of the plural if nouns / adjectives ending in -*al*, -*ail* + article contracted to *au* → *aux* /o/: *aux, journaux, travaux, anormaux*	— loan words or words from Latin: — words ending in -*ex* /ɛks/, -*ax* / aks/, -*ox* /ɔks/: *duplex, jukebox, relax, thorax*	silent except in liaisons where it is pronounced /z/ e.g. *aux enfants* /ozɑ̃fɑ̃/ — *dix, six* (see 6.1.4)

	S/P	Examples	Exceptions	Special cases / comments
		-ix /i/: perdrix, prix -oix /wa/: choix, voix others: portefaix /ɛ/, flux /y/, houx /u/	– Greek words ending in /ɛ̃ks/: sphinx, lynx (Gr. then Lat.), larynx, Aix /ɛks/	
z	S	– 2nd person plural e.g. avancez ! /avɑ̃se/; Vous y étiez ? /etje/ – assez, nez, chez, rez-de-chaussée – raz-de-marée, riz	loan words: blitz, ersatz, jazz, gaz, quiz, showbiz	

17.5.4 Phonemes in French and English

Although French and English have the same alphabet, their respective phonemes do not correspond to one another.

▶ Phonemes such as *r* /ʁ/, *u* /y/, *ui* /ɥ/, *gn* /ɲ/ and the nasal vowels *an* /ɑ̃/, *en* /ɑ̃/, *in* /ɛ̃/, *on* /ɔ̃/, *un* /œ̃/ do not belong to the phonetic system of English: *la rue* /laʁy/, *régner* /ʁeɲe/, *huit* /ɥit/.

▶ *-ill-* transcribes the semi-consonant /j/: *soleil* /sɔlɛj/, *émailler* /emaje/, *verrouiller* / veʁuje/, *cédille* /sedij/, *fille* /fij/.

Exceptions

ville /vil/, *Lille* /lil/, *tranquille* /tʁɑ̃kil/, *bacille* /basil/, *codicille* /kɔdisil/, *distiller* / distile/, *mille* /mil/, *pénicilline* /penisilin/, *million* /miljɔ̃/, *milliard* /miljaʁ/, *billion* / biljɔ̃/ etc.

17.5.5 Silent and aspirated h

There are two sorts of *h* when it is in initial position: 'silent' and 'aspirated'. Both are in fact silent, but they affect pronounciation differently.

▶ Silent *h* has no influence on its environment. It is as if the word begins with a vowel. Therefore liaison (see 17.10) and elision apply: *l'habitude* /labityd/, *les habitudes* / lezabityd/, *j'habite* /ʒabit/, *ils habitent* /ilzabit/.

▶ Aspirated *h* has not been pronounced since the eighteenth century, but the influence it has on its environment – non-liaison and non-elision – has remained: e.g. *la hache* / laaʃ/, *les haches* /leaʃ/, *les hackeurs* /leakœʁ/, *le hameau* /ləamo/.

In English a few common words begin with silent *h*, e.g. 'heir', 'honest, 'hour', but in general *h* is aspirated, e. g. 'harvest', 'heavy', 'holiday'.

The English phonemes /ɪ/ (ship) /r/ (tree) /ŋ/ (ring) /ʌ/ (but) /θ/ (think) /ð/ (that) /ʊ/ book are not present in French.

17.5.6 Nasal vowels

▶ The group vowel + nasal consonant /n/, and to a lesser extent /m/, before a consonant or at the end of word nasalizes in /ɑ̃/, /ɔ̃/, /ɛ̃/ and /œ̃/: *danse* /dɑ̃s/, *penser* /pɑ̃se/, *sapin* / sapɛ̃/, *garçon* /gaʁsɔ̃/, *emprunt* /ɑ̃pʁœ̃/. The nasal consonant /n/, is not heard.

▶ The sounds -*in*- /ɛ̃/ versus -*un*- /œ̃/ can be difficult to distinguish for those who are unaccustomed to them: *un lapin* [œ̃ lapɛ̃], *cinq parfums* /sɛ̃k paʁfœ̃/

Exceptions

Loan words such as 'gentleman' /dʒɑ̃tləman/ and all English words ending in -man or -men + ombudsman, abdomen, backgammon, Pokémon, Shogun, Simoun (= simoon), pachtoun (= pashtun)

▶ English nasalized vowels like, 'can't', 'won't', 'long', 'singing' or 'change', are, variously, /kɑːnt/ /wəʊnt/ /sɪŋɪŋ/ /tʃeɪndʒ/. While the French articulation of this sound is wholly via the nose, in the English pronunciation, the air flows through the mouth and the nose at the same time; this allows the nasal consonant to be heard lightly.

17.5.7 Silent e

▶ The letter -*e* at the end of a word is not pronounced: *livre* /livʁ/, *librairie* /libʁeʁi/.

▶ It can be also found between two vowels:

  ▶ in nouns derived from verbs ending in -*ier*, -*uer*, -*yer*: *tutoyer* → *tutoiement* / tytwamɑ̃/; *manier* → *maniement* /manimɑ̃/; *payer* → *paiement* /pɛmɑ̃/; *remercier* → *remerciement* /ʁəmɛʁsimɑ̃/; *se dévouer* → *dévouement* /devumɑ̃/; *éternuer* → *éternuement* /etɛʁnymɑ̃/

    ▶ in the future and conditional tenses of these same verbs: *vérifier* → *vérifierai* / veʁifiʁɛ/, *vérifierais* /veʁifiʁɛ/.

▶ -*e* is, however, pronounced in short words like *je* /ʒə/, *me* /mə/, *te* /tə/, *de* /də/, *le* /lə/, *ce* /sə/.

17.5.8 Liaison

Making a liaison

Liaison is one of the features of spoken French. It consists, in specific cases, of sounding the final silent consonant of a word by pronouncing it with the initial vowel of the word which follows, e.g. deux ans (pronounced deu zans /døzɑ̃/).

When liaison takes place, it is made within groups of words: noun groups [determiner + noun], verb groups [subject + verb], prepositional groups [preposition + noun group].

In a case of liaison:

Silent final consonants	Are pronounced	
d, t	[t]	*un grand écran*
f	[f] [v]	[v] (only in) *neuf ans* and *neuf heures* otherwise [f] *neuf ingénieurs*
g	[g]	*un long étui* (exception: *Bourg en Bresse* **g** = /**k**/)
n	[n]	*un animal*
p	[p]	(these two words only) *beaucoup* and *trop*: *trop aimable !* *beaucoup exagéré*
r	[r]*	
s, x, z	[z]	*trois enfants de deux ans*

* When *r* is present in the final sequences -*rc*, -*rd*, -*rs*, -*rt*, liaison does not take place: *le nord-est, une part entière, un court entretien, un bord ébréché, un corps en mouvement, un clerc efficace, elle se dirige vers eux, envers et contre tout.*

Exceptions

Liaison is made after the following words: *leurs*, *divers*, *plusieurs*, e.g *leurs achats, plusieurs étés, des jours heureux.*

Depending on the circumstance, liaison may be compulsory, not allowed or optional.

Compulsory liaison

Letters in blue are to indicate liaison.

▶ In a noun group, between a **determiner** (possessive demonstrative, interrogative, exclamative, indefinite adjective and a number, [*aucun, tout, quelques*]) and the **noun**:

   des états d'âme; les amis de nos amis; Quelles histoires vont-ils raconter; Tout homme a droit au respect; trois abricots

▶ Between an adjective and a noun:

   un grand homme; les terribles évènements

▶ After certain prepositions (e.g. *chez, sous, sans, en, dans, avant, dès*):

   en Angleterre; sans étui; dans un an; dès hier; chez elle

▶ In certain fixed expressions:

de temps en temps; *c'est-à-dire*; *mot à mot*; *nuit et jour*; *tout à coup*; *avant-hier*; *tout à l'heure*

▶ Between the personal pronoun (*on, nous, vous, ils, elles*) and the verb, or the verb plus the inverted personal pronoun:

Vous avez raison; *Sont-elles arrivées ?* *Que dit-on de lui dans le journal ?* *On y tient à nos photos !*

▶ After *être* and *avoir*:

Nous sommes arrivés et ils nous ont offert à boire; *C'est un tableau de Picasso*; *Vous étiez à la mi-temps*

▶ A verb ending in a vowel, followed by its inverted subject *il* or *elle*, introduces the consonant *t* between the two:

A-t-il pris son remède ? *ira-t-il mieux ensuite ?* *Se porte-t-il bien ?*

▶ A verb ending in a vowel followed by *en* or *y* adds the consonant *s*, pronounced /z/ at the end of the verb (it does this to avoid confusion with the present participle *cherchant*):

Cherches-en d'autres ! *Penses-y !*

▶ After a short adverb:

Pierre est devenu plus aigri. Anne est bien installée.

▶ After quand (*-d* is pronounced /t/):

Quand est-ce qu'il commence son stage ? *Quand on lit, le temps passe vite*

▶ After *comment*, in a single case:

Comment allez-vous ?

Liaison that is not allowed

Liasion is not made:

▶ between two groups of words:

Nous sommes allés / aux vendanges / en septembre.

▶ before aspirated *h*:

des haricots; *en haut*; *sans honte*; *les hérons*; *les hamsters*

▶ after the conjunction *et*:

un jour et une nuit; *et elles avaient raison*

▶ after a word ending in -er, including infinitives ending in -er:

rester à table; *ce diner était exquis*; *le courrier accumule du retard*

▶ after a singular noun:

un champs éclairé par la pleine lune; *le corps électoral*; *un étudiant en vacances*

▶ after a subject that is not a personal pronoun + verb:

Les avions ont décollé à l'heure. Les étudiants ont-ils pris de quoi écrire ? Les comptes indiquent une erreur.

▶ after the verb:

Elle tient à la vérité. Ils ont mis un peu plus de lait ?

▶ after an adverb + adjective:

C'est complètement incompréhensible !

▶ after -s in a compound word:

des fers à repasser; *des fours à pain*

▶ after certain prepositions: *selon, hormis, ci-inclus*, and prepositions ending in -rs, such as *vers, à travers, hors*:

á travers un champs de blé; *ci-inclus une lettre explicative*

▶ before the semi-vowel /j/ (yod) and the word *oui*:

des yaourts, trois yacks (except with words of Latin origin, e.g. *les yeux*)

▶ before *un, huit, onze* and derivatives, *huitaine, huitième, onzième*:

trois-huitièmes; *neuf-onzièmes*; *les dix huit* /dis ɥit/ *ans, devant pour la photo, SVP !* (to be differentiated from *dix-huit* /dizɥit/)

▶ after *quand* and *combien* used interrogatively:

Quand a-t-il dit qu'il venait ? Combien avez-vous dépensé ce weekend ?

Optional liaison

This allows differentiation between two meanings:

des savants américains (*savant* = noun)

de savants américains (*savant* = adjective, therefore liaison is made)

The adverbs *bien* and *rien* are not followed by liaison when they function as nouns.

Tu es un rien excessif dans ton jugement !

Un bien acquis malhonnêtement.

APPENDIX: A GLOSSARY OF COMPUTING TERMINOLOGY

administrateur (m) *de site / de serveur*	webmaster
adresse universelle (f)	uniform / universal resource locator (URL)
améliorer	to upgrade
appliquette (f)	applet
article (m) / *contribution* (f) *de forum* (m)	news item / news posting / news article
barre d'outils (f)	toolbar
barre de défilement (f) / *ascenseur* (m)	scroll bar
barre des menus (f)	menu bar
barrière de sécurité (f)	firewall
boite de dialogue (f)	dialog box
catalogue (m) / *répertoire* (m)	directory
clavier (m)	keyboard
clic (m)	click
clic droit (m)	right click
(se) connecter (à)	to connect (to)
copie sur papier (f) / *tirage* (m)	hard copy
corrompu(e)	corrupt
courriel (m)	e-mail
curseur (m) / *pointeur* (m)	cursor
défilement (m)	scrolling
diffusion sur la toile (f)	webcasting, netcasting
disque (m) / *disquette* (f) *de sauvegarde*	back-up disk / disquette
disque dur (m)	hard disk
données (f pl)	data

double-clic (m)	double click
écran (m)	screen
effacer / supprimer	to delete
en ligne	online
erreur (f) / *bogue* (m) / *bug* (m)	bug
extension / module d'extension (f)	plug-in
FAQ / foire aux questions (f), *fichier des questions courantes* (m)	FAQ / frequently asked questions (file)
fenêtre du navigateur (f)	browser window
fenêtre pop-up (f)	pop-up box
fichier (m)	file
fond (m) *d'écran*	wallpaper
formater	to format
forum (m)	newsgroup
fouineur (m)	hacker
fournisseur (m) *d'accès*	internet service provider
frimousse (f) (familiar)	emoticon / smiley
glisser-déposer	drag and drop
grappe (f)	cluster
hameçonnage (m)	phishing
haute définition / résolution (f)	high resolution
hors-ligne	offline
hypertexte (m)	hypertext
icône (f)	icon
imprimante (f)	printer
imprimante à jet d'encre (f)	printer (inkjet)
imprimante à laser (f)	printer (laser)
imprimante matricielle (f)	printer (dot matrix)
imprimer	to print
infolettre (f)	newsletter
installer	to install
intégré(e)	built-in

interface (f)	interface
internaute (mf)	cybernaut / internet user
internet (m)	internet network / internet / Net
lecteur (m) *de disquettes* (f)	disk drive
liste (f) *de signets* (m)	hotlist
liste déroulante (f)	drop-down menu
logiciel (m)	software
logiciel de diagnostic (m)	diagnostic program
logiciel (m) *de navigation* (f)	browser
mandataire (mf)	proxy server / proxy
matériel (m)	hardware
mémoire (f)	memory
mémoire RAM (f) / *mémoire vive*	RAM
mise à niveau (f)	upgrade
mot (m) *de passe*	password
mouchard (m)	cookie
navigateur (m)	browser
octet (m)	byte
onglet (m)	tab
ordinateur (m)	computer
ordinateur personnel (m)	personal computer (PC)
page d'accueil (f)	home page
page sur la toile (f)	webpage / web page
par défaut	default
pare-feu (m)	firewall
passerelle (f)	gateway
pirate (m)	hacker / cracker
police de caractères (f)	font
raccordement (m) *numérique asymétrique* (*RNA*)	asymmetric digital subscriber line (ADSL)

raccourci (m)	shortcut
redémarrage du logiciel (m)	reboot
relancer, réinitialiser	to reboot
réseau (m)	network
retour à zéro (m)	reset
sauvegarde (f)	back-up
sauvegarder	to back up
scanner	to scan
scanner (m)	scanner
sélectionner	to select
serveur (m)	file server
serveur mandataire (m)	proxy server, proxy
signet (m)	bookmark
site (de la toile / sur la toile) (m)	website / web site
souris (f)	mouse
système d'exploitation (m)	operating system
tableau de commande (m)	control panel
tableur (m)	spreadsheet
témoin (de connexion) (m)	cookie
la toile / toile mondiale (f)	World Wide Web

Note

Many French computing terms are translated from English. IT specialists often use English terms, even when an official French version of a term exists.

VERB TABLES

All French verbs belong to one of three groups, whose endings are *-er* (group 1), *-ir* (group 2) and either *-re, -oir* or *-ir* (group 3). Note that verbs with *-ir* endings may be found in groups 2 (e.g. *finir*) and 3 (e.g. *sortir*) and that one *-er* verb, *aller*, belongs to group 3.

Regular verbs are those that follow a predictable model in all forms of the verb. **Irregular** verbs exhibit changes which are not predictable; the forms of irregular verbs should be learned.

Each verb consists of two parts, a **radical** (or stem) which imparts the meaning of the verb and an **ending**, which is variable according to person, tense and mood. For example, in the infinitive of the verb of the group 1 *chanter*, the radical is *chant-* and the ending *-er* (see 10.2.1). Regular verbs have one radical only, which is invariable; irregular verbs may have several radicals, which can be seen in the different forms taken by the verb.

1 -er group

Chanter *(to sing)*

Indicative

	Present	**Imperfect**	**Simple past**	**Future**
Je / j'	chant**e**	chant**ais**	chant**ai**	chant**erai**
Tu	chant**es**	chant**ais**	chant**as**	chant**eras**
Il / elle	chant**e**	chant**ait**	chant**a**	chant**era**
Nous	chant**ons**	nous chant**ions**	chant**âmes**	chant**erons**
Vous	chant**ez**	vous chant**iez**	chant**âtes**	chant**erez**
Ils / elles	chant**ent**	chant**aient**	chant**èrent**	chant**eront**

	Compound future	**Conditional**	**Compound conditional, first form**	**Compound conditional, second form**
Je / j'	**aurai chanté**	chant**erais**	**aurais** chanté	**eusse chanté**
Tu	**auras** chanté	chant**erais**	**aurais** chanté	**eusses** chanté

	Compound future	Conditional	Compound conditional, first form	Compound conditional, second form
Il / elle	**aura** chanté	chant**erait**	**aurait** chanté	**eût** chanté
Nous	**aurons** chanté	chant**erions**	**aurions** chanté	**eussions** chanté
Vous	**aurez** chanté	chant**eriez**	**auriez** chanté	**eussiez** chanté
Ils / elles	**auront** chanté	chant**eraient**	**auraient** chanté	**eussent** chanté

	Compound past	Pluperfect	Past anterior
Je / j'	**ai** chanté	**avais** chanté	**eus** chanté
Tu	**as** chanté	**avais** chanté	**eus** chanté
Il / elle	**a** chanté	**avait** chanté	**eut** chanté
Nous	**avons** chanté	**avions** chanté	**eûmes** chanté
Vous	**avez** chanté	**aviez** chanté	**eûtes** chanté
Ils / elles	**ont** chanté	**avaient** chanté	**eurent** chanté

Subjunctive

		Present	Compound past	Imperfect	Pluperfect
Que	je / j'	chant**e**	**aie** chanté	chant**asse**	**eusse** chanté
Que	tu	chant**es**	**aies** chanté	chant**asses**	**eusses** chanté
Qu'	il / elle	chant**e**	**ait** chanté	chant**ât**	**eût** chanté
Que	nous	chant**ions**	**ayons** chanté	chant**assions**	**eussions** chanté
Que	vous	chant**iez**	**ayez** chanté	chant**assiez**	**eussiez** chanté
Qu'	ils / elles	chant**ent**	**aient** chanté	chant**assent**	**eussent** chanté

Imperative

	Present	Past
(Tu)	chant**e** !	**aie** chanté !
(Nous)	chant**ons** !	**ayons** chanté !
(Vous)	chant**ez** !	**ayez** chanté !

423

Participle

Present	Past
chant**ant**	chant**é**

Infinitive

Infinitive	Past infinitive
chant**er**	**avoir** chant**é**

2 *-ir* group

Bâtir *(to build)*

Indicative

	Present	Imperfect	Simple past	Future
Je / j'	bât**is**	bât**issais**	bât**is**	bât**irai**
Tu	bât**is**	bât**issais**	bât**is**	bât**iras**
Il / elle	bât**it**	bât**issait**	bât**it**	bât**ira**
Nous	bât**issons**	bât**issions**	bât**îmes**	bât**irons**
Vous	bât**issez**	bât**issiez**	bât**îtes**	bât**irez**
Ils / elles	bât**issent**	bât**issaient**	bât**irent**	bât**iront**

	Compound future	Conditional	Compound conditional, first form	Compound conditional, second form
Je / j'	**aurai** bâti	bât**irais**	**aurais** bâti	**eusse** bâti
Tu	**auras** bâti	bât**irais**	**aurais** bâti	**eusses** bâti
Il / elle	**aura** bâti	bât**irait**	**aurait** bâti	**eût** bâti
Nous	**aurons** bâti	bât**irions**	**aurions** bâti	**eussions** bâti
Vous	**aurez** bâti	bât**iriez**	**auriez** bâti	**eussiez** bâti
Ils / elles	**auront** bâti	bât**iraient**	**auraient** bâti	**eussent** bâti

	Compound past	Pluperfect	Past anterior
Je / j'	**ai** bâti	**avais** bâti	**eus** bâti
Tu	**as** bâti	**avais** bâti	**eus** bâti
Il / elle	**a** bâti	**avait** bâti	**eut** bâti
Nous	**avons** bâti	**avions** bâti	**eûmes** bâti
Vous	**avez** bâti	**aviez** bâti	**eûtes** bâti
Ils / elles	**ont** bâti	**avaient** bâti	**eurent** bâti

Subjunctive

		Present	Compound past	Imperfect	Pluperfect
Que	je / j'	bât**isse**	**aie** bâti	bât**isse**	**eusse** bâti
Que	tu	bât**isses**	**aies** bâti	bât**isses**	**eusses** bâti
Qu'	il / elle	bât**isse**	**ait** bâti	bât**ît**	**eût** bâti
Que	nous	bât**issions**	**ayons** bâti	bât**issions**	**eussions** bâti
Que	vous	bât**issiez**	**ayez** bâti	bât**issiez**	**eussiez** bâti
Qu'	ils / elles	bât**issent**	**aient** bâti	bât**issent**	**eussent** bâti

Imperative

	Present	Past
(Tu)	bât**is** !	**aie** bâti !
(Nous)	bât**issons** !	**ayons** bâti !
(Vous)	bât**issez** !	**ayez** bâti !

Participle

Present	Past
bât**issant**	bâti

Infinitive

Infinitive	Past infinitive
bât**ir**	**avoir** bâti

3 -re group (also -oir and some verbs ending in -ir)

Attendre (to wait for)

Indicative

	Present	Imperfect	Simple past	Future
Je / j'	attend**s**	attend**ais**	attend**is**	attend**rai**
Tu	attend**s**	attend**ais**	attend**is**	attend**ras**
Il / elle	attend	attend**ait**	attend**it**	attend**ra**
Nous	attend**ons**	attend**ions**	attend**îmes**	attend**rons**
Vous	attend**ez**	attend**iez**	attend**îtes**	attend**rez**
Ils / elles	attend**ent**	attend**aient**	attend**irent**	attend**ront**

	Compound future	Conditional	Compound conditional, first form	Compound conditional, second form
Je / j'	**aurai** attendu	attend**rais**	**aurais** attendu	**eusse** attendu
Tu	**auras** attendu	attend**rais**	**aurais** attendu	**eusses** attendu
Il / elle	**aura** attendu	attend**rait**	**aurait** attendu	**eût** attendu
Nous	**aurons** attendu	attend**rions**	**aurions** attendu	**eussions** attendu
Vous	**aurez** attendu	attend**riez**	**auriez** attendu	**eussiez** attendu
Ils / elles	**auront** attendu	attend**raient**	**auraient** attendu	**eussent** attendu

	Compound past	Pluperfect	Past anterior
Je / j'	**ai** attend**u**	**avais** attendu	**eus** attendu
Tu	**as** attendu	**avais** attendu	**eus** attendu
Il / elle	**a** attendu	**avait** attendu	**eut** attendu
Nous	**avons** attendu	**avions** attendu	**eûmes** attendu
Vous	**avez** attendu	**aviez** attendu	**eûtes** attendu
Ils / elles	**ont** attendu	**avaient** attendu	**eurent** attendu

Subjunctive

Que		Present	Compound past	Imperfect	Pluperfect
Que	je / j'	attend**e**	**aie** attendu	attend**isse**	**eusse** attendu
Que	tu	attend**es**	**aies** attendu	attend**isses**	**eusses** attendu
Qu'	il / elle	attend**e**	**ait** attendu	attend**ît**	**eût** attendu
Que	nous	attend**ions**	**ayons** attendu	attend**issions**	**eussions** attendu
Que	vous	attend**iez**	**ayez** attendu	vous attend**issiez**	**eussiez** attendu
Qu'	ils / elles	attend**ent**	**aient** attendu	attend**issent**	**eussent** attendu

Imperative

	Present	Past
(Tu)	attend**s** !	**aie** attendu !
(Nous)	attend**ons** !	**ayons** attendu !
(Vous)	attend**ez** !	**ayez** attendu !

Participle

Present	Past
attend**ant**	attend**u**

Infinitive

Infinitive	Past infinitive
attend**re**	**avoir** attendu

Irregular verbs

Note

Where *derivatives* or *similar verbs* are listed, these verbs are conjugated in the same way.

Avoir (to have)

▶ *avoir* is conjugated using four different radicals: *a(i)*, *av-*, *eu-*, *au*.

▶ *avoir* is the only group 3 verb which does not end in *-s* in the first person singular of the present indicative.

► Note the third person plural of the present indicative: *ils ont.*

► *avoir* has an irregular ending in the present subjunctive: *que j'aie*, etc.

► The imperative of *avoir*, *aie !*, etc., is formed from the present subjunctive and **not** the infinitive.

► The present participle, *ayant*, is **not** formed from the first person plural of the present indicative.

avoir						
	Present indicative	**Imperfect**	**Future**	**Simple past**	**Present subjunctive**	**Imperative**
J'	*ai*	*avais*	*aurai*	*eus*	*aie*	
Tu	*as*	*avais*	*auras*	*eus*	*aies*	*aie !*
Il / elle	*a*	*avait*	*aura*	*eut*	*ait*	
Nous	*avons*	*avions*	*aurons*	*eûmes*	*ayons*	*ayons !*
Vous	*avez*	*aviez*	*aurez*	*eûtes*	*ayez*	*ayez !*
Ils / elles	*ont*	*avaient*	*auront*	*eurent*	*aient*	
Present participle	*ayant*					
Past participle	*eu*					

Être (to be)

► *être* is conjugated using **six** different radicals: *s-*, *e-*, *ét-*, *f-*, *soi-*, *sui-*.

► Note the irregular first, second and third persons plural of the present indicative: *nous sommes, vous êtes, ils sont.*

► The imperative of *être*, *sois !* etc., is formed from the present subjunctive and **not** the infinitive.

► The present participle, *étant*, is **not** formed from the first person plural of the present indicative.

► Despite being a group 3 verb, *être* forms its past participle in *-é*: *été.*

être						
	Present indicative	**Imperfect**	**Future**	**Simple past**	**Present subjunctive**	**Imperative**
Je / j'	*suis*	*étais*	*serai*	*fus*	*sois*	
Tu	*es*	*étais*	*seras*	*fus*	*sois*	*sois !*

être						
	Present indicative	Imperfect	Future	Simple past	Present subjunctive	Imperative
Il / elle	est	était	sera	fut	soit	
Nous	sommes	étions	serons	fûmes	soyons	soyons !
Vous	êtes	étiez	serez	fûtes	soyez	soyez !
Ils / elles	sont	étaient	seront	furent	soient	
Present participle	étant					
Past participle	été					

Acheter (to buy)

Similar verbs: *amener* (to take), *mener* (to take, lead), *emmener* (to take [away]), *promener* (to take out), *lever* (to raise), *enlever* (to remove), *geler* (to freeze), *peser* (to weigh)

▶ In the present indicative and present subjunctive, the *e* of the penultimate of group 1 verbs becomes *è* in all persons except *nous* and *vous*.

acheter	Present indicative	Present subjunctive
J'	achète	achète
Tu	achètes	achètes
Il / elle	achète	achète
Nous	achetons	achetions
Vous	achetez	achetiez
Ils / elles	achètent	achètent
Present participle	achetant	
Past participle	acheté	

Aller (to go)

▶ *aller* is an irregular verb belonging to group 3. It is the only group 3 verb to form the ending of the simple past with the letter *-a*, like verbs of the first group.

▶ *aller* is conjugated using three different radicals: *v-*, *ir-*, *all-*.

▶ Note the third person plural of the present indicative: *ils vont*.

▶ Despite being a group 3 verb its past participle ends in *-é*: ***allé***.

aller	Present indicative	Future	Simple past	Present subjunctive	Imperative
Je / j'	vais	irai	allai	aille	
Tu	vas	iras	allas	ailles	va !
Il / elle	va	ira	alla	aille	
Nous	allons	irons	allâmes	allions	allons !
Vous	allez	irez	allâtes	alliez	allez !
Ils / elles	vont	iront	all**èrent**	aillent	
Present participle	allant				
Past participle	allé				

Boire *(to drink)*

▶ *boire* is conjugated with three different radicals: ***boi-***, ***buv-*** and ***b-***.

boire	Present indicative
Je	bois
Tu	bois
Il / elle	boit
Nous	buvons
Vous	buvez
Ils / elles	boivent
Present participle	buvant
Past participle	bu

Conduire *(to lead, drive)*

Similar verbs: *construire* (to build), *luire* (to shine), *nuire* (to harm)

▶ The past participles of *luire* and *nuire* are *lui* and *nui* respectively; they are invariable.

▶ The simple past of *luire* is *je luis . . . nous luîmes . . . ils luirent*.

conduire	Present indicative
Je	conduis
Tu	conduis
Il / elle	conduit
Nous	conduisons
Vous	conduisez
Ils / elles	conduisent
Present participle	conduisant
Past participle	conduit

Connaître *(to know)*

Similar verbs: *apparaître* (to appear), *croître* (to grow)

▶ Verbs ending in *-aître* and *-oître* had a circumflex accent on the *i* when it preceded a *t*. With the new spelling regulations the circumflex accent has now disappeared.

▶ These verbs are conjugated like verbs ending in *-ir* (e.g. *finir*), with the infix *-iss-*.

connaître	Present indicative
Je	connais
Tu	connais
Il / elle	connaît
Nous	connaissons
Vous	connaissez
Ils / elles	connaissent
Present participle	connaissant
Past participle	connu

Craindre *(to fear)*

Similar verbs: *atteindre* (to achieve, reach), *dissoudre* (to dissolve), *éteindre* (to put out), *joindre* (to attach, get hold of), *peindre* (to paint), *résoudre* (to solve)

▶ These verbs keep the *d* in the future and conditional tenses only.

craindre	Present indicative	Future
Je	crains	craindrai
Tu	crains	craindras
Il / elle	craint	craindra
Nous	craignons	craindrons
Vous	craignez	craindrez
Ils / elles	craignent	craindront
Present participle	craignant	
Past participle	craint	

Croire *(to believe)*

▶ The *i* in *croire* becomes a *y* before *a* and *o*, and before *i* in the imperfect indicative and the present subjunctive.

croire	Present indicative	Imperfect	Present subjunctive
Je	crois	croyais	croie
Tu	crois	croyais	croies
Il / elle	croit	croyait	croie
Nous	croyons	croyions	croyions
Vous	croyez	croyiez	croyiez
Ils / elles	croient	croyaient	croient
Present participle	croyant		
Past participle	cru		

Courir *(to run)*

Derivatives: *accourir* (to run up), *concourir* (to compete), *discourir* (to hold forth), *encourir* (to incur), *parcourir* (to travel), *recourir* (to have recourse), *secourir* (to help)

▶ These verbs form their future and conditional by doubling the *r*.

courir	Future	Conditional
Je	cour**r**ai	cour**r**ais
Tu	cour**r**as	cour**r**ais
Il / elle	cour**r**a	cour**r**ait
Nous	cour**r**ons	cour**r**ions
Vous	cour**r**ez	cour**r**iez
Ils / elles	cour**r**ont	cour**r**aient

Devoir *(must, to have to)*

Derivative: *redevoir* (to owe)

▶ These verbs have a circumflex accent in the past participle in the **masculine singular** only: *dû, redû*.

▶ They lose *-ev-* in the three singular persons of the present indicative, the past simple, the imperfect subjunctive, the past participle, and the imperative singular.

▶ Note that these verbs are rarely used in the imperative.

devoir	Present indicative	Future	Past simple	Imperfect subjunctive	Imperative
Je	dois	devrai	dus	dusse	
Tu	dois	devras	dus	dusses	dois !
Il / elle	doit	devra	dut	dût	
Nous	devons	devrons	dûmes	dussions	
Vous	devez	devrez	dûtes	dussiez	
Ils / elles	doivent	devront	durent	dussent	
Present participle	devant				
Past participle	dû, dus, due, dues				

Dire *(to say)*

Derivatives: *redire* (to repeat), *contredire* (to contradict), *dédire* (to retract), *interdire* (to ban), *maudire* (to curse), *médire* (to speak ill of), *prédire* (to predict)

▶ The second person plural form in the present tense of *dire* and *redire* is *dites* and *redites* respectively, **but** in the derivatives *contredire*, *dédire*, *interdire*, *maudire*, *médire* and *prédire* this form is *-disez*, e.g. *vous me contredisez*, etc.

dire	Present indicative
Je	dis
Tu	dis
Il / elle	dit
Nous	disons
Vous	dites
Ils / elles	disent
Present participle	disant
Past participle	dit

Écrire *(to write)*

▶ Note the irregular past participle of *écrire*: *écrit*.

écrire	Present indicative
J'	écris
Tu	écris
Il / elle	écrit
Nous	écrivons
Vous	écrivez
Ils / elles	écrivent
Present participle	écrivant
Past participle	écrit

Espérer *(to hope)*

Similar verbs: *céder* (to give up), *compléter* (to complete), *considérer* (to consider), *posséder* (to possess), *préférer* (to prefer), *répéter* (to repeat)

▶ In the present indicative and present subjunctive, the *é* of the penultimate syllable become *è* in all persons except *nous* and *vous*.

espérer	Present indicative	Present subjunctive
J'	espère	espère
Tu	espères	espères
Il / elle	espère	espère
Nous	espérons	espérions
Vous	espérez	espériez
Ils / elles	espèrent	espèrent
Present participle	espérant	
Past participle	espéré	

Faire (to do, make)

Derivatives: *contrefaire* (to forge), *défaire* (to undo), *refaire* (to redo), *satisfaire* (to satisfy), *surfaire* (to overrate)

▶ *faire* is conjugated using three different radicals: *fai-*, *f(i)(a)-*, *fe-*.

▶ Note the endings of the second and third persons plural of the present indicative: *vous faites*, *ils font*.

▶ *faire* changes its radical in the subjunctive.

faire	Present indicative	Future	Simple past	Present subjunctive
Je	fais	ferai	fis	fasse
Tu	fais	feras	fis	fasses
Il / elle	fait	fera	fit	fasse
Nous	faisons	ferons	fîmes	fassions
Vous	faites	ferez	fîtes	fassiez
Ils / elles	font	feront	firent	fassent
Present participle	faisant			
Past participle	fait			

Lire *(to read)*

Derivative: *élire* (to elect)

lire	Present indicative
Je	lis
Tu	lis
Il / elle	lit
Nous	lisons
Vous	lisez
Ils / elles	lisent
Present participle	lisant
Past participle	lu

Manger *(to eat)*

Similar verbs: *changer* (to change), *nager* (to swim), *voyager* (to travel), *loger* (to lodge), *partager* (to share), *ranger* (to tidy)

▶ Verbs whose infinitive ends in **-ger** keep the **e** before **o** or **a**

manger	Present indicative	Imperfect	Simple past	Imperfect subjunctive	Present participle
Je		mangeais	mangeai	mangeasse	mangeant
Nous	mangeons				

Mettre *(to put)*

Derivatives: *transmettre* (to transmit), *soumettre* (to subdue), *permettre* (to permit), *admettre* (to admit)

▶ These verbs are conjugated using two radicals: **met(*t*)-**, **m-**.

▶ They lose one **t** in the three singular persons of the present indicative.

Mettre	Present indicative	Imperfect	Simple past	Imperative
Je	mets	mettais	mis	
Tu	mets	mettais	mis	mets !

Mettre	Present indicative	Imperfect	Simple past	Imperative
Il / elle	met	mettait	mit	
Nous	mettons	mettions	mîmes	mettons !
Vous	mettez	mettiez	mîtes	mettez !
Ils / elles	mettent	mettaient	mirent	
Present participle	mettant			
Past participle	mis			

Mourir (to die)

▶ This verb forms its future and conditional by doubling the *r*.

▶ In the singular persons of the present indicative and present subjunctive, *-ou-* changes into *-eu-*.

▶ Note the past participle *mort*.

mourir	Present indicative	Future	Conditional	Present subjunctive
Je	meurs	mourrai	mourrais	meure
Tu	meurs	mourras	mourrais	meures
Il / elle	meurt	mourra	mourrait	meure
Nous	mourons	mourrons	mourrions	mourions
Vous	mourez	mourrez	mourriez	mouriez
Ils / elles	meurent	mourront	mourraient	meurent
Present participle	mourant			
Past participle	mort			

Naître (to be born)

▶ The past participle of *naître*, despite it being a verb of group 3, ends in *-é*: *né*.

▶ *naître* had a circumflex accent on the *i* when it preceded a *t*. With the new spelling regulations the circumflex accent has now disappeared.

naître	Present indicative
Je	*nais*
Tu	*nais*
Il / elle	*naît*
Nous	*naissons*
Vous	*naissez*
Ils / elles	*naissent*
Present participle	*naissant*
Past participle	*né*

Ouvrir *(to open)*

Similar verbs: *couvrir* (to cover), *offrir*, (to offer), *souffrir* (to suffer), *assaillir* (to attack), *cueillir* (to pick), *tressaillir* (to quiver, start) and their derivatives

▶ Although these verbs belong to group 3 (mostly *-re*), they are conjugated like verbs in group 1 (*-er*) in the present indicative, the present subjunctive and the imperative.

▶ The past participles of *ouvrir, couvrir, offrir, souffrir* end in *-ert* (*ouvert*, etc.), whereas the past participles of verbs ending in *-llir* is *-i*: *cueilli*, etc.

ouvrir	Present indicative	Present subjunctive	Imperative
J'	*ouvre*	*ouvre*	
Tu	*ouvres*	*ouvres*	*ouvre !*
Il / elle	*ouvre*	*ouvre*	
Nous	*ouvrons*	*ouvrions*	*ouvrons !*
Vous	*ouvrez*	*ouvriez*	*ouvrez !*
Ils / elles	*ouvrent*	*ouvrent*	
Present participle	*ouvrant*		
Past participle	*ouvert*		

Partir *(to depart)*

Similar verbs: *sentir* (to feel), *mentir* (to lie), se *repentir* (to repent), *sortir* (to go out), *dormir* (to sleep)

partir	Present indicative
Je	pars
Tu	pars
Il / elle	part
Nous	partons
Vous	partez
Ils / elles	partent
Present participle	partant
Past participle	parti

Plaire *(to please)*

Derivative: *déplaire* (to displease)

Similar verb: *taire* (to silence)

	plaire	taire
Je	plais	tais
Il / elle	plait	tait
nous	plaisons	taisons

Prendre *(to take)*

Derivatives: *apprendre* (to learn), *comprendre* (to understand), *surprendre* (to surprise)

▶ These verbs have regular endings but note the changes in the radical: **prend-, pren-, prenn-, pri-**.

prendre	Present indicative	Imperfect	Simple past	Present subjunctive	Imperative
Je	prends	prenais	pris	prenne	
Tu	prends	prenais	pris	prennes	prends !
Il / elle	prend	prenait	prit	prenne	
Nous	prenons	prenions	prîmes	prenions	prenons !

(continued)

(continued)

prendre	Present indicative	Imperfect	Simple past	Present subjunctive	Imperative
Vous	prenez	preniez	prîtes	preniez	prenez !
Ils / elles	prennent	prenaient	prirent	prennent	
Present participle	prenant				
Past participle	pris				

Pouvoir *(can, to be able)*

▶ The ending *-s* is replaced by *-x* in the first two persons of the present indicative.

▶ The future and conditional of *pouvoir* are formed with a double *r*.

pouvoir	Present	Future	Conditional
Je	peux	pourrai	pourrais
Tu	peux	pourras	pourrais
Il / elle	peut	pourra	pourrait
Nous	pouvons	pourrons	pourrions
Vous	pouvez	pourrez	pourriez
Ils / elles	peuvent	pourront	pourraient
Present participle	pouvant		
Past participle	pu		

Recevoir *(to receive)*

Similar verbs: *apercevoir* (to catch sight of), *décevoir* (to disappoint), *percevoir* (to perceive)

▶ These verbs have a cedilla under the *c* before o and **u**.

recevoir	Present
Je	reçois
Tu	reçois
Il / elle	reçoit

recevoir	Present
Nous	recevons
Vous	recevez
Ils / elles	reçoivent
Present participle	recevant
Past participle	reçu

Rire *(to laugh)*

Derivative: *sourire* (to smile)

▶ *rire* has two *i*s in the first two persons plural of the imperfect indicative and the present subjunctive.

rire	Present indicative	Imperfect	Present subjunctive
Je	ris	riais	rie
Nous	rions	riions	riions
Vous	riez	riiez	riiez

Savoir *(to know)*

▶ *savoir* is irregular in the indicative, the subjunctive, the imperative and the participles.

▶ The present participle, *sachant*, is **not** formed from the first person plural of the present indicative.

savoir	Present indicative	Future	Simple past	Present subjunctive	Imperative
Je	sais	saurai	sus	sache	
Tu	sais	sauras	sus	saches	sache !
Il / elle	sait	saura	sut	sache	
Nous	savons	saurons	sûmes	sachions	sachons !
Vous	savez	saurez	sûtes	sachiez	sachez !
Ils / elles	savent	sauront	surent	sachent	
Present participle	sachant				
Past participle	su				

Suivre *(to follow)*

Derivatives: *poursuivre* (to pursue), *s'ensuivre* (to ensue)

▶ These verbs lose the *v* in the first three persons of the present indicative and the imperative singular.

▶ *S'ensuivre* is conjugated in the third person singular and plural only: *il s'est ensuivi, ils s'ensuivent.*

suivre	Present indicative
Je	suis
Tu	suis
Il / elle	suit
Nous	suivons
Vous	suivez
Ils / elles	suivent
Present participle	suivant
Past participle	suivi

Vaincre *(to defeat)*

Derivative: *convaincre* (to convince)

▶ These verbs have a *c* in the singular of the present indicative: *il vainc*. The *c* changes into *qu* before a vowel.

vaincre	Present indicative	Simple past	Future	Imperative
Je	vaincs	vainquis	vaincrai	
Tu	vaincs	vainquis	vaincras	vaincs !
Il / elle	vainc	vainquit	vaincra	
Nous	vainquons	vainquîmes	vaincrons	vainquons !
Vous	vainquez	vainquîtes	vaincrez	vainquez !
Ils / elles	vainquent	vainquirent	vaincront	
Present participle	vainquant			
Past participle	vaincu			

Valoir *(to be worth)*

Derivatives: *équivaloir* (to be the equivalent of), *prévaloir* (to prevail), *revaloir* (to get even with)

▶ *valoir* has four different radicals: ***val-, vau-, vaud-*** in the future and conditional; ***vaill-*** in the three singular persons of the present subjunctive.

▶ The ending *-s* is replaced by *-x* in the first two persons of the present indicative.

▶ In the present subjunctive *prévaloir* (to prevail) is *que je prévale*.

▶ *Falloir* (to be necessary) is conjugated like *valoir*, but it is only used impersonally: *il faut, qu'il faille, il a fallu*.

valoir	Present indicative	Future	Imperfect	Present subjunctive
Je	vaux	vaudrai	valais	vaille
Tu	vaux	vaudras	valais	vailles
Il / elle	vaut	vaudra	valait	vaille
Nous	valons	vaudrons	valions	valions
Vous	valez	vaudrez	valiez	valiez
Ils / elles	valent	vaudront	valaient	vaillent
Present participle	valant			
Past participle	valu			

Venir *(to come)*

Derivatives: *revenir* (to come back), *devenir* (to become), *convenir* (to suit), *intervenir* (to intervene), se *souvenir* (to remember)

Similar verbs: *appartenir* (to belong), *mantenir* (to maintain), *obtenir* (to obtain), *retenir* (to keep), *soutenir* (to support), *tenir* (to hold)

▶ *venir* has four different radicals: ***vien-, ven-, vin-, viendr-***.

▶ A *d* is inserted in the future form of these verbs.

venir	Present indicative	Future	Simple past
Je	viens	viendrai	vins
Tu	viens	viendra	vins

(continued)

(continued)

venir	Present indicative	Future	Simple past
Il / elle	vient	viendras	vint
Nous	venons	viendrons	vînmes
Vous	venez	viendrez	vîntes
Ils / elles	viennent	viendront	vinrent
Present participle	venant		
Past participle	venu		

Vivre *(to live)*

▶ Note the irregular past participle of *vivre*: *vécu*.

vivre	Present indicative
Je	vis
Tu	vis
Il / elle	vit
Nous	vivons
Vous	vivez
Ils / elles	vivent
Present participle	vivant
Past participle	vécu

Voir *(to see)*

Derivatives: *entrevoir* (to glimpse), *revoir* (to see again), *prévoir* (to foresee)

▶ These verbs form their future and conditional by doubling the *r*.

Exception: *prévoir*: *je prévoirai* and *je prévoirais* respectively.

voir	Present indicative	Future	Conditional
Je	vois	verrai	verrais
Tu	vois	verras	verrais
Il / elle	voit	verra	verrat

voir	Present indicative	Future	Conditional
Nous	voyons	verrons	verrions
Vous	voyez	verrez	verriez
Ils / elles	voient	verront	verraient
Present participle	voyant		
Past participle	vu		

Vouloir *(to wish, want)*

▶ The ending *-s* is replaced by *-x* in the first two persons of the present indicative.

▶ The radical *voul-* becomes *voudr-* in the future and conditional tenses, *veuill-* in the present subjunctive except the *nous* and *vous* forms, and in the second persons singular and plural imperative.

Vouloir	Present indicative	Future	Present subjunctive	Imperative
Je	veux	voudrai	veuille	
Tu	veux	voudras	veuilles	veux ! / veuilles !
Il / elle	veut	voudra	veuille	
Nous	voulons	voudrons	voulions	voulons !
Vous	voulez	voudrez	vouliez	voulez ! / veuillez !
Ils / elles	veulent	voudront	veuillent	
Present participle	voulant			
Past participle	voulu			

ANSWERS TO EXERCISES

Chapter 2 Nouns

1. 1. une agnelle 2. un ami 3. une conseillère 4. une poule 5. le directeur 6. une élève 7. une épicière 8. le fermier 9. ma grand-mère 10. cet étalon 11. un marchand 12. mon père 13. sa tante 14. une paysanne

2.

a) Animate nouns which do not differentiate between male and female	b) Nouns which have only one form for masculine and feminine	c) Animate nouns having different words for male and female	d) Nouns whose feminine form is a modification of the masculine form	e) Homonyms whose meaning varies according to the gender
crocodile, araignée, sentinelle, recrue, victime, mannequin, perroquet, altesse	acrobate, architecte, artiste, camarade, concierge, élève, enfant, secrétaire, stagiaire, pianiste, Russe	coq, vache, brebis, grand-père, oncle, nièce, jument, chèvre, roi	chat, infirmière, tigre, ami, danseur, Anglais, Espagnole, Indienne, boulanger	moule, livre, voile, poste, pendule, critique, parallèle, mémoire, somme

3. Il y a eu trois incidents en deux **après-midis** dans trois **villes** des **environs**. J'ai pu lire tous les **détails** dans les **journaux** locaux ce matin. Comme c'était l'époque des **festivals**, de nombreux **bus** transportaient les **festivaliers** à travers la ville. De jeunes **cyclistes nu-tête**, sur des **vélos** aux **pneus** usés, jouaient à des **jeux** imprudents, comme par exemple faire des **demi-tours** brusques sur la chaussée. Soudain, à 50 m d'ici un bus fit irruption, et en moins de 2 **sec.** il alla heurter légèrement l'un des **jeunes** avec son rétroviseur, au niveau des **yeux** et le fit tomber sur les **genoux**. Heureusement le jeune quitte pour **quelques éraflures** et **quelques bleus**. Il y eut plus de peur que de mal.

Chapter 3 Determiners

1. 1. cette 2. ce . . . cette 3. ces . . . cette 4. ces . . . ce 5. ces . . . ces 6. cette 7. Ce 8. cette 9. ce 10. Cette

2. 1. Ma 2. Mes 3. Sa / Leur 4. mon 5. Ma 6. sa . . . mon 7. Mon 8. Nos
   9. Notre . . . mon 10. votre
3. 1. ma / la . . . une 2. Le . . . ma . . . le 3. de l' 4. une / ma . . . le . . . une 5. de la
   6. l' . . . une . . . le 7. Une . . . au . . . la . . . la . . . des 8. de l' . . . de la . . . du . . . des
   9. La . . . les . . . l' 10. du . . . du . . . mon . . . les 11. Ce . . . au . . . un . . . mon

Chapter 4 Pronouns

1.
   1. Elle joue sur la plage.
   2. Ses parents la surveillent.
   3. De temps en temps les parents jouent avec elle.
   4. La famille y passe l'été. Elle en part à l'automne.
   5. Les parents lui ont offert un petit bateau gonflable.
   6. Ils le lui montrent.
   7. Il y fait monter l'enfant.
   8. Elle ne veut pas les garder.
   9. « Donne-les-lui », disent-ils.
   10. Elle les ôte. Puis elle les leur tend.

2. 1. leur 2. lui 3. leur 4. en 5. en 6. y 7. les 8. leur 9. les 10. se
3. 1. vous 2. Moi 3. elle 4. lui 5. Nous 6. Eux 7. Elles 8. toi 9. moi 10. moi
4. 1. le tien 2. la sienne 3. la leur 4. les leurs 5. des siens 6. des vôtres 7. les siennes 8. la nôtre 9. le mien 10. le sien

Chapter 5 Adjectives

1. 1. turque . . . iranienne 2. favorite . . . meilleure 3. belle . . . multicolores 4. radieuse
   5. patiente . . . petits enfants 6. jeune . . . courte 7. vieille 8. longues . . . seule
   9. brève 10. vert . . . clair . . . roses . . . épaisse . . . auburn
2. 1 Seule / femme

(only) one woman	*une seule femme*
a lonely woman	*une femme seule*

2. Jeunes / mariés

newly married (couple)	*des jeunes mariés*
young married people	*des mariés jeunes*

3. Belle / famille

a beautiful family	*une famille belle*
in-law family	*une belle-famille*

4. Sale / tête

a nasty face	une sale tête
a dirty face	un tête sale

5. Propre / voiture

his / her clean car	sa voiture propre
his / her own car	sa propre voiture

6. Cher / bijou

my beloved jewel	mon cher bijou
my expensive jewel	mon bijou cher

7. Ancienne / usine

a former factory	une ancienne usine
an old (in age) factory	une usine ancienne

8. Sacré / endroit

a (hell of a) place	un sacré endroit
a holy place	un endroit sacré

9. Curieux / enfant

a nosy / inquisitive child	un enfant curieux
a strange child	un curieux enfant

10. Pauvre / homme

the poor man!	le pauvre homme!
a poor (not wealthy) man	un homme pauvre

3. Examples of possible answers:
   1. Ma meilleure amie est assez jolie.
   2. Elle a une apparence plutôt athlétique.
   3. Sa tête est ronde mais pas joufflue.
   4. Ses yeux, en amande, sont bleu clair.
   5. Elle a les cheveux roux et légèrement frisés.
   6. Ses bras sont longs et un peu musclés.

7. Elle n'aime pas vraiment les peaux tatouées.

8. Elle est d'humeur assez calme mais dynamique.

9. Elle est généreuse et à la fois posée et combative.

10. Mais parfois elle semble tellement froide, même indifférente.

Chapter 6 Numbers

1. 1. cent vingt et une pages 2. trois cent quatre-vingts 3. l'an mille huit cent 4. page quatre cent 5. cent vingt pages 6. deux cent mille 7. deux cents millions d'euros 8. tous les vingt ans 9. deux millions deux cent vingt mille trois cents 10. quatre-vingts millions

2. 1. huit milliards 2. six mille 3. un virgule neuf million 4. deux virgule un millions 5. quatre miles à l'heure 6. trois milles nautiques 7. neuf divisé par trois égale(nt) trois 8. huit moins un égale(nt) sept 9. quatre fois / multiplié par six égale(nt) vingt-quatre 10. un plus un égale(nt) deux

3. 1. quatre-vingt-dix-neuf 2. cent soixante et onze 3. cent soixante-douze 4. mille deux cent quatre-vingt-six 5. trente-trois 6. sept cent soixante-dix-huit 7. cent quatre-vingts 8. quatre-vingt-dix-sept virgule soixante-deux 9. cent quatre-vingt-onze 10. deux cent quatre-vingt-un

4. 1. page trente et un 2. trente et unième page 3. page trois cent 4. ligne quatre-vingt 5. premier jour 6. vingt et unième semaine 7. quatre-vingt-unième semaine 8. soixante et onzième semaine 9. quatre-vingt-onzième semaine 10. l'an huit cent

Chapter 7 Adverbs

1. nonchalamment . . . silencieusement . . . généralement . . . rarement . . . tranquillement . . . simplement . . . Habituellement . . . parallèlement . . . soigneusement . . . inévitablement . . . précipitamment . . . Inopinément . . . violemment . . . étrangement . . . vraiment . . . attentivement . . . délicatement . . . Rapidement . . . hâtivement . . . bonnement . . . indubitablement

2.

A	5	B	7	C	8	D	3	E	9
F	1	G	2	H	10	I	6	J	4

3.
1. Oui, je l'ai beaucoup aimé.
2. Non, je n'y vais pas souvent.
3. Elle chante très bien.
4. Oui, elle l'attend toujours.
5. Oui, j'y vais quelquefois.
6. Non, je ne l'ai pas vraiment lu.
7. Oui, je tiens absolument à y aller.
8. Oui, il est parti brusquement.
9. J'en mange assez.
10. Non, il n'est pas aussi fort qu'avant.

Chapter 8 Negation

1.

    1. Le jardinier ne taille pas les arbres.

    2. Il n'a pas eu le temps d'arroser les fleurs auparavant.

    3. Il ne commence jamais sa journée par les fleurs.

    4. Dans sa cabane, il n'a rien.

    5. Il n'a même pas une meule pour affûter les lames.

    6. Ne doit-il pas affûter les lames ?

    7. Pas les sécateurs, non !

    8. Demain il ne lui restera plus beaucoup à faire.

    9. Il ne lui faudra pas préparer les engrais.

  10. Ne pas répandre les produits non plus.

2.

    1. Il n'a vu personne.

    2. Il ne lui reste que trois jours de révision.

    3. Il n'a rien mangé depuis ce matin.

    4. Il n'est allé nulle part aujourd'hui.

    5. Il ne va ni au cinéma ni au théâtre / Il ne va ni au théâtre ni au cinéma.

    6. Il n'a guère le temps de dormir.

    7. Il n'a nullement envie de plaisanter.

    8. Je n'ai rien compris à son discours.

    9. Elle ne s'en souvient jamais.

  10. Nous espérons ne rencontrer personne.

3.

    1. Ils ne seront pas là avant le week-end.

    2. Je n'ai pas bu / pris un seul café depuis deux jours.

    3. Je n'ai jamais mis les pieds ni en Asie ni en Afrique.

    4. Ils n'ont pas de boulanger dans ce village.

    5. Ce n'est pas un magasin.

    6. Ils n'en ont vu nulle part.

    7. Pas une plante ne peut survivre sans eau.

    8. Ils m'ont fait travailler pour rien.

    9. Ils sont irlandais, n'est-ce pas?

  10. Il est parti sans rien acheter.

4.

    Je ne suis pas heureux. Je n'ai pas de dîplomes et ma vie ne s'annonce pas bien. Je n'aurai même pas de maison, ni de jardin ni de voiture.

    Je ne fumerai jamais de gros cigares. Je n'aurai pas d'amis sincères. Mes parents ne seront plus là pour garder les enfants.

    Je n'aurai pas assez d'argent pour envoyer mes enfants étudier à l'étranger. Ils ne fréquenteront pas les plus grandes écoles.

Ils ne voyageront jamais. Ils ne connaîtront pas toutes les grandes cultures du monde. Ils ne seront pas souvent épanouis et personne ne les aimera. Ils n'auront pas beaucoup d'amis sur Facebook. Ce ne sera pas la fête tous les jours.

Chapter 9 Verbs I

1.

	Verb	Tense	Example	1	2	3	4
1.	aller	present	*Ils vont à Londres ce samedi.*			X	
2.	penser	present	*Nous pensons aux vacances.*		X		
3.	poster	compound past/ perfect	*Tu as posté la lettre hier?*	X			
4.	avoir besoin	present	*Je n'ai besoin de rien pour l'instant.*		X		
5.	dédicacer	compound past/ perfect	*Elle a dédicacé son livre à sa fille.*				X
6.	voyager	compound past/ perfect	*Nous avons voyagé dans / par toute l'Europe.*			X	
7.	passer	present	*Je passe mes vacances en France.*	X			
8.	jouer	present	*Est-ce que tu joues aux échecs ?*		X		
9.	jouer	present	*Est-ce que vous jouez du piano ?*		X		
10.	travailler	present	*Il travaille le bois.*	X			

2.
1. Les étudiants ont été appelés par leur nom.
2. Ils ont été installés dans différentes salles d'examens.
3. Les identités ont été contrôlées par les surveillants.
4. Puis les enveloppes ont été décachetées (par eux).
5. et les sujets ont été distribués (par eux).
6. Une bouteille d'eau par table a été autorisée.
7. Tous les portables avaient été mis dans une boîte en entrant.
8. et les vestes avaient été laissées aux porte-manteaux.
9. Les étudiants n'étaient pas autorisés par le règlement à sortir avant une heure.
10. Une copie fut rendue par un étudiant bien avant les autres.

3.

	Verb	Example	1	2	3
1.	se dégrader	*La situation s'est dégradée / se degrade.*	X		
2.	se saluer	*Ils ne se sont pas salués.*		X	
3.	se battre	*Ils se sont battus comme des chiffonniers.*		X	
4.	se voir	*De tels événements se voient rarement.*			X
5.	se demander	*Elle se demande ce qu'elle va faire.*	X		
6.	s'entraider	*Elles s'entraident chaque fois qu'elles le peuvent.*		X	
7.	s'appeler	*Nous nous appelons Claude tous les deux.*			X
8.	se chercher	*Elle se cherche un emploi convenable.*	X		

Chapter 10 Verbs 2: tenses of the indicative

1.

    1. j'ai pris
    2. j'y suis retournée
    3. nous aurons repris
    4. je serais bien . . . repartie
    5. il faut
    6. je pourrais
    7. je leur ai déjà beaucoup demandé
    8. il fut . . . je demandais
    9. je préférerais
    10. on verra . . . j'aurai trouvé

2.

    1. Ce café **était** trop mauvais, je **ne l'ai pas bu.**
    2. On a bien **ri** hier, mais il **n'a pas fait** beau de toute la journée.
    3. En quelle année vous-êtes **vous mariés?**
    4. Vous êtes **arrivés** pendant que je **dormais.**
    5. Je **n'ai pas entendu** le téléphone, j'**ai dormi** toute la matinée.
    6. Nous **sommes allés** la voir trois fois mais elle n'**était** jamais là.
    7. Je **voulais** bavarder avec lui mais il **est parti** trop vite.
    8. Où **êtes-vous allé** hier pendant que j'**écrivais** mes lettres?
    9. Hier il **a emprunté** la voiture de ses parents car ses amis l'**attendaient** depuis une heure.
    10. J'**aimais** bien lire le journal les matins au petit déjeuner quand j'**étais** en stage.

3.

1. Je **dormais** quand soudain le telephone **sonna**.
2. Ils **arrivèrent** au moment où je me **lavais** les mains pour passer à table.
3. Nous **avions** l'habitude de lui rendre visite souvent.
4. En entendant le bruit, le chat **prit** la fuite.
5. Dès que je **sortis** sur le balcon, l'oiseau **s'envola** dans un éclair.
6. Tous les matins en sortant je **faisais** attention à bien fermer la porte.
7. En un instant les nuages **s'accumulèrent** et il **se mit** à pleuvoir. Nous **dûmes** courir nous abriter.
8. Ils **rentraient** chaque jour en autobus.
9. Grand père **s'arrêtait** toutes les demi-heures pour reprendre son souffle.
10. Il se **couchait** tard tous les soirs, mais il **comprit** très vite qu'à ce rythme son travail en patirait.

Chapter 11 Verbs 3: the imperative, the infinitive, participles

1.

1. Je lui ai dit **de se dépêcher**.
2. On nous a dit **de laisser tomber** les sucreries.
3. Ils nous ont recommandé **de faire nos** courses après 18 heures.
4. Le médecin nous a recommandé **de manger** des fruits et des légumes.
5. Le médecin m'a conseillé **de me peser** régulièrement.
6. Le médecin m'a conseillé **de prendre mon** pouls tous les matins.
7. Le médecin m'a dit **de ne pas maigrir** trop vite.
8. Le médecin m'a répété **de ne pas me faire de soucis et de me reposer**.
9. Mon mari m'a dit **de ne pas croire** tout ce que disent les médecins.
10. J'ai dit à mon mari **de s'occuper de ses** affaires.

2.

1. Le professeur nous a demandé: « **n'oubliez pas les livres!** »
2. Il nous a conseillé: « **ne buvez pas trop de café!** »
3. Le professeur nous a conseillé: « **révisez bien le cours!** »
4. Il nous a suggéré: « **laissez de côté les trois premiers chapitres!** »
5. Il nous a précisé: « **pensez bien à apporter une pièce d'identité!** »
6. Il a répété: « **ne commettez pas la même faute que l'an dernier!** »
7. Il a dit: « **apportez un dictionnaire!** »
8. Il a dit: « **évitez tout appareil électronique à l'examen!** »
9. Il a dit: « **ne soyez pas surpris par le sujet d'examen!** »
10. Il a dit: « **souhaitez-nous bonne chance!** »

3. 1. courant 2. adhérents 3. adhérant 4. fatigante 5. brûlants 6. parcourant
7. précédant . . . reposants . . . suivant 8. encourageants 9. fatigants . . . précédents
10. chantant

Chapter 12 Verbs 4: the subjunctive

1.

infinitive	je / j'	tu	il / elle	nous	vous	ils / elles
jouer	joue	joues	joue	jouions	jouiez	jouent
finir	finisse	finisses	finisse	finissions	finissiez	finissent
rendre	rende	rendes	rende	rendions	rendiez	rendent
avoir	aie	aies	ait	ayons	ayez	aient
être	sois	sois	soit	soyons	soyez	soient
dormir	dorme	dormes	dorme	dormions	dormiez	dorment
recevoir	reçoive	reçoives	reçoive	recevions	receviez	reçoivent
construire	construise	construises	construise	construisions	construisiez	construisent
écrire	écrive	écrives	écrive	écrivions	écriviez	écrivent
aller	aille	ailles	aille	allions	alliez	aillent

2. a. aille b. viennes c. comprenne d. ait e. permettiez f. partions g. soit h. puissiez
3. a. vienne b. avez c. arriviez d. va e. racontions f. soit g. aient h. aie
4. Possible answers:

Je crains que Claude ne soit très en colère et j'ai bien peur qu'il aille jusqu'à la séparation.

Claude, je regrette qu'on se soit disputé ! Je ne voudrais pas qu'on se sépare.

Je suis fâchée qu'il n'ait pas téléphoné ni écrit une seule fois depuis trois semaines.

Claude, avant que tu ne partes tu avais promis d'écrire !

Pourvu que Claude ne vérifie pas son compte en banque tout de suite, il va certainement exiger que je rembourse la somme.

Claude, il est temps que je t'explique ! Je suis vraiment désolé que le cheval ait perdu la course. J'aurais voulu que tu gagnes beaucoup d'argent pour que tu puisses te payer cette guitare.

Chapter 13 Prepositions

1. 1. dans . . . dans . . . à 2. de chez . . . à . . . de . . . 3. sur . . . sur . . . à
   4. . . . en . . . à . . . chez 5. dans . . . Dans . . . au 6. au . . . par . . . à 7. avec . . . de
   8. au . . . à . . . sur 9. autour 10. par . . . sous
2. 1. chez 2. chez 3. à l' 4. chez 5. à l' 6. chez 7. à la 8. à 9. à la 10. chez

3.

1.

	à	dans	chez	en	sur
être	Paris	la rue	le dentiste	avance	le trottoir

2.

	à	dans	chez	en	vers
aller	pied	sa chambre	mon oncle	Normandie	le sud

3.

	à compter de	à l'exception du	entre	après	avant de
Quand?	la semaine prochaine	jeudi après-midi	2 et 3 heures	le déjeuner	récupérer les enfants

4.

	pour	en	[no preposition]	aux	par
passer	un avare	sixième	l'aspirateur	choses sérieuses	Marseille

5.

	à	du	après	pour	de
venir	l'apprendre	grec	son chef	s'excuser	loin

Chapter 14 Conjunctions

1. 1. car 2. ni . . . ni 3. et 4. mais 5. car 6. donc 7. ou 8. et 9. or . . . donc 10. puis
2. 1. quand 2. Parce qu' 3. Plutôt que 4. parce qu' 5. que 6. à mesure que 7. Bien qu' 8. pour que 9. tant que 10. Selon que
3. 1. mais 2. pour que 3. quand 4. ni . . .ni 5. ou 6. si 7. comme si 8. Dès que / aussitôt que 9. autant que / tant que / aussi longtemps que 10. donc

Chapter 15 Relative pronouns

1. 1. dont 2. qu' 3. qui 4. que 5. qui 6. qui 7. qu' 8. qu' 9. que 10. dont
2. 1. qui / lequel 2. qui 3. qui / laquelle 4. auquel 5. lequel 6. laquelle 7. quoi 8. quoi 9. Auquel 10. qui
3. 1. [Ce] dont 2. [Ce] à quoi 3. [ce] qui 4. [ce] dont 5. [ce] qui 6. [ce] à quoi 7. [Ce] qui 8. [Ce] qu' 9. [ce] que 10. [Ce] de quoi

Chapter 16 Questions and exclamations

1.

1G	2A	3I	4F	5J	6D	7E	8C	9B	10H

2. 1. Qui 2. Que 3. Comment 4. Combien 5. Quel 6. Qu'est-ce qu' 7. Où 8. Laquelle 9. Qu'est-ce qu' 10. Lequel

3.

Possible questions		Responses
1. *naissance*	*Quand est-ce qu'elle est née ?*	*En mai 1989*
2. *naissance*	*Où est-ce qu'elle est née ?*	*À Helsinki*
3. *langue*	*Quelle langue est-ce qu'Isabel parle à la maison ?*	*À la maison ? Le suédois !*
4. *éducation*	*Est-ce qu'elle a été une très bonne élève ?*	*Oui, une très bonne élève*
5. *études*	*Est-ce qu'elle étudie ?*	*Oui, le droit*
6. *études*	*Où est-ce qu'elle étudie ?*	*À l'université de Helsinki*
7. *études*	*Pour combien est-ce qu'elle en a encore ?*	*Pour encore 3 ans*
8. *vie sociale*	*Est-ce que Camilla est sa meilleure amie ?*	*Oui, Camilla est sa meilleure amie*
9. *vie sociale*	*Combien est-ce qu'elle a d'amis en tout ?*	*Des amis ? Au moins trois.*
10. *carrière*	*Qu'est-ce qu'elle voudra faire après sa licence ?*	*Après sa licence ? elle voudra faire un master*

INDEX

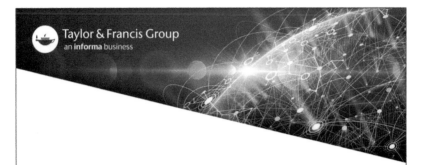